Narrative and Media

Narrative an   :luding
film, televis   ırch in
structuralis   image
analysis, the   l offers
interpretive   ·ticular
media form   isation
are realised

As the bc   ia continue to dis   : seam-
lessly transl   ions of
these strate

Narrative and Media

Helen Fulton
with
Rosemary Huisman
Julian Murphet
Anne Dunn

CAMBRIDGE
UNIVERSITY PRESS

CAMBRIDGE UNIVERSITY PRESS
Cambridge, New York, Melbourne, Madrid, Cape Town,
Singapore, São Paulo, Delhi, Mexico City

Cambridge University Press
The Edinburgh Building, Cambridge CB2 8RU, UK

Published in the United States of America by Cambridge University Press, New York

www.cambridge.org
Information on this title: www.cambridge.org/9780521617420

First published 2005

A catalogue record for this publication is available from the British Library

Library of Congress Cataloguing in Publication Data

Fulton, Helen Elizabeth.
Narrative and media.
Bibliography.
ISBN 0 521 61742 1.
ISBN 9 780521617 420.
ISBN-13 978-0-521-61742-0.
ISBN-10 0-521-61742-1.
1. Mass media.   2. Narration (Rhetoric).   3. Structuralism.
4. Poststructuralism.   I. Title.
302.23

ISBN 978-0-521-61742-0 Paperback

Contents

20 Conclusion: postmodern narrative and media

Figures and tables

Figures

Tables

Contributors

Helen Fulton has recently been appointed Professor of English at the University of Wales, Swansea, after teaching for a number of years at the University of Sydney. Her teaching and research areas include grammar, discourse analysis, narrative theory and medieval studies.

Rosemary Huisman is Honorary Associate Professor in the Department of English, University of Sydney, where she was also Head of Semiotics until 2003. Her research brings together contemporary literary, semiotic and linguistic theory in the exploration of textual production and interpretation in different media, discourses and genres. A practising poet, she has also produced major publications on the semiotics of poetry, from Beowulf to contemporary Australian writing.

Julian Murphet lectures in the Department of English, University of Sydney, where he teaches American literature, film and critical theory. He is the author of two books on contemporary American literature, and has published widely in postmodern culture and the interrelations of visual and literary media.

Anne Dunn is Senior Lecturer in the Department of Media and Communications at the University of Sydney. Before embarking on an academic career, she spent more than twenty years in commercial and publicly owned media, as a writer, researcher, journalist, producer, director and manager, including freelance work with magazines and newspapers. She is the current president of the Australian and New Zealand Communication Association.

Acknowledgements

The authors would like to thank the following people and publications who have given permission for work to be reproduced in this book: *Australian Women's Weekly*; *Daily Telegraph* (Sydney); Clare Dyer/*The Guardian* for 'Media will pay for trial collapse'; Lucy Gough, *The Mermaid's Tail*; *New Idea* cover of 6 October 2001; Jon Henley/*The Guardian* for '*Garçon*! You're slow, surly and at last you've admitted it'; Alec Russell, 'Americans see war as mistake' copyright © Telegraph Group Limited 2004; Ben Sills/Reuters for 'Basque nationalists issue challenge to Madrid'; *Sydney Morning Herald*; Rhett Watson/*Sunday Telegraph* (Sydney) for 'Town living in fear over mining deal'; cover of *Who* magazine, 8 October 2001, reproduced with permission of *Who* magazine, Time Inc.; Miranda Wood for 'Pregnant women urged to take iodine'.

Chapter 1

Introduction: the power of narrative

Helen Fulton

In a world dominated by print and electronic media, our sense of reality is increasingly structured by narrative. Feature films and documentaries tell us stories about ourselves and the world we live in. Television speaks back to us and offers us 'reality' in the form of hyperbole and parody. Print journalism turns daily life into a story. Advertisements narrativise our fantasies and desires.

As long as human beings have had the power of speech, they have been speaking in narratives, goes the theory (O'Shaughnessy & Stadler 2002: 127). Yet there is nothing natural or universal about narrative, which is a form of representation. As such, it is historically and culturally positioned to turn information and events into structures that are already meaningful to their audiences. Since the media are now the major controllers of narrative production and consumption in the Western world, the stories that seem the most 'natural' are the ones to which the media have accustomed us.

This book is about the ways in which contemporary media structure narrative and how the processes of production and signification that characterise media narratives can be theorised. Beginning with a historical survey of narrative theory, which focuses on structuralism and its post-structuralist responses (chapters 2 and 3), the book then examines film as a major producer of narrative (chapters 4 to 9). These chapters look at the ways narrative elements such as plot, character, voice and point of view are constructed and manipulated in feature films to produce different kinds of meanings and to address audiences in specific ways.

The sections on television (chapters 10 to 13) pick up the concept of genre and the ways in which television genres are distinguished by aspects of narrative construction, particularly the uses of space and time. Two chapters on radio (chapters 14 and 15) emphasise the narrative possibilities of sound, rather than vision, as a semiotic code in which reality can be constructed. The final sections (chapters 16 to 19) examine the ways in which information is translated into the discourses and genres of news and magazines, and the semiotic possibilities of multimodal texts that use both written language and image.

Many of the concepts and terms appearing in bold type throughout the book are gathered together into the glossary for reference. Some of these concepts, as well as ideas and examples, occur more than once in different chapters, often deployed or theorised in different ways. The idea of genre, for example, is discussed at various stages in the book as a discursive construct, an industry marketing tool and an effect of technological strategies. By contextualising narrative within a range of analytical traditions and practices related to media texts, we hope to maximise the possibilities for deconstructing this most pervasive of representational systems.

The domain of this book is cultural and media theory. Its theoretical approach is broadly post-structuralist, which understands meaning, or the process of signification, as socially and culturally produced and situated. Post-structuralism itself is a set of theories about the relationships between text and meaning; in order to be realised as a useful analytical system, these theories need to be activated by at least a basic understanding of linguistic and visual signs. Drawing mainly on the linguistic theory of Michael Halliday, this book provides a set of techniques and terms for the semiotic analysis of media texts. At the same time, it offers a consideration of industry-related issues that affect the production and consumption of media texts.

Semiotics has had a chequered career in the burgeoning field of cultural studies, to which media studies are normally assigned, or by which they have been appropriated. The idea of semiotics as a method of analysis is perennially popular in media and cultural studies, but the large majority of its devotees ignore its inescapable grounding in language. Routinely reduced to such a vague and oversimplified form as to be useless, semiotics, fully realised as the study of linguistic and visual signs positioned in a cultural and historical context, still remains the only systematic approach to explaining how, rather than just what, texts mean. If cultural studies is not to disappear into a vacuum of superficial rhetoric and ambit claims about the hegemonic function of the media, it has to be buttressed by a theorised approach to language, signification and the production of ideology. One of the aims of this book is to provide an introduction to such an approach and to demonstrate its potential for media consumers and practitioners alike.

There are a number of common themes that recur throughout the different sections of the book and represent the theoretical positioning of its authors. The first is the idea of narrative as cultural production, something that is deliberately produced and sold as an economic commodity. The second concerns the audiences of narrative and how they are positioned as the subjects of story. Finally, the

Barthesian idea of stories as 'myths' we tell about ourselves and our social order, and how we are positioned ideologically, forms a detectable undercurrent to many of the chapters. These ideas can be elaborated and summarised briefly here.

Narrative as cultural production

It is a truism, but nevertheless true, that all media have a primarily economic function. Their job is to produce and disseminate commodities that can be bought and sold. Even state-owned media, such as the ABC in Australia and the BBC in Britain, although not dependent on advertising revenue, compete for market share of audiences to guarantee their funding. They also earn income from selling programs and associated merchandise such as CDs, DVDs, videos and other products, including books and clothing, which are related to their broadcast output. Commodification was theorised by Marx, who used the terms 'use value' and 'exchange value' to distinguish between the function of an object and the value it acquires as a commodity in the marketplace. In terms of film's essential function as a medium of entertainment, a feature film by an unknown director might have much the same use value as a movie directed by Francis Ford Coppola, but the exchange values of the two films will be vastly different. Most media products have an exchange value disproportionate to their use value because they are not simply 'used' by audiences (paying and non-paying) but exchanged as commodities by producers, distributors, advertisers and other kinds of customers in the media marketplace.

The economic function of the media, to generate profits, undermines the idea of narrative as some kind of innate or universal structure common to all humanity. Narrative in the media becomes simply a way of selling something. This means that the economic structure of media industries determines their output, the kinds of stories they can tell. The feature film industry makes money from distribution, box-office sales and sponsorship, increasingly in the form of product placements as a kind of indirect advertising. Not only did the brand name of Calvin Klein appear on the visible waistband of Michael J. Fox's underpants in *Back to the Future* (1985), but also it then became the subject of an ongoing joke in the film when his companion assumed this was his own name and began calling him 'Calvin'. Only money can buy that kind of publicity.

The consequence of this economic structure is that film narratives have to be 'commercial'; that is, they have to fit a standard pattern and set of expectations, or what is often termed a **genre**. Genres themselves are not 'natural' or inevitable, but have a practical function: to create a market and an audience. Movie reviews, in print or in TV programs, work to place films into generic categories for us so that we can decide which ones to see, although our 'choice' is already restricted by what is available and what producers have decided that we want to see.

Generically coded films are not only easier to sell to audiences but are also easier to associate with merchandise and spin-off products such as books, toys and clothing. Writing about the Hannibal Lecter films as a 'franchise', Australian journalist Sandra Hall said (jokingly, one hopes): 'We don't yet have a line in Hannibal steak knives . . . but give him one more film and a cookbook will surely follow' (*Sydney Morning Herald*, 26–27 October 2002). 'Cross-over' films, such as the *Lord of the Rings* trilogy, which were produced and edited in such a way as to fit into both the 'fantasy' and 'children's' genres, both of which provide lucrative pathways to related merchandise, are highly prized and much sought-after by commercial film studios.

Unlike film, commercial television makes its money almost exclusively from paid advertising in designated and clearly marked 'ad breaks' in the programming. TV programs are therefore designed and generically identified to bring together mass audiences of particular demographic types, which can then be 'sold' to advertisers who want to reach such audiences. Since audience sectors are defined and distinguished on the basis of their assumed VALS (values and lifestyle), television narratives have to display and reinforce the same sets of VALS as the desired audience. It is no accident that advertisements for toys and fast food dominate children's programs, or that advertisements for gardening products and funeral homes tend to cluster during traditional detective mystery dramas. It is not that demographically distinct audiences exist, sitting patiently in their homes waiting to be addressed, rather that generically coded programs and their associated advertisements call such audiences into being through their narrative strategies.

The print media – newspapers and magazines – are also driven largely by advertising revenue, including classified advertising. They therefore need to create media products that do not simply cater to readers and consumers but which will attract advertising around, and sometimes into, the stories themselves. 'Advertorials' embed product promotion within the editorial: that is, the actual 'stories', which are visually coded, with large headlines, bylines, columns and pictures, to look like the 'real' content of the newspaper or magazine. Many feature articles about celebrities and their lifestyles are coded to look like 'news' but are in fact indirect advertisements for their latest film or book, together with the various brands of clothing or cosmetics that they apparently use. Special supplements or weekly regular features, such as 'good food' guides or technology sections, are included not merely as a service to readers, or even as mechanisms to attract and retain more readers, but mainly to provide a tailor-made venue for advertisers to promote specific types of products.

Media narratives do not exist, then, simply to entertain us, the consumer, to tell us stories in order to amuse us, or to provide us with a service and a range of choices from which we can make our selection. They are constructed in order to support the huge business empires that run most of the media outlets, geared specifically to creating profits from the commodification of media products.

Constructing the audience

When we consider the audiences for media texts, it seems obvious that in a literal sense they are people like us, watching television, going to the movies, buying newspapers. But from a theoretical perspective, an audience is called into being by a particular discourse, or 'interpellated' by the text, to use Althusser's term. In other words, an audience doesn't exist until a text addresses it; and by the same token, texts don't simply address a pre-existing and knowable audience. They actually construct a virtual audience, defined by Pertti Alasuutari as 'a discursive construct produced by a particular analytic gaze' (Alasuutari 1999: 6). The virtual audience is the audience that is sold to advertisers. Whether or not the virtual audience is then realised as an actual group of consumers who buy the products is one of the great gambles of the free market.

As actual individuals who use media products, the extent to which we feel ourselves to be part of an audience depends on whether or not we feel addressed by a media text. Does it speak to us directly? Does it use a language we recognise as ours? Do we feel included in the world view and attitudes articulated by the text? Magazines and television genres, including advertising, use narrative to construct very distinct audiences, segmented mainly by age and gender, but these are virtual audiences who might not correspond exactly to literal audiences. Editorial discourses in 'women's magazines' might call up a virtual readership of young women, while the sexualised discourses of the advertising might speak to a literal audience of young men.

A literal mass audience is unknowable, beyond small groups of individuals, and even then empirical and ethnographic studies of audience reception, using focus groups or real people in their homes, can be made to work only by assuming that individual readers are fully aware of their reading practices and processes of signification. On the other hand, by looking at the discursive relationship between text and constructed audience, it is possible to assess the ideological role of media narratives in producing the empowered readers that we imagine ourselves to be. As the audiences for media products, we are discursively positioned by media texts as 'sovereign consumers'; that is, consumers who have the power to make our own purchasing decisions and choices, pandered to by a subservient market eager to win our patronage. This positioning, or subjectivity, is manifested most clearly in advertising, which tells the same basic story: there is a problem that can be solved by the product. The problem might be material, such as stains on our clothing that need to be removed by a stain-remover, or it might be a crisis of identity, such as the lack of a partner or the onset of middle-age (both to be controlled with cosmetics or a new car). In all cases, and regardless of the coded demographic of the advertisement, the audience is positioned as freely choosing individual consumers, consciously making choices about how to improve their lives.

Because of the connection between media narratives and economic imperatives, most media narratives work persuasively in the same way as advertisements, to interpellate the audience as coherent and unified individuals empowered to make appropriate choices on their own behalf. The crucial factor is freedom, a concept that regularly occurs in many media narratives: free choice, free competition, free market and a free subject of discourse who can move directly from sign to referent, from text to meaning, without pausing for signification. Media texts therefore appear to be both denotative, offering us a window on reality, and connotative, asking us to recognise ourselves as individuals who choose to participate in a certain lifestyle. But because the 'reality' we are shown is itself constructed, even the denotative level is also connotative, persuading us that we need to change in order to match up to the reality around us. From a post-structuralist perspective, denotation and connotation are effects of discourse, mediating reality in different ways but both equally detached from it.

Contemporary cultural studies tend to reinforce the ideology of the sovereign consumer by emphasising the power of the individual to 'make their own readings' (Fiske 1987: 236). This assumption is based on the theory that individuals represent a single coherent subjectivity, that they 'know who they are' and can choose how to respond to a text. This subjectivity is, however, an effect of discourse. We are discursively encouraged by media texts to think of ourselves as singular, unified, individual, able to resist dominant or preferred meanings and to negotiate our own. This is the kind of stable subjectivity constructed for us by most media narratives, because once placed in this subject position we are ready to be sold something. It is a position that invites us to read texts superficially, just for entertainment, to enjoy some and reject others without any effort of analysis or interpretation, in order to confirm our status as freely choosing 'private' individuals. We read media narratives as consumers – which is how we have been positioned.

Narrative as 'myth'

Roland Barthes articulated the importance of language in the formation of ideology when he described **myth** as 'a type of speech . . . a mode of signification', which he located within semiology, the science of signs (Easthope & McGowan 1992: 14). For Barthes, myths represented a **metalanguage**, a second-order or connotative discourse that enables us to speak about the first-order or denotative level of signification. Myths therefore function as symbolic, ironic or metaphorical commentaries on what we understand to be literal meanings, offering us alternative readings imbued with ideological flavour. It is easy to see how media narratives, particularly those of film and television, might operate as myths, the stories in which we encode truths about ourselves and our society.

From a post-structuralist viewpoint, there is a major theoretical flaw with much of Barthes' early work, and that is his distinction between denotation and connotation, or first-order and second-order systems of signification. Although it is undoubtedly logical that one 'signified' can also stand as the 'signifier' of another sign, this process does not operate merely on two or three levels, but as a chain of signification limited only by social usage. In other words, there is no denotation but only connotation, since denotative language – appearing objective, unmediated, reflective – is as ideologically positioned as language that we would regard as highly connotative and subjective. The belief in a denotative level of expression is itself a piece of ideology.

The Barthesian idea of myth can therefore be reinterpreted simply as narrativised ideology, the formulaic articulation and naturalisation of values, truths and beliefs. What media narratives achieve is precisely this kind of mythologising, the presentation of ideological positions as if they were natural and normative. Yet it is the Barthesian model of the two levels of meaning, the literal and the symbolic, that structures most media narratives, either by drawing attention to double layers of meaning, as in feature films, or by an apparent omission of second-order meaning, as in objective news journalism. In analysing media texts, we need to interrogate the ideological myths that are told at every level.

The mythical function of most media narratives is to return us to a stable subjectivity, to remind us of who we are and what reality is. Classic Hollywood movies and realist television dramas reinforce such myths as the existence of innate morality and gender, the natural opposition between 'good' and 'bad', and between 'male' and 'female', as clearly defined and unproblematic categories. Their narrative structures assert myths, or ideologies, of the episodic nature of life, where natural or inevitable resolutions are reached and points of closure can be achieved. News reporting mythologises, and therefore normalises, the existence of universal truths and an objective reality that can be retrieved and represented without ideological mediation. By constructing these powerful narratives of who 'we' are, the media separate 'us' from 'them', those others who don't share or understand the stories we know and believe to be true.

Media myths are, by and large, the myths of late capitalism in Western societies, which function to produce the coherent subjects of capitalist economies. As subjects, we are prepared to keep working to maintain the status quo of power as long as we have access to the media products and consumer items that construct and reinforce our identities. Media narratives tell us stories about who we think we are, and in so doing they skilfully reproduce the freely choosing consumers of global capitalism. Only by understanding the mythic nature of these narratives, constructed in language and image as signifying systems, can we begin to choose whether to accept the seamless identity laid out for us or to find its contradictions and resist.

Part 1

The basics of narrative theory

Chapter 2

Narrative concepts

Rosemary Huisman

Narrative is realised in many different media. In this book we look at narratives in film, in television, in radio and in various media of popular print culture. These could be called 'mass media' in that all are assumed to be shown or broadcast to a scattered and diverse audience.

I want to begin here, however, with a narrative in a very different medium: a handwritten letter from one person to another person. This is a much simpler textual situation than that of many of the media texts we will later consider, yet, in an introductory way, we can identify certain features of this letter and its relation to its social context as exemplifying more general 'concepts of narrative'. In the comments following the letter, the concepts, when first mentioned, are in **bold**. In the latter part of this chapter and in the next, chapter 3, many of these concepts are more generally described (see also the glossary, at the end of the book).

Introducing some concepts of narrative

In 1830 Isabella Parry 'went to live at Port Stephens on the edge of the settled areas north of Sydney', capital of what was then the British colony of New South Wales. Isabella's husband Edward had been knighted for his involvement in Arctic exploration; now he was appointed Commissioner of the Australian Agricultural Company. Isabella's letters home have been preserved. On 19 December 1831 she wrote to her mother in England:

We have lately experienced another disadvantage of a newly cultivated country, and have witnessed what I have only heard of before, and read in Cooper's novels – I mean the burning of the woods, and it is, indeed, a fearful and extraordinary sight. For the last fortnight, the whole country around has been in a blaze, and between this place and the Gloucester, a distance of more than seventy miles, there is scarcely a blade of grass left: it is one continued black plain, and the stems of the trees are all scorched and blackened. We were in hopes we should have escaped, near the house, but, after two or three days, we saw there was but little prospect of our avoiding the general destruction. Just as we were coming home from church, last Sunday, a man came running to say that the fire had reached his house, and was rapidly approaching our garden. Immediately all hands were sent off to save the poor garden, and, I am happy to say, succeeded, though it was only by a few minutes. Edward made them set fire to a broad space all round, and this was only just completed when the fire reached the place we had burnt, and, finding no food to supply its flames, turned off in another direction.

(Clarke & Spender 1992: 45)

What is Isabella doing here? Clearly she is telling her mother a story. She and her husband have had an actual experience. Now she is telling that experience in language, the principal semiotic means humans have for signifying meaning. Because she is in Australia and her mother is in England she uses the written **mode** of language. If she and her mother were together she could have told her story in the spoken mode. But even in speaking directly to someone in the same location, the story of the experience is obviously not the same thing as the experience itself; the medium always mediates the message.

Isabella also refers to her experience of other people's stories of similar events, from both 'factual' and 'fictional' sources. Longer-term inhabitants of the colony have told her of their experience of 'the burning of the woods': in '[we] have witnessed what I have only heard of before', 'hear' implies the spoken mode of language. And she has also read such stories 'in Cooper's novels'. The author referred to here must be the American James Fenimore Cooper, born in 1789, whose books, *The Pioneers* (1822) and *The Last of the Mohicans* (1826), feature terrible 'forest fires', which threaten the small settlements of the American frontier. (I will return to the mythology purveyed in these novels.)

The novel has been the narrative **genre** most typically studied in traditional narrative studies; it is a genre of the **discourse** of prose fiction or, more generally, of literary discourse. Isabella's text here is an instance (an instantiation) of the genre of letter, a genre that can be used in different discourses. Here, writing to her mother, the discourse is 'personal', a personal letter (compare a 'business letter'). Similarly her conversations with other colonists could be classified as personal discourse, although realised in a different genre (that of conversation) and mode (the spoken mode). The names we give texts as known objects are usually the names of genres: she sent her mother a letter, they were having a conversation, she had been reading a novel.

A distinction introduced by the French linguist Emile Benveniste was that between the speaking **subject** and the subject of speech. The speaking subject is identified with the producer of the text, while the subject of speech refers to the first-person pronouns actually in the text, 'I', 'we' and their oblique cases ('me', 'us' and so on) (Silverman 1983: 43–53). When the text is one we understand to be a narrative, then the producer of that text can be called a narrator. For her letter, Isabella is both the 'speaking subject', the narrator, and the 'subject of speech', the one to whom the pronouns in the narrative refer. She is a first-person narrator, being one of the characters in her own story. (Characters are sometimes referred to as 'narrative existents'.) But compare this simple letter with a novel or the script of a play. Then first-person pronouns, the subject of speech, will be used in the dialogue of characters to refer to themselves. Moreover, for the novel, while both the narrator (who tells the narrative) and the author (who writes the narrative, including the narrator's role in it) are 'speaking subjects', the two cannot simply be equated (the author Dickens is not Pip, who narrates the story of *Great Expectations*). In the play or film, the narrator might be effaced altogether, or occasionally present (as in the film 'voice-over'). This is a complex area of narrative theory.

In the letter as we have it, Isabella is the narrator of the story. A story is always mediated from some perspective, the phenomenon of **focalisation**. Isabella tells the story very much from her own perspective so she is the focaliser as well as the narrator, although frequently signifying herself and her husband as a unified subject: 'we' is a frequent grammatical subject in her letter. A subtle distinction here is that Isabella is the narrator in the present of writing her letter, but she relates the past experience from her perspective on it at that time. Her focalisation is in the past, her narration is in the present. Literary genres are more likely to distinguish narrator clearly from focaliser, as when a third-person narrator tells a story from the perspective of a character.

Temporality is usually seen as an essential ingredient of narrative. In Isabella's story, we see the importance to her of the temporal organisation of actions or events. She tells a simple chronological sequence, in which the linguistic sequence signifies the sequence in which she experienced the events. Time meanings proliferate, realised, for example, in adverbs ('lately'), in verbal groups ('have witnessed', 'is', 'was approaching'), in prepositional phrases ('for the last fortnight'), in a clause ('when the fire reached the place we had burnt'). However, all events are not equal in Isabella's eyes, and it is interesting to see how she paces her narrative so as to give most prominence to the actions or events that she, as narrator, saw as the climax of her story. Gérard Genette (whose work is discussed further in chapter 3) used the concept of **duration** to describe 'steadiness of speed' in the narrative: 'the speed of a narrative will be defined by the relationship between a duration (that of the story, measured in seconds, minutes, hours, days, months, and years) and a length (that of the text, measured in lines and in pages)' (Genette 1980: 87–8). I find the term **pacing** helpful to describe relative changes of duration in the narrative, as exemplified in the following discussion.

In her first sentence, Isabella introduces this story cohesively by implying that previous stories of colonial life have been told to her mother: 'another disadvantage' – one disadvantage in the context of others. She refers to stories heard from others, novels read, in the past. Her placing of this particular experience in a larger context of experience is like a chapter in a novel or even an episode in a television series. The structure of this sentence is unusual. It begins with an evaluation of the event as a 'disadvantage' (a device that might be intended to promote a particular emotional context of reception, that of sympathetic anticipation from her mother reading), tells us that this is Isabella's first direct encounter with the event (the reference to others' stories and novels), only then, finally, tells us what event is being referred to, and concludes with a strong statement of her emotional response to seeing the fire, as a general opinion (not 'it was a fearful sight' but 'it is a fearful sight'). This first sentence is a mini-narrative summary with a delayed climax – what the event was – but it has the temporality of Isabella's mental understanding surrounding the event, not her physical experience of it, for there is no sense of chronological sequence. The sentence is telling us about Isabella's past mediated experience (from conversations and novels) and present opinion, not about the event that takes place in between. In the terminology of linguistic accounts of narrative structure we could call this the 'abstract'.

Isabella's telling of the particular event begins with the second sentence, and it is from here that Genette's notion of duration is helpful. The next two sentences (the orientation) condense time – the events and description of the last two weeks are compacted. The area around is blackened, they lose hope of avoiding destruction of their own home. Then in the fourth sentence, Isabella's storytelling slows down to a specific day and time and place (the complication), 'Just as we were coming home from church, last Sunday', and the most specific detail of the story is given, 'a man came running to say that the fire had reached his house, and was rapidly approaching our garden'. Notice the (past) continuous forms of the verbal groups (came running, was approaching) – the meaning of this verb form is that an action is in progress, is going on. This is comparable, in verbal terms, to a camera tracking an action – the duration is extended over the action. Note, too, that Isabella projects the man's speech, although indirectly (direct speech would be: 'a man came running to say, "The fire has reached my house!"'). This is the climax of her tale – in a serial cliffhanger (like the old Saturday afternoon film serial or the contemporary soap opera season) the episode would break off at this point.

Isabella continues her story with the narrative order in the chronological sequence of events, but in summary (she does not describe each individual action in the burning of the firebreak) except for the climactic temporal detail. The time of completing the firebreak and the time of the fire reaching the firebreak are emphatically equated at a single moment in time: 'and this [the firebreak] was only just completed when the fire reached the place we had burnt . . .' (the resolution of the narrative structure). The editors of *Life Lines* (Clarke & Spender 1992), the collection in which this extract from Isabella Parry's letter appears, break off the extract at this point. I imagine Isabella's letter continues, but the editors judged this extract, as a text, to be a complete narrative episode. This is both because of the cohesion of the text (it is internally cohesive about the one subject matter, the fire) and because the text exhibits a recognised narrative structure of abstract (here including evaluation), orientation, complication and resolution, noticeably marked by the change of pacing in the narration.

One choice of language particularly marks Isabella as 'English' in her lexicon. This is her phrase 'the burning of the woods'. In Modern Australian, that could only be 'bushfire'. Isabella had grown up in England, and came to Australia in 1829, two years before she wrote this letter. Other visitors of about that time noticed the local usage. In 1833 W. H. Breton wrote, in *Excursions in New South Wales*, 'The only convenient way of travelling in the "bush" is on horseback. Bush is the term commonly used for the country *per se*: "he resides in the Bush", implies that a person does not reside in, or very near, a town. It also signifies a forest' (from the entry under bush in *A Dictionary of Australian Colloquialisms*, Wilkes 1978: 65).

James Fenimore Cooper was aware of the difficulties of describing natural phenomena in the New World to readers in the Old. At the end of chapter 38 of his novel *The Pioneers* (1822), he appended the following footnote:

> The probability of a fire in the woods similar to that here described has been questioned. The writer can only say that he once witnessed a fire in another part of New York that compelled a man to desert his wagon and horses in the highway, and in which the latter were destroyed. In order to estimate the probability of such an event, it is necessary to remember the effects of a long drought in that climate and the abundance of dead wood which is found in a forest like that described. The fires in the American forests frequently rage to such an extent as to produce a sensible effect on the atmosphere at a distance of fifty miles. Houses, barns, and fences are quite commonly swept away in their course.

This is quite an extraordinary intrusion into the narrative diegesis; the novelist breaks into the fictional world of the novel to give factual information.

Narrative and the structuring of experience

In scholarship since the 1970s, the term 'narrative' has been taken up in various ways. Some are to do with the detailed examination of the narrative of an individual text, such as this discussion of Isabella Parry's letter so far. This has been the traditional focus of literary studies. Some, however, are more concerned with so-called **metanarratives** (after the work of Jean-François Lyotard 1984), the grand master stories (I use the patriarchal term deliberately) dominant in a culture. These are the stories, or myths, through which a culture tells itself its ideology, its idea of what is natural in its social order. A critique of such narratives (such as those of class, ethnicity and gender) has been the focus of cultural studies. I want now to discuss this understanding of narrative both in regard to Isabella Parry's letter and, at greater length, in regard to the novels of James Fenimore Cooper. These texts are distant in time from the contemporary media with which the remainder of this book deals, but not so distant from some 'myths' that still have contemporary currency.

In the first paragraph of the previous section, I wrote: 'the story of the experience is obviously not the same thing as the experience itself; the medium always mediates the message.' But you could also say that your understanding of the experience itself is structured by the kinds of stories with which you are familiar. For example, you might not be familiar with the Old English poem *Beowulf*, in which a monster Grendel invades a Danish hall to eat warriors, and Isabella Parry did not know it (the first edition with a Modern English translation appeared in 1837), yet her choice of language personifies the fire as just such a greedy monster: '[the fire] finding no food to supply its flames, turned off in another direction.' Older than *Beowulf*, this tale of the monster who comes out of the wilderness to devour humans in their small 'civilised' settlements resonates with the stories of folk tale, the sense of precarious social order threatened by natural chaos. In Isabella's account, notice her phrase 'newly cultivated country'. And it is 'our garden', 'the poor garden', which is threatened by the fire. This is a colonial economy, in which what is valuable is equated with what has been newly established and controlled.

Moreover this colony, with its convicts and free settlers, has a clearly distinguished class structure. The power relation of Sir Edward Parry, Isabella's husband, to others in the situation is clearly told in the choice of language. In 'all hands were sent off' we see the rhetorical figure of synecdoche (the part for the whole) in the word 'hands' for 'people' – it is indeed as 'hands' that these people are useful to Isabella and her husband in this crisis. In the passive voice 'were sent off', the someone who has sent the people off is not explicit in the grammar, although from the later causative verbal group, 'Edward made them set fire to a broad space . . .' we can infer it was Edward, or a deputy representing his power. Those who give orders and those who are ordered are clearly distinguished in the narrative when the actions of fighting the fire are told, but, in the fortunate result, all are conflated into one social unit in the first-person subject of speech: 'when the fire reached the place *we* had burnt'.

We can trace similar metanarratives of colonial ideology in the writings of James Fenimore Cooper and his father, Judge William Cooper. In chapter 2 ('To the frontier') of *A Private Life of Henry James*, Lyndall Gordon describes the Cooper family's move into 'the wilderness of western New York'. Judge Cooper, with (impractical) eighteenth-century ideals of fraternity, established a settlement, Cooperstown, there. Gordon writes:

American myth took off in this place. There was the myth of an uninhabited wilderness, though in actual fact the land had been wrested from Iroquois peoples displaced from hilltop settlements where women had conducted a flourishing agriculture – women's work did not impress the invaders as a claim to land . . . At the heart of the myth of the untrammelled wilderness stalked a mythical character . . . the wandering backwoodsman who precedes the settlers.

(Gordon 1999: 11)

This is Natty Bumppo, 'bonded in spirit and the dignity of nature to his red brother, Chingachgook or Great "Sarpent"', who both feature in five books of James Fenimore Cooper, of which the most famous is *The Last of the Mohicans*.

Gordon continues, 'On the heels of the lone woodsman comes the practical man with ready fists in the cause of civilisation – the image the Judge projects in his own story.' The latter is *A Guide to the Wilderness* (1810), which, Gordon says, 'tells the primordial frontier story with the unfussed brevity of a man of action', who wrote 'fire and fishing tackle were my only means of subsistence . . . In this way, I explored the country, formed my plans of future settlement and meditated upon the spot where a place of trade or a village should afterwards be established' (p. 12). But these are not only stories of colonisation. They not only exclude the indigenous people, they also exclude women. Gordon comments:

These are men's stories. Women are invisible or peripheral, locked in the dominant plot of enterprise and political battle. Beyond that plot, their lives and feelings are not on record, as though they had no meaning in their own right; there is not a word on the experience of women in William Cooper's account of his settlement, though without women such a community could not have existed.

(p. 12)

If colonial women – like Isabella Parry, say – had no narrative existence (were excluded as speaking subjects or subjects of speech), then it is scarcely surprising that the Iroquois women with their 'flourishing agriculture' did not constitute a presence.

Gordon's book belongs to a 'factual' genre of narrative, that of biography. In retrospect, her concern with the metanarratives of patriarchy, as evidenced in the repression of women's history in the public (published) narratives of colonisation (even if women's stories continued, like Isabella's, in personal letters), explains her choice of title for her book. The title *A Private Life of Henry James* has the subtitle, *Two Women and His Art*. The book is not so much about the detailed everyday activities of James, as one might first assume, as about James' interactions with the two women and their involvement with his life, professionally and personally. The feminist focalisation of Gordon's text illuminates how 'private' has been understood as 'concerning the female', so that the conventional history of James tends to repress the contribution of these women. This ideology, in which 'public' and 'private' have been identified with 'masculine' and 'feminine' respectively, is persistent; we meet it again in the discussion of television narratives in chapter 13.

Diegesis and mimesis

These concepts are used in overlapping, rather than identical, ways by various theorists, beginning with Plato and Aristotle. For Plato, **mimesis** and **diegesis** are two ways of presenting a story (that is, both are within narration). These terms are credited to Socrates, in the third book of Plato's *Republic*, when Socrates is talking about two ways of representing speech. With diegesis, 'the poet himself is the speaker and does not even attempt to suggest to us that anyone but himself is speaking'. With mimesis, the poet tries to give the illusion that another – whom we might call a character – speaks. (T. S. Dorsch (1965: 11) prefers the translation 'impersonation' to the more usual understanding of 'imitation'.) Mimesis is etymologically related to the English word 'mirror': it is as if the character is reflected directly to us. Thus direct speech is more mimetic, since the character's exact words are given. In contrast, indirect speech is more diegetic, as we know the poet or writer is telling us about the character's speech.

For Aristotle, tragic drama is

> a representation of an action that is worth serious attention, complete in itself and of some amplitude; in language, enriched by a variety of artistic devices appropriate to the several parts of the play; *presented in the form of action, not narration*; by means of pity and fear bringing about the purgation of such emotions . . . the representation is carried out by men *performing the actions.*
>
> (McQuillan 2000: 40; my italics)

Here Aristotle contrasts the process of telling, the form of narration, with 'doing', 'the form of action'. In the drama, as he is describing it, there is *no* narration or telling of the action because the actors *do* the action. Or, to be more precise, the actors *represent* the action by performing the action. (Performing is a simulation of doing.) A fight will be represented by the actors performing fighting. Speech of the characters will be represented by the actors performing speaking. The body of the actor becomes the medium of semiotic expression of the character. (This is a contentious issue in modern films in relation to the representation of sexual acts.)

This is mimesis for Aristotle: the Greek word *mimesis* can be glossed in English as 'showing', and the drama on the stage shows us directly the actions and speech of the characters. The performed drama has a particularly complex relation of speaking subjects. While Aristotle describes the speaking subject of the actor, through whose body the 'subject of speech' – the first-person pronouns – of the character's speeches are spoken, a modern critical account would also point, at least, to the effaced speaking subjects of playwright/narrator in telling the story of the drama. The concept of agency, as discussed for television in chapter 12, further illustrates the complexity of 'speaking subjects' in the production of media texts.

For Aristotle, epic has the form of narrative, that is of telling. The narrator tells us the story or stories (he allows the epic to be longer and episodic, like the *Iliad* and *Odyssey*, compared to the unity of the drama) and also tells us the speech of characters. Here we recognise Plato's distinction between diegesis (poet telling) and mimesis (poet effacing self behind the direct speech of characters), so the epic has sometimes been described as a 'mixed mode' – both diegetic and mimetic. This description mixes both Plato and Aristotle's understandings of diegesis and mimesis. (For a subtle reading of Aristotle's vocabulary, see Lowe 2000: 6–13.)

In twentieth-century narratology, diegesis is sometimes used to refer to 'that which is told' – in a novel, for example, to the fictional world, the fictional 'reality' that is perceived in the telling, the **Umwelt** of the characters. In traditional novels, an authorial comment might break into this world, disrupting the 'suspension of disbelief' traditionally ascribed to the absorbed reader of the novel (as in the example from Cooper's novel). However, novels described as 'postmodern' typically inhibit the reader's construal of a 'realistically' coherent diegesis by disrupting the conventions of coherent character or temporality (for example, Thomas Pynchon's novel, *The Crying of Lot 49*). Each of the mass media has its own practices and techniques relevant to diegesis: for example, commercial television, with its juxtaposition of segments of fictional narrative (the diegesis of series and serials) and segments of advertising (feigning a direct address to the viewer, that is, mimesis) can be described as inherently 'postmodern'.

Using the noun *diegesis* and the adjective *diegetic* Gérard Genette coined an impressive arsenal of terms. For example, of the Russian-doll structure of narratives within narratives he says:

> We will define this difference in level by saying that any event a narrative recounts is at a diegetic level immediately higher than the level at which the narrative act producing this narrative is placed. M. de Renoncourt's writing of his fictive *Mémoires* is a (literary) act carried out at a first level, which we will call extradiegetic; the events told in those *Mémoires* (including Des Grieux's narrating act) are inside this first narrative, so we will describe them as *diegetic* or *intradiegetic* the events told; the events told in Des Grieux's narrative, a narrative in the second degree, we will call *metadiegetic*.
>
> (Genette 1980: 228; Genette's italics)

This use of diegesis/diegetic ultimately derives from Plato's category of the voice of the teller, the poet. For further examples of compound terms, such as 'autodiegetic', see McQuillan's glossary of narrative terms (McQuillan 2000: 314–29).

Intertextuality/heteroglossia

The concept of intertextuality/heteroglossia was first described by the Russian Mikhail Bakhtin, who said famously (in English translation): the word knows where it has been. He saw interpretation as an interaction between speaker and listener. What draws their understanding together (a 'centripetal force') is the shared verbal situation, which he calls dialogue. On the other hand, what pulls each back towards an idiosyncratic understanding ('a centrifugal force') is the individual's previous experience of language (heteroglossia). Each speaker's previous experience of the use of the word is different, to a greater or lesser extent, from that of another speaker (quoted in Clark & Holquist 1984: 290–1).

Intertextuality, Julia Kristeva's term derived from her reading of Bakhtin, usefully describes the 'echoes', vague or more specific, that the reader/viewer perceives in a media text (Moi 1986: 35–61). The very concept of genre refers to a recognised intertextuality, conventional similarities between different texts. Intertextual reference might, however, be a passing similarity; for example, the contexts in which I had previously met 'woods' rather than 'bush' gave the word an intertextual meaning for me, which I described as 'English'. And again television series have played with intertextuality, for example, introducing into an episode of one sitcom a character from another sitcom.

Semiotics

We can distinguish two main usages of this term:
1 the study of semiosis (compatible with a post-structuralist understanding)
2 the study of signs (structuralist understanding).

Sense 1 is associated particularly with the work of the American philosopher Charles Sanders Peirce (1839–1914). Semiosis is to semiotics as language is to linguistics: that is, the former is the phenomenon and the latter is the study of the phenomenon. 'Semiosis' refers to the meaning-making practices of a species; for humans, language is the most complex vehicle for making (realising) meaning, but physical gestures, facial expressions, dress, choice of car, brand of beer – any sensible matter (accessible to the senses) or perceivable behaviour can be imbued with cultural significance.

Sense 2, more appropriately called 'semiology', is associated with the work of the French-speaking Swiss linguist, Ferdinand de Saussure (1857–1913). See chapter 3 for a discussion of his influence on structuralist narratology.

Peirce's triadic understanding of the sign

Except for Umberto Eco, scholars in Europe have been relatively unfamiliar with this model, yet it is more compatible with recent theories of narrative than the

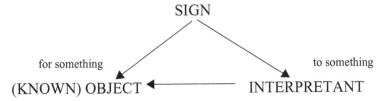

Figure 2.1: Pierce's triadic understanding of the sign.

Saussurean sign. In its minimal definition, the Peircean sign is anything that stands *for* something *to* something. What the sign stands for is its (known) object; what it stands *to* is the interpretant, as illustrated in figure 2.1.

A sign signifies something else (the known object) because this signification has a meaning (interpretant) that is understood by the interpreter. The Peircean sign (sometimes called the representamen) is realised in some perceivable vehicle (a linguistic sign like a spoken word, a hand gesture, any physical or virtual object, such as a photographic image or the digital pattern received on a television screen). Humans have a capacity for 'unlimited semiosis' because the interpretant can itself be understood as a sign and then be interpreted in its turn as signifying another known object. This is the very mechanism of metaphor.

Interpretation takes place within a context (Peirce's 'grounds', rather like Kristeva's 'intertextuality') of individual subjectivity and cultural conventions, the semiotic world or *Umwelt* of the interpreter. Known objects are culturally known; they may be understood to have an external existence ('factual') or to exist in the cultural world of the imagination ('fictional'). Nonetheless, the cultural concepts 'chair' and 'Hamlet' are equally objective, in the sense of being known objects.

The difficult point here is that although the subjectivity of the interpreter (his/her performance of cultural experience) is part of the interpretant (an idea, a mental concept), the known object is outside that subject, is understood to exist 'objectively'. Yet this 'objective' does not equal 'external, non-semiotic', whereas the traditional dualism of subject and object drew a simple line between 'internal' and 'external' (Deely 1990: 50–9).

Peirce described three kinds of relation between the sign and its known object: that of icon, of index and of symbol. These are still culturally understood – the icon to look like its object (compare the image called an ikon in the Russian Orthodox tradition), the index to be associated with its object (comparable to metonymy), and the symbol to be an entirely arbitrary association of sign and object, like the linguistic sign (Chandler 2002: 38–42). Accessible introductions to Peirce's thought are difficult to find; for brief comments, a bibliography and a relevant extract see Innis 1985: 1–19. (Paul Cobley introduces the Peircean sign in the last five pages of his book, *Narrative* (2001: 223–8), under the subtitle 'The future of the narrative sign'.)

Saussure's dyadic understanding of the sign

This is the well-known dichotomy of signifier and signified. The signifier corresponds to a linguistic vehicle and the signified to the interpretant, in Peirce's terms. Saussure described his linguistics as part of psychology; what he omitted from that dichotomy was any reference to the objective world. Unfortunately, Saussure's sign has been used loosely, sometimes as if 'signified' referred to the object, rather than to the idea. This is rather like nailing the word 'tree' to a tree! Other dichotomies, such as literal meaning/metaphor or denotation/connotation, are subject to the same criticism; that is, it is an illusion to claim that some meanings, described as literal or denotative, have a direct dyadic relation between signifier and object. Umberto Eco has written: 'the rose is a flower but . . .', meaning, but maybe in this context it is not (such as the biblical 'rose of Sharon', taken to refer to a woman in the context of *The Song of Solomon*). Eco coined the phrase 'unlimited semiosis' to refer to this open-ended possibility of human interpretation (Eco 1984: 68).

The French theorists Gilles Deleuze and Felix Guattari use the term 'rhizome' to describe the possibilities of unlimited semiosis. As Eco describes it, quoting them, 'a rhizome is a tangle of bulbs and tubers appearing like "rats squirming one on top of the other"' (Eco 1984: 81–2). Peirce once wrote that interpretation continues until the necessity to act. This might be why literary narratives, understood not to relate to 'facts', invite or are allowed to provoke more 'symbolic' interpretation. Conversely, the interpretative mediation (the 'spin') given events in 'factual' discourses, such as the narratives of television news, is not always acknowledged.

Umwelt

The biologist Jakob von Uexküll originally used this term for the environmental reality for a living organism: that is, it refers to the part of the environment that is meaningful and effective for a given species. For humans, objective reality is constituted by the known objects (in Peirce's sense) of their cultural *Umwelt*. There is no unmediated direct access to a reality external to human semiosis (Deely 1990: 59–62). However, if that cultural reality becomes too inconsistent with the external reality, as Peirce says, 'reality will have its way with us'. The history of medical practice gives many examples of unfortunate 'objective' practices, such as bleeding an already weak patient. The *Umwelt* of a fictional world, as in the novel, can be referred to as the diegesis of the novel; that is, the world of telling.

Iconography/*mise en scène*/setting/location

In 'realist' narratives of any media, the ***mise en scène*** and iconography are important in establishing and/or signifying the historical and social settings and the geographical location (both 'factual' and 'fictional': think of the cuts from newsreader to filmed catastrophe in the evening news, or the 'on location' shots in the police series *The Bill*, as the police yet again pound down the outdoor corridors of the council estates). In the factual situations of a culture, known objects cluster together. If a producer of a fictional discourse (narratives of prose fiction, drama, film, television) wants to signify that situation, then a selection of known objects associated with that situation will be told or shown.

The selection might be minimal; for example, in a play I have seen recently, *Far Away* by Caryl Churchill, two characters stand on a bare stage making hats. They have a hat stand each and an elaborate hat on the stand, which they are working on, with pins, paint and two spray-gun or stapler-like implements that hang from the ceiling. The **mise en scène** (literally, French for 'put in scene') establishes the social situation of milliners, those who make hats. There are several 'blackouts' between short scenes; in each scene, the hat is now more advanced in preparation: that is, of course, the actual hats have been replaced by stage hands during the blackout. In terms of the diegesis (the fictional world) of the drama, the development of the hats tells the passing of time. The hats are ridiculous, hyperbolic exaggerations of hats.

Audience members, who are listening to the chat between these two workers, most, I assume, straining to make some sort of cohesive narrative sense, have already seen a disquieting first act. With so little on the stage, the iconography of the hats – that is, what the hats stand for – must be very significant. But what? What story are we being told, and how do the hats fit in? (After the play, I overheard the classic remark, 'What was all that about?' so unlimited semiosis can take people far or nowhere!) I leave you to give your own interpretation. After the exchanges between the milliners, we then had a long, very long, sequence of people, six at a time, processing from the left, stopping, and a cow-bell was heard, moving off to the right. Each person wore an absurd hat – we recognised the two 'our' milliners had been working on, completed – and a pair of orange pyjamas. A placard with a number – say 3726 – hung around their necks, and their hands were tied.

Rhetorical figures

Traditional rhetoric divided its terms for stylistic features into two: difficult figures (tropes) and easy figures (also called figures of speech). Easy figures might be, for example, just the repetition of the same word (*repetitio*), but difficult figures were said to alter the meaning of a word and so to require cognitive processing. Synecdoche, metaphor and metonymy (the Greek names) remain the three most commonly identified tropes. Metaphor depends on one thing representing another; metonymy uses one thing (smoke) that is associated with another (fire); synecdoche uses a part of the thing (hand) for the whole (person). It is of course misleading to talk in terms of 'thing'; using a Peircean understanding of the sign, we can say that, to an English speaker, a sign (say the word 'smoke') usually implies the interpretant/idea (smoke) that signifies the known object (the observable phenomenon). The experience of that observable phenomenon is associated with the experience of another observable phenomenon, which is signified by the interpretant/idea (fire); thus the idea (smoke) becomes in turn a sign for another triadic relation, that to the interpretant/idea (fire) and the known object, the observable phenomenon. It is true that this is a very long-winded explanation, but it reminds us that a figure like metaphor or metonymy is not just a relation of things, or a relation of signifiers (as was sometimes suggested in the early days of post-structuralism, using the Saussurean term), or even just a relation of interpretants.

This explanation is not meant to imply that the interpreter 'solves' the trope; that is, arrives finally at its meaning, the final interpretant. The human capacity for unlimited semiosis, within the cultural context of the *Umwelt*, means that interpretation has no necessary end. Moreover, the possibility for cultural (and personal) transformation – even change in the *Umwelt* – derives in large part from the possibilities of reinterpreting metanarratives, stories of being, which have been taken for granted in the dominant cultural ideologies.

Temporality

Temporality has been seen as central to narrative since the time of Aristotle. The problem is that 'time' is not a singular concept. Structuralist studies, discussed in chapter 3, assumed that it was a simple chronological sequence in order to theorise the category of 'story', events ordered in chronological sequence. However, there are potentially at least six varieties of temporality. First, there are the three temporalities of ordinary human experience: sociotemporality (a culture's understanding of its history and being over time), human mental temporality (the personal present, which includes memory and prediction – this is the temporality of the first paragraph of Isabella Parry's letter) and organic (living) temporality (this most closely corresponds to that of the structuralist's 'story'). Second, there are the three temporalities of the non-organic physical world that humans can come to understand through scientific technology and mathematics: material temporality (that of space/time and gravity), probabilistic temporality (of quantum theory) and atemporality (of electromagnetic radiation) (Fraser 1999: chapter 2). Narratives that have been characterised as 'postmodern' typically exploit the 'non-human' temporalities of probabilistic and atemporal telling (Did that happen? Who was that? Is that the same character as the one who . . .?). The viewer/reader's traditional expectations of narrative coherence are upset by such temporal displacement.

What is particularly relevant to this book, in its focus on different mass media, is the way in which the technological and commercial circumstances of production can affect the temporal structure of the narrative (for example, the non-linear narratives of television, discussed in chapters 12 and 13).

Narrative structure and linguistics

Narrative is treated as a genre in many linguistic studies and its genre or text type described in terms of narrative structure. Taken alone, this approach is inadequate (see Cortazzi 1993: chapter 3), but it can be especially helpful in studying the pacing (changes of duration) in a text. It works best with oral personal narratives; William Labov originally described such structures in his study of black youths' stories in Harlem (see especially Labov 1972: chapter 9, 'The transformation of experience in narrative syntax'). Table 2.1 shows Cortazzi's transcription of the most typical structure (p. 45).

Table 2.1: Cortazzi's transcription of the most typical narrative structure.

STRUCTURE	QUESTION
Abstract	What was this about?
Orientation	Who? When? What? Where?
Complication	Then what happened?
Evaluation	So what?
Result	What finally happened?
Coda	(Returns the listener to the present; for example, 'That's it.')

Speech

Speech was an area of close structuralist analysis for the literary narratives of prose fiction. Boris Uspensky, in his detailed study of Tolstoy's novel, *War and Peace*, identified four levels of what he called 'point of view' in the novel: that on the ideological plane, that on the phraseological plane, that on the spatial and temporal plane, and that on the plane of psychology. Seymour Chatman combined these planes with the speech categories of speech act theory. Genette differentiated the 'speech' of narrators and characters under his general category of Voice.

Drawing on the work of these authors, figure 2.2 is a diagrammatic representation of differences of voice, correlated with the narrative roles of author (production)/implied author (interpretation), narrator and character. In the figure, 'tagged' refers to an explicit projecting clause, such as 'she said', 'she thought', while 'free' refers to the absence of such a tag. The vertical axis roughly indicates the position of a speech act on a continuum from diegesis to mimesis – in Plato's sense, from telling to showing, which Genette used to indicate closeness or distance from the narrator. As this is a model for written texts, those fictional texts

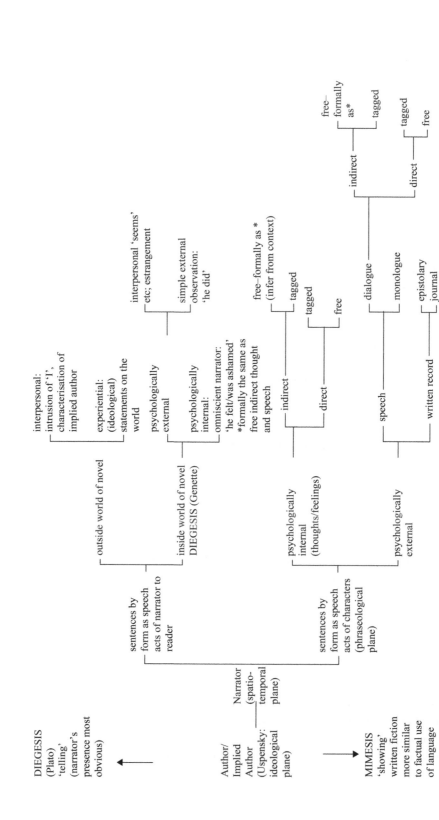

Figure 2.2: Differences of voice

that are 'impersonations' of written factual texts (such as a novel written as a journal or diary or letters) are closest to the mimetic, 'showing' end (Uspensky 1973; Chatman 1975; Genette 1980).

If you look closely at the central area of figure 2.2, you will see that the structuralist distinction between speech acts of narrator and character breaks down (the dichotomy is deconstructed). The psychologically internal speech act of an omniscient narrator describing a character ('he felt ashamed') looks the same as (is formally identical to) the free indirect speech or thought (the character thinks or says 'he felt ashamed', without a tag). You, the reader, will interpret the same clause, 'he felt ashamed', as spoken by the narrator or the character – or as ambiguous – on the grounds of your understanding of the previous textual context. This would be an important topic in a book devoted to literary narrative; Virginia Woolf, for example, makes particularly complex use of this narrative potential to blur voices from narrator to character and between characters.

In other media, such as theatre, film and television, where we see characters speak directly to each other, this verbal device is less relevant (although a character could report indirectly the speech of another character). The critical focus in those media shifts to an interest in the ideological plane, an interest in the world/diegesis of the media text and the implied cultural values of its 'implied author'/production. This shift in focus, together with the application of concepts introduced in this chapter, will be discussed with particular reference to film and television narratives in subsequent chapters.

Conclusion

Narratives in any medium or genre – oral or written, novel or letter, film or soap opera – are ways of structuring and representing lived experience. Just as we can describe experience only through the language we have available to us, so we make use of existing narrative patterns to structure and make sense of new experiences. Most narrative theorists, from Aristotle onwards, have used concepts of language to define what narrative is, and the complexities of diegesis and mimesis, narrator and focaliser, temporality and chronology, can be interpreted by a semiotic analysis of signifying elements.

This chapter has begun to draw attention to the limitations of structuralism as a means of explaining narrative in terms of binary oppositions or levels of construction (where the 'underlying structure' is privileged over superficial manifestations of storytelling). We have also suggested that these limitations can be counterbalanced to some extent by a post-structuralist consideration of the ideological work performed by narrative. Structuralist narratology and its post-structuralist critique form the main topic of the next chapter.

Chapter 3

From structuralism to post-structuralism

Rosemary Huisman

Martin McQuillan, editor of *The Narrative Reader*, describes the usual history of narrative theory as a story:

> Histories of narrative theory tend to follow a familiar pattern . . . The story goes: In the beginning there was Aristotle who theorised 'plot', then there came the novelists who theorised their own plots, then after some false starts (Propp, Benjamin, Bakhtin) narrative theory really took off with narratology (the structuralist-led 'science of narrative'). However, like the dinosaurs, narratologists died out and were replaced by more mobile, covert forms of narrative theory within a 'post-structuralist' diaspora. Narrative theory now lives on, embedded in the work and tropes of post-structuralism.
>
> (McQuillan 2000: xi)

In this Darwinian account, McQuillan parodies the oversimplification of the 'evolution' of narrative theory. The linear storyline is too simple because it assumes a reductive Enlightenment myth of progress, where what comes after necessarily replaces and is better than what came before. (Conversely, by those critics who shudder at the word 'post-structuralist', or its stylistic companion, 'postmodernist', the same succession of theories can be interpreted as a story of decadence and decay.)

In this chapter I describe some of the major differences between theories. It is well to remember that people have different purposes in analysing narrative, and some theories better suit different purposes. This is particularly so in relation to the study of commercial media texts, as the discussions in the following chapters will illustrate.

The beginnings of narrative theory

The work of Aristotle (384–322 BCE) most relevant to later narrative study is known as his *Poetics* (edited in Dorsch, 1965; extract in McQuillan 2000: 39–44). The scope of the *Poetics* is a study of the kinds of poetry practised by the Greeks: epic poetry, dramatic poetry and lyric poetry. From chapter 6, Aristotle discusses tragic drama (which is always written in poetry), and it is this discussion that is most pertinent to an analysis of narrative.

Aristotle identifies 'six constituents' of tragedy: plot, character, diction, thought, spectacle and song. It is **plot** (*mythos*) that Aristotle sees as the most important. By plot he means 'the ordered arrangements of the incidents': that is, the 'representation of the action'. Character is important, but secondary to plot. For Aristotle, character motivates the action, so that a character is not just a performed being but also a being with particular traits essential to the motivation and development of the plot. Thus brave actions require a character with the trait of bravery. (The classicist N. J. Lowe (2000: 7) gives a new translation of the sentence in which *mythos*/'plot' is defined in this way.)

Further, says Aristotle, the good plot is well constructed, unified and memorable. And finally the good plot has incidents that are causally related – what happens as a result of something else. The good plot is not just incidents ordered by chronology, one incident merely happening after another. For a historical example, consider the telling of the Arthurian legends by the fifteenth-century English writer Thomas Malory. His earlier tales of the Knights of the Round Table are fairly linear, one incident merely following another, but the last Book, of the final battles between Gawain and Lancelot, and the death of Arthur, has an intricate weaving of incident, one causing another, towards the final tragic outcome of the destruction of the Round Table (Vinaver 1977).

Next in McQuillan's story of narrative theory come the novelists who 'theorised their own plots'. The early novels, from the eighteenth century and into the nineteenth century, typically focused on the individual. The kind of theory that accepts this focus on the individual we might call a humanist theory – humanism being a term often used for social values that emerged after the Renaissance. We remember the early novels with their titles typically of the individual whose fortunes they follow: Samuel Richardson's *Clarissa*, Henry Fielding's *Tom Jones* and so on. The picaresque novel, as exemplified by much of *Tom Jones*, has a series of episodes linked in plot only by the presence of the main character. This is an episodic structure associated with the classical epic, but now one through which the 'development' of Tom as an individual can be read.

Another novelist whom McQuillan might have had in mind is Laurence Sterne, in his novel *Tristram Shandy*. It would be a good idea to look at this novel if only to decide that the late twentieth-century term 'postmodern' might be the most accurate description of the style of this eighteenth-century author! Shlovsky, a member of the same 'formalist' school as Propp, commented, 'The first impression upon taking up Sterne's *Tristram Shandy* and beginning to read it is one of chaos' (McQuillan 2000: 63–7). (Incidentally, I use 'postmodern' as a term of style and 'post-structuralism' as a term of theory, although 'postmodern' is often used for either, especially in the USA.) In their works, both Fielding and Sterne at times 'speak directly' to the reader about the direction or possibilities of their characters' adventures, 'theorising their own plots'.

The development of structuralism

McQuillan's next point is what he calls 'false starts' in narrative theory. I'm not sure what he implies by this phrase, unless he means that later scholars did not continue to develop in the direction of these theories. Of the three he mentions, Propp, Benjamin and Bakhtin, the first is always included in introductory accounts (as below) because his work is part of a school of early twentieth-century literary study that does influence later narratology. Mikhail Bakhtin (1895–1975), Russian like Propp, was mentioned in the previous chapter in relation to intertextuality/heteroglossia. (For a helpful introduction to Bakhtin's theory of the novel, see Clark & Holquist 1984: chapter 13.) Finally, Walter Benjamin (1892–1940) wrote (in German, often translating from French) subtle imaginative criticism of the prose fiction of Kafka and Proust; most relevant to the concerns of this book is his essay, 'The work of art in the age of mechanical reproduction'. Here is a sample, in which he ponders the context of reception of the mass audience:

> Mechanical reproduction of art changes the reaction of the masses toward art. The reactionary attitude toward a Picasso painting changes into the progressive reaction toward a Chaplin movie. The progressive reaction is characterized by the direct, intimate fusion of visual and emotional enjoyment with the orientation of the expect. Such fusion is of great social significance. The sharper the decrease in the social significance of an art form, the sharper the distinction between criticism and enjoyment by the public. The conventional is uncritically enjoyed, and the truly new is criticized with aversion. With regard to the screen, the critical and the receptive attitudes of the public coincide. The decisive reason for this is that individual reactions are predetermined by the mass audience response they are about to produce, and this is nowhere more pronounced than in the film. The moment these responses become manifest they control each other.
>
> (Benjamin 1969: 234)

Vladimir Propp (1895–1970) was a member of the literary school known as Formalism, which developed in Russia in the second and third decades of the twentieth century. It was the first school definitely to turn away from the 'humanist' understanding of narrative. Rather than centre their interest on action or event, like Aristotle, or the social progress of one character, like the eighteenth-century novelists, the formalists wanted to identify what formally made a text a literary text. One important answer for them was 'defamiliarisation': the literary text deliberately using language in such a way as to be unfamiliar, so as to draw attention to the text itself. (A famous example was Tolstoy's use of a horse as narrator in his novel *Kholstomer: The Story of a Horse*, published in 1886.) However, in order to recognise the unfamiliar, they had to know what was familiar, stereotypical, expected. To explore this issue, Vladimir Propp studied the Russian fairy tale (not the folk tale, incidentally, although the book of his study is translated into English as *The Morphology of the Folktale*).

Propp's 'discovery' was that there were thirty-one possible functions for events in the fairy story. Not every story had every function, but what functions they did have always came in the same order. Examples are (the Roman numeral indicating their position in the thirty-one functions): XI 'The hero leaves home', XVI 'The hero and the villain join in direct combat', XXXI 'The hero is married and ascends the throne'. Propp's thirty-one functions, with their invariable sequence, effectively describe the maximal narrative of the Russian fairy tale. Each function is centred on one (or more) actions; in this regard Propp's analysis is similar to that of Aristotle, with its insistence that plot was a representation of action.

Character was secondary to plot in Aristotle's account, but characterisation (having the appropriate traits to motivate the plot) was still important. However, for Propp, in the fairy tale, characters are formal devices required by functions. The thirty-one functions bring into being seven spheres of action for *dramatis personae*, such as the hero, the villain and the donor, someone who provides the hero with a helpful piece of knowledge or an actual object. The fourth sphere of action includes both 'a princess' and 'her father'. This is because the princess is defined so passively, as 'a sought-after person', that she contributes nothing to the action. That usually pertains to her father who, for example, assigns difficult tasks. We can compare this formalist method with the humanist approach to narrative – rather than being centred on the character as an individual, as in the humanist approach, Propp's analysis makes the character a formal necessity of the plot. For a heroic action to occur, there must be a hero to do it; for the hero to be deceived, there must be a villain to practise deception.

Propp's work was ground-breaking in its time, but very slowly disseminated. It was published in Russian in 1928 but not translated into French until the late 1950s, when its method was appropriated into French structuralism. English speakers encountered it even later in that context. It has been quoted in narrative studies ever since, but has considerable limitations from the perspective of post-structuralist critique. The thirty-one abstracted functions, forming a model or **langue**, are not the same as the events of the specific text, the **parole**. Thus the same textual event – say, 'the hero receives a ring' – might be interpreted as having a different function in different texts: perhaps XII 'The hero is tested . . . which prepares the way for his receiving either a magical agent or helper', or XIX 'The initial misfortune or lack is liquidated'. Each function is a meaning abstracted by Propp; it is not directly in the words of the text. Thus there is nothing objectively in the form – as formalists would originally have claimed. *Langue* does not pre-exist *parole*, but is simply another example of *parole* as text. Propp has subjectively inferred the meanings of the specific events in order to produce his thirty-one functions. And there is no guarantee that another reader would infer exactly the same functions. A number of cultural studies theorists reproduce Propp's thirty-one functions and regard them as relevant to the contemporary analysis of popular culture (Lacey 2000: 46–64). I suggest that the method, rather than the content of the functions, might be helpful for some purposes, such as the study of reiterative sitcom narratives from the perspective of agency (see chapters 12 and 13). But bear in mind the criticism by Hernstein Smith, which is discussed below.

We now reach McQuillan's non-false start, a flurry of activity: 'narrative theory really took off with narratology (the structuralist-led "science of narrative")'. In his glossary to *The Narrative Reader*, McQuillan gives the following as the more specific, historically circumscribed definition of 'narratology' (sense 1): ' . . . the structuralist-led theory of narrative which seeks to identify what all, and only, narratives have in common. Narratology examines the nature, form and function of narrative across genre and media. By proposing narrative as a[n] object of rigorous scientific inquiry ("ology") narratology seeks to produce a comprehensive and universal narrative grammar. Term first proposed by Todorov (1969)' (McQuillan 2000: 324).

In his 'chronology of narrative theory in the twentieth century', McQuillan gives 1950–60 as the beginnings of structuralist narratology and 1960–70 as its high point. But these dates refer to work appearing in French. It is not until the decade 1970–80 that, as McQuillan puts it, 'narratology is well established as an interest in the English-speaking world' (McQuillan 2000: 312) – and by this time new intellectual developments are beginning to displace it in the French-speaking world. Yet to understand later developments it is still necessary to understand what is being extended, or reacted against.

To understand the basic assumptions of structuralist study of narrative we must move further back in the century than this history suggests. French structuralism develops from the theories of the French-speaking Swiss linguist Ferdinand de Saussure, who died in 1913. Nineteenth-century linguistics was primarily descriptive and historical. It focused on the history of an individual language and its relations with other languages (English with other Germanic languages, or French with other Romance languages). Saussure, however, wanted to study language scientifically, as he understood science. He tried to reconceptualise what language study could be. His solution was to study language as a structure. To do this he abstracted from all the different uses of language an underlying system – what he thought of as an understanding of language that was cognitive, psychologically real, to all the speakers of that language, and which enabled them to speak or write any particular use of the language. (He understood 'scientific' linguistics to be part of psychology.) He called this underlying structure *la langue*, and contrasted it with any of the particular uses of the language by an individual speaker or writer, which he called *la parole*. So to produce an instance of *la parole*, the speaker/writer had to know *la langue*, the abstract structure of the language (Saussure 1966; Culler 1976).

Saussure's method for analysing language was essentially dualistic. As described in the previous chapter, his psychological model of the sign had two aspects: a linguistic signifier, such as the idea of a spoken word, and a cognitive signified, a mental concept. Typically he identified dichotomies, such as *la langue* and *la parole*, in which one aspect was more abstract than the other. Features of the system *la langue* were to be mentally abstracted, or inferred, by consideration of many examples of *la parole*; that is, the actual speaking of language. Another dichotomy, essential to the identification of his sign, was that of paradigm and syntagm (also called selection and combination). For example, consider the following two sentences:

1. Saussure's sign is dyadic; the interpretative aspect of his sign is known as 'the signified'.
2. Peirce's sign is triadic; the interpretative aspect of his sign is known as 'the interpretant'.

In each individual sentence, the relation between the words in that sentence is syntagmatic, one word after another. (The whole sentence could be called a 'syntagm', a combination of words.) However, by comparing the two sentences, we can see both similarities and differences. The grammatical structure of each sentence is identical, but the meanings obviously differ, because sentence 1 has *Saussure*, *dyadic*, *signified*, in the same places in the structure as sentence 2 has *Peirce*, *triadic*, *interpretant*. The words that can occur at the same point in the structure, from which you can choose (such as *Saussure* and *Peirce*), belong to the same paradigm. It is obvious that the paradigm is more abstract, because you don't hear/see it directly, whereas you can see or hear the sequence of words. More generally, the structuralist paradigm grouped together, under some unifying concept, items from which the speaker/writer chooses one member. For example, the paradigm 'colour' (unifying concept) includes the items red, green, pink, blue and so on (see Hodge & Kress 1986 for a discussion of Saussurean dualism).

Saussure's university lectures were published posthumously, in 1915. By complicated means, via the Prague school of linguistics (which had itself been influenced by Russian studies of language, including Formalism), by the 1950s Saussure's understanding of dualisms such as *la langue* versus *la parole* had begun to influence French intellectual thought. This influence was described as 'structuralism'.

Returning to the work of Propp, we can see how it relates to a structuralist understanding of language and text. Propp studied the syntagmatic axis of the fairy tale, the combination of functions in the sequence of the narrative. His work is not strictly structuralist, for a fully structuralist account closely studies the paradigmatic axis as well. In comparison, the analysis of cultural forms by the anthropologist Claude Lévi-Strauss is unambiguously structuralist.

Table 3.1: Lévi-Strauss: paradigm and syntagm in the myth of Oedipus.

Paradigm 1	Paradigm 2	Paradigm 3	Paradigm 4
Cadmos seeks his sister Europa, who has been ravished by Zeus			
		Cadmos kills the dragon	
	The Spartoi kill one another		
			Labdacos (Laios' father) = *lame* (?)
	Oedipus kills his father Laios		Laios (Oedipus' father) = *left-sided* (?)
		Oedipus kills the Sphinx	
			Oedipus = *swollen-foot* (?)
Oedipus marries his mother Jocasta			
	Eteocles kills his brother Polynices		
Antigone buries her brother Polynices, despite prohibition			

Lévi-Strauss published his very influential paper, 'The structural study of myth' (in French), in 1958 (Lévi-Strauss 1977: 206–31). The formalists, like Propp, wanted to identify formal indications of 'literariness' in the literary text, but they were not concerned with thematic interpretation, the more traditional aesthetic goal of literary criticism, for they considered it too 'subjective'. However, Lévi-Strauss saw structuralist procedures as a way of being 'objective', 'scientific' (like Saussure) in studying the interpretation of myth. He set out to study particular tellings of a myth (like the particular instances of *la parole*) to identify a myth system (like *la langue*, the language system).

Lévi-Strauss takes the narrative syntagm, the sequence of the story of the myth of Oedipus, and tries out paradigmatic arrangements that will bring together similar 'bundles of relation' (as he calls paradigms). Table 3.1 is reproduced from his account (p. 214):

Reading from left to right, line by line, in the usual way is 'telling the myth': it gives you the syntagm of the myth system, the order of events in the story. However, Lévi-Strauss claims, reading the vertical columns is 'understanding the myth'; it enables him to read the paradigmatic structure of relations. For Oedipus, this structure consists of two sets of dichotomies. The first, between paradigms 1 and 2, have an antithetical relation of meaning: paradigm 1 is concerned with the 'over-rating of blood relations', paradigm 2 with the 'under-rating of blood relations'. The second dichotomy, between paradigms 3 and 4, again has an antithetical relation: paradigm 3 is concerned with 'the denial of the autochthonous origin of man' (autochthonous = Greek *auto*, 'self' + *kthon*, 'from the earth'; that is, self-generating, without predecessors), whereas paradigm 4 is concerned with the 'persistence of the autochthonous origin of man'; that is, a repudiation of human sexual origin. Lévi-Strauss then reads the meaning of the myth in the culture's capacity to reconcile, in the sense of balancing, these contradictory dichotomies. Essentially, Lévi-Strauss sees mythic thought as attempts to overcome contradictions between belief and experience, so that a culture can maintain its beliefs, its cosmology, even while they are contradicted by experience.

The analysis of the 'themes' of a narrative into binary oppositions, like the antithetical paradigms of Lévi-Strauss's interpretation, was extensively used in narratological studies. In the second edition of *Reading Television*, Fiske and Hartley still find it a helpful way to understand the ideology of a television series (Fiske & Hartley 2003: 142). However, the post-structuralist critique of Lévi-Strauss, like that of Propp, points to Lévi-Strauss's subjective interpretation of the myth in order to abstract his opposing paradigms. His explanation of paradigms 3 and 4 (which I do not reproduce here; see Lévi-Strauss 1977: 215) derives from his disciplinary expertise as an anthropologist. Like the expert interpretation of a literary scholar (such as Genette on Proust) it is suggestive and stimulating, but it cannot be said to be objectively 'in' the myth.

The French structuralist study of narration, or of 'narratologies', inspired as it was by Saussure's study of language system rather than language use, and by the formal analyses of the Russian formalists, typically used discourse only as raw data from which to infer abstract narrative structures. A glance at structuralist accounts reveals the diagrams and reductionist figures with which such discussions are illustrated. (For an introductory account, see Rimmon-Kenan 1983: chapter 2, 'Story: events'.) Consider the work of Tsvetan Todorov, the Bulgarian who first translated Propp into French, and who wrote in French. Todorov described five points in a narrative structure (note how this is an underlying structure, like Saussure's *la langue*, abstracted from the telling of any particular narrative, like Saussure's *la parole*):

a state of equilibrium at the outset – situation 1
a disruption of the equilibrium by some action
a recognition that there has been a disruption
an attempt to repair the disruption
a reinstatement of the equilibrium – situation 2

(Lacey 2000: 23–45, 101–2)

(Compare this abstracted structure with the linguist Labov's abstracted narrative structure, described in chapter 2 above.) In some ways, Todorov wanted to return to generic descriptions similar to those of Aristotle. Aristotle gave a two-part description of the basic sequence of a narrative: from misery to happiness or from happiness to misery. Todorov's scheme seems to envisage a three-step development: from equilibrium to disruption to equilibrium.

In the early 1970s, Todorov was one of those who directly equated the *langue* and the *parole* of Saussure with the study of narrative. They spoke of a 'narrative grammar', the abstract system that was a kind of *langue* of the narrative. This enabled the specific tellings by the individual who knew the abstract narrative grammar, which were a kind of *parole*, like the specific utterances of an individual who knows the abstract grammar of the language. Various terms became fashionable for naming the *langue* of narrative as contrasted with the *parole* of narrative. The terms 'plot' and 'story' are sometimes contrasted in this way. In this usage 'story', or the chronological order of events, is an inferred *langue* of narrative, inferred on the single grounds of chronological sequence, sequence in physically experienced time. 'Plot', in contrast, is used of the narrative sequence in the actual telling – that is, the *parole* of narrative – in which the linear sequence of time may be disordered for various purposes (for example, the detective story or film, which typically begins with the discovery of the body, and then reconstructs – by telling or showing – earlier events).

The grounds for inferring the story sequence in time are least problematic when they are causal, rather than merely chronological. In the Western film, we expect the shot in which the hero and villain draw their guns to precede the shot in which the villain crumples and falls to the earth while the hero clutches his bleeding shoulder, and we derive this expectation from our knowledge of cause and effect in the physical world of time outside language. (In *Through the Looking-Glass* Lewis Carroll played with just such expectation in his account of the White Queen, who surprises Alice because she screams *before* she pricks her finger.) For Aristotle, as I have said, a good plot had incidents that were causally related – not merely incidents ordered by chronology, one incident just happening after another.

Taken over from Russian narrative study into French narrative study was another influential naming of narrative *langue* versus narrative *parole*. This was a contrast of *l'histoire* with *le discours* or, in English, 'story' and 'discourse'. 'Discourse', comparable to *la parole*, referred to the particular telling of the story, whereas 'story', comparable to *la langue*, referred to what was common to different tellings of 'the same story'. The vocabulary in this area can be very confusing. Here are equivalences, with references to meanings in McQuillan's glossary in bold and Bal's usage, commented on below, in parentheses:

- **discourse**/narrative/*récit*/*sjuzet*/(Bal and Rimmon-Kenan *text*) – the particular telling

- **story**/*l'histoire*/*fabula*/(Aristotle *logos* meaning 1) (Bal *fabula*) – the events in chronological order
- **plot** (Aristotle: *mythos*, also comparable with discourse) (Bal *story*) – the causally related order of events in a particular telling.

The most confusing word is perhaps 'plot' as it has an everyday sense of a summary of the story, whereas in structuralist use it refers to the specific ordering of the events. In chapter 13, 'Soap operas and sitcoms', you will see that 'plotline' is used interchangeably with 'storyline'. Table 3.2 shows the confusion of story(-line) and plot(-line).

Table 3.2: Storyline and plotline.

Story	Storyline
1 = narrative, what is told in full	1 = plotline, one thread (one of many in the complete narrative) concerning the same characters and their interaction centred on a narrative complication.
2 = plot, what is told in summary	2 = story 2 (plot, what is told in summary)
3 = storyline 1	
4 = (structuralist use, abstracted) events in a chronological order, but note Bal's intermediate use	

In addition to story and text, Rimmon-Kenan organises her chapters with a third term, taken from Genette: *narration*. This refers to the 'act or process of production', both real (the author) and internal to the text (the narrator) (Rimmon-Kenan 1983: 3–4). Figure 2.2, 'Differences of voice', illustrates 'narration'.

'Bal' is Mieke Bal, writing in *Narratology: Introduction to the Theory of Narrative*. Bal makes use of the three levels that are implicit in the structuralist talk of two sets of dualisms, plot and story, and discourse and story. The most underlying level of story in the structuralist analysis is the events in chronological order. She calls this *fabula*, from the Russian tradition. An intermediate level in which the events are ordered as they will be in the final narrative, she calls 'story' (i.e., what has been called 'plot' in the simple dualism). And the actual particular telling of the ordered events, the discourse, she calls 'text' (Bal 1985, 1997). One's head begins to spin! However, in general, those describing a structuralist model of narrative (like H. Porter Abbott in *The Cambridge Introduction to Narrative*, 2002) have found just two levels adequate: an 'underlying' story/*fabula*, and a 'surface' telling/discourse/text/*sjuzet*, in which events might be disordered from the story. Note those words 'underlying' and 'surface': such notions are characteristic of structuralist talk, implying a pre-existing model or structure that has in fact been retrieved from particular texts.

The post-structuralist critique

I have particularly mentioned the work of Bal because she is one of those many people who found themselves moving from a structuralist to a post-structuralist understanding from the 1980s. The first edition of her book, *Narratology*, appeared in English in 1985 (she had published in the late 1970s in Dutch). In this first edition Bal is an avowed structuralist. The second edition, thoroughly revised, came out in 1997, and it is worth reading at least the preface to see her change in perspective. She writes, 'I was more and more uneasy about the tone of it [the first edition], the references to "being sure" and all those remnants of the positivistic discourse of my training that inhere in structuralist thought.' Bal does not reject the usefulness of structuralist analysis, but she now recognises the contingency, the particular perspective or purpose, the subjectivity, that any such analysis takes up.

Mieke Bal's later interests also illustrate a general tendency in post-structuralist work on narrative: she writes in the preface, '. . . my recent work has been less oriented towards literary narrative than to narrative in such diverse domains as anthropology, visual art, and the critique of scholarship.' So McQuillan's generalisation, which I quoted at the beginning of this chapter, 'Narrative theory now lives on, embedded in the work and tropes of post-structuralism', doesn't imply a falling-off of interest in narrative theory. On the contrary, the relevance of narrative theory is now seen in any area of human semiosis; that is, where humans make meaning (such as in popular culture, as in much of this book).

From post-structuralist criticisms of structuralist studies of narrative – that Propp's functions and Lévi-Strauss's paradigms were not objectively in the text, and that Bal herself became uneasy about her positivistic training – you might already have inferred – subjectively of course! – the post-structuralist perspective. The word 'de-construction' (it originally had a hyphen), as used by the French philosopher Jacques Derrida, is frequently associated with post-structuralist talk; one can (at least) gloss deconstruction as the undoing of the dichotomy of subject and object, the recognition of the subject in the object. 'The structure is the object plus the subjective intelligence of the observer; the structure is a **simulacrum** of the object. In other words, the experience and understanding of the observer are built into the observation. The experience and understanding of the interpreter are built into the interpretation' (Spivak 1976: lvii). Structuralist studies of narrative are certainly useful for gaining insights and making generalisations and comparisons – which is the role of any theory, to give us helpful ways of talking about an object of study – but they do not have the objective status that, in their heyday, was given to them by structuralist theorists. Remember Peirce's understanding of the sign, discussed in chapter 2 above. The structuralist objectivity derived from a simple dualism of external: internal to the observer/interpreter. In contrast, for Peirce, objectivity is always mediated, the interpreter interpreting within the semiotic world of his/her *Umwelt* – which, to a greater or lesser extent, might coincide with external reality.

A helpful example of deconstruction is given by Barbara Hernstein Smith, in her study of the many versions of 'Cinderella'. Her paper deconstructs the structuralist opposition of story and discourse: the notion that there is an objectively general underlying story associated with many particular surface discourses/tellings. From the post-structuralist perspective, the story is not 'underlying' – it is just another version that the teller has told for a particular social purpose. Smith writes:

> Not only will different summaries of the same narrative be produced by people with different conventions, habits, and models of summarising, but even given the *same* conventions, their summaries will be different if the motives and purposes of their summarising are different. Thus one would present a different plot summary of a given novel if one's motive were to advertise it to potential buyers or to deplore its sexism to a friend and still different if one were summarising the novel in the course of presenting a new interpretation of it or of writing a critical biography of its author. Each of these summaries would simplify the narrative at a different level of abstraction, and each of them would preserve, omit, link, isolate, and foreground different features or sets of features in accord with the particular occasion and purposes of the summarising. It is evident . . . that each of these summaries would . . . be another version of the novel: an abridged, and simplified version . . .
>
> (Smith in McQuillan 2000: 141)

Think of the Reader's Digest abridged versions of novels, of the comic book versions of Shakespearean plays . . .

Structuralist studies of narrative, then, focused on the text as an object of study. Post-structuralist studies, with their awareness of the perspective, the subjectivity of any interpretation, have paid explicit attention to the **subject**: that is, the human being doing the producing or interpreting of narrative. A concern with the subject has led in much contemporary work to a focus on ideology – the ideology of those producing text and the ideology of those interpreting it, as readers or viewers. A very influential text of this kind is *The Postmodern Condition*, by Jean-François Lyotard, which appeared in 1984. In his lengthy gloss on 'Narrative', McQuillan gives a comment on Lyotard as item 7:

> For Lyotard, narrative is a mode of knowledge . . . Knowledge is articulated and communicated in society in the form of narratives. Therefore, narratives define the possibilities of knowledge and, hence, action in any given society. Thus, narratives are legitimised by the very fact that they exist. A knowledge of the narratives of a community or society distinguishes an indigenous person from an outsider.
>
> (McQuillan 2000: 323)

From that last sentence, you could infer why Mieke Bal, in 1997, could say her study of narrative had moved from a concern with literary texts to include anthropology.

The French literary and cultural critic Roland Barthes moved from structuralist towards post-structuralist practice in his approach to narrative. (His early paper, 'Introduction to the structural analysis of narratives', was very influential. McQuillan 2000: 109–14.) He was one of the first to do so. In his early work, in the 1960s, he drew diagrams of inferred narrative structure and talked of story and discourse, but in his book *S/Z* (published in 1970, in French) Barthes makes a consciously idiosyncratic analysis of a novella by Balzac. Emphasising the contingency of any particular reading of a text, Barthes names five codes – with no claim that these are absolute codes, just ones he finds useful – and then exhaustively discusses his own interpretation of the novella, making explicit the way in which his own particular experiences and history as a reader are contextualising the narrative for him (that is, giving him a context of reception in which to make sense of the narrative), so that the text is meaningful for him (Barthes 1974). Describing Barthes' 117 pages (approximately) analysing the thirty-three-page story, Lacey comments that this is 'impressive . . . and mad' (Lacey 2000: 72–7).

The advantage of reading such a study as *S/Z* is that it allows you to follow the traces of highly informed reading by a very intelligent and very erudite reader – a kind of modelling of imaginative reading, from which, if one is accustomed to more frugal reading practices, one can learn. The best kind of literary criticism is exactly like this – not telling you how a text is, but modelling for you how it might be read.

Since 1980, the narrative theory of the French scholar Gérard Genette has been particularly influential because it is 'the most thorough attempt we have to identify, name, and illustrate the basic constituents and techniques of narrative' (Jonathan Culler's foreword in Genette 1980: 7). Genette's analytic categories were derived from his close work on Marcel Proust's novel, *La recherche du temps perdu* (*In Search of Lost Time*). Table 3.3 gives an overview, without detailed terms. (For a brief discussion, see Cortazzi 1993: 93–7; see also the section on diegesis and mimesis in chapter 2 above.)

Because Genette's terms describe features *in* the text, his theory is in the structuralist tradition. As Culler observes, in his foreword to Genette's most famous book, *Narrative Discourse: An Essay in Method*, '[This major work] is one of the central achievements of what was called structuralism. The structuralist study of literature . . . sought not to interpret literature but to investigate its structures and devices' (Genette 1980: 7–8). In comparison, traditional readers attempt to interpret literature whereas post-structuralist or postmodern critics attempt to identify the ideology of the interpreter (whether speaker, writer, listener or reader) or investigator (another critic or theorist). As the opening paragraphs of this chapter imply, these three approaches do not form a linear progression, but can coexist usefully for different purposes, as long as the user recognises the relevance and

Table 3.3: Genette's set of categories for analysing narrative.

TENSE	MOOD	VOICE
Order The order of events in the narrative compared to the chronological order of events	**Focalisation** The perspective from which the narrative is told, the one who 'sees', as opposed to the one who 'tells' (the narrator). A refinement of the traditional concept 'point of view' (Rimmon-Kenan, 1983: chapter 6).	**Narrators** Figure 2.2 Speech acts of narrator
Duration Compares how long a narrator dwells on events when telling them in the narrative with how long those events might take if actually experienced.	**Distance** Diegesis and mimesis, as indicated on figure 2.2	**Speech** Figure 2.2 Speech acts as acts of characters
Frequency Number of mentions of an event in the narrative		

theoretical implications of all three approaches. For example, Genette's detailed structuralist study of Proust might enable many readers to develop a more subtle interpretative response to the complex writing of that author.

At the same time, Genette's comments can have unexpected resonance with postmodern notions one might have about the kind of media discussed in this book. For example, '[We observe] the increasing discontinuity of the narrative. The Proustian narrative tends to become more and more discontinuous, syncopated, built of enormous scenes separated by immense gaps, and thus it tends to deviate more and more from the hypothetical "norm" of narrative isochrony' (Genette 1980: 93). (Isochrony: a 1:1 **duration**, or a direct equivalence between story time and plot time; see Julian Murphet's discussion of isochrony in chapter 5.) The unexpected resonance here is with the commercial television production of the soap opera (see chapter 13), except with an inversion of size and length of time (the soap opera narrative typically cuts from one short scene to another, each 'showing' what different characters are doing or saying at much the same time). However, as that chapter elaborates, this is the soap opera norm, rather than the structuralist notion of the 'hypothetical "norm" of narrative isochrony'.

Narrative and time

Despite the differences between various theories described so far, they share a common feature: they all assume that narrative is somehow about time. In most accounts of narrative before about 1980, time is assumed to be a meaning through which narratives are understood to be coherent, but this assumption receives little direct attention. In contrast, however, the movement to post-structuralism (even if not specifically theorised) sees time become the principal focus of narrative study. In his book-length study, H. Porter Abbott asks in his first chapter, 'Narrative and life': 'What does narrative do for us?' (The 'us' is human beings.) He answers 'many things' but that 'if we had to choose one answer above all others, the likeliest is that narrative is the principal way in which our species organises its understanding of time' (Abbott 2002: 3). As early as 1983, the publication date in French (although still trailing the vocabulary of a structuralist scholarly context – remember intertextuality!), Paul Ricoeur writes, on the first page of his massive three-volume study, *Time and Narrative*: 'The world unfolded by every narrative work is always a temporal world. Or . . . time becomes human time to the extent that it is organised after the manner of narrative; narrative, in turn, is meaningful to the extent that it portrays the features of temporal experience' (Ricoeur 1984: 3).

The general assumption that narrative is about time might derive, yet again, from the work of Aristotle. As already described, Aristotle considered the most important aspect of narrative was plot – 'the ordered arrangements of the incidents' – and that in the most effective plots these incidents are causally related: what happens, happens as a result of some previous incident. Now time is of the essence in causality – the cause precedes the effect. The most effective plots are thus evaluated by a criterion dependent on time meaning relations between incidents.

Aristotle assumed that less effective plots will also be ordered by time but that inferior plots will have mere temporal sequence in their incidents. Ideally, 'these [plot discoveries or reversals] should develop out of the very structure of the plot, so that they are the inevitable or probable consequence of what has gone before, for there is a big difference between what happens as a result of something else and what merely happens after it' (McQuillan 2000: 44). But this confusion between mere chronological sequence and causal connections is just what can be exploited to make narrative sense. This confusion is so traditional that it has a medieval Latin name, *post hoc ergo propter hoc*. I quote McQuillan's glossary:

> According to Barthes (reading Aristotle), narrativity is sustained by the confusion between what-comes-after-X and what-is-caused-by-X (e.g. 'The family left Glasgow and Jane became sad' in which Jane's sadness is assumed to derive from the family leaving Glasgow). Scholasticism identifies such confusion between chronology and consequence with the Latin tag *'post hoc ergo propter hoc'* [after thing therefore because of thing].

(McQuillan 2000: 326)

In language, this potential confusion is particularly associated with parataxis; that is, clauses joined by 'and' (sometimes immediately adjacent, without 'and') as, for example, in each of the following two sentences:

He fell to the ground and the gun went off.
(He fell to the ground; the gun went off.)

The gun went off and he fell to the ground.
(The gun went off; he fell to the ground.)

For each sentence we assume a different temporal relation between the same events, and are likely to assume a causal relation in the second sentence ('he fell because he was shot'). If, however, the two clauses are joined by a subordinating conjunction, such as 'when', which makes the meaning relation explicit, then the clauses can follow in either order but be understood with the same time meaning relation:

He fell to the ground when the gun went off.
When the gun went off he fell to the ground.

Note that 'when' has a temporal meaning, but not necessarily a causal one – in narrative context, he might be startled by the explosion rather than wounded. We are more likely to understand a causal relation from the simple parataxis ('the gun went off and he fell to the ground'), although, as always with language, a particular textual or situational context might suggest another interpretation to the reader or listener.

Yet this principle of *post hoc ergo propter hoc* was what early film-makers discovered to be the very stuff of editing to construct a 'narrative'. In 1917 the young Russian film-maker Lev Kuleshov shot film of two people looking off screen and then, in quite a different place, he shot film of an electric pylon. Then he edited the two shots together. Now the people appeared to be looking at the pylon. Kuleshov was amazed to discover that he had created a 'new geography', a 'new place of action'; that is, the narrative coherence perceived in the sequence of shots in film had created a visual fiction. In a study of narrative composition, Nick Davis comments, 'Like other early film-makers, Kuleshov seems to have been puzzled and intrigued by the propensity of shots in juxtaposition to "show" what had not been present in the same shots individually' (Hawthorn 1985: 25).

In another famous experiment Kuleshov took one close-up of a well-known actor, then juxtaposed that single shot successively with images of a woman's body lying in a coffin, a bowl of hot soup, a small girl playing with a teddy bear and so on. 'Audiences viewing these miniature sequences "saw" an appropriate affective response – "sorrow", "hunger", "fatherly pride" and what have you – registered in the actor's facial expression, though this was in fact unchanged' (Davis in Hawthorn 1985: 25). In this second account we see the way a viewer, in perceiving coherence between the two shots, actually writes in their own life experience of events and feelings and attributes some psychological state to the first image of the male actor in order to generate a meaning link between the successive shots: 'The man looks sorrowful because he has lost his wife.'

Alfred Hitchcock, who studied the early Soviet film-makers closely, 'even demonstrated Kuleshov's idea during a 1965 television program, filming himself with a suggestive smile, then intercutting the image first with tender-hearted footage of a mother and a baby, then with a beautiful young woman in a sexy bikini, winkingly making his point that the order and arrangement of the images – the editing – drastically altered the message' (McGilligan 2003: 75–6). Strictly speaking, what is altered is not the message but the sequence of shots to which a viewer gives coherence from their own experience. Only a post-structuralist account – one that acknowledges the 'subject in the object' – is adequate to describe the subjectively coherent interpretation a producer or a viewer can make of an edited film.

Conclusion

The history of narrative theory is itself a narrative told in chronological order, forming links that are both temporal and causal. Post-structuralism is a necessary consequence of the limitations of structuralist analysis, repositioning the subject as the producer of meaning in a text. This brief account of the development of narrative theory draws attention to the importance of linguistic concepts to an understanding of narrative structure, starting particularly with Saussure's structuralist opposition between *langue* and *parole*, paradigm and syntagm. This chapter also reiterates the central function of time as a structuring principle in narrative, one whose meaning is as much a product of subjective interpretation as any other aspect of narrative.

Part 2

Film as narrative and visual mode

Chapter 4

Stories and plots

Julian Murphet

There are many ways to think about film as a medium; its narrative properties represent only one component of a very complex whole. For example, it would be perfectly legitimate to approach film from its technological aspect, or to consider its function in sustaining a certain political culture, or to concentrate on its pictorial aesthetic qualities, or on its musical, rhythmic or chromatic properties. Nevertheless, both within the purview of this book, and more generally in the way we tend to think about and discuss the medium, films are predominantly considered as narrative forms. Indeed, it would be possible to contend that film was the dominant narrative medium of the twentieth century; a fact not without its own interesting history, some of which we will glance at below.

As a narrative medium, film – like other narrative media: epics, novels, dramas, operas and the various media considered in this book – has established many interlocking conventions to make its storytelling comprehensible. Many of these conventions concern the unique art of editing: the splicing together of different shots to make one coherent narrative whole. But other conventions have to do with how the image is composed 'within the frame' of any given shot. Traditionally, these two distinct areas in film aesthetics are known as, respectively, **montage** and *mise en scène*. Narrative conventions in the cinema articulate these two domains: there are rules for the way shots should be assembled to provide the greatest narrative efficiency, and rules for the way individual shots should be composed to direct attention to the relevant narrative information. However, in undertaking an investigation of the narrative dimension of film, it is arguably best to begin with the raw narrative unit of the medium: the shot.*

Shots as proto-narratives

Film's ability to reproduce actions in a photographically realistic space is the most important property it brings to the telling of stories. In every other medium, a far greater amount of effort has to be expended to create the 'illusion' of a believable milieu: words describing places and faces; theatrical sets 'suggesting' Tosca's tower or Elsinore. From the moment of the first short films by the Lumière brothers, however, the miraculous narrative advance of the cinema was apparent: *there it is,* happening before your eyes. A real train pulls into a real station and stops; a real factory opens its gates and out pours a real stream of industrial labourers; a man in a real garden bends over his blocked hose and is sprayed by real water when his hidden tormentor lifts his foot from the hose. The suspension of disbelief is immediate; we no longer have to be lulled into a sense of security by an eloquent narrator, or gradually accept that that prop really is what it purports to be. To be sure, nothing is as simple as it seems, and no doubt a cultural predisposition to see flat images in a rectangular space as 'three dimensional' is an advantage in 'seeing the real' in film; yet, all quibbling aside, the apocryphal stories of the first viewers of the Lumières' *L'Arrive d'un train en gare* (1895), rushing away from the projection in fear for their lives, are 'true' in the sense that they underline this basic fact – film is compellingly 'realistic', and its shots elicit more immediate credence than any other narrative medium.

The question is: is *L'Arrive d'un train en gare* properly 'narrative'? A train pulls towards us from a distance, and stops, at a station platform where passengers mill around. This is the establishment of a scene and the completion of an action. At this very early stage in the development of cinematic narrative, there was no need for further elaborations of plot; the mere presentation of an uninterrupted moving visual image was enough. The effect of the Lumières' 'arrival of the train' suggests that the mechanical succession of briefly illuminated frames, at sixteen or twenty-four frames per second, can establish a unity of place, a unity of time and a unity of action (Aristotle's three narrative unities) without any formal effort on the part of the putative 'storyteller' or of the viewer. The train entering the station 'happens' in a way that mere still photography or painting cannot match and, more to the point, in a way that verbal narration cannot match either. The action

---

* It is, however, true that since the development of digital visual technology, and especially of digitally animated feature-length films, the 'shot' as such has ceased to exist as the relevant unit of narrative analysis. In fact, these films (such as *Toy Story* and *Antz*) continue to appear as though they are made up of shots, because the directors and animators want to adapt the new technology to existing habits of perception and comprehension, even though the medium itself has transcended the unit of the shot, and with it the necessity of cutting.

is integrated, seamless, complete, self-contained, repeatable and consistent. The arrival of the train does *not*, apparently, *have to be narrated*; it just 'happens'. It has become as 'natural' and organic an event as the blowing of wind through the leaves or the ripple of water on a pond. In this respect, cinema really introduces a revolution into the art of narrative. It 'naturalises' the conventional; it sidesteps the inevitably artificial reduction of an action to a sequence of words, and gives us instead a mesmerising visual unity – because the artificiality is purely mechanical, it announces itself only when the projector breaks down.

So, can we really call the event as represented in this film 'narrative' at all? In the words of H. Porter Abbott, it will suffice for a narrative: 'in my view [he says] the capacity to represent an event, either in words or in some other way, is the key gift and it produces the building blocks out of which all the more complex forms are built' (Abbott 2002: 12). I agree with this, but I think it pays to differentiate between such bare events as the arrival of a train at a station and the complex narrative of *The Great Train Robbery* (Porter 1903), or Hitchcock's *Strangers on a Train* (1951). It is in this respect that I recommend the concept of proto-narrativity: a proto-narrative represents an event, but is not yet a narrative proper. It might become one, but only when it is combined with other, connected represented events. In a 'proto-narrative' some action happens, and this event provides a unit for larger compositions, as a sentence does in prose, but without requiring the complex linguistic conventions of prose narrative. You don't seem to have to be 'literate' in any language to 'get' this seamless action, as you need to be literate to 'get' the sentence 'a train pulled into the station'; just as you will need to be 'film literate' to 'get' *Strangers on a Train*. *L'Arrive* offers us a proto-narrative, and it does so by a calculated act of framing – through *mise en scène*.

For the film is, despite all its appearance of immediacy and absence of conventions, still a deliberately staged, focused and framed episode, with some kind of 'author' or narrator hovering over it. The imitation of action in film is so powerfully persuasive, and its *modus operandi* so purely technical, that the traditional function of narrator seems severely weakened: who is narrating the trivial arrival of the train at the station? It seems to be nothing other than a moving slice of reality, unmediated and pure. Nevertheless, this is indeed an illusion. At the very least, someone has mounted a camera at a specific spot at a specific time to capture a specific event in a particular way. What if the camera had been pointed at the sky at this moment, or taken the shot two minutes later, after the train had left? As well, there really is something like a 'story' here, and arguably one with meanings: 'Look, here's a train, on time! Isn't France wonderful? The French trains and the French cinema are two wonderful, modern things, and see how they go together – so much to enjoy!' In a single shot, this is just part of the story being told, by two brothers who made a fortune out of such simple proto-narratives. The first business of narrativity in the cinema is *framing the event* in a shot, and every such framing is, already, a story of sorts: the minimal but indispensable unit of film narrative.

Putting shots together

Now, if you want to construct a larger narrative out of several proto-narrative shots, how are you going to justify the leap between various points of view that each cut entails? Each shot in the representational cinema has its own perspective, duration, logic and justification. And each cut radically disrupts this integrity. The fact that we, today, rarely notice the cut as such (and students often need to be trained to tell where cuts fall) is a product of intensive conventionalisation, a testament to the degree to which the radical disruptions of the editorial process have been naturalised and integrated into our cognisance of filmic narrative form. To a large extent, the history of narrative film has been one continuous effort to naturalise its conventions to the degree that we can experience it 'like a novel' or 'like a stage play'.

How so? Helen Fulton considers the developed conventions of 'visual cohesion' in film form in part 4 of this book; in this section, I will be approaching film's narrative conventions under the more traditional and 'literary' auspices of 'plot', narrative time, voice and point of view. In each case, however, the point is that the potential for film to elaborate an entirely new perspective on things (a mechanical, analytical, 'inhuman' perspective) is constrained and curtailed by an overarching effort to 'humanise' the medium, render it subservient to the rules of human psychology and causality as these had been canonised by centuries of spoken, written and enacted narrative forms.

> The first impulse [in early cinema] was simply to turn the camera on some interesting subject, staged or real, and let it run. In terms of structure, the earliest films . . . are simply brief recordings of entertaining or amusing subjects in which the camera was made to obey the laws of empirical reality. That is, *it was treated as an unblinking human eye, and there was no concept of editing because reality cannot be edited by the human eye.*
>
> (Cook 1996: 8–9; my emphasis)

As David Cook here implies, as soon as you introduce the narrative logic of film construction, and splice two or more shots together, all at once you lose the comfortable analogy between machine and bodily organ. No matter how hard you try, in real life it is impossible to 'see' the visual cut from the outside of a train rushing past, to the inside, where Cary Grant and Eva Marie Saint are sitting down to lunch in the dining car (in *North by Northwest*; Hitchcock 1959). This transition, this editorial cut, is fundamentally *inhuman*. It suggests that the 'point of view' of narrative film is radically different from that of all previous media – the immediate leaps one is constantly making from shot to shot have no parallel for the human eye or any other human sense. It is the manufactured visual experience of a machine, and if we 'assume' this point of view, then we are in effect identifying with a piece of technology.

Edited film thus offers the first instance of a properly 'post-human' perspective, and the remarkable thing has been the degree to which this 'post-humanism' has been repressed and denied by the dominant forces in film production since its invention. But always remember: it could have been otherwise. In the Soviet Union, during the 1920s, many experiments were made to liberate the film medium from classical modes of narration. The Soviet avant-garde in cinema realised that film could achieve radically 'post-human' effects, and tried to build up new laws of construction that would allow the camera, and the process of editing, a maximum degree of freedom. The apex of this achievement is a film called *Man with a Movie Camera* (USSR, Dziga Vertov 1929), which not only allows the camera to take up an amazing number of 'inhuman' positions on everyday life in revolutionary Russia but also combines its images in ways that are not tied to any character other than the camera itself. In this film the machine, the camera, is the hero, and human beings are only a small part of the world it can perceive: a world of machines, natural forces, buildings, light and shade, ideas and symbols. The idea of tying this unprecedented freedom of perception down to something as tired and conventional as a 'story' was anathema to the film's director, who called himself Dziga Vertov, after the sound made by film passing through the projector's shutter mechanism. In his wonderful manifesto of 1922, he wrote:

We consider the psychological . . . film-drama – weighted down with apparitions and childhood memories – an absurdity.

. . .

We proclaim the old films, based on the romance, theatrical films and the like, to be leprous.
Keep away from them!
Keep your eyes off them!
They're mortally dangerous!
Contagious!

. . .

The 'psychological' prevents man from being as precise as a stopwatch; it interferes with his desire for kinship with the machine.

(Vertov 1984: 5–7)

This kind of futuristic utopianism, although it provided the blueprint for some of the most exciting films ever made, was never likely to catch on in the West, and in the USA especially. There, above all, the dominant domain of the cinema has ever been the domain of human psychology, human action, human sentiment and human cliché; in a word, the world of 'stories'. The question is: how did the US cinema, and all of its imitators, manage to channel a machine-like perspective on the world into another version of human psychology? How did Hollywood transform a machinic and technical point of view into a human and narrative one?

In order to draw crowds, and generate profits, the new medium conformed to existing ideas about what 'entertainment' and storytelling were. First, this meant always carefully preparing and planning the 'story' of what would be shot before the camera began to roll. The act of writing would therefore precede and determine the process of cinematography, in order to eliminate wasted, 'random' or unplanned incidents. Second, it meant adapting pre-existent styles of performance from the stage to the exigencies of the newer medium. Viewers like to identify with human beings, and stage acting offered a ready-made model of such identification; in particular, the stage's cult of the 'star' was quickly adapted to the cinematic medium. Time and again since the heyday of the 1920s, narrative has proven subordinate to star power in the creation of cinematic product in the USA. Third, and most importantly, it meant that, in the construction of complex narratives out of basic shot units, fundamental narrative principles derived from the long history of narrative form would be applied to the nascent medium. To borrow a well-known, if theoretically vulnerable, distinction from narrative theory, we could say that, in the elaboration of the codes of film narrative, the distinction between **story** and **plot** was of paramount importance in dictating what would be shot, how it would be shot, and how the shots would be assembled.

Plots and stories

In the world of film studies, the word most often used for the 'story' of a film is the Greek word for 'recounted story', *diegesis*. Narrative film, we might say, privileges the frame of the diegesis: it fosters, during our viewing experience, the apprehension of a single, consistent, integral imagined world, in which actions connect with one another causally, and through which, generally, one central character makes his or her way from an initial state to a different, final state. The 'implied world' of the diegesis is most often structured around a 'major' chain of events, concerning the central character(s), and usually some 'minor' chains of events connected tangentially to the main line, and it is in order to make this world clear, apparent and believable that most of the conventions of film narrative construction were developed. Such an approach to storytelling is entirely derived from oral, written and performed narrative.

And, as with all other narrative media, it is still convenient to make a distinction between this 'implied world' of the diegesis and the actual projected celluloid (or written words, or stage performance) before our eyes and ears. No one would wish to argue that the 'world' of *Bambi* (Hand 1942) or *Pulp Fiction* (Tarantino 1994) is 'real'; yet the films themselves certainly are, and one of their main effects is to make it compelling for us to believe in their implied worlds for the duration of any screening (and, in our private reflections, for any time thereafter). The 'trick' of all good narrative consists in collapsing this inevitable distinction (artificial presentation, believable diegesis) into the 'right kind' of distance for its implied audience, and the name most generally given to this 'trick' is plot. *Plot* is the wherewithal of narrative construction. It is the higher-order art of selection, combination, exaggeration, distortion, omission, acceleration, retardation, implication and so on, whereby a basic story (or chain of events) is restructured to become interesting and compelling to a certain audience. *Pulp Fiction* is an excellent example of a film that deliberately 'plots' its material in unexpected and arresting ways (arranging incidents out of chronological order; repeating key incidents; adding non-diegetic elements such as the box drawn by Uma Thurman's fingers when she says 'square'; and so on) in order to seduce a media-savvy audience into its diegesis while also keeping an appropriately ironic distance from it. *Bambi* on the other hand is a perfect instance of 'classical' narrative form, where the 'plot' never intrudes too visibly to distract its young viewers from the diegesis, but maintains a quiet grip on proceedings nevertheless.

Plots and stories, then; but there are stories and there are stories. The 'story' of such a film as *The Usual Suspects* (Brian Singer 1995) is relatively dense with inconsistent information, and its articulation, reconstructed painstakingly from the plot, is no easy matter. In this regard it is an 'unusual suspect' in the history of Hollywood film, which relies heavily on legibility and simplicity. Hollywood story construction, to quote David Bordwell, is premised on very simple laws: 'causality, consequence, psychological motivations, the drive toward overcoming obstacles and achieving goals. Character-centred – i.e., personal or psychological – causality is the armature of the classical story' (Bordwell, Staiger & Thompson 1985: 13). To be sure, as Singer's film shows, we have evolved since the days of 'classical cinema' proper (the high point of which was probably 1939); yet there is little doubt that these same laws, suitably modified to a more canny and media-conscious spectatorship, apply equally well to most Hollywood products today. What has changed, I feel, is the quality and nature of the plotting. In what remains of this chapter, I want to focus on three distinct historical examples of 'Hollywood' film, one 'classical', one 'modernist' and one 'postmodernist', to see how film plotting has altered in response to the evolution of the global filmgoer while persisting in framing very basic and elemental 'storylines'. These three examples are: *The Birth of a Nation* (Griffith 1915), *Citizen Kane* (Welles 1941) and *Memento* (Nolan 2000). No matter how far these films, progressively, get from immediately apparent laws of psychological cause and effect (to the extent that the last precisely inverts this order), we can still locate a classical story logic behind each of them.

Classical narration

In *The Birth of a Nation*, D. W. Griffith, who pioneered so many of the finer details of narrative construction in his early shorts, and here virtually invented the 'feature length' film, prioritised strong structural dualisms (North v. South, black v. white, male and female, blonde and brunette, etc.) in the story material. This was to make sure that the endurance test of three hours' viewing-time was not made helplessly complicated and alienating for an audience used to quick, five- to ten-minute presentations. Clear oppositions underlie almost every major scene, and the stark visual contrast of black and white on monochrome stock was raised into the film's central political, ideological and 'racial' crux. But more importantly still, he carried his dualistic, melodramatic temperament across into the business of plot construction and editorial rhythm.

The film's opening scenes are a good illustration of the way in which Griffith would conceive of his plotting in the film as a whole. After a brief, 'historical' prelude (no more than mobile tableaux explained with intertitles), Griffith installs us spatially in the home and then gardens of the Stoneman household, the 'Northern' half of his two-family historical romance. There a letter is penned that promises a visit to the 'other', Southern family, the Camerons, in Piedmont, Virginia. Griffith then cuts to Piedmont and to the Camerons out on the porch, receiving the letter. The subsequent scene concerns the arrival of the Stoneman brothers at the Cameron house. Very crudely, this is a working example of Griffith's method of fusing shot sequences within an evolving dramatic unity: two distinct locales are first of all paralleled, then stitched together by revealed diegetic intent (the letter proposing the visit), and by achieved synthesis (the visit itself), which mingles elements of both, discrete sets (Stoneman/North; Cameron/South). In this way, and throughout his landmark film, Griffith canonised certain habits of construction (of 'plotting') that laid the foundations for much US film to come. From the rather simplistic and melodramatic story materials that he took from his source novel, Dixon's *The Clansman*, Griffith extrapolated a bipolar and coercive editorial rhythm, predicated on patterns of dualistic alternation, disjunction and synthesis.

This rhythm was called 'parallel alternate montage', and nowhere is its logic better witnessed than in the thrilling climax of *The Birth of a Nation*. Two principal lines of action, each consisting of two opposed forces, are coordinated and unified by Griffith in an inspired logic of intercutting and mutual implication. The first line concerns Ben Cameron at the head of the mounted legion of 'Night Hawks' (or Ku Klux Klan), riding towards Piedmont to save the town from the outrages of 'crazed Negroes' and Elsie Stoneman from the lascivious clutches of her father's trusted mulatto conspirator, Lynch. 'Meanwhile', in the words of David Cook, in the second line of action,

> Negro militiamen have discovered the cabin containing Dr Cameron, Margaret [Cameron], and Phil [Stoneman], and have besieged it with every intention of murdering its occupants. Shots of this action are now intercut with shots of the torrential ride of the Klan, Negroes rioting in the streets of Piedmont, and . . . Lynch's impending rape of Elsie Stoneman; so that we have a suspense-filled, multi-pronged, 'last-minute rescue' elaborately wrought of four simultaneous actions converging toward a climax. Griffith heightens the tension of his montage by decreasing the temporal length of each shot and increasing the tempo of physical movement as the sequence traces towards its crescendo.
>
> (Cook 1996: 91)

Griffith so orchestrates his material that two distinct 'stories' finally converge at a single point, at once emphasising the difference between the two series of events, and demonstrating their ultimate harmony within a higher-level unity once narrative closure is reached. Griffith's plotting mechanism, which proved to be so persuasive and influential, has always to do with the restoration of unity, accord and organic harmony out of alternating rhythms of discord, animosity and opposition. His legacy, looming so large in the history of US film, is a formidable formal ideology: the excitement of a threat to order, of difference and dissonance, will always be contained and becalmed by a flexible organic unity. His plots grip us with their strong parallelisms and the breathlessness of the accelerating speed of their cuts, but only to reassure us with their final resolutions.

Classical Hollywood plotting owes much to Griffith's inaugural act in *The Birth of a Nation*. The function of a 'good' Hollywood plot is to concentrate the spectator's attention on a story with this basic trajectory: a given state of affairs is interrupted by some 'cut' in the real; readjustments and losses occur, but finally a new, improved state of affairs emerges from the central character's wrestling with that 'cut' in things (for example, Ben Stoneman's invention of the Ku Klux Klan eventually overcomes the threat to Southern order and to his own beloved, represented by black enfranchisement). The 'cut' is usually a villain of some sort, but could just as well be an impending disaster, a medical emergency, a threat to an expected union and so on. A Hollywood 'plot' focuses our attention on this story by manipulating our interest and identification through devices I will discuss in chapters 5, 6 and 7 (point of view and voice, above all), but more importantly through coercive rhythms of construction that automatically guide our sympathies towards imperilled situations and characters. 'Good plotting' always emphasises the darkness, power and malignancy of the story's villain, disaster or disorder, and underlines the goodness and undeserved suffering of the hero, by cutting back and forth between the two fields of action in such a way as to underscore this dualism as an opposition, a Manichean struggle between right and wrong, good and bad. The 'good' is always a human (or humanised) character, an individual self, struggling to survive and 'do the right thing' in adverse circumstances; the 'bad' is whatever threatens the personal integrity and security of this self. Classical plotting privileges this simplification of the world through not-so-subtle patterns of rhythmic organisation, tonal accentuation, musical accompaniment, 'colour' and field dynamics that have become all but invisible to us during a century of familiarisation and habituation.

Modernist narration

What cultural history knows as 'modernism' was the first great movement to question these habits of viewing installed by 'classical' narrative form. This questioning went ahead on two fronts, both at the level of the story material itself and, more importantly, at the level of its organisation, its 'plotting'. In fact, however, as far as the US cinema is concerned, the first aspect of this modernist desta-bilisation of classical norms really could not take root. It took the European modernists (such film-makers as Godard, Resnais, Bergman, Rossellini and so on) to dismantle the hegemonic story regime of cause-and-effect psychological determinism emanating from Hollywood. By filming stories predicated on polit-ical causation, collective social dialectics, the impossibility of a single point of view, and spiritual profundities, the Europeans effectively launched a wholly dif-ferent type of cinema, often in a kind of loving opposition to the dominant US films. In the USA itself, it was much harder to make the break from classical story structure; what did emerge, however, most unexpectedly, and as though in antici-pation of the revolution that would finally take place in US films thirty years later, was one work that broke free from the dominant Griffith-style plotting of Holly-wood cinema and cleared an effective space of resistance. That film was *Citizen Kane*.

Citizen Kane is not particularly remarkable for its story. As in many another exemplary fictional 'biopic', *Kane* tells the story of one man's vaulting ambition and its destructive consequences for his personal integrity and those around him. It situates cause and effect strictly within the domain of human psychological motivation (except for the social cause of the 1930s Depression), and focuses on a very limited cast of interrelated characters, in a few major spaces (the *Inquirer* office, the Kane household, Susan's apartment, Xanadu and so on). There is noth-ing path-breaking about any of this. What has made *Kane* the most revered film in US cinema history is its plotting, the art of its construction.

Borrowing its form loosely from the generic field of detective fiction, *Kane* splits its story materials into two distinctive, if overlapping diegeses: the seventy-five-year life of Charles Foster Kane, up to and including his death, and the subsequent week-long journalistic investigation into his final words. This second diegetic frame provides the rationale for the organisation of the first frame, which is the 'story' proper: the story of Kane's life. In this sense, it makes some sense to speak of the faceless reporter Thompson as the 'plotter' of the primary story material, just as a detective is the 'plotter' of his investigation of a crime. The plot 'comes after' the story and arranges its pertinent details into some arresting order. *Citizen Kane* makes an issue out of its own plotting: Thompson is sent on his quest for Rosebud because the first 'plotted' version of Kane's story – the 'News on the March' newsreel – is felt to be defective and incomplete. Rawlson and his team of editors and journalists feel that the story could be 'better told'; the story of the newsreel is tired and uninteresting. So, what Thompson is effectively told to do, under the guise of a search for more story information, is come up with a better way to plot a seventy-five-year life in a five-minute newsreel (or a two-hour film, which is what we see).

A good way to think about the convenient but controversial analytic distinction between 'story' and 'plot' is in terms of necessity and contingency: story is what *has* to happen, the incontrovertible sequence of events that gives the narrative its identity (for example, *Casablanca* would not be *Casablanca* if Ilsa stayed with Rick at the end). Plot, however, is the domain of choices and alternative possibilities in the way that that necessary material is presented. The thing to remember about all plots is that they *could have been done differently*. One of the delightful aspects of *Citizen Kane* is its tongue-in-cheek flirtation with this fact. Early on, Thompson pays Kane's widow, Susan Alexander Kane, his first visit in the hunt for Rosebud. It makes good professional sense to go straight to the woman who shared many of Kane's late years in the search for clues. However, Susan's homodiegetic narration of the final part of the story near the film's beginning would ruin the aesthetic orchestration of the narrative that Orson Welles had in mind: after the trial run of the newsreel, a loosely chronological retelling of the life, from boyhood, through early adulthood, middle age and old age.

So, in order to stall this part of the story, Welles makes sure that Susan is hopelessly drunk with grief at the bar, unable to answer Thompson's questions. Thompson therefore has to go to the Thatcher diaries first, and has to visit Bernstein and Leland before he can return to Susan, who is at last in a position to answer his queries. In this way, Welles has dangled before us an alternative plot, which would have begun with Susan, then taken an altogether different path through the story material, perhaps strictly retrogressive. Such an alternative plot would not have altered any of the primary story material but would radically have affected its emotional valency and meaning in the 'telling': if the snowbound boy Kane, shouting 'The Union forever!', were left until near the film's end, the affective power of the Rosebud revelation would be severely diminished. Similarly, if the jaded and increasingly monstrous Kane of the Leland section were to precede the jubilant and visionary Kane of the Bernstein section, the significance of either section would be altered: it is harder to mourn the depleted enthusiast if we do not yet know that he existed.

In these and other ways, *Kane* encourages us – *pace* the Griffith-style of film-making – to imagine alternative plots, to try our hand, even, at playing director. It is a film that foregrounds the 'constructedness' of its plot, its contingency and openness to variable constructions, above all by granting us a surrogate viewer/director in Thompson, whose haphazard quest through thickets of tonally and factually inconsistent material mirrors both our own and that of the director, who, like Thompson, is obliged to put things into *some* order, if not *the* order.

Postmodern narration

Christopher Nolan's *Memento* (2000) is a dazzling display of postmodern plotting. Eschewing the modernist regard for synthetic totalities, as much as the 'classical' regard for dualisms and organic rhythms, Nolan's film makes a virtue of its own insular epistemology and inverts the very structure of chronology. We experience the narration from the point of view of a character, Leonard Shelby, who suffers from short-term memory loss, and to accentuate the fact that Shelby cannot remember anything for longer than ten minutes, Nolan has constructed his narrative segments (his scenes) in *reverse* order. Beginning, literally, at the end (and in a sequence shown in reverse), the film is then plotted such that each successive scene occurs (in 'story time') just *before* the previous scene. We could represent this in the following way:

Memento
Story: A – B – C – D – E – . . . V – W – X – Y – Z.
Plot: Z – Y – X – W – V – . . . E – D – C – B – A.

This is not literally the plot of *Memento*, however, for strewn between several of these scenes are snippets of another scene, shot in black and white, in which Shelby tells someone over the telephone the sad story of 'Sammy', another character who suffers from short-term memory loss. These scene fragments are filmed in the 'proper' chronological order, but are taken from a scene that precedes the rest of the story and, crucially enough, are finally revealed to be the 'back story' about Shelby himself (who is exposed to have been 'Sammy').

Here, we can see that the story itself, and its inclusion of the characterological detail of 'short-term memory loss', amounts to little more than what the structuralists called a 'motivation of the device'. Nolan clearly wanted to 'make a movie backwards', and the memory loss merely provides him with a narrative excuse to do just that. The fact that so much of *Memento*'s narrative information depends upon Shelby's writing (tattoos, graffiti, commentary, dossiers) and Polaroid photography, further emphasises the film's status as a reflection on narrative, rather than simply a narrative itself – Nolan wants us to think about how we employ verbal and visual techniques to make our lives coherent and meaningful, in ways that are little more than fictional, rather than give way to the sheer flux of being.

Through its ingenious plotting, *Memento* manages both to enthral us with an essential *film noir* mystery (Who is Shelby? What are his real motivations?) – thus remaining in the territory of classical story 'cause and effect' logic – *and* to make us question that logic and our dependency on it in a world full of fabricated images, messages and identities. The radical inversion of story and plot 'sequencing' might also make us question this very distinction. For, if we were to write *Memento* 'forwards' – if we were to plot the story material in its 'correct' chronological order (which we can do on DVD) – what would emerge from this process would be *unrecognisable* as *Memento*. That is to say, the identity of the narrative would be so radically transformed; the suspense so thoroughly destroyed; the mystery traduced; the motivation banal; the device of memory loss incomprehensible – that we would in effect have a completely different film, even though the shots were the same and the 'story' material identical.

Conclusion

And is not this the case, ultimately, for every film? I suggested above that 'plot' is the arena of narrative choice, of contingency, whereas 'story' was the world of necessity. But in every achieved narration, contingency becomes necessity – the 'final cut' is what the film is. It might help us analytically to make these distinctions and separate 'story' from 'plot' to aid our understanding of how narrative functions, but the case of *Memento*, and of *Kane*, and of *Birth of a Nation*, make it perfectly clear: the plot is the story. A *Citizen Kane* in which we began with Susan's story and worked backward to Thatcher's would not be Orson Welles' *Citizen Kane*; it would be a very different narrative with very different meanings and implications. A *Memento* in which the whole story ran forward instead of backward is not a film we would even want to watch; from it, all the magic of the film would have evaporated; it would be banal and uninteresting. This is as much as to say, echoing a phrase by Peter Brooks, that we 'read for the plot' (Brooks 1992), not for the story; or rather, to repeat what I have just said, the story *is* the plot. We are interested and gripped not by the constituent elements of the story, in their ideal order and transparent set of relations, but by the way in which this order and these relations are gradually and teasingly revealed through the narration. Abstracted from their plot, the 'story elements' are about as interesting as names in a telephone book; immersed into their narrative setting, these elements can be as surprising as the revelation that 'Sammy' is Shelby, or as moving as when we learn that the dying words of one of the world's wealthiest men is the name of a poor child's sleigh.

Chapter 5

Narrative time

Julian Murphet

To begin with the very obvious, all storytelling is necessarily extended in time: narrative is a *temporal* mode. To tell a story is to articulate represented events in a sequence, putting one thing after another, drawing causal connections between them, until we have moved (as Aristotle said) from beginning, to middle, to end. And this takes time; it occupies and could even be said to 'flesh out' time. Narrative has generally been thought of as a pleasurable way of spending time, or filling it, and from time to time we are even conscious of going to the movies to 'kill time'. From the moment our caregivers start telling us bedtime stories, we are woven into narrative textures and use these textures to orient us in our daily experience of time. The fact is that our very notion of time, the way we represent it intimately to ourselves, is entirely bound up with the forms of narrative to which we have been exposed. Try to imagine your own personal history 'outside' some kind of narrative shape; the closest you can get is a set of simultaneously juxtaposed images, from which precisely the element of time is missing. Narrative is the medium in which we 'think time', although it might as well be said that time itself, if we can imagine it outside human consciousness, has nothing narrative about it. You might say that narrative is the 'sense organ' we have collectively evolved to detect and record the passing of time and, like all sense organs, it is highly selective and restricted in what it perceives of the 'real world'.

Like theatre, dance and music, film is a medium that works through time. This does not mean that it is inherently a narrative medium, just as neither music nor dance is inherently narrative, but it does predispose the film medium to narrative uses. Whether or not any film 'text' is recognisably a narrative one, it is always, to use a phrase coined by the great Russian film-maker Andrei Tarkovsky, 'sculpted in time' (Tarkovsky 1986). This beautiful image brings to light the inextricable blending of temporal and spatial elements in film; Tarkovsky rightly suggests that, unlike literary narrative, which is entirely linguistic and in some sense immaterial, film has an ineluctable material and spatial dimension: the 'shots' on celluloid strips; the mechanism that passes them over the lens of the projector; the light that casts its shadows on to the screen and our eyes; the illusion of real space. These elements 'sculpt' the time that we experience in film, moulding our sense of pace, duration, continuity and temporal sweep.

Story time, plot time, screen time

Recall the distinction made in chapter 4 between *story* and *plot* – despite understandable misgivings, this division has been useful in orienting the study of narrative texts. And as far as the temporal dimension of texts is concerned, there is a logical and convenient distinction to be made between the *time of the story* and the *time of the plot*. The 'time of the story' would be the period covered by all of the events narrated during the film, including (if it is mentioned or implied to be important) the birth of the lead character, and all the key events that have shaped her life as we see it enacted before us. Remember that the 'story' itself is a rather ideal phenomenon. We never 'get it', directly, as such; it is something we construct during the narration, filling in gaps as we go, and we can never finish this task until all the pieces have been supplied. The story has a temporal order all its own, which corresponds more or less to our conventional understanding of time in the world; a series of connected events organised around a few major transformations, which begins at a certain point, carries through its middle and arrives finally at its end. Often this story time is marked by days, months, years and then hours, minutes and even seconds, to make it easier for us to reconstruct its 'original' and sequential occurrence.

Nevertheless, it is not the 'story' that we are presented with, it is the plot itself, which has played with and distorted the time of the story to suit its own ends. It is plot time with which we are confronted, and this has a logic that often flies in the face of our conventional understanding of time in the world. Not only can plot time be 'out of order' (arranged in a non-chronological sequence) but also it can slow itself down to an unworldly crawl, or accelerate to a frantic blur, or even skip years altogether without a word. So, if 'story time' appears to obey our everyday sense of time as a series of moments succeeding one another in an irreversible order, then 'plot time' obeys only its own sense of what is most appropriate for the increase of pleasure and the maximisation of aesthetic effects. The clearest and most often cited illustration of this difference is the time taken by a detective to unearth all the clues and piece together the crime (plot time) and the time of both the crime itself and its subsequent investigation (story time). Plot time is thus almost always 'shorter' than story time.

Furthermore, we should add to this convenient distinction a third dimension of narrative time in the cinema: the time of the actual presentation, or screen time. Film is distinct from previous narrative media in that the speed of its projection is mechanically fixed. Oral and written narratives are clearly highly flexible in the 'speed' of their delivery, whereas theatrical forms are less flexible but are certainly open to wide variations in the pace of their presentation. As the first narrative medium of the mechanical age, film has a rigidly determined 'time of presentation': owing to the standardised mechanism of projection, no matter where you see *Rashomon* or *Citizen Kane*, you will be seeing it, literally, for exactly the same period, down to the last half a second (allowing for some speed variation in transfers to video, and of course the 'dead time' of commercial interruptions on television). This fact has meant that screen time is a very significant factor at the level of film production. Literally every second counts, as it were, and costs a great deal of money; so film-makers have mastered the 'art' of timing as no previous group of storytellers ever had to. Alfred Hitchcock was famous for knowing exactly, to the order of fractions of a second, how long to hold a shot before cutting, and this was in large part owing to the enormous pressure on each of his productions to make every second of screen time 'pay'.

So, with this initial tripartite conception of 'narrative time' in film (story time, plot time and screen time), we can now begin to enquire how films manage to exploit each level, and the relations between them, for a range of effects. It is only insofar as there *are* dynamic relations between these three levels that time becomes 'interesting' in film. The actual machinery of film-making is 'stupid' as regards time: the apparatus records and projects time mechanically, most often at twenty-four frames per second. The optical illusion on which film depends means that the raw experience of 'watching film' is not all that different from just keeping your eyes open. To illustrate this, it is worth considering the experimental films of Andy Warhol, who turned the banality of film's mechanical relationship to time into an aesthetic *modus operandi*. In such films as *Sleep* (1963; 321 minutes of a man sleeping) and *Empire* (1964; 485 minutes of the Empire State Building on a single day), Warhol simply allows his camera to record the passing of time. Of course things 'happen' in *Empire* (clouds pass, the day darkens, shadows lengthen . . .), but none of this could be described as 'eventful'. *Empire* is a non-narrative film (there is no 'story' and no 'plot'; this is the kind of film that directly calls these categories into question) whose screen time is inflated into a numbing end in itself.

Such an extreme serves to mark a horizon beyond which human tolerance probably does not extend: generally we do not go to the cinema to *experience* screen time but, strictly, to *forget it*. In the earliest of films, this could be guaranteed by the extraordinary novelty of witnessing a banal, everyday event projected on to a screen. The arrival of a train at a provincial station, or the exodus of workers from a factory, has for us some of the intolerability of a Warhol epic; but for the first spectators, the mesmerising fact of such an event's projection, of *moving pictures*, overwhelmed the experience of 'screen time'. Since that moment, however, a more sophisticated set of relations between the three orders of time introduced above has had to be developed to make the passing of ninety or 120 minutes a more compelling experience than watching paint dry.

Unique speeds

Before getting to the formal analysis of variable narrative speeds, it is worthwhile to draw attention to certain technical properties of the medium that make for aesthetic distortions of temporality, even before narrative intrudes. Our film viewing over many years has familiarised us with the following phenomena: the slow-motion shot, the accelerated shot and the freeze frame. Each of these effects is the product of a discrepancy between the screen time of a given event or image and its diegetic temporality – the time it 'would really take' in the implied world of the narrative. And each conveys different affective and psychological information about the narrator's (or film-maker's) intention towards the content of the shot. Stanley Kubrick's *Full Metal Jacket* (1987) includes a scene in which Gunnery Sergeant Hartman is shot by Private Gomer Pyle. At the point of impact, Kubrick slows down the shot to draw out the immensity of the moment in existential terms for all concerned: the victim, the perpetrator and the witness (Private Joker) all 'feel' the event as radically outside the experience of normal time, and so do we.

Godfrey Reggio's *Koyaanisqatsi* (1983) and *Powaqqatsi* (1988) are non-narrative films, but they employ extensive use of slow-motion and accelerated shots. By slowing down the projected shots of threshing rituals or mining practices in Third and Fourth World nations, Reggio seeks to 'dignify' the labour of his filmed subjects. Projected in 'real time' (that is, the speed at which it was filmed), the episode in the open-cast gold mine in *Powaqqatsi* might stress the ant-like and inhuman quality of the labour, but decelerated to the glacial speed at which it is screened in the film, the labour assumes colossal and tragic proportions; the anonymity and degradation of these workers becomes heroic and moving. In some of the sections devoted to the hectic and wasteful life of the postmodern city, however, Reggio speeds up his shots, precisely to emphasise the 'mass' and insect-like conditions of urban life today. These accelerated shots dehumanise the 'Western', white peoples, even as the slow-motion shots 'humanised' the darker, 'Southern' peoples in the films. Such effective use of the variations between 'screen' and 'story' time in film draws on a century of such experiments, although these effects are rarely used well in narrative cinema, either because they look clichéd and crass or because they draw undue attention to the cinematic apparatus and to the conventionality of the presentation.

The freeze frame is a very special case, virtually impossible in any other medium, where 'screen' time becomes infinitely greater than 'story' time. At the end of the first scene of Martin Scorsese's *King of Comedy* (1983), after Rupert

Pupkin has 'saved' Jerry Langford from his adoring fans and bundled them both into the waiting car, the film suddenly stops when a flash from a camera outside lights up the interior of the car. It is at this moment that Scorsese rolls his titles. The effect is startling: the frenetic action ceases, calm descends over the screen; but it is a calm filled with something like comic dread. Caught in the flashlight of a deranged adulation, star and fan together occupy a complex space that they will both dance across for the rest of the film: who is the 'king of comedy'? Who has control? What events will be precipitated by this encounter? The freeze frame allows these questions to emerge from the arrested situation, as no other narrative device could. The end of François Truffaut's *Les Quatre cent coups* (1959) is justly famous for freezing the image of young Antoine escaping his school, and leaving it at that. By terminating the narrative before any neat 'conclusion' could be imposed on it, Truffaut has kept a door open for Antoine's freedom; by terminating the film on a freeze frame of his ecstatic face, Truffaut does more: he immortalises Antoine's freedom. It is no longer a narrative 'option', it is an aesthetic fact, which will live forever as art.

Duration

These are some medium-specific examples of narrative relations of **duration**; that is, relations of speed between the three orders of narrative film time. To describe these complex relations of speed, it will be useful to introduce some critical concepts first pressed into service by the French theorist Gérard Genette. First we will consider the difference between 'isochronic' and 'anisochronic' film texts, and then, under the umbrella of this latter term, we will turn to the variable speeds of narration in the distinct categories of the 'scene', the 'summary', the 'ellipsis' and the 'pause' (Genette 1980: 86–112).

Any film text in which the 'story time' exactly equalled the 'plot time' and both were the same as the 'screen time' would be what Genette calls an 'isochronic' text. In the isochronic text, plot and story time would perfectly overlap, and the speed of narration would be absolutely constant and identical to the 'velocity' of real time. There would be no acceleration or elimination of unnecessary details; nor would there be any interpolated background information. There would be just the steady flow of all relevant events at an even, unexpurgated pace. Do any such films actually exist? At first glance, we might think that Alfred Hitchcock's 1948 film, *Rope*, qualifies as an 'isochronic' film. It is composed of what appears to be a single, continuous shot, and the action of the film takes exactly as long to occur on the screen as it would in 'real life' – it is apparently a case of a film whose 'story', 'plot' and 'screen' times are perfectly equal.

But this is not the case: every time a character speaks of an event that happened before the scene takes place, the 'story' of the film immediately exceeds its 'plot' length and screen duration. Insofar as any information about the prior relations between the two young men and the Jimmy Stewart character is crucial to an understanding of their motivations in the film (and the 'time' of that relation stretches back months and even years into the past), the 'time of the story' dwarfs that of the 'plot'. What we have in *Rope* is isochrony of plot and screen time, but not of plot and story time. It is always worth remembering that the 'master text' of so much Western culture, Sophocles' *Oedipus Rex*, unfolds before us much as *Rope* does: in a continuous present tense, where things happen without apparent 'editing'; yet much of what happens is that information about the past is uncovered that needs to be told within the narration. Aristotle's famous 'unity of plot' basically means an isochrony between the time of the plot and the time of the presentation; it does not mean that 'story time' should be equal to either of these. Indeed, the purely 'isochronic' film text is a kind of hypothetical limit, which would look something like an Andy Warhol film.

Almost all films are therefore 'anisochronic', and manipulate the relations between plot and story time in various ways. Films necessarily vary the speed of their delivery according to aesthetic criteria and in the interests of plot development. It would be quite useless in a detective film to dwell in a monotonous tempo on all the minute-to-minute actions of Sherlock Holmes; useless, because it would mire the viewer in a morass of unnecessary detail, banality and tedium. As the adage in Hollywood has it, 'Cut to the chase'. We want to know what Holmes discovers, what he deduces from his discoveries and what he does about them; along the way, we might happen to find him bantering with Watson or snuffing cocaine, but these moments are important usually for their contrastive nature. The rhythm of the delivery is carefully judged to create the maximum impression of both believability and efficiency. Thus the speed of the text varies according to the specific arc of its plot, the way it allows us to discover its underlying 'story' in the most pleasurable way.

Still, it is worth stating that, in cinema, the pleasure of looking at things can be substituted for traditional narrative devices to an extent probably not present in any other narrative medium. Experiments with narrative speed are not always and everywhere necessary. Part of the pleasure of a film such as *La règle du jeu* (Jean Renoir 1939) consists in simply gazing into the deep spaces of the big house; to derive this pleasure, we require the narrative pace to slacken and give way, which it accordingly does. *Citizen Kane* (Orson Welles 1941) is hardly an isochronic text: its experiments with narrative time are some of the most radical ever tried in a commercial film. But there are key moments when this text, like most others, tends asymptotically towards the condition of pure isochrony: the conversation between Leland and Kane after the election debacle, the scene in which Kane tears apart Susan's room at Xanadu, the conversation between Kane and Susan in the enormous parlour, and so on. In these scenes, the duration of the telling 'matches' the duration of the story events. The principle here is 'realism', and Genette is right to say that, in almost every realist text, the 'scenes' – the set pieces in which characters actually relate to each other in conversational 'real time' – aspire towards the state of isochrony. It is in the spaces 'around' the scenes – in the setting-up, the transitions, the explanations, the descriptions and so on – that narrative speed picks up or becomes retarded.

Getting between scenes requires variations in narrative speed. However, even within scenes, strange things can happen to narrative time. One possibility is that a cut puts us slightly 'back' in story time, either to increase tension or to help the viewer orient herself, or for other aesthetic effects. In many early films, you will find that one shot in which a character closes a door is followed by another in which the door is still closing. This is what we would call today 'bad editing': a continuity error. But things are not always so simple. In Sergei Eisenstein's *Battleship Potemkin* (1925) there is a scene in which a sailor, disgusted with cleaning up unsoiled dishes, smashes a plate against a table-top. Only, this simple action is made up of many short, differently angled shots; and in the montage of the scene, it seems to happen many times, in a rapid pulse of succession. Eisenstein shakes us out of our simple habits of perception, both to convey an impression of pure muscular dynamism and to suggest much larger, allegorical dimensions for the action of smashing a plate. At the comic end of the spectrum, *Monty Python and the Holy Grail* (Gilliam & Jones 1975) features a sequence in which Sir Lancelot is approaching Swamp Castle. The music and the galloping action accentuate the heroism of his quest to rescue an imprisoned maiden, and to increase the drama still further, the editing mimics many an adventure movie in cutting between long shots of Lancelot's approach and reaction shots of the castle guards. Each time we cut back to Lancelot, we see him further back than he was at the end of the last shot of his charge; narrative time is stretched out in a mockery of film 'suspense' until, out of nowhere, the brave knight is pell-mell among the guard, running them through with his sword.

More often, what happens in cinema is that we simply cut from one scene to another, eliminating dead time. This is what Genette called a narrative ellipsis: a radical reduction of plot time to an absolute zero, while the intervening story time can be anything up to several millennia. The most extreme and exciting example of this in commercial cinema is the moment in Stanley Kubrick's *2001: A Space Odyssey* (1968) when the shot of a bone hurled into the air by a Neanderthal is followed by the shot of a spacecraft drifting slowly through the void: here a few million years of story time are radically compressed into a single narrative cut. Ellipses are rife throughout *Citizen Kane*, and we need only mention the great moment when the scene of Kane, Leland and Bernstein huddled in front of the window of the *Chronicle*, which ends with a close-up of the photograph of the *Chronicle* personnel, is magically succeeded by an identical shot of the same men now posing for a picture as the staff of the *Inquirer*. An indefinite number of years has intervened, probably something like six or seven, during which time, the ellipsis silently tells us, the *Inquirer* has supplanted the *Chronicle* as the city's premier journal and Kane has bought up the latter's staff. It is a perfectly economical ellipsis, using identical framings to condense years of story time into a single cut. The art, as so often in film storytelling, is one of economy: expressing the greatest possible amount of information in the least possible time, without losing the audience for a moment. These famous cuts are testimony to the artistic genius that has evolved to do precisely that in the commercial cinema.

Next down the scale of narrative tempo is what Genette describes as the summary; the speed of which we can describe by saying that, in it, story time is significantly greater than plot time. In a conventional summary, rather than just omitting all the detail as in an ellipsis, a brief survey of typical events over a considerable period of time is condensed into a few robust passages. A summary is, in Genette's words, 'the narration in a few paragraphs or a few pages of several days, months, or years of experience, without details of action or speech' (Genette 1980: 95–96). Here again, story time is vastly more extensive than narrative time, but not to the point of infinity, as in an ellipsis. Nineteenth-century novels are full of summary passages. Indeed, although scenes might enjoy the quantitative supremacy in classic realist fiction, summaries are if anything more 'typical' of such texts as those of Dickens, George Eliot, Thomas Hardy and Balzac. Summaries were, until the various revolutions of the twentieth century, 'the most usual transition between two scenes, and thus the connective tissue *par excellence* of novelistic narrative, whose fundamental rhythm is defined by the alternation of summary and scene' (Genette 1980: 97).

How do summaries work in film? *Citizen Kane* contains many of them, and they all take the form of what we call a 'montage'. We will look a little later at the remarkable pastiche of a newsreel near the beginning, the 'News on the March' montage, which is a summary, in advance, of the entire narrative of Kane's life. There are other summaries as well: for example, the summary of Kane's encounters with Thatcher, taken from the Thatcher diaries, which elegantly allows Kane to grow from mere boy to successful young man in a matter of seconds, and the summary of Susan's bored obsession with jigsaw puzzles. But by far the most extraordinary of the summaries in this film is the legendary sequence describing the marriage of Charlie Kane to Emily Norton. This too is a montage, a collation of short clips, all set around the breakfast table in the Kane household where, over what must be a number of years, the marriage declines from rapturous love into silent mutual contempt. It is a textbook illustration of how to do a summary in the medium of film, and that might well be what is most 'modernist' about it. It takes what elsewhere would have been a simple, humble transitional device and transforms it into an end in itself, advertising its own technical brilliance at the same time as it performs a humdrum operation between major scenes.

Finally, Genette proposes a fourth category of narrative tempo: the descriptive pause. This, the 'slowest' of narrative durations, is the other extreme from the ellipsis, which is the 'fastest'. Here, it is story time that reduces to a zero and narrative time that dilates to unpredictable lengths. In a novel – and indeed in all verbal storytelling – it is occasionally incumbent upon the narrator to suspend proceedings altogether so that he or she can spend some time describing the situation at hand: be it the room, the dress, the weather, the avenue, the state of play or what have you. Such descriptions are not strictly necessary to narrative development, but they lend a considerable air of authenticity, atmosphere and detail to a narrative, and became particularly indispensable in the eighteenth and nineteenth centuries for filling pages in those voluminous triple-decker novels.

The remarkable thing about narrative's transition to the medium of film is that, to a most extraordinary degree, the descriptive pause becomes an irrelevancy. The medium is so visually rich – and every shot contains so much 'descriptive' information (with the kind of immediacy the older realist novelists would surely have relished: 'a picture tells a thousand words') – that it is generally no longer necessary to have a camera pan around a room before the action can take place in it: we can have the room 'described' to us *at the same time* as we watch the action unfolding in it. Action and description have become *fused*. You can see how difficult, indeed impossible, this is for a novelist. The novelist has to be extremely selective and careful about what she tells us about the environment of an action or scene, and she has to deliver this information in the absence or suspension of the action itself; it makes for a lot of hard work and tough aesthetic decisions about relevancy, tempo and economy. Yet, with the simple act of rolling a motion picture camera, all the essential descriptive information merges into a visual synthesis with the scene itself. Thus the 'speed' of filmic narration is vastly 'quicker' than novelistic narrative because the only substantial 'tempo' of classical narrative that is 'slower' than isochronic parity, the descriptive pause, is more or less redundant.

Nevertheless, the cinema has not been able to avoid description altogether. There is usually what is called an 'establishing shot' at the beginning of each major scene, a long-distance shot that situates the action in a knowable environment; this shot is a pretty familiar cinematic version of the novelistic 'descriptive pause'. But more importantly, even while it might have discovered a miraculous economy towards objective description, film is radically impoverished when it comes to the description of emotional or psychological states. The moving picture is not (or not obviously; we will consider this further in chapters 6 and 7) a 'subjective' medium. Films exceed the theatre's capacity to 'describe' *affective* states by virtue of their discovery of the 'close up', where the actor's face can be witnessed at such proximity that any reasonably familiar emotion can be seen writ large upon its sensitive surface; but when it comes to complex *moral, psychological* or *philosophical* states, films have most often had to resort to the clumsy descriptive pause of the 'voice-over'.

Citizen Kane of course employs quite a few descriptive pauses, from the opening camera crawl over the fence at Xanadu towards the window over Kane's death-bed, through the trick shot that descends through the skylight of the nightclub where Susan sings, to the elaborate final crane shot of the abandoned detritus of the Kane fortune, which finally discovers the snow sled for us, just as it is being burned. These are classic cinematic 'descriptions' and again, typically, they make a virtue of necessity and foreground their own formal elegance. But when it comes to describing emotional complexes, *Kane* is quite subtle; most of its effects in this regard are generated out of the device of having five separate sources of narration, each with a subjective spin on events. Thus, in their respective dialogues with the faceless Thompson, the narrators manage to impart crucial psychological 'descriptions' of Kane, themselves and others. I will mention only two of these. When, at the end of her section, Susan is told by Thompson, 'All the same, I feel kinda sorry for Mr Kane', she snaps right back at him: 'Don't you think I do?' It is a confession that changes the entire complexion of her story and adds a pathos otherwise swamped by her inebriated egotism. Earlier, during Mr Bernstein's narration, the ageing chairman of the board indulges in a retrospective narrative about his youth; it is what Genette would call an 'extradiegetic' narrative with no bearing on anything but Bernstein's own character and generous heart. He describes a girl he saw only once, long ago, on a passing ferry, and declares, 'I'll bet a day hasn't gone by since that I haven't thought of that girl.' This functions as a glorious 'descriptive pause' about the inner life of Kane's irrepressible 'yes-man'.

Order

The next set of relations between the time of narration and story time to be considered is that of order – in a way the most obvious and objectively verifiable temporal relation between narration and story. Actually, rather few narratives strictly adopt the same order of events as the story itself. The idea, in most cases, is to play around with the order of story events in a variety of ways, to increase pleasure and heighten the epistemological impact of certain items of information. Genette insists that we begin by accepting the notion of anachrony. This concept covers every instance in the text that makes for a discrepancy between story sequence and plot sequence; or, as he puts it, 'various types of discordance between the two orderings of story and narrative' (Genette 1980: 36). Beginning with this general concept, Genette goes on to outline the two major species of anachrony, prolepsis and analepsis.

Prolepsis, the rarer of these two species, refers to 'any narrative manoeuvre that consists of narrating or evoking in advance an event that will take place later' (Genette 1980: 40). I want to suggest that we can 'read' the opening of *Citizen Kane* (that is, everything before our immersion in Thatcher's diaries) as an extended prolepsis. Strictly, however, this is not true: this is actually the film's present tense, which begins with Kane's death. Nevertheless, functionally, the opening sequences have the effect of proleptic anticipation of the end of the film's main story: the life of Charles Foster Kane. The first thing to 'happen' is Kane's death, and this is immediately followed by a mock newsreel that proceeds to outline all the major incidents in the protagonist's life; a series of rapid-fire prolepses to help us find our way through the various narrative versions of that life to come. Kane is born poor, inherits the world's third-richest gold mine, interests himself in the *Inquirer*, becomes the first 'yellow journalist', controls a media empire, marries a president's niece, has an affair with a singer, runs for office, fails, divorces, remarries, launches a singing career, builds a colossal mansion, divorces again and dies. This is the entire story of the film's central narrative. Why does Welles want to employ this device of prolepsis so richly and disconcertingly, and 'give it all away', spoiling the element of suspense (although he retains that element for the 'Rosebud' mystery story)?

There are several possible answers to this question. First, perhaps Welles recognised that suspense is a rather vulgar narrative ploy and that there are other, more worthwhile reasons for wanting to watch a film like this – for instance, the interest is much more in the polyphony of voices that attempt to tell the story of this text than in the story itself. *Citizen Kane* is an exercise in ambiguity and relativity; it is less 'about' the life of Charles Foster Kane than it is 'about' a multiplicity of viewpoints on that life, all coloured by personal interests and tonalities. Second, in a sense everyone in 1941 'knew' the story of *Citizen Kane* already: it was essentially a thinly veiled version of the life of America's first media baron, William Randolph Hearst. As such, it was more or less in the public domain already, and the device of telling the entire story at the beginning serves more to authenticate the *déjà-vu* nature or 'already-knownness' of that story than to reveal something secretive in advance. But perhaps most importantly, for all the narrative ingenuity and radicalism of this film, *Citizen Kane* is less concerned with that aspect of itself than it is with its own sense of style.

So much for prolepsis, although it is worth bearing in mind that the various film genres employ what we might want to call 'virtual prolepses', and that a musical score in a movie can use certain motifs as 'musical prolepses'. In a traditional Western, the very appearance of an unshaven, black-garbed, cigarette-smoking ruffian virtually ensures his eventual demise at the hands of the hero, or, in a contemporary horror film, there is almost no doubt that the first defeat of the monster or psycho-killer will have to be repeated by a second, authentic killing. Genres function according to their satisfaction of expectations that they themselves install in us, and, often enough, those expectations are met so precisely that to speak of generic 'virtual prolepses' is not unreasonable. As for music, the application of a certain repeated minor-key motif to a hospitalised child in a movie more or less writes his death certificate, and so on: prolepses can happen via suggestion and iconic symbolism as well as by direct representation.

By far the most common type of anachrony is the type known as analepsis. An analepsis is a violation of the temporal order of a story that narrates for us something that has happened before the given moment we have reached in the story. Owing to the hegemony of film in the twentieth century, we have commonly come to call these narrative incidents 'flashbacks'. And flashbacks are everywhere; they are part of the bread-and-butter technical arsenal of every storyteller. Tracing the Western narrative tradition, for convenience's sake, back to Homer, already there the analepsis is not merely an occasional device but is elevated to a supreme level of structural importance: mention a hero, a warrior of any worth, and Homer will fill you in on his back story. Structural analepsis is part of the genetic code of the Western narrative tradition, and there is scarcely a tale told that does not use it in some degree.

From the archetypal flashback Rick Blaine has in *Casablanca* (Curtiz 1942) of his glory days with Ilsa Lund in Paris before the Germans invaded, to the remarkable film *Memento* (Nolan 2000), which is composed entirely of scenes presented in the reverse order of their story sequence, analepsis runs right through film history. Why is it such a common feature? First, analepsis can increase the dramatic impact of a revelation about the past by leaving it to a moment when it is particularly pertinent: we find out about Rick's romantic past only when the narrative urgency of the Laszlos' escape elevates it to a matter of major complication. Second, an analepsis can cast a different light on a character that the present circumstances of the story do not permit: Rick is a very different man in free Paris from the man he is in Vichy Casablanca; without the flashback, we would not otherwise know that he is capable of smiling and laughing. Third, an analepsis can restore to present memory what might have been forgotten in the long duration of a narrative. And so on.

To reverse what I had previously suggested, in *Citizen Kane*, the Charles Foster Kane story is, in one critical respect, entirely analeptic. Since Kane's first action is to die, everything about him that follows is a series of flashbacks to his life. It could be said that, in a sense, the film is both proleptic and analeptic at once. What Orson Welles has done is to create a very complicated filmic 'tense', where the present-tense narrative, Thompson's quest for Rosebud, is actually a cipher and a red herring: it is not even the equivalent of a detective story's present tense, because the mystery is essentially banal and meaningless. Rather, the film's story as such is the Kane story and the nature of its telling by various of its participants. So that we are obliged to occupy a very curious position, in which the present is drained of all its intensity, and the past assumes the magnitude of genuine reality. This effect is entirely typical of Welles' work, and it warrants closer study. Suffice it to say that a film composed almost entirely of analepses can nevertheless be felt to have the immediacy and open-endedness of the present tense.

Frequency

The third and last of Genette's major temporal categories in narrative is frequency. In certain narratives, it is of the utmost importance how often this or that event is represented, and, most often, repetitions of narrative actions and events are motivated in the plot by differences in 'point of view', which we will consider in chapter 7. Akira Kurosawa's *Rashomon* (1950) repeats the same 'event' – although precisely what that event is is the question of the film – from three different perspectives, in order to explore the subjectivity of competing truth claims. In many films, certain events are not exactly 'repeated' but are meant to be typical of a particular character, and so recur. It is vital that we know that Rick does not drink with his customers in *Casablanca* in order that his violation of this rule for Ilsa assumes its proper importance. Therefore the 'non-event' of his drinking with customers is repeated in the plot before Ilsa's arrival. In Gus Van Sant's *My Own Private Idaho* (1991), River Phoenix repeatedly falls asleep in narcoleptic seizures to underline his disconnection from narrative agency.

Repetition works in various ways in the film medium, and perhaps the most outstanding instance of it in US cinema is Welles' shooting of an identical event in *Citizen Kane* (Susan's première in the opera *Salammbo*) from two entirely different perspectives: first, the vantage point of Leland, looking down bored from the box, and second, that of Susan herself, from the stage, strutting in anxious dread before an invisible and hostile house. Here, by repeating the event, Welles is able to demonstrate radically disjunct perspectives on it and open the medium to relativity. In some films, repetition is elevated into an end in itself. In Francis Coppola's masterpiece, *The Conversation* (1974), Gene Hackman's Harry Caul plays a recorded conversation over and over again, filtering it of all imperfections, until he can deliver the finished recording to his clients: each repetition gets Caul one step closer to his final version, revealing nuances to his attentive ear. Probably no film has devoted so much of its narrative time to a repeated episode, although Harold Ramis' *Groundhog Day* (1993) takes repetition as a metaphor for everyday life in the USA and milks the device for every drop of comic life that it offers.

Conclusion

Narrative is the way in which we organise both time and space in relation to each other. As a multimodal form, film is able to create the possibility of multiple temporal and spatial zones whose relativities become meaningful during the course of the viewing. In order to see how the time–space mechanism works in individual films, we can use the concepts of story time, plot time and screen time to locate ourselves in the filmic chronology. Duration, as a means of controlling pace and significance, positions events and characters within the spectrum of our attention, giving them more or less time to be noticed by us, while the order and frequency of events controls the way in which information is measured out to us and, to some extent, how we might react to it. Through these manipulations of narrative time, film overcomes the limitations of its essential linearity to suggest the semantic and symbolic possibilities of multiple chronologies.

Chapter 6

Narrative voice

Julian Murphet

The relations between narration proper and the points of view of the characters being narrated are every bit as complex as the relations between story time and 'plot' time. In any narrative form, there is a spectrum of what we can call 'distances' between a narrator's 'voice' and the mental and sensory states of his or her characters: from alpine and godlike superiority, through gradations of nearer proximity and outright identity to the point where the characters know more than the narrator. This spectrum of relations clearly hinges on a question of apparent 'knowledge', although we also know that, in some ultimate sense, the film 'knows itself' throughout; it *produces* various narrators to tantalise us with their different degrees of knowledge.

Consider for a moment the intricate patterns of knowing and unknowing in Brian Singer's *Usual Suspects* (1995). One principal narrator, 'Verbal' Kint, spins a dizzying yarn to one principal narratee, Dave Kujan. Internal to Kint's story, various other narrators tell their stories (Keaton, Kobayashi and so on). Meanwhile, external to it, Kujan interrupts with his own versions of some events, while a survivor of a mysterious waterfront atrocity is telling, in Turkish, the story of seeing Keyser Söze. By interlacing these distinct voices, Singer achieves a formidable density of narrative texture and moreover works towards his astonishing final revelation: that Kint is himself Keyser Söze, and that almost everything he has been telling Kujan (and us) is a welter of lies, fiction and misrepresentation. Here, the narrative voice of Kint 'knows' everything but has told us, effectively, nothing. Visually, we have been 'seeing' everything from the point of view of Kujan, who hears Kint's voice and translates it into the moving images on the screen. We take away the single solace of knowing who Kint is, just as he disappears from the narrative net. The larger question remains: who is telling the story of Kint and Kujan? What is the 'narrating instance' of the film itself, at a higher narrative level than that of these diegetic interlocutions?

Written and filmed voices

This example brings to light some differences between traditional oral and written narrative forms and film narrative, which arise principally over the place of the 'narrating instance'. There seems relatively little difficulty in accepting that a character speaking in a film functions as a narrator in much the same way as a character speaking in a novel does. However, what about the higher-order narrator within whose voice all these lesser voices are orchestrated? A novel's narrating instance is that variable but omnipresent voice that, throughout, mediates the panoply of other voices; it is the voice that describes a room, introduces a character, expatiates on a relation. Broadly speaking, in the cinema, it is the camera that 'mutely' does all this for us.

Consider some of the complexities of approaching the 'narrating instance' of Alfred Hitchcock's film, *Rebecca* (1940). First, we are called upon to enter the narrative through the explicit, almost hypnotic voice of Joan Fontaine, who tells us of a dream she had of Manderley, and whom we accept is playing a fictional character who had a dream of Manderley. Add to this already complex voice the declared fact that this film is based upon a novel by Daphne du Maurier, whose title flashes up imperiously in the opening credit sequence: so that we have to read the 'voice' of the film's prologue and narration throughout as in some sense du Maurier's as well. And then, of course, the overriding knowledge for us that this is a 'Hitchcock movie' and that therefore the voice of Alfred Hitchcock, the recently transplanted Englishman in America, will have to be figured into the equation. And quickly many more 'voices' come rushing in for consideration: the 'voices' of Philip MacDonald and Michael Hogan, just two of the men who collaborated on the adaptation of du Maurier's novel; the 'voice' of Franz Waxman, whose romantic score underlines Fontaine's voice-over; the 'voice' of Lyle Wheeler, the man who built the model of Manderley that we see during the voice-over; and of course the 'voice' of George Barnes, the director of photography, who literally produced the shots. But this strange, hybridised polyphony of 'voices' is not really one of which most of us are aware when watching *Rebecca*. Our awareness, even of Fontaine's narrating function, dwindles immediately the plot is underway, and we are caught in the middle of the action. And this is a very different experience from that of reading du Maurier's novel, when the voice of the narrator is never out of our heads.

In watching films, we are only rarely aware of being told something by a human being. Generally, if we are aware of any kind of medium of the message of a film, it is the mechanical medium itself: the apparatus of camera, celluloid, projector, genre, technology, all of which join together into some utterly impersonal and subjectless machine. When we are sitting in the cinema, or at home, watching the latest Jackie Chan movie, it scarcely occurs to us to ask: who is *narrating* this? We know we are being told a story, and we might even know that there is a director and a screenwriter (although we almost certainly cannot remember their names), but it doesn't seem to make much sense to make a link between these two orders of knowledge. If we think of the director or screenwriter at all in the viewing of a Jackie Chan movie, it is probably only as functionaries hired to supply a certain coherence to the succession of action sequences that are the real point of the film. It is the machine that tells us the story: the machine of the genre and of the industry itself, which supplies narratives the way the automobile industry supplies cars.

This kind of experience of narrative in the cinema – a kind of generic, industrial, machine-like experience – has long been a constitutive part of going to the movies. And this seriously undermines the putative presence of a narrative 'voice' in much commercial film. Narration in the commercial cinema consists of broadly recognisable and repetitive patterns of presentation: a privileging of the rules of visual coherence Helen Fulton will be exploring in chapters 8 and 9; simple plots with clear oppositions; no attention drawn to the apparatus itself; an erasure of any overt stylisation; a pretence to 'objectivity' and anonymity of voice. The whole idea of enjoying film directors as sources of expressiveness in the cinema has historically been a minority experience, confined largely to intellectuals and cineastes. The rather different idea of enjoying a film for its efficiency and effectiveness of narration, its 'voice' or style as such, is less rare, but still on the margins of cinema-going experience, and reserved for very particular kinds of film. By and large, for most movie-going people around the world, film is a *narrative medium without a narrator*.

It is important to emphasise, in this respect, the radical distinction between film as a narrative medium and any of the language-based forms of narrative. In a novel, a long poem, a fire-side story or a verbal drama, the fact that what is being presented to us comes in the form of words makes it almost 'natural' that we should posit a human consciousness as an agency behind the narration. Narration and narrator suggest each other and support one another in the verbal narrative forms – even if we recognise, as we must, that every 'narrator' in a literary text is a construction. Construction or not, we consumers of verbal narratives generally enjoy those occasions when someone seems to be revealing him- or herself – like Oz – behind the surface of the narration. Why is this? Why isn't our experience of verbal narratives the same kind of impersonal, machine-like experience as audio-visual narratives in the cinema? It is because we all use language every day and are ourselves constantly occupied in the business of telling stories, to one another and to ourselves. We recognise the activity as our own, and wherever we see this activity taking place, we tend to assume that someone more or less like ourselves is taking responsibility for it.

Until such time as carrying digital video cameras around with us everywhere and making instant visual representations to tell our stories is as natural to us as speaking sentences, this will not be the case for visual narratives.* Films and videos do not appear to come to us from a narrator because we do not produce our own narratives in this medium – or at least most of us do not. It still appears to us as a specialist and industrial activity – most of us would have only a very dim idea of how James Cameron 'told us' the story of the *Titanic* using extremely complex digital effects (in fact I daresay even James Cameron probably has a very dim idea of how he did so). We could not frame our own narratives in that way, the way we can all probably tell a version of the *Titanic* story off the top of our heads in language or even, at a stretch, 'act it out' using our bodies. The film version seems highly technical and depends upon massive hardware beyond the reach of all but the wealthiest. There is a vast economic gap between the producers and the consumers of film narrative, and until the day when this gap narrows to the point where we can all happily 'narrate' using audio-visual technology, we will always be in a relatively passive and subservient position *vis-à-vis* that technology.

So we tend not to recognise a narrator in commercial cinema. And indeed much of the narrative power of the cinema depends upon the erasure of a subject position from the narrative. Narrative cinema strives to be overpowering in its diegetic realisation: it overwhelms us with 'realistic' visual information, kinetic energy, sound and the rapid pulses of frequent cutting. And none of these effects seems to flow from a human subject. They come from the system, the industry, Hollywood. Hollywood has evolved a form of storytelling that depends on remarkably old-fashioned plot devices and narrative structures, but without the humanising element that made those structures breathe in the older forms. And for want of a better term, we had better think about this 'humanising element' of narration, that aspect of narration that seems to proceed directly from a human consciousness, in terms of the grammatical category of **voice**.

When we say that a narrative text has a 'voice', all we really mean is that it proceeds from a narrator and that that narrator imparts some of his or her own personality to the narrative. Another way of saying this is that narrative texts are generally 'accented' and located in some way. But to arrive at some conception of what this means, we have first to define what we mean by 'narrator' as opposed to 'author'. This distinction is as old and fundamental as the hills, but a little amplification cannot hurt. The author of a text is, of course, that historical, real-life agent responsible for producing the text: the person who physically wrote it. The narrator, on the other hand, is the 'consciousness' we can detect internal to the text, who from time to time puts a spin on the narrative and offers value judgements and sympathies as a supplement to the story. This 'consciousness' is a

---

* It might be the case that, as digital visual technology and mobile phones become more and more tightly integrated, wealthy citizens of the First World will indeed 'communicate' through moving pictures. The speed of technological developments is rapidly calling all of our habits and codes of communication into question.

construction: it is produced in literature through language, more or less deliberately through a series of aesthetic decisions by the author, and cannot be simply
identified with that person. In films, too, the sense of a 'consciousness' hovering
over *The Godfather* (Coppola 1972) or *Kill Bill: Vol. 1* (Tarantino 2003) is an effect
of highlighting certain habits of storytelling – Coppola's 'narrator' is an amalgam
of certain lenses, certain colours, certain rhythms of editorial composition that
tends towards a 'nostalgic realism'; Tarantino's is a choppier, more frenetic and
stylistically variegated 'narrator', who is recognisable through habits of excess
and stylistic flamboyance. In every case, the narrator is a property of the text, not
the other way around – it is something, rather like the story itself, that we induce
and put together from the narrative discourse before us.

Person and temporal location

We can analyse 'voice' in the cinema through a variety of coordinates. First, 'person': narrators can be broadly in the 'first-person' voice or the 'third-person' voice.
Even in literature, however, these distinctions are not as important as they might
first seem to be. The same 'voice' can be detected across these grammatical boundaries, and there is virtually no sustained first-person narration that is not, also
and even predominantly, a third-person narration. Anyone who talked exclusively
about themselves would not be a very interesting narrator. And, at the same time,
even when writing strictly in the third person, there are ways of registering a
very particular narrative 'consciousness' without the literal use of 'I'. But the term
'first-person narrative' covers all those texts, including *Rebecca*, where there is a
subjective 'I' who from time to time takes up a first-person account of his or her
actions and thoughts. And a 'third-person narrative' is one where this grammatical figure, the 'I', is absent. Second-person narratives are extremely rare in film
and not very effective.

The second coordinate to consider is temporal location. It matters very much
whether the voice of the narrative comes after, is simultaneous with or (very rarely)
comes before the events of the story being narrated (or, another possibility, combines present and past-tense narration in new permutations). It matters because
this position of the narrative voice in time, the equivalent of a grammatical tense,
greatly affects our understanding of the story. Basically, there are four types of
narrating relative to temporal position:

1 *subsequent* (past-tense, classical)
2 *prior* (predictive, future-tense)
3 *simultaneous* (present-tense), and
4 *interpolated* (inserted past-tense amid present-tense action).

Most commonly, of course, the narrative voice is positioned at a temporal point
sometime after the cessation of the main events of the story: the voice can tell us
the story because the story is essentially finished, and we can accept the authority

of the voice because of this expiration of the events and thus their inaccessibility to us. The voice, in a typical past-tense narration, is our only access to knowledge of the events it narrates. Indeed, logically, in literature this is the only narrating type that makes any real *sense*, since we cannot picture how a present-tense narrative (at least, in its first-person variety) could actually come to be written unless it is only about interior moods, and predictive or prophetic, future-tense narration is surely unreliable unless it comes from God Himself. Only subsequent narration fulfils the 'realistic' expectations of readers, and this is why most novels and stories continue to be written in this tense. Not in film, however, which, even when prefaced by some attestation to its already having happened, appears always to unfold in 'real time', just as events do in the theatre: so an interesting point is that if the subsequent tense is the most typical temporal location of *literary* narrative voice then the simultaneous tense is the most typical temporal location of *filmic* narrative voice.

Let us think for a moment about David Fincher's 1999 film, *Fight Club*. Here, we enter the diegesis very much through the 'voice' of Edward Norton's nameless narrator, who spins us his story about looking for authenticity in ritualised forms of violence. Although the voice-over, when it intrudes, is couched in the past tense, the compelling power of cinematic visualisation 'cancels' that pastness and irresistibly transforms the tale into a 'present-tense' narration. This greatly enhances the power of the final realisation that the narrator and Tyler Durden (Brad Pitt) are one and the same person. Although they are played by different actors, and interrelate like other characters in the film, we 'buy' the fact of their identity because the voice in which their story is presented is subjective and (functionally) present tense – and *the present tense of this subjectivity is precisely one in denial of his being a split personality*. Told in the past tense, this revelation would have been felt as a cheat – the narrator would have known 'all along', and would have been misleading us; whereas the immediacy of filmic narration means that we identify spontaneously with Norton's limited field of knowledge and accept this sudden reversal of narrative fortune for Brad Pitt's character. Fincher has used a formal property of the film medium to counteract a potential formal embarrassment in his narrative.

The 'anterior' or 'prior' tense is properly rare in film narrative because in 'giving things away' it destroys some of Hollywood's favourite effects: mystery, suspense and surprise. More importantly, perhaps, this tense raises very interesting problems about agency and free will, both of which are sacred to Hollywood models of psychological causality. The witches in Shakespeare's *Macbeth* make various future-tense narrative propositions about the Scottish laird, demonstrating the degree to which narrative prediction might actually shape subsequent events. Is it the case that Macbeth does what he does because he is told the prophecy? Or that he simply fulfils his objective fate, to which the witches have divine access? This question is properly undecidable and suggests that the prior tense enjoys some very intriguing narrative possibilities, many of which are anathema to classical Hollywood narration. Still, whenever a soothsayer or prophet appears in a film, it is almost invariably the case, as in for example *The Matrix* (1999), that what he or she says will come to pass, in some manner. Hence the prophetic mode has not vanished from contemporary narrative; instead, it seems stronger than ever. What this means *vis-à-vis* Hollywood's tendency to privilege psychological causality has yet to be determined.

Diegetic location

The third coordinate of narrative voice is that of diegetic location. Narrators can be internal to the diegetic world of the text; for instance, the narrator of *The Great Gatsby*, Nick Carraway, is a character in the story itself, but one with the added responsibility of telling it all from his own perspective. The same is obviously true of our principal narrator in *Rebecca*, the nameless character who speaks to us in the beginning about her dream of Manderley, and who occupies a chief place in the narrative. This is what Genette would call a homodiegetic narrator: a narrator involved in what is being narrated. Clearly, we also recognise this type of narrator from *Fight Club*, *Memento* and *The Usual Suspects*; it is a frequently employed narrative location, for the simple reason that it tends to grip spectators' attention more immediately. The fact that a narrator participates and is interested in the narrative, by virtue of his or her direct implication in its unfolding (at both levels), seems to impel us more effectively into the implied world of the diegesis. But there are potential drawbacks as well, such as the high risks involved in both *Fight Club* and *The Usual Suspects* – risks deriving from these narrators' limited knowledge and our perplexed relation to it. A film in which a homodiegetic narrator is exposed as having misled us can be very dissatisfying. For example, early reactions to Wiene's *Das Kabinett des Doktor Caligari* (1920), which turns on an ultimate revelation that the homodiegetic narrator is a madman in an asylum undergoing treatment for pathological delusions, were extremely negative. We tend to be intolerant towards stories that end by saying, 'It was only a dream' – which is effectively what both *Fight Club* and *The Usual Suspects* do. It is a miracle of narrative style that in both cases we are not turned off.

When we think of narrative 'voice' in film, we tend to think of the voices of homodiegetic character narrators who literally speak to us as the film unfolds. An excellent example of 'voice-over' narration is the film *Sunset Boulevard*, which is narrated to us, in a more sustained way than usual, by a very world-weary and jaded Hollywood screenwriter. (By the end of the film, we realise why he is quite so world-weary. He is the dead man we see floating in the pool just after the title sequence.) If we look carefully at the film's opening as an illustration of narrative voice in the cinema, what we see is a complex articulation of different registers. First, visually, we have two camera shots: one long, mobile tracking shot, which gets us from *Sunset Boulevard* to the swarming police and journalist activity, then to the swimming pool itself; followed by another, extremely unusual static shot upwards from the bottom of the swimming pool, with the dead man at the centre of the frame. Viewed silently, this transition suggests a narrative 'voice' predisposed towards shocking dénouements, abrupt shifts in shot register and the cynical urbanity of a violent society. There is a florid rhetoric of the image here: from fluid to static, from long to three-quarter shot, from horizontal to vertical line, from bustle to rigor mortis.

But the addition of the soundtrack amplifies all of this with the fatality and cynical ironies of the *film noir* voice-over: it is a voice inherited directly from the radio serials of the 1930s and 1940s and the 'Black Mask' pulp fiction of the 1920s. This literal voice also implies the addition of a *subsequent* narrative tense to the immediate, *simultaneous* tense on the visual track. Thus a very strange vocal position is implied; what we are seeing has already happened. When, by the end of the film, we learn that the narrator is no other than the dead man himself, this voice is elevated to an even further level of distinction: it is the voice of the dead, the ghostly revenant, who always speaks from a position of justice and retribution.

On the other hand, narrators can be *external* to the world of the text. Most novels are narrated by an 'omniscient narrator' who seems to know everything about the inner and outer lives of the characters and the whole world that they inhabit. This kind of narrator does not 'belong' to that world, and is called extradiegetic. Stanley Kubrick's *Dr Strangelove, or How I Learned to Stop Worrying and Love the Bomb* (1963) begins with a voice-over narrator of this sort, describing the flotilla of Cold War bombers and their fail-safe positions as a prelude to the war story that unfolds. The extradiegetic voice is characterised by a cold, 'objective' and disinterested view of the mechanics of geopolitics – a tonality that we come to associate with the film's narration as a whole. Martin Scorsese's adaptation of Edith Wharton's *Age of Innocence* (1993) has an extradiegetic narrator – Joanne Woodward – as an intermittent presence throughout, intervening to clarify the scrupulously gradated moral hierarchy of the social milieu of New York. In this case, the voice is highly ironic, and charged with a melancholic fatalism that, again, carries over into the way we 'hear' the 'voice' of the film's narration, even when the narrator is not speaking.

In either case, the fact is that the voice-overs give way to other cinematic means of storytelling: cinematography, *mise en scène*, montage, production design, plot construction, performance styles and so on, all of which are 'bound together' by a stylistic consistency. Kubrick's film, although it ceases to be literally 'narrated' after the first few minutes, nevertheless has a 'voice', a recognisably cynical, chilly, distant and mordantly amused satirical mode of presentation that is consistent throughout the film. At no point does Kubrick allow for any sentimentality, any affective immersion in his characters' lives; his three parallel lines of action harmonise by way of an equivalent misanthropy; the clinical precision of the cinematography, its meticulously focused close-ups of machines and objects, and symmetrically framed long shots of spaces, remove us from the realm of psychology; throughout, the ticking clock of the bombers' missions and of the terrifying Doomsday Device hangs over the narrative as a palpable dread; and the thematic accent on the inhuman machinery of codes, communications, representation, war and annihilation drains the narrative of any human intentionality. In these and other associated ways, the narrative voice of *Dr Strangelove* is 'identifiable', although we are speaking of 'voice' very loosely and analogously here; it remains a good way of conceiving of the narrative 'unity' of a film's obviously very scattered mode of production (hundreds of cast and crew members, thousands of shots, several weeks of shooting time, months of post-production and so on). The narrative 'voice' is that associated set of stylistic decisions which allows this heteroclite and unpredictable mode of production to be consumed as one, unified, two-hour narrative experience. Wherever it is located, 'homo-' or 'extradiegetically', the voice locates us in the implied diegetic world, luring us into it by eliminating, as far as possible, discrepancies of style, tone or mood.

Narrative presence

Narrative voice is the accumulated presence of markers such as those we identified in *Dr Strangelove*, in any narrative text – it is all those moments where some kind of identity peeks out from behind the curtains of representation and declares itself. And we can now turn to the fourth consideration about narrative voice: namely, the issue of narrative presence. The narratologist Rimmon-Kenan has suggested a six-stage growth chart of degrees of narrative presence (Rimmon-Kenan 1983):

Least narrative presence, or 'voice'
1 description of settings
2 identification of characters
3 temporal summaries
4 definition of characters
5 reports of what characters did not think or say
6 commentary – interpretation, judgement, generalisation.
Most narrative presence, or 'voice'

 This graded scale can aptly be applied to literary narrative, but is there really such a spectrum of 'presence' in film narrative voice? The cinema seems to 'do' the first two stages automatically, and we saw in the previous chapters how stage 3 could be achieved. But it is when we get to stages 4, 5 and 6 that the 'voice' of a film narrative usually cedes to the homodiegetic narration of some character within the world of the text – one character will describe another, indulge in a voice-over soliloquy or pass some kind of judgement on the proceedings of the narrative. One particularly galling instance of this last device is a scene at the end of Brian De Palma's misjudged adaptation, *The Bonfire of the Vanities* (1990), in which a judge (Morgan Freeman) summarises and adjudges every participant in the film's action. What galls here is the sense that what Freeman is saying is *exactly* what the film's implied 'narrator' wants to say, and this unwonted identity of homodiegetic and extradiegetic voice falls utterly flat. The very fact of the inhumanity of the cinematic apparatus tends internally to bear down upon and flatten any attempt to 'humanise' its mode of articulation. And yet films do 'comment' on and appraise their own contents, and do so constantly; how is it that this maximal zone of narrative 'presence' is indicated and felt in the cinematic text?

There is a host of devices for registering narratorial interpretation and judgement in film narrative. We can only touch on a few of these here, but these examples should suggest and call to mind a slew of other, similar techniques for making an interpretive, if invisible and silent, narrative voice palpable. Sergei Eisenstein, one of the cinema's greatest 'rhetoricians', worked arduously towards a specifically cinematic mode of commentary on the action of his films, because he wanted them to teach revolutionary lessons. To this end, he theorised a device he called the 'montage of attractions'. At the end of his film *Strike* (1924), he offered a scene in which an armed troop of police massacres a defenceless and hungry mass of industrial strikers and their families; in order to 'comment' on this atrocity, he intercut graphic shots of cattle being slaughtered in an abattoir. This kind of blunt cinematic metaphor worked effectively (in 1924) to pass judgement on the proceedings: one was left in no doubt as to what the narrator 'thought' about police butchery since precisely *that* ('police butchery') was the thought produced by the montage. However, this kind of effect had a limited period of effectiveness; the crude splicing of two distinct objects or phenomena in an instant visual metaphor rapidly became hackneyed. Other, equally grandiose modes of cinematic rhetoric could be achieved at the level of *mise en scène*. If we want to know what the narrator of *Ivan the Terrible, Part One* (Eisenstein 1945) 'thinks' about Ivan's relation to his people – its mixture of tyranny and care – we need only examine the famous final shot of the film, which juxtaposes Ivan's extraordinarily angled and foregrounded silhouette with the twisting line of approaching subjects massing to his defence in the far background. This extreme contrast of lines and of scale, held for the duration of a long shot, forcefully 'comments' on what would otherwise be a simple narrative fact – needless to say, such effects are derived almost entirely from the history of Western painting.

Less aggressive means of commentary have also been developed. Music is often employed to pass judgement on the action on the visual track: from the crudity of character-based Wagnerian 'leitmotifs' to the 'dialectical' and contrapuntal use of music in the films of Jean-Luc Godard, music is a very useful non-verbal way of guiding, or challenging, an audience's identification with the moral interpretations of the film's implied 'narrator'. Effects of lighting and of colour also frequently make interpretive glosses on what appears on the screen. The colour palette of Andrei Zvyagintsev's *Vozvrashcheniye* (*The Return*, 2003) is subdued into a virtual monochrome, making patent the 'narrator's' dispassionate and emotionally drained voice at the level of chromatic tonality; whereas, at the other extreme, the work of Christopher Doyle and Zhang Yimou on *Ying xiong* (*Hero*, 2002) transformed the legendary tale of dynastic China into a colour tone-poem, with each vivid hue (orange, red, blue, green and so on) becoming a virtual character in the diegesis – here, chromatic formalism supplies a dense mythic tone to the narrative voice. Horror films tend to be shot in a lot of darkness, giving the 'voice' of their narration a sepulchral and malevolent tonality; musicals tend to be bright and airy, thus eliminating negativity from the implied 'commentary' on what transpires. And so on. From these few and bare examples, a range of other, similar effects can be induced, all of which manage to create a degree of rich narrative presence in a film's unfolding. Although we tend not to 'read' these effects as transparently as we do the overt verbal commentary of a literary narrator, there is no question that the film medium has discovered a wide variety of means for the 'subjectification' of the narrating instance, the 'voice' in which any particular story is told.

Author or narrator?

It is interesting to ask to what extent such narrative 'voices' are or are not related to the authors who are ultimately responsible for producing them. Some theorists have argued that there must be an intermediate category between the textual 'narrator' (a property of the text) and the textual 'author' (the actual living being(s) who made it). This intermediate category would be that of the 'implied author'. Once you have seen the whole of a series of films by a director, be it Nicholas Ray or Akira Kurosawa or James Cameron or any other, you have already begun to develop a rather complicated image of any one of them. You might be able to identify the specific narrators of *Rashomon*, *The Seven Samurai* and *Ran* (three Kurosawa films), each of which is a different construction for the purposes of that specific film; but also you might be able to identify, among all of the films, an abiding set of narrative concerns, recurrent patterns, obsessions, formal turns and so on, which add up to something more than a 'narrator'. But neither is this the author. You've never met Akira Kurosawa, and you never will; you have no access to him as a biographical personality.

But, somewhere between this man and the individual narrators of his films, there is what we call an 'implied author': the image we have of Kurosawa, something we strive to define and defend in our essays, against other versions of the 'implied Kurosawa' made by other readers and critics. And it might well be that what we mean by narrative 'voice' is as much a property of this larger, more general figure as it is of specific textual narrators. There are similarities of voice between these narrators, and there is an overarching satisfaction in turning to other texts by this 'implied author' and discovering in them some of the same vocal qualities we recognise and value from other texts. And this is, interestingly, one of the few defensible ways of identifying narrative 'voices' in the cinema: not so much through specific film narrations as through career-long habits of presentation and expression that, in retrospect, can be shown to have had a kind of expressive consistency. This is what the movement known as 'auteur theory' was all about; taking the lifetime's work of a director working in various, unrelated genres and identifying a peculiar mode of film discourse, a 'voice', working behind and on the surface of all of the separate films.

Citizen Kane is an excellent example of a film narrative composed of multiple homodiegetic narratives, each of which is associated with a particular voice that we hear, connected to a body that we see; and in the end, all four are couched within the 'extradiegetic', silent narrative voice of some implied narrator above and beyond the limited points of view of the characters. Thompson's various interviews, with Bernstein, Leland, Susan Alexander and Raymond the butler, and his consultation of the Thatcher diaries, construct a patchwork quilt of reminiscences, all shot through with the subject positions and narrative 'voices' of his various interviewees. But the question is: once the initial set-up, the direct, interview situation with Thompson, has been passed through, does each of the five narrators really have his or her 'own voice' in the section of the film that tells his or her story? For instance, take the example of the breakfast-table montage sequence. The segment begins and ends with a shot of Jed Leland in the nursing home, musing about Emily Norton and her marriage to Kane; thus it is entirely 'framed' by a specific, elderly, nostalgic and somewhat cynical narrative voice.

But once we are into the montage proper, and the direct narrative voice has died away, does the 'visual language' of the framing and editing carry on the same voice, or construct a rather different one? The question is virtually impossible to answer: the point is that, by framing the montage sequence with two bookends of direct narratorial voice, Orson Welles has created the *impression* that the breakfast-table sequence is a visual surrogate for Leland's voice – even though he could never actually have witnessed any of the scenes we see. The double irony of the scene is that not only is Leland not directly 'narrating' it for us in anything other than a virtual sense but also *all* of the incidents summarised in it must ultimately have depended on Kane's narration of them to Leland in the first place. The 'narrating instance' is thus incredibly complex at this point; what we get is:

'Orson Welles' directing . . .
Thompson's interview version of . . .
Leland's narrative of . . .
Kane's narrative of . . .
his marriage to Emily Norton.

Only the very 'top' level, the level of Welles' direction, is specifically filmic and visual. And the final question is, of course, how we can justifiably posit such a narrator in images and shots? We are given some licence by the title sequence at the beginning and the credit sequence at the end, two 'extradiegetic' references to an 'implied author', named Orson Welles, whom *Citizen Kane* is ostensibly 'by'. And then, too, our attention is definitely being drawn here, as in most scenes in the film, to an irrepressible, virtuosic presence, whose flamboyant sense of style exceeds the bare necessities of pure narrative logic; and what is narrative voice but this addition of a 'something extra', above and beyond the simple needs of narrative reason, a signature of narratorial activity, judgement, style and ideology, bound up in the narration itself? We have seen this in *Dr Strangelove*, and I think we see it all over *Citizen Kane*, and over *Rebecca* as well: the imprints of an organisational, playful and manipulative hand on a medium not tied to the linguistic medium.

Conclusion

Whatever the complexities of the more obvious forms of homodiegetic narrative voice in *Kane* and the cinema at large (use of voice-overs especially), it seems that there is also, if not always, something like a metadiegetic narratorial voice at work in film as well. It might not be recognisably present in Jackie Chan movies, but it is arguably there in films by Welles, Hitchcock and many others who tried to turn cinema into an authorial medium, despite its industrial mode of production. But perhaps a better way of phrasing this is to suggest that we adapt Rimmon-Kenan's table of degrees of narrative presence to film narration as well: the average Hollywood movie exists on the same vocal level as Ernest Hemingway's texts do (that is, refining itself out of existence, not commenting, seeking to vanish from consciousness), while the more assertive directors achieve more of the 'commentary' and 'judgement' that we associate with a George Eliot type of narrator.

Chapter 7

Point of view

Julian Murphet

In previous chapters I have mentioned an important difference between narratives executed through language and those executed through film. We can 'identify' readily with verbal narratives because they occur in the very medium in which we ourselves think and speak. When J. D. Salinger's narrator in *The Catcher in the Rye* writes, 'I sat in the chair for a while and smoked a couple of cigarettes . . . Boy, I felt miserable. I felt so depressed, you can't imagine' (Salinger 1994: 89), the ease of our identification is directly related to the fact that *this is exactly how we might describe ourselves*. In the case of film, however, we are presented with the products of a technology that is not intrinsic to our comportment in the world. We neither think nor, normally, communicate in celluloid, video or digital imaging. The animated spectacle of a cowboy-doll and a toy space ranger wrestling under the wheels of a semi-trailer in *Toy Story* (Lasseter 1995) is not a narrative sequence we would be able to execute ourselves; as soon as we represent it, it has entered the realm of language. I have suggested that, to the extent that we are compelled to 'identify' with filmic narratives, we are in fact identifying with a series of machines. In some, 'experimental' films, such as Michael Snow's *La Région centrale* (1971), this strange, android identification is explicitly acknowledged – we find ourselves embroiled in the free-wheeling perceptual field of a mechanised camera. In such films, our point of view on the world is profoundly and openly technological; alienation from a humanist perspective is one of the points of this kind of work. By and large, however, this 'becoming machine' of our cinematic spectatorship is repressed and translated into a 'human' perspective by a host of conventions designed to comfort and flatter us rather than jolt us out of our routine behaviour.

In this chapter, we examine how mainstream cinema developed means for encouraging our belief that what we see projected on the screen is a matter of human psychology, human desires and human sense perception. In the language of narratology, what we will be asking is: how is it that film narratives are 'focalised' such that they resemble novelistic and theatrical representations? What specific technical devices have allowed film narratives to project their worlds through the imagined eyes and thoughts of their characters?

Identification, projection

The first point to make is that there seems to be a very basic psychological urge to project one's own desires into the visually compelling spectacles of film narrative; almost despite one's higher intellectual functions, one is predisposed to 'mistake' film images for one's own mental images. It has been universally observed that, once the basic conventions have been mastered, virtually everyone automatically 'identifies' with the actions of a film's central characters and assumes their motivations as one's own. This process of identification has been analysed by many critics and scholars, perhaps none more memorably than Christian Metz, who compared the cinema screen to the field of dream, and analysed the infantile pleasures of sheer looking involved in film spectatorship (Metz 1982). The 'primordial wish' of pleasurable looking in the cinema is to 'recognise' oneself on the screen, to see anthropomorphic images of the human form, and either assume the identity of those images or consume them as a kind of fuel for one's self-image.

Following Metz, we might wish to speculate on the fundamentally 'scopophilic' (gaze-loving) nature of all film-going and issue some strong critical cautions about what is at stake in such immediate and overpowering psychological investment. Laura Mulvey, in a landmark essay, explored the dependence of identification in the cinema on 'preexisting patterns of fascination already at work within the individual subject and the social formations that have molded him' (Mulvey 1992: 963–4). Specifically, she demonstrated the clear continuity between the 'patriarchal unconscious' and the basic operation of film as a medium: commercial film clearly has privileged a 'male gaze' and has produced a great many scenes whose basic logic is the pleasure of looking at a woman's body image.

It could be argued that, to the extent that there *must* be 'a girl' in all films following the classical Hollywood format, all Hollywood film is predicated parasitically on woman's '*to-be-looked-at-ness*' (Mulvey 1992: 967). Thus, the process of identifying with cinematic narratives can be said to implicate the viewer all the more deeply in his or her own social and psychological 'constructedness' by archaic patriarchal patterns of perception. The most important technical requirement of this kind of identification is that the cinematic apparatus (the technology required to keep the illusion in place, and all its social institutions and conventions) does not announce itself, remains hidden, erased from the visual and auditory domain.

In all of this, narrative *per se* in film is far less important in securing effects of identification than it is in the verbal media. We 'identify' willy-nilly with the projected images, owing to primary processes of psychological construction and what Jacques Lacan called the 'Imaginary'. Narrative devices merely extend and perfect what is already a potent absorption of the viewer in the image-field itself, *as though its point of view were his or her own*.

Scopophilia

David Lynch's film, *Blue Velvet*, is a powerful meditation on the relation between cinematic spectatorship and compulsive looking, or scopophilia (as are other notable films, not least *Peeping Tom* and *Psycho*). Cinema has been described as 'essentially pornographic' (Jameson 1992) and, to that extent, *Blue Velvet* is a very useful guide to the disturbing relations between our habits of identification in film, the often violent or exploitative nature of its contents, and the 'vanishing mediator' of the cinematic apparatus itself. As suggested above, in conventional narrative film, it is of paramount importance that the camera, the celluloid, the projector and all the other equipment that go together to make the spectacle *disappear* from view and from consciousness. The technological apparatus is eliminated from the very perceptual field it enables. At the same time, we can say that this apparatus is retained, subliminally, as a kind of prophylactic barrier between us and the latent trauma in what we see. The camera vanishes, but is preserved as a kind of existential guarantee, both that the spectacle on show is a production and that we ourselves will not be caught watching it. The apparatus is, in this sense, a double barrier between the viewer and the viewed; a barrier all the more effective in being imperceptible.

The great central scene in *Blue Velvet* concerns a young amateur sleuth, Jeffrey Beaumont, who has broken into an exotic singer's apartment to gather clues connected to a case he has stumbled across. While he is there, the woman (Dorothy Valens) returns from her nightclub, and he is obliged to slip into her closet, from which hidden vantage point he watches her undress. During this part of the scene, Lynch has the camera literally adopt Jeffrey's optical perspective, and cuts between 'point of view' shots through the closet slats and close-ups of his fascinated face. Here, we are presented with a perfect initial analogue for the process of cinematic spectatorship and 'identification': slipping into a dark space, we guiltlessly peer at a displayed body. The closet door, with its one-way louvred vision, is a fitting symbol of the cinematic apparatus. What we 'identify' with in this part of the scene is Jeffrey's invisible position of 'scopic power'; his power to gaze without being seen. The correlative of this power is precisely the spectacle of the disrobing woman, the object of the gaze *par excellence*. In this pure model of cinematic voyeurism, the 'subject' of the gaze is an invisible masculinity; its object is an all-too-visible femininity. The process of 'identification' is an assumption of this subject-object, masculine-feminine complex, a weave of desiring pulsions and attractors.

The greatness of the scene, however, is what follows this set-up. Before Jeffrey or we know what is happening, Dorothy Valens has opened the closet and exposed the lurking voyeur. At knifepoint, she forces him to kneel, then to strip naked. His own, hitherto secret desire is turned directly back upon him, as she kisses his penis and stabs him in the cheek simultaneously with the command 'Don't look at me!' Here, all at once, Lynch has exposed and traumatised the inherent libidinalism, the 'essential pornography' of the cinematic gaze. The voyeur's zone of invisible security is ruptured; the hoarded, 'closeted' desire is loosed into the space of the spectacle; the object-woman claims the desire to look, and the power of the phallic blade, as her own. With whom do we identify now? As before, surely, with Jeffrey; yet this identification has entered the realm of dread. From the comfortable squirm of potential discovery, to the full glare of exposure, the godhead of scopophilic power is radically dismantled: 'Don't look at me!' We find ourselves looking up into the shuddering face of the naked youth instead, from the hungry eyes of Mrs Valens; and everything changes.

Focalisation

All of which is meant to demonstrate that there are very complicated ethical issues in the process of cinematic identification, of looking in the dark at bodily images that do not look back. With that said, however, it clearly remains to analyse the technical and formal mechanisms whereby effects of identification are secured in the film medium. **Focalisation** is the anchoring of narrative discourse to a specific subject position in the story: the projection of a diegesis through the interested 'point of view' of a given character. To a large extent, the question of 'identification' in the cinema is the question of 'point of view' and focalisation. Narrative point of view need not be fixed, either to one spot or to one character – focalisation can and often does shift all around its diegetic world, like a spotlight travelling around a stage, highlighting first this actor, then that one; first this prop, then that one. But insofar as a narrative becomes fixed to one position or another, even as it roams, it has been focalised. If, however, the narrating instance is one that *does not* attach itself to a character within the world of the text, or is 'extradiegetic', the problem of focalisation does not arise. Who is the extradiegetic narrator, and where does he or she stand? These are questions only of *voice*. Focalisation becomes an issue when we shift into the diegetic world and begin to have our perceptions and thoughts shaped by the characters who attract and direct narrative discourse.

Memento is a clear example of a film relying strictly on a fixed focalisation: for the duration of the film, we never leave Leonard Shelby's 'point of view'. This is a crucial component of the film's meaning, for if we were to leave that very narrow range of narratorial knowledge for even an instant, the plot would collapse and the power of the final revelation be seriously diminished. *The Usual Suspects*, like most films, employs what should be called variable focalisation – because the focal point shifts between several different characters, even if one dominates the whole. And this is also the case of Hitchcock's *Rebecca*: although it appears to be a fixed focalisation, in fact the focal point shifts from Joan Fontaine's character to Maxim de Winter towards the end of the film. One further species of focalisation is the class of multiple focalisation, where different points of view narrate the same story events. The two most famous examples of this are Robert Browning's long poem *The Ring and the Book*, which presents multiple eye-witness accounts of the same criminal case, and Akira Kurosawa's film *Rashomon*, which does the same sort of thing. On the surface, it might seem as though *Citizen Kane* is an example of multiple focalisation rather than variable focalisation, but because in fact the various narrators take on different periods in Kane's life, rather than telling it all individually, it does not fully attain to this category.

To begin with only the most obvious device for focalising narrative in the cinema, first-person voice-over (a vestige of older or parallel media, like the radio and illustrated lecture) saturates the image in the peculiar intonations, grain and 'psychology' of a given character's voice. Voice-overs are essentially rather easy and 'cheap' means of identification since all they really require is a simultaneity of sound and image, but they remain effective because they offer a non-strenuous way of 'humanising' the film image. This, ironically enough, is precisely why the 'Director's Cut' of Ridley Scott's *Blade Runner* (1997) is so superior to the original cinema-release version of 1982: by eliminating the derivative 1940s, *noir*-style voice-over of Harrison Ford that heavily focalises the original, Scott achieves a relative 'de-subjectification' of the film's point of view – it is this that increases our suspicion that Dekker is after all not a human at all but an android like the ones he hunts down. It is not that we fail to 'identify' with Dekker (identification is secured by other means) but that we no longer do so as 'deeply' as we did, and this is better for the narrative.

Close-up

There is, however, a more visual formal feature of the cinema that allows for a remarkable and unprecedented degree of 'identification' with a character – and this is, of course, the facial close-up. A close-up literally fills the screen with the details of a face: the subtle expression of the eyes, the cast of the mouth, the furrows on the brow and so on. Film was the first narrative medium in which this degree of intimacy with the face of another became possible. We can think about the close-up as a device for focalising two kinds of experience: perception and emotion. In terms of focalised perceptions, the close-up plays a very useful role. By intercutting 'objective' perceptions of objects and spaces with close-ups of a character's face, a new kind of focalisation is made possible: not direct focalisation or strict optical 'point of view' (POV) shots, but what I want to call *associative focalisation*. We associate the filmed perceptions with the face we see in successive shots. They fuse and form a single, complex image in the mind. Whenever we watch a close-up of a face followed by a close-up of an object, we are seeing the object as it were through the eyes of the face. The name for this editorial trick in the cinema is the 'eye-line match'.

In terms of affections, of feelings and emotional states, the close-up plays an even greater role. In fact there are few representational devices as powerful as the film close-up for recording emotional states in their extensive physical detail. We are easily focalised by a character whom we see up close in a state of grief, panic, hunger, hilarity or whatever. Hitchcock makes great use of this in *Rebecca*, as close-up after close-up shows the increase in nervous tension, fear and humiliation on Joan Fontaine's face. Two of the most powerful moments of focalisation in the film happen when Fontaine's face turns from anxious but expectant joy to crushed embarrassment and pain, on both occasions when Maxim doesn't respond well to what she is wearing. Another is when we see her about to faint in the courtroom: we get an extreme close-up of her eyes, glazed over by a gauze on the lens, conveying the effect of her own dizziness, even as we look at her.

An interesting point about this boundary between associative and affective focalisation is that it is a very blurred one. In one of the most famous psychological experiments ever conducted in the medium, Lev Kuleshov spliced close-up shots of the face of Mozhukhin, a famous Russian actor, with several different shots: a bowl of soup, a teddy bear, a young girl and a child's coffin. In each case, the audience read the emotions on the face of the actor as *direct* reactions to the other shots: he was hungry, aroused, amused, saddened. Of course, the irony was that the shots of Mozhukhin's face were identical. Here, the associative power of editing had exceeded the direct, iconic power of the affection image in the close-up. The point is that, with some clever combination of the two, effects not too far removed from the free indirect discourse of a Henry James can be achieved.

When filming *Rebecca*, Hitchcock made a very interesting decision about the way to film Mrs Danvers. In an interview, he put it this way:

> Mrs Danvers was almost never seen walking and was rarely shown in motion. If she entered a room in which the heroine was, what happened is that the girl suddenly heard a sound and there was the ever-present Mrs Danvers, standing perfectly still by her side. In this way the whole situation was projected from the heroine's point of view; she never knew when Mrs Danvers might turn up, and this, in itself, was terrifying. To have shown Mrs Danvers walking about would have been to humanize her.
>
> (Truffaut 1985: 129–30)

It is not that Mrs Danvers really was a kind of ever-present ghost; it is that, combined with the distressed close-ups of Joan Fontaine's face, and with the constant framing of Danvers looming over Fontaine's seated figure at a table, the always unexpected appearance of Danvers was the final touch in Hitchcock's establishment of a closed psychological space in the film. Danvers is seen not objectively but as Fontaine sees her. And she would not be as frightening as she is without the nervous close-ups of Fontaine to underline our fear.

Optical POV

Another technique for focalising film narrative on a specific subject position is of course to shoot the film as if from the point of view of a character, taking literally the comparison of the camera with a human eye. Many films have attempted this effect of perceptual subjectivity from time to time, as part of the overall narrative structure, but very few have tried it throughout a film. The first classic example of such an attempt is the 1946 film, *Lady in the Lake* (Montgomery 1947); almost the entire film is shot as if from the eyes of the character Philip Marlowe. Shots like this are called 'optical point of view' or POV shots, and their combination with a voice-over narration might be thought to effect a pretty comprehensive focalisation of the narrative. But the irony is that identification does not work so happily with a consistency of literal camera POV. For some strange psychological reason, it is the case that the unrelenting optical point of view of a character alienates us as often as it draws us in: the simple fact is that a machine lens and an organic lens are two very different phenomena, and any time a mechanical lens is pretending to 'have a body', it can easily seem ridiculous.

In *Rebecca*, the optical POV shot is not often used, but when it is, it is especially effective. The first view we have of Maxim, standing precariously at the top of a cliff outside Monte Carlo, is from the POV of Fontaine, whom we have not even seen yet, only heard. The first appearance of Mrs Danvers, a haunting, sudden close-up, is again framed as a POV shot. But perhaps the most extraordinary POV shot in the film comes towards the end, at the very moment when Maxim is telling the story of Rebecca's final minutes in the cottage. So caught up is Fontaine's character in the narrative she has been waiting such a long time to hear that we move from a close-up of her face to a POV shot that looks around the interior of the cottage *as though Rebecca were still there*, moving about the way Maxim is describing her actions. At the centre of the frame is an absence, an absence that moves: we are asked to adopt the extreme psychological state of Fontaine's character and project 'the most beautiful creature we have ever seen' into this space. We inhabit the POV of the nameless narrator, whose compulsive wish to see and compare herself to the dead Rebecca is most eloquently expressed in these vacant shots from her desperate perspective.

Synthesis and limitation

Altogether, *Rebecca* is a remarkable exercise in film focalisation. We begin in the narrator's dream space – another very effective means of establishing imaginative identification. Our first view of Manderley, of the gates and the drive and the great house itself, is entirely from the position of the narrator's nocturnal dreams of the past. The voice-over that accompanies these shots is measured and hypnotic and focalised very particularly: 'Last night I dreamed of Manderley again . . . I looked upon a desolate shell with no whisper of the past about its staring walls . . . We can never go back to Manderley again, but sometimes, in my dreams, I do go back, to the strange days of my life, which began for me in the south of France . . .' By the end of this voice-over, which is the last such intrusion in the film, we know several things about our narrator: she no longer lives at Manderley, she often dreams of it, she is involved with another (she speaks of a 'we'), and her life, described as 'strange', effectively began where we finally see her, screaming 'NO!' at Laurence Olivier leaning over a precipice. Combined with the visual message of the dream flashback, we know that this house exerts considerable pressure on her unconscious, and we are about to find out why.

For most of the rest of the film, until the revelation scene in the beach cottage, this focalisation is preserved intact. Most of the drama of the film depends upon a very limited range of narrative information: Joan Fontaine does not know the real story of Rebecca. With her, and solely from her point of view, we piece together select pieces of evidence and come to the same conclusion she does: that her new husband is still madly in love with his dead wife. The whole narrative logic of the film depends upon this repression of the POVs of other characters. Everyone else of any significance in the film – Maxim, Frank Crawley, Jack Favell, Beatrice and Giles, the dread Mrs Danvers, even old Loony Ben – everyone else knows the truth: that Rebecca was a promiscuous and unfaithful sexual predator whom her husband despised and almost killed. In being focalised by the nameless narrator, we too are forced to adopt this extremely limited narrative range, and the effect is – to say the least – exasperating. When Beatrice turns conspiratorially to Fontaine after lunch and says, 'Oh, but you know the whole story, of course', the immediate response is that, no, she doesn't; but if this character had any gumption, and any class, she would ask! She doesn't. She surmises and hypothesises, but will never act like the mistress of the house and simply press for information. Her passivity and gaucherie are very annoying, and not only for us but for her narrator as well.

Thus, although we are for a large part of the film exclusively focalised by one of the dimmest characters in film history, there exists a latent tension between this focal lens and the invisible, meta-diegetic narrator who is presenting her POV for us. For brevity's sake, we will call this invisible narrator 'Alfred Hitchcock' (of course, he isn't *totally* invisible, and he makes his patented cameo when Jack Favell is making his trunk call to Danvers from London). To give you a sense of what I mean, here is another excerpt from the interview of Hitchcock by François Truffaut, on the subject of *Rebecca*:

HITCHCOCK: It's not a Hitchcock picture; it's a novelette, really. The story is old-fashioned; there was a whole school of feminine literature at the period, and though I'm not against it, the fact is that the story is lacking in humour . . .

TRUFFAUT: . . . you've said that the picture is lacking in humour, but my guess would be that you must have had some fun with the scenario, because it's actually the story of a girl who makes one blunder after another . . . I couldn't help imagining the working sessions between you and your scriptwriter: 'Now, this is the scene of the meal. Shall we have her drop her fork or will she upset her glass? Let's have her break the plate . . .'

HITCHCOCK: That's quite true; it did happen that way and we had a good deal of fun with it.

(Truffaut 1985: 130–1)

This suggests some very interesting narrative dynamics between the narrative focal lens and the invisible hand of the film narrator. Hitchcock simply does not like his diegetic narrator; so he will signpost this exasperation not by breaking the focalisation (if he did this, the narrative would unravel) but by torturing his narrator, playing sadistic games with her, even as she maintains a tight grip on the narrative reins. Throughout the film, she is dismissively referred to as a child; she bites her nails when out for a drive with Maxim, and is reproved for it. When she sits down to a table in the restaurant at Monte, she knocks over a vase of flowers; when she sits down to her desk in the morning room, she breaks the china Cupid and hides the shards; when she is confronted by the breakfast service at Manderley, she doesn't dare eat lest she embarrass herself further; her sketches are bad and uninteresting; when she walks with Maxim, she insists on going directly to the cottage that is most traumatic to him; when she dresses for dinner, she looks ridiculous; and so on. There is a long chain of explicit humiliations and *faux pas*, which we are invited sadistically to enjoy as the compensation for so little narrative information.

In other films, the exploration of point of view is more fluid and provocative than it is in the narrow narrative world of *Rebecca*. One of the more fascinating films of recent years has returned to the film-length optical POV, in a single unbroken shot, and the 'dream space' of a first-person fixed focaliser, to meditate profoundly on the relationship between image and memory, narrative and history. This is Alexander Sokurov's film *Russian Ark* (2002).

Russian Ark seriously challenges the naive presupposition that a consistent identification of the camera with a single characterological perspective leads to a similar psychological identification between the viewer and that character. In fact, quite to the contrary, what we find in this film is that, far from 'identifying' with the nameless first-person drifter through the Hermitage, we are evacuated through his eyes into the space itself, to be 'focalised' by any number of faces drifting past us. In the exquisite ball sequence, for instance, it is not the narrator we find ourselves focalised by (indeed, he has precisely fallen silent and withdrawn into a purely receptive state), but the French diplomat, the short, fair-haired young officer, the conductor, the lady in white, the spy and so forth, in the order in which they appear before us and conduct us through the dance. Despite being rigorously shot from the optical POV of the narrator, it is this literal 'focaliser' who vanishes from the psychological, affective and physical milieu, liberating us to assume the perspective and desires of these virtually random others, in what amounts to a gaseous deconstruction of any singular or consistent narratological frame.

Once again, this powerfully demonstrates the critical function of the close-up and medium shot as focalising devices in film narrative. Precisely insofar as the optical first-person 'point of view' effectively erases the explicit focaliser from the visual field, he or she fails to engage the viewer in anything other than a literal way. What happens instead is that the faces and three-quarter bodies that occupy the visual field of the narrator assume disproportionate focalising functions. Sokurov makes this explicit throughout his film by 'splitting' the narrator function in two: the nameless first-person narrator/dreamer and his companion figure, the French diplomat, whose constant and riveting visual presence (his towering height; the leanness of his frame, darkness of his clothes and expressiveness of his face in close-up and three-quarter shots) becomes a surrogate for the invisible narrator, despite the fact that they are in constant dispute over most of the issues the film raises. The narrator and the diplomat are worlds apart psychologically, emotion-ally and intellectually; yet owing to the fact that one is embodied and the other is not (is just an eye and a voice), they become a complex whole, a pseudo-couple, which allegorises the dialectic the film most wants to represent: between the im-perial visibility of European culture and the elusiveness of the Russian 'soul', existing in its shadow.

Conclusion

Most cinema claims us not through the cold mechanical eye of the camera but through the sensitive faces of others registered in its visual field. Whether those faces are the exquisitely and relentlessly studied expressions of Falconetti in Carl Dreyer's *La Passion de Jeanne d'Arc* (1928) or the digitally animated visages of Docter, Silverman and Unkrich's inhuman comedy *Monsters, Inc.* (2001), we are focalised less by the literal 'point of view' of the camera on the diegetic world than we are by these expressive windows into the psychological life of sentient and affective beings. More than a century of mechanically reproduced machine art has not diminished the extraordinary hold on our imaginary lives of faces and the souls they appear to manifest.

Chapter 8

Novel to film

Helen Fulton

The process of reworking a written text, such as a novel, into an image-based text, such as a film, reveals the different narrative conventions of the two media. In this chapter, I am primarily interested in the ways in which the narrative conventions and techniques of film work to create meanings, so that a novel and its film adaptation, although clearly related, tend to have different themes and goals. I will be referring mainly to two films, *The English Patient* (written and directed by Anthony Minghella, 1996) and *The Lord of the Rings*: *The Fellowship of the Ring* (directed by Peter Jackson, screenplay by Frances Walsh, 2001), and the corresponding novels, *The English Patient* by Michael Ondaatje (1992) and *The Lord of the Rings*, Part 1: *The Fellowship of the Ring* by J. R. R. Tolkien (1949).

Issues of adaptation

The novelist John Irving, who wrote the screenplay for the film *The Cider House Rules* based on his own novel, has said, 'Even when you don't have to lose much in an adaptation from book to screen, you always lose something. Screenwriters learn to compensate for what they've lost . . . In an adaptation, you can't be too literally wedded to the novel. You have to take advantage of what a film can do' (*Guardian*, 28 January 2005, 'Friday Review', p. 11).

What Irving is getting at here is that the process of film adaptation, like the process of linguistic translation, is itself a creative act of authorship that results not in a variant version but in a distinctively original text. The opening scene of a novel, for example, might not be the best opening scene for a film of that novel, which has to draw the viewing audience immediately into the location, the time setting and the fictional world of the protagonists, so the screenwriter has to find another way in, often by inventing a scene. The film of *The English Patient* opens with the desert rescue of Almásy from his burning plane, showing us his terrible injuries. This scene introduces us to the main character and how he came to be cared for by Hana in the Italian villa, linking the two main strands of the film, the desert and the villa. Michael Ondaatje's novel, *The English Patient*, opens with Hana in the villa and takes us through a series of brief scenes alternating between the desert rescue and the villa, but the physical landscapes and appearance of each locale, so striking a feature of the film, are marginalised in the novel. Instead, each scene reveals a little bit more to us about these two characters, their states of mind and, most significantly, those cultural and discursive points of reference – what Pierre Bourdieu calls 'habitus' (Bourdieu 1979) – that define and distinguish them.

Such a process of adaptation confirms that the narrative modes of novel and film operate according to different logics of storytelling. And the existence of these different logics, each appropriate to its own mode and context, reminds us that there is no 'natural' or 'obvious' way of telling a story. How a story is told depends not only on cultural and linguistic conventions but also on the parameters of the specific medium through which it is articulated. Dudley Andrew suggests that 'the analysis of adaptation . . . must point to the achievement of equivalent narrative units in the absolutely different semiotic systems of film and language' (Andrew 2000: 34), but I would argue that it is not possible to construct 'equivalent narrative units' in the different media, since each operates according to its own narrative logic. In this chapter, I am concerned not so much with the actual processes by which a novel is turned into a film as with the narrative conventions of film and how they create meanings that might differ from those of the preceding novel.

Narrative theory has traditionally dealt with written texts, occasionally with oral texts, such as folk tales (as in Propp's schematic theory), and assumptions about what narrative is have therefore been based on these particular kinds of storytelling modes. In analysing filmic narrative, we need to rethink the established conventions of narrative. For example, the process of editing is crucial in constructing the narrative sequence of a film, whose individual shots are rarely filmed in sequence. The 'director's cut', which restores scenes omitted from the commercial version, the collections of extra scenes marketed on DVDs and the Oscar awards for 'best editor' all draw our attention to the role of the editor and the significance of the editorial process in movie-making.

But this process of editing, of cutting and pasting, refocusing dialogue, reordering scenes, which is often just as significant in the crafting of a novel, and which might be done by professional editors as well as by authors, is almost entirely elided from analytical accounts of narrative structure. Debates about different manuscript versions of texts, such as the many emendations and print versions of James Joyce's novel *Ulysses*, centre on the issue of authenticating the 'original' version of the text, a debate that never happens in relation to differently edited versions of the same film. Critical analysis of a novel seeks a single, coherent and uniquely gifted authorial voice, such as that of J. R. R. Tolkien in *Lord of the Rings*, echoes of whose scholarly institutionalised persona are readily retrievable from his writings. Although early film criticism modelled the director on the literary author as the *auteur*, the single gifted originator of the text, more recent criticism (not to mention industry reward systems) acknowledges the multivocal perspective of film, shared among writers, directors, editors and even actors.

A theory of narrative based on an assumption of univocal, singular, coherent authorship is inevitably different from one based on an assumption of multivocal shared authorship. As Robert B. Ray has put it, 'Fearful of seeing literature's narrative role usurped by the movies, and under the sway of New Criticism's religious reverence for "serious art" . . . critics typically used adaptation study to shore up literature's crumbling walls' (Ray 2000: 46). A post-structuralist view of film narrative, on the other hand, acknowledges the decentring of authorial responsibility that in turn decentres meaning. Such a model of authorship, with its implications of editorial and directorial interventions and the likelihood of multiple versions with no 'original' text, has to frame our expectations of what filmic narrative is and how it operates.

It is also important to remember that both novel and film can do things that the other cannot or, as Seymour Chatman put it, 'What novels can do that films can't (and vice versa)' (Chatman 1980). A novel mainly *tells*, through diegesis; a film mainly *shows*, through mimesis. So in relation to character and motivation, for example, a novel can explain, through an 'omniscient narrator', why characters perform certain actions, and even what they are thinking and feeling while they are doing them. A film can show characters performing actions, but cannot easily comment on those actions from an external perspective, except through an interventionist device such as voice-over. These differences in the modes of representation effectively produce two quite different texts, undermining the hierarchy of 'original' novel and secondary film, or what Imelda Whelehan calls the 'unconscious prioritising of the fictional origin over the resulting film' (Cartmell & Whelehan 1999: 3). The structuralist view of adaptation, in which novel and film are regarded as having the same underlying 'story' (or *langue*) realised in different 'plots' (or *paroles*) (McFarlane 1996: 23), is unable to explain the discursive and semiotic strategies by which the two texts are related and yet quite distinct.

In terms of focalisation – the perspective from which events are narrated – a film has less control than a novel over different viewpoints. A third-person external narrator in a novel can give the viewpoints of several characters during a single event. In a film, we do not always know how characters interpret events, whose viewpoint is privileged or what their inner thoughts are. Film characters are always in front of a camera; they have only public personae, they are never alone. The only external narrator is the camera, which represents the viewpoint of the director, the cinematographer and the editor as well.

Table 8.1: Novel and film.

	NOVEL	FILM
FIELD	Structure – 'story'	Structure – 'story'
	Description of settings	*Mise en scène*, sound
	Transitivity	Composition and vectors
TENOR	Characters (motivated)	Characters (public)
	Focalisation	Focalisation
	Modality	Camera techniques
MODE	Chronology – 'plot'	Chronology – 'plot'
	Chapters	Shots, sequences
	Verbal cohesion	Continuity editing, sound

We can summarise the narrative features of novel and film in table 8.1, which compares aspects of the two modes of storytelling. Those aspects of filmic narrative listed in the right-hand column are discussed in this chapter and chapter 9.

Structure: field and mode

The strategies for constructing a coherent visual world within which a film can be 'read' as real and meaningful can be expressed as aspects of **field**, **tenor** and **mode** (Halliday 1978: 110; see also Rosemary Huisman's chapter 12 in this book). The field of subject matter is created diegetically through action, *mise en scène* and sound, as well as through the structuring of the 'story', the basic sequence of narrative events. The tenor, the range of social relations and attitudes constructed by the narrative, is expressed diegetically through dialogue between characters, and visually, or mimetically, by means of camera techniques and focalisation. The mode, the textual means by which a message is organised into a coherent whole, is achieved by the construction of 'plot' in scenes and sequences, editing and various technical applications of camera and sound.

As a mode of representation, film typically has a fairly simple structure, consisting of a linear progression made up of individual shots organised into sequences of juxtaposed images. A novel, on the other hand, could have a considerably more complex narrative structure than a film, which has to be followed at one sitting by a viewing audience. The 'field' of a film, the subject matter and content, is therefore presented in a particular 'mode' or style of organisation, laid out along a linear time frame. The mode of description characteristic of novels is replaced by the mode of visual and auditory signifiers that create the 'field' of the film.

Seymour Chatman argues that a dual time frame – the distinction between chronological 'story' and reordered 'plot' (or 'discourse' as Chatman calls it) – is a fundamental property of narrative found in both novel and film (Chatman 1978). This distinction, however, can be made in relation to all kinds of utterances, not just narratives, since the disjunction between the chronology of an event and the manner of its telling is a function of representation. Like other kinds of structuralist binaries, notably *langue* and *parole*, this distinction is also problematic because of the difficulty of drawing an absolute line between what is 'story' and what is 'plot'.

Many screenwriters adapting a screenplay from a novel break the narrative down into what they see as the essential chronological elements of the 'story' before reordering them into a 'plot'. However, there is no single 'story' (or *langue*) lying behind or beneath all versions of a text that will then yield multiple 'plots' (or *paroles*), depending on the writer. Just as a *langue* is socially defined and constructed within discourse, and is therefore as unstable and plural as a *parole*, so the 'story' of a novel or film can be reconstructed differently by different interpreters. Events that might seem an essential part of the 'story' to one interpreter could be omitted or abbreviated or assimilated into other events by another interpreter working within a different cultural framework or with a different purpose (Smith 1980).

Rather than considering films such as *The Lord of the Rings: The Fellowship of the Ring* and *The English Patient* as 'versions' of the respective novels of the same names, we need to read their textual logic, the ways in which field, tenor and mode construct meaning, in terms of the specific mode of film. The 'story' of a film, that is, the chronological summary of events, can be retheorised as its 'field', that is, the semantic content and subject matter. The concept of 'plot', as the particular ordering of events in a specific text, can be retheorised as an aspect of 'mode', the way in which the elements of a narrative are organised into a coherent chain of events.

The 'field' of a film – which events and locations are actually shown – tends to be much simpler than the 'field' of a preceding novel. At the same time, the 'mode' – the way in which the events are selected and ordered – inevitably differs quite markedly between novel and film because of the different demands of the two media. The novel *The English Patient* layers multiple locations and time frames into an intricate pattern that works at both horizontal and vertical levels, dismantling any easy distinction between 'field' and 'mode', or indeed between 'story' and 'plot'. Instead, the reader is challenged to decipher the events of the book just as Hana tries to decipher Almásy's copy of Herodotus into which he has pasted all the fragments of his life, in random order.

To make the film version of 1996, the director and screenwriter, Anthony Minghella, working to the demands of the mainstream commercial movie industry, used aspects of the 'field' and techniques of filmic 'mode' to create a clear distinction between 'story' and 'plot'. He stripped out many of the scenes from the novel and reordered the remaining events into three main narrative sequences, one set in the present, in the villa where the English patient lies dying, one set in

the past, tracing the love affair between Almásy and Katharine, and a third centred around the figure of Caravaggio that brings past and present together into a
disturbing continuum.

In the film *The Lord of the Rings: The Fellowship of the Ring* there is only one
main storyline, or semantic field, whereas the novel has several. Some have been
left out entirely, such as the Tom Bombadil episode; others have been abbreviated
or incorporated into the main narrative, such as Gandalf's story of Saruman, told
by him as a flashback in the novel but featured as part of the main action in the
film. The main effect of these changes is to remove many of the novel's 'fields',
and therefore its themes, and replace them with other preoccupations generated
by the film. Novel and film, while drawing on some of the same semantic fields,
conform to different narrative logics, or 'modes', and therefore construct different
meanings.

The novel is structured as two books, with most of the first set in the Shire
and leading up to the meeting with Strider towards the end of Book 1. Much
of Book 1 consists of folklore, genealogy, self-contained stories and narratives of
past adventures, forming a rich texture that works to suggest the totality of life
in the Shire, with its own distinctive history, geography and world view. Tolkien's
career as an academic medievalist has clearly influenced his creation of a lost
society whose reality belongs to the past and can be reconstructed only through
its surviving texts.

Book 2 of the novel focuses on the adventures of the fellowship of the ring,
but here again there are interspersed accounts of the history and politics of the
warring groups. Many of these accounts are delivered by characters in direct
speech, rather than by the narrator, such as Glóin's tale of Sauron's threat (Book 2,
chapter 2), drawing attention to the orality of knowledge and memory in this
created world. This kind of textuality – the 'back stories', the distinction between
orality and literacy, the detailed construction of an entire culture, with its own
history and beliefs – is necessarily absent from the film version.

The film is structured as a typical adventure movie, in the form of a journey
or quest. After a relatively brief introductory section, the main content of the film
follows the journey of the band of heroes. The Proppian structure of the hero-
quest, elaborated by Joseph Campbell in *The Hero with a Thousand Faces* (1949),
and taken up by such directors as George Lucas (writer and director of the *Star
Wars* series, 1977 to the present) and Steven Spielberg (director of the *Indiana
Jones* series, 1981–89, co-written by George Lucas and Philip Kaufman), has been
foregrounded as the main structuring device of the film. The various 'back stories'
are either omitted, abbreviated, brought in to the main action or summarised
as voice-overs, clearing the way for a central narrative structure with a strong
forward propulsion provided by the motif of the quest.

The choice of episodes taken from the novel depends largely on whether they
can be shaped into distinct sequences that have a clear time frame and carry the
action of the story forward. The linear structure of film, as part of its 'mode',

also demands points of climax that are clearly signposted. Typically, 'Hollywood' movies (made according to a defined set of technical and aesthetic conventions by studios for maximum commercial profit) infix two points of climax at intervals of roughly a third of the running time. The first point of climax is left only partially resolved, generating a renewed development of the plot, while the second resolves the main issues and leads to the end of the film.

Because the novel of *The Lord of the Rings*: *The Fellowship of the Ring* is organised as a multilayering of numerous tales and anecdotes, there are many points of climax, often based around the deaths or woundings of major characters. The loss of Gandalf on the bridge of Khazad-dûm, for example, forming the climactic moment of Book 2, chapter 5, is one of a series of such moments that often prefigure the end of a chapter. This pacing of the classic adventure novel, as a set of chapters ending with a suspenseful 'cliffhanger', owes a great deal to popular cultural forms, particularly the serialised magazine and comic story, a format that reappeared in the television age with the weekly serial, both drama and soap opera, where each episode ends on an unresolved moment of suspense (see Rosemary Huisman in chapter 12).

In the film, the points of climax are provided by the two set-piece battle scenes, which are characteristic devices of action movies. The different pacing of the novel and the film, produced partly by the number and placement of the points of climax, directs us to the main message or theme of each text, alerting us to what is significant and what are the major issues and generators of tension. A further indicator of meaning is provided by the point of **closure**, that moment in a narrative when the story can end only in one way, when other possibilities are closed off. According to Martin McQuillan, 'All narratives end, but not all provide closure' (McQuillan 2000: 324), and, in the case of such serial texts as *The Lord of the Rings* (novels and films), we might expect the point of closure to be withheld until the very last text in the series. Yet as 'stand-alone' texts, each novel and film does not simply end but has its own point of closure that works to inform us of the major ideological preoccupations of the text.

In the novel *The Lord of the Rings*: *The Fellowship of the Ring* the point of closure is Frodo's realisation (in Book 2, chapter 10) that he must go on alone. Putting on the ring, he has a vision of such terrible war and destruction that, when he manages to remove the ring, his mind is made up: he must break up the fellowship and continue alone:

> Frodo rose to his feet. A great weariness was on him, but his will was firm and his heart lighter. He spoke aloud to himself. 'I will do now what I must,' he said. 'This at least is plain: the evil of the Ring is already at work even in the Company, and the Ring must leave them before it does more harm. I will go alone. Some I cannot trust, and those I can trust are too dear to me . . . I will go alone. At once.'
>
> (*The Fellowship of the Ring*, Book 2, chapter 10)

With this resolution of Frodo's dilemma, the book can come to an end, prefiguring a new stage of the journey to be continued in the next book. This moment of closure draws attention to the casting of Frodo in the role of the ordinary hero, the individual who, faced with unexpected dangers, performs as a hero without consciously inhabiting the persona. Tolkien's model of the everyday hero was drawn not from medieval literature and folklore, in which heroes tend to be over-determined and instantly recognisable, but from the men of his own day who had fought in two world wars and shown exceptional courage and fortitude. In the character of Frodo, Tolkien idealises the heroic possibilities of the ordinary man, the innate skills of leadership that reside in some and not in others, regardless of social class. At the same time he re-erects the class-based structure of 'officers and men' in his portrayal of the relationship between Frodo and his friends, Sam, Merry and Pippin. Sam, in particular, is constructed as the perfect batman, loyal, sensible, cautious, ready to follow his leader unquestioningly despite personal misgivings. Although Frodo has determined to journey on alone, we are not surprised that the novel ends with Sam firmly accompanying him.

In the film version, the point of closure is an incident that does not occur in the novel, namely the temptation of Aragorn. This scene confirms the positioning of Aragorn, rather than Frodo, as the filmic hero and naturalised leader of the quest. Frodo is the ordinary person selected by fate to do a difficult job; Aragorn is the traditional hero of medieval literature. Like Arthur, he is aristocratic, a trained warrior, leader of an army, destined to rule. The economics of commercial cinema dictate that an action movie must have a personable action hero. Frodo cannot be transformed into such a hero without losing his essential otherness, so Aragorn is elevated into a larger and more prominent role. The 'temptation of the hero' is a conventional motif of hero cycles ranging from Jesus to Lancelot, and the location of Aragorn in this context works to affirm his heroic status. To bring the film to a dramatic end, the episodes of the attack of the Orcs and the death of Boromir are moved from their place at the beginning of Part 2 of the novel sequence, *The Two Towers*, to provide a conventional ending for an action film. Aragorn's hand-to-hand combat with the Orc reinforces his heroic status and centrality to the world of the film (as opposed to that of the novel), while the deathbed confession of Boromir again recalls the chivalric behaviour of medieval knights.

We can see a significant difference in the points of closure occurring in *The English Patient* as novel and film. The film, as a commercial vehicle, is firmly structured into one of the major genres of 'Hollywood' film; that is, romance. Its point of closure, one of the signposts that tells us it is a romance, is the death of Katharine and Almásy's return for her body, accompanied by soaring music and dramatic visuals of the orange desert and the white robes flowing around Katharine's body. The ending comes with the death of Almásy himself, having relived the contours of the desert and the love affair that took place within it. The novel, however, eludes a simple generic categorisation. It is more open-ended, finishing on a final leap in the chronology with Kip and Hana separately thinking back to the villa ten years after the war. The point of closure is Hiroshima, marking the end of the war and the end of Kip's belief in the 'British Empire' and the values that sustained him during the war. It is at that point that he sees through what Bronwen Thomas has called 'the mirage of cultural imperialism' (Thomas 2000: 208). The novel, then, is marked not simply as a romance – like the commercial vehicle of the film – but as a rumination on some of the larger themes of twentieth-century life, such as war, memory and identity.

Points of climax, moments of resolution, the point of closure and the ordering of events therefore tell us how to 'read' a text and to recognise its preoccupations. By selecting particular events – the 'field' – and arranging them into coherent sequences marked by points of climax and closure – the 'mode' – each of these films creates a very different fictional world from that of the corresponding novels. The different points of closure determine what each text is about and how we are to read it: the ordinary heroism of Frodo and the idea of essential goodness and evil in the novel are submerged beneath the commercial fantasy of the action hero in the film, the 'superman' who can win wars and save civilisation.

Setting

Where the filmic action takes place is an important aspect of the 'field', structuring our sense of the 'reality' of the film and our expectations of what might occur in it. Setting can be considered to comprise location, encompassing particular physical and geographical sites, and *mise en scène*. This term, used in both theatre and film, describes the immediate surroundings and composition of individual shots in a film, and provides a visual realisation of what in a novel is usually described in words. The various settings of a film help to achieve a seamless fictional world through a powerfully iconic visual medium.

Each *mise en scène*, which normally lasts through a sequence of shots (although an effect of dramatic or comedic pace can be achieved by cutting rapidly backwards and forwards between different *mises en scène*), comprises a physical location, interior or exterior, costumes and props. It also includes those elements that will be picked up by the camera as the shot is filmed: the bits of 'business', or specific actions performed by the characters in the shot, the lighting and the colour (Nelmes 1996: 93–4).

We can also include the specific composition of each shot: where the characters and props or physical objects are positioned and their relationship to each other. The spatiality of the *mise en scène*, allowing a number of people and objects to be seen in the same shot, provides an important site of signification: what we are supposed to notice first and how we are to rank the visual items in order of significance has to be carefully controlled through composition, lighting and focus (McFarlane 1996: 27–8). A symmetrical composition, with characters positioned equidistantly from each other or lined up with specific props, can suggest formality or romantic fantasy, as in musicals. Asymmetrical arrangements tend to look less posed and therefore more realistic, as if we are observing people as they would normally behave.

The actual or imaginary lines that connect the characters and objects – such as Almásy watching Katharine's arrival by plane, or Gandalf on the bridge of Khazad-dûm – are the narrative '**vectors**' that literally point to the main participants of the action and show us how they are connected (Kress & van Leeuwen 1996: 56–8). These vectors are the visual equivalent of grammatical **transitivity** in verbal language, the arrangements of participants in clauses that indicate who is doing what to whom (and sometimes how and why) (Fowler 1996: 220–32; Goatly 2000: 59–65).

In Tolkien's *Lord of the Rings*, Gandalf's power is indicated by his relation to the bridge, which he cracks with one blow of his staff: 'At that moment, Gandalf lifted his staff, and crying aloud he smote the bridge before him' (Book 2, chapter 5). In both verbal processes, 'lifted' and 'smote', Gandalf is the agent exercising power over the goals, 'staff' and 'bridge'. In the visual *mise en scène* of the film, Gandalf's location on the bridge, and the vectors departing from Gandalf towards the bridge and the staff, convey the same relationship of power between agent and goal.

In Ondaatje's *English Patient*, Almásy describes being part of a group of men who see Katharine arrive with Geoffrey Clifton, her husband: 'He sat in his two-seater plane and we walked towards him from the base camp. He stood up in the cockpit and poured a drink out of his flask. His new wife sat beside him . . . I watched the friendly uncertainty scattered across his wife's face, her lionlike hair when she pulled off the leather helmet' (p. 142). The transitivity patterns place Clifton at the centre of the action, the alpha male who owns his wife as he owns his plane. He sits in 'his' plane, stands up in the (gendered) cockpit, pours a drink from 'his' flask, while the others walk towards him, drawn towards him as a focal point. Katharine, described pedantically and jealously by Almásy as 'his [i.e. Clifton's] new wife' merely sits beside him. Almásy himself is the watcher, observing without acting. In the film version of this scene, a similar set of relations between the characters is conveyed by the *mise en scène*. When Clifton's plane has landed, we see Almásy standing apart from the others, watching from a distance, with a reactional vector line implied between his vision and the plane. But he is also wearing sunglasses, hiding his eyes, and he has emerged from the seat of a car so that the door cuts across his body, forming a physical vector between him and the others, visually indicating his isolation and his initial hostility towards Clifton and 'his wife'.

Through the manipulation of *mises en scène*, different hierarchies, different 'worlds' and different 'realities' can be conveyed. In *The Lord of the Rings: The Fellowship of the Ring*, the hatching of the Orcs in Isengard takes place in a diabolic orange glow. The world of Saruman, by contrast, is depicted in shades of grey and black, colours that are cold and suggestive of evil. Much of the journey takes place in settings that are dark, with vertical vectors of trees, mountains or rocks, and made of hard-edged stony surfaces. The contrast with the early scenes set in the Shire, where the colours and lighting are strong and bright, the vector lines are low and horizontal, and the surface textures of grass and crops are soft, helps us to realise the sacrifice that Frodo and his friends have made in undertaking the quest. It also creates the 'reality' that there are two different kinds of world, the good and the evil, that these worlds are easily distinguishable and that we therefore have a choice about which we inhabit.

I have already identified three main narrative sequences in the film of *The English Patient* – Almásy and Hana in the villa, the love story in the desert and the story of Caravaggio – and these three threads are intertwined and yet clearly distinguished by the use of different and instantly recognisable key settings. The world of the villa is revealed to us throughout the film as bare, crumbling, over-grown, bathed in cool shades of red and blue. Hana and the other characters around her wear wartime clothing, uniforms or cheap utilitarian dresses and sturdy shoes. The shots are mostly interior, suggesting domesticity but also con-finement and loss of autonomy. The 'props' are mainly domestic, or connected with Hana's task of nursing the English patient, but there are occasional and sig-nificant interruptions of such objects as the piano and the wall painting, and the book of Herodotus, which all suggest the remnants of a lost culture. In the setting of the villa, we see that this is what Western culture has come to, the 'old world' of Europe broken down by war and neglect.

The desert scenes, on the other hand, are huge, open, airy and exotically 'other'. The orange colours of the desert merge with the wide blue of the sky and the dun colours of the desert clothing. The costumes of the Westerners, expensive tailor-made clothing specially adapted for desert living, mark their difference from the native Africans on the expedition, while their 'props' – their tents, maps, jeeps, planes and cameras – indicate the technological mastery of the West over the uncivilised East. Most of Caravaggio's story is shown to us in scenes bathed in bright white light, bleached of colour, suggesting their location in the past but also their dreamlike quality, as if their 'reality' is unreliable and deceptive. This is one of the ways in which Caravaggio is presented to us as enigmatic, not entirely trustworthy, his motives obscure.

Through these different settings and *mises en scène*, the cultures of East and West are constructed as entirely different, in fact quite oppositional, with no con-ceivable point of contact except through the Western technology of mapping, which is a form of cultural appropriation. In the novel, however, villa and desert are less clearly distinguished, rarely described in detail, but merely suggested in occasional images of rooms and gardens, spaces and caves. Less significant in the novel, which interrogates people rather than places, the settings constantly spill into each other, merging in Almásy's mind as he gradually recalls the last years of his life, the war, the desert expeditions and his relationship with Katharine.

In the novel, Almásy explicitly rejects a cultural appropriation of the desert and defends the scientific curiosity that brought him and his friends to the desert: 'We seemed to be interested only in things that could not be bought and sold, of no interest to the outside world' (p. 143), an image that connects us at once to the life of the villa, similarly enclosed and of no interest to the outside world. By separating the two locations into visually distinctive settings, the film breaks apart what was in the novel a narrative continuity, from villa to desert and back again. By setting East against West, the film forces Almásy to be one or the other, and he is positioned as a Westerner. Yet in the novel, Almásy's identity and his own self-definition are a central mystery, and one that is never properly solved, an area of obscurity that highlights the dislocation of war, the artificiality of national boundaries and the problematic issues of cultural and national identity as the main themes of the narrative.

Setting, in the form of location and *mise en scène*, is therefore another site of meaning in film, determining how we 'see' events and the kinds of 'reality' that are created for us. Although the semantic fields of novel and film are similar, the ways in which they are realised visually in the film construct experiential meanings that belong to a quite different kind of narrative, a Westernised romance that positions the East as 'other'. In the novel, East and West are almost indistinguishable, blending into each other, as ideological halves of the same whole.

Conclusion

The process of adapting a novel into a film demonstrates the limitations of a structuralist understanding of narrative as divisible into 'story' and 'plot'. The 'story' that seems to underpin both a novel and its filmic version has to be reduced to such bare bones to fit both texts that it becomes little more than a statement of genre and a recognition of character. At the same time, the manifestation of 'plot' in each version is realised in such different semiotic forms that it is almost impossible to think of the two texts as being in any way 'the same'. The privileging of the 'authorised' text, the novel written by a single known author, over the multimodal team-produced work, as most films are, overestimates the coherence of the author as subject and underestimates the complexity of meaning available through the narrative logic of film.

Chapter 9

Film narrative and visual cohesion

Helen Fulton

In the previous chapter, I discussed ways in which the structures of film narrative are able to create meanings, themes and concerns that could be different from those expressed in a corresponding novel. In this chapter, further examples from the two films *The Lord of the Rings: The Fellowship of the Ring* and *The English Patient* will focus mainly on tenor and mode and how they are realised in film, particularly through sound, character, focalisation and cohesion. By examining the technical production of these effects, we can see how they provide complex sites of signification for viewing audiences.

Sound

The sound of a film is one of its most versatile signifiers, since it contributes to field, tenor and mode as a powerful creator of meaning, mood and textuality. Diegetic sounds are those that belong to the on-screen 'reality', able to be heard by the characters on screen, such as dialogue, sound effects (the striking of the staff on the bridge) and ambient noise (the noise of the sandstorm in the desert). Non-diegetic sounds come from outside the filmic world, and are not 'heard' by the characters. These conventionally include soundtrack music and voice-overs.

While dialogue clearly contributes to the tenor of a film, as the main means by which relations between characters and their attitudes to each other are constructed, sound effects and ambient noise, over-determined by technology, help to construct the semantic field. In the mines of Moria, the arrival of the Balrog, the fire demon, is announced with stomping and growling and the noise of fire and flames, preparing us as well as the characters in the film for the worst, and reminding us of the vulnerability of the heroes. Like the Balrog, the sinister Black Riders are heard before they are seen, and we know from the sound effects that they will appear on horseback. By contrast, the soothing sounds of elven music emanating from Rivendell reassure us that this is a welcoming place where no dangers await.

Voice-over is used in both films to indicate viewpoint (an aspect of tenor) and to move the film through long periods of time. The early history of the Shire and the finding of the Ring are told at the beginning of *The Lord of the Rings: The Fellowship of the Ring* in the form of a voice-over by Galadriel who, as an immortal elf, might be supposed to know everything that had happened in the past. Non-diegetic music is particularly significant in *The English Patient*, such as the scene of Almásy's removal of Katharine's body from the Cave of Swimmers, referred to in chapter 8. Earlier in the film, when Almásy and Katharine are flying above the desert in different planes, the diegetic noise of the planes is replaced by a non-diegetic soundtrack of orchestral music, which suggests an emotional connection between the two characters despite their physical separation, and which also addresses us, the viewing audience, directly in a shared space outside the diegesis.

Sound is also significant as an element of narrative cohesion, helping to link scenes together or, alternatively, to mark a sudden change of location or mood. At one point in *The English Patient*, Hana is playing hopscotch outside in the garden in the dark, and the noise of her jumping feet is picked up on the soundtrack and blended in to the noise of drumbeats in the desert, heard by Almásy in his memory, and this sound, gradually predominating, leads us in to the next scene of Katharine in the desert telling the story of Candaules and Gyges. The merging of sounds made by Hana into sounds associated with Katharine indicates both the differences between these two women and their connection in Almásy's life.

Characters

The characters of a film, as in a novel, form part of the field but also contribute to the **tenor**, the interpersonal function of the text, through their interactions and dialogue. Any representation of individuals in the form of fictionalised characters rests on a theory, however unconscious, of individualism. In many novels, the motivation and emotions of characters are described by the narrative voice, whether by the narrator or by one of the characters themselves. They are therefore constructed as having an inner life that is essentially their own and under their own control, suggesting that such characters are theorised as the unique individual of liberal humanist philosophy who precedes the social formation and exists separately from it. This is the kind of individual imagined by Tolkien in his representation of Frodo, for example:

He sat down upon the stone and cupped his chin in his hands, staring eastwards but seeing little with his eyes. All that had happened since Bilbo left the Shire was passing through his mind, and he recalled and pondered everything that he could remember of Gandalf's words. Time went on, and still he was no nearer to a choice.

(Book 2, chapter 10)

Frodo is positioned outside the social order, thinking about his current situation as if from the outside, with his power of thought limited only by his memory, and his course of action determined by his own choice.

In film, however, internal motivations and emotions have to be conveyed externally and visually, through gesture and expression, or directly through dialogue. Characters in film therefore take on a more public and social aspect, embedded in the social order rather than operating outside it. They are in fact positioned as social subjects, constructed through discourse. The filmic mode of representing individuals suggests a theory of individualism in which individuals are 'types' rather than uniquely different, and their behaviour can be explained in terms of their social context and positioning. The filmic character, in other words, tends more towards the post-structuralist concept of the individual, compared to the liberal humanist characters found in the realistic novel.

Filmic characters also have considerably less dialogue than their novelistic counterparts. The 'reality' of a film partly depends on short scenes and brief exchanges that get straight to the point, setting a brisk pace that keeps viewers alert. The character of Boromir, for example, has a lot more to say in Tolkien's novel than he does in the film version, and is our main source of information about the different peoples of the fantasy world, such as elves, half-elves, wizards and so on. Not only do we find out more about Boromir as a character from these accounts (as part of the tenor of the novel) but we are also given a semantic field, the sense of political complexity in the fantasy world, which is elided from the film, where politics are reduced to heroes and villains. Boromir's stories enable us to read the novel allegorically, as a comment on post–World War II Europe, yet it is virtually impossible to read the film as any kind of political allegory or commentary on contemporary events.

In the adaptation of novel to film, a certain amount of character reassignment is inevitable. Both narrative and economic imperatives are at work here, since both the story and the budget have to be kept simple. But more subtle forces are also at work in the commercial movie industry, such as the need to foreground celebrity actors and to tailor a film to meet the conventions of a recognisable and successful genre. In Tolkien's novel, Frodo is rescued by Legolas, but in the film, it is Arwen who rescues him, providing an opportunity to foreground one of the film's most bankable actors (Liv Ullmann). The lack of female characters in Tolkien's novel has had to be redressed in the film by giving those few characters bigger parts, not from any feminist scruples but in order to give the film a greater box-office appeal. At the same time, the character of Aragorn has been given a considerably expanded role in the film, replacing Frodo as the main hero of the narrative. If Frodo were the hero, the film would resemble the genre of children's fantasy movie, reducing its potential audience. With Aragorn as the hero, played by a lesser-known but visually striking actor and buttressed by impressive digital effects, the film becomes an action movie with all the potential profits associated with that genre.

Focalisation

Focalisation refers to the viewpoint or perspective from which the narration is told, positioning narrative voices, who may or may not be characters in the story, in relation to events and to each other. We can therefore regard focalisation as an aspect of 'tenor' in a text; that is, a way of constructing interpersonal meanings that indicate relations and attitudes among the participants inside and outside the narrative events. The camera, standing in for the external third-person narrator of a novel, conveys the modality of what is being shown and what is being exchanged between the characters; that is, the extent to which the various propositions and events appear to be truthful and certain, and how we might evaluate them (Kress & van Leeuwen 1996: 159–80).

The usefulness of the term 'focalisation', developed by Genette and subsequently taken over by a number of narrative theorists (Genette 1980; Bal 1983, 1997), in relation to the visual aspect of movie texts has been debated by various theorists. Lowe asserts that the 'proper usage' of the term 'is confined to the spoken and written word', and prefers the term 'viewpoint' or 'point of view' as the 'more traditional and inclusive usage' (Lowe 2000: 46 n. 15). Griffith, on the other hand, rejects the 'virtual equation of the camera with the point of view' as too simplistic (Griffith 1997: 47). Toolan suggests 'orientation' as 'a usefully wider, less visual, term' than focalisation (Toolan 1991: 68). With regard to film and other visual media such as television, the term 'focalisation' is useful in reminding us that there are both focalisers, those participants who 'see' what is going on, and focalised, those participants (people or objects) who are seen.

Julian Murphet has already touched on some aspects of focalisation in chapter 7, defining it as 'the anchoring of narrative discourse to a specific subject position in the story'. Murphet follows Rimmon-Kenan in distinguishing between focalisation, or 'seeing', and narration, or 'speaking', as separate activities (Rimmon-Kenan 1983: 71–3). Writing specifically about film, Murphet defines focalisation as an aspect of diegesis – what is going on in the filmic world – and narrative voice as a description of where the narrator is located, either inside or outside the filmic world.

Both aspects of narrative can be described by collating the different focalising positions and types of focalisers with the location of the narrative voice in relation to the diegesis; that is, the telling of the story. An extradiegetic narrator is speaking to us outside the events of the story, whereas a homodiegetic narrator is a character within the story whose narration is normally marked as direct speech. A heterodiegetic narration is a 'story within a story', an event outside the diegesis that is told by a character within the diegesis.

So when Gandalf tells Frodo about the magic rings (Book 1, chapter 2), he is functioning as a homodiegetic narrator, one who speaks as a character within the story, and who is therefore positioned as more or less knowledgeable and empowered in relation to other characters. Strider's account of Beren and Lúthien (Book 1, chapter 11) positions him as a heterodiegetic narrator; that is, as a character in the story who is recounting another story that is outside the main narrative. This is also the focalisation of Katharine in *The English Patient* when she reads the story from Herodotus of Candaules and Gyges (pp. 232–4), observed by Almásy as the internal focaliser and first-person narrator. His observation of her, as the unintended audience, puts him in the viewing position of Gyges and therefore draws out the prophetic significance of the classical story.

These three narrative positions – extradiegetic, homodiegetic, heterodiegetic – can be realised through a number of focalising strategies. An extradiegetic narrator can 'see' the story from an external or internal position. The third-person narrator of *The English Patient* is situated outside the diegesis and yet adopts an internal perspective that is able to reveal information, thoughts and emotions available only to characters in the story. This is the 'omniscient' narrator of fiction, constructed in this scene describing Caravaggio: 'Caravaggio enters the library. He has been spending most afternoons there. As always, books are mystical creatures to him. He plucks one out and opens it to the title page. He is in the room about five minutes before he hears a slight groan' (p. 81). Although the narrator is extradiegetic, the narrative voice has its own view of the action, its own focalisation. The narrator 'sees' Caravaggio entering the library, notices the way he 'plucks' one of the books from the shelf, and is aware of how many minutes have passed, even though Caravaggio is alone in the room. This is the focalisation through which we, the reader, make our assessment of Caravaggio. It is also a privileged, or first-order, focalisation since the narrator has access to knowledge not shared by others. At the same time, the narrator constructs a second-order internal focalisation emanating from Caravaggio himself. We are told that 'books are mystical creatures to him' and that 'he hears a slight groan', as if it is only by chance that Caravaggio is not telling us these things himself.

Tolkien often adopts a similar kind of extradiegetic internal focalisation in *The Lord of the Rings: The Fellowship of the Ring*, commenting on the concerns and fears of many of the characters, such as the extract about Frodo quoted above. But he also assumes at times an extradiegetic external focalisation, notably in the Prologue, where his ethnographic description of the various hobbit peoples positions him, and us, outside their world, explicitly denying any special claims to inside information about them. Although extradiegetic narration is typically in the third person, it can also be in the first person, as it is in much of *The English Patient*. The different facets of Almásy suggested by his various epithets – the English patient, Almásy, the dying man, the surveyor – are also conveyed through the different focalisations through which he narrates his story. He can be either an external or an internal focaliser, speaking in either the first or the third person, and occasionally both at once ('When Almásy was like this we usually dispersed, but this was Madox's last night in Cairo and we stayed', p. 244). He positions himself sometimes extradiegetically, sometimes homodiegetically, when he speaks to Hana or Caravaggio in first-person direct speech, and sometimes heterodiegetically.

This range of focalisations, along with the points of view of the other characters, illustrate the possibilities both of variable focalisation, where different events are seen from different viewpoints, and mulitiple focalisation, where the same event is shown from different perspectives. The death of Katharine in the Cave of Swimmers is described twice by the extradiegetic narrator, once from Katharine's point of view ('She had dragged herself into a corner, had wrapped herself tight in the parachute material . . . She would have hated to die without a name', p. 170), and once from Almásy's ('On the floor of the Cave of Swimmers, after her husband had crashed their plane, he had cut open and stretched out the parachute she had been carrying', p. 248). Later, Almásy is narrating the event in the first person, telling both us and Caravaggio about the physical contacts between the lovers, almost their last: 'I pulled her out of the plane Clifton had called *Rupert* and carried her up into the rock caves. Into the Cave of Swimmers . . .' (p. 257). The extradiegetic narration describes Katharine's focalisation and then Almásy's actions, practical and controlled, while Almásy's own version draws on memory and intimacy to give a different account of what happened.

While the extradiegetic narration of Tolkien's novel offers a fixed focalisation, supported by a range of variable focalisations situated homodiegetically, the variable and multiple focalisations of *The English Patient* construct a rich texture of interpersonal meaning. As readers we become aware that constructing the events of the past is contingent on memory and that all knowledge is partial and ideologically positioned. At the same time, we are presented with a theory of the individual as unstable, incoherent and discursively produced. The focalising strategies that produce this type of individual in Ondaatje's novel contrast with the fixed narrative perspectives of Tolkien's novel, which result in the creation of seamless, coherent and stable identities.

Narrative subtleties of this kind, involving a variety of narrative voices positioned differently within the narrative and outside it, create a hierarchy of focalisations that is replicated in the medium of film through a variety of camera techniques. The camera is the extradiegetic narrator, located externally as an invisible narrator but also able to suggest internal focalisations through camera angles and *mises en scène* as well as the actual speech and action of characters. In both the films, focalisation is variable, following the perspectives of a number of different characters in speech as well as visually. Multiple focalisation is realised by different camera angles, which position us to see the action from a number of different viewpoints. In the scene from *The English Patient* where Katharine recites the story of Candaules and Gyges to the circle of listening men, the camera seems to spy on Katharine from the darkness beyond the audience, tracking around the back of the scene, with Katharine facing almost straight to camera. The camera does not simply represent the internal focalisation of Almásy, who is shown watching Katharine covertly; it also acts as an external voyeur on our behalf, allowing us to watch as Katharine unwittingly reveals herself like Candaules' wife.

In this sequence, then, the camera is the focaliser, constructing interpersonal meanings about the relationship between Almásy and Katharine. She is lit by firelight and facing straight ahead, revealed to the watchers and hiding nothing. Almásy is shown in profile and in shadow, positioned in front of her as audience and watcher. The scene is shot mainly in distance or middle-distance, indicating the reserve between them, the fact that they do not know each other very well, while the close-up of Clifton's face, brightly lit by the fire, beaming and proud, suggests the confidence of his ownership of Katharine and his absolute ignorance of what is about to happen. Almásy and Katharine do not appear in shot together until the final scene of the sequence, alerting us to the inevitability of their love affair. The use of colour and lighting in this sequence conveys the different shades of modality. The dim lighting and shadows created by the fire reduce the **modality** – the assertion of truth – so that we are not sure exactly what we are being told or whose authority is privileged. Katharine's uncertainty and Almásy's confusion, already indicated through their body language, are also enhanced visually by the uncertain light. On the other hand, Clifton's brightly lit face conveys a high modality, giving us a high level of certainty and confidence about the meaning of this shot: it conveys, without any doubt, Clifton's clear belief that his wife is devoted to him.

The various kinds of focalisation can be summarised in relation to the diegetic positioning of the narrative voice, as in table 9.1, which draws partly on McQuillan's definitions (McQuillan 2000).

Camera techniques

Ways in which the film camera is used to create particular shots, along with related technical elements such as colour and lighting, are another aspect of the 'tenor' of a film. Camera techniques communicate interpersonal meanings to the audience that tell us something about how we should 'read' the individual characters, and about the social relationships operating between them. The use of a handheld camera, for example, rather than a fixed camera, creates a sense that the viewpoint

Table 9.1: Summary of focalisation.

Focalisation	Extradiegetic narration (outside the diegesis)	Homodiegetic narration (character in diegesis)	Heterodiegetic narration (extradiegetic story told within diegesis)
External Observation of characters, no privileged knowledge	External third person narration; camera in film; documentary voice-over	First-person narration	Character located externally to extradiegetic story
Internal Perspective of characters is known	'Omniscient' third person narrator; film voice-over; 'straight to camera' narration	First person direct speech; handheld camera	Character located internally to extradiegetic story
Fixed Events seen from one perspective	Single narrator or fixed camera	First person narration; privileging of one viewpoint	One character narrating an extradiegetic story
Variable different events seen from different perspectives	More than one narrative voice or camera angle	Viewpoints of different characters are foregrounded	A number of extradiegetic stories recounted by different characters
Multiple Same event seen from different perspectives	Different narrative voices represented; same filmic event repeated from different angles	Several characters give versions of same event	Different characters narrate same extradiegetic story

is located within the diegesis and is giving us an internal perspective on the action, one that is therefore more 'authentic', but less privileged and authoritative, than an externally located viewpoint.

Both *The English Patient* and *The Lord of the Rings: The Fellowship of the Rings*, as films, are made in the style of 'Hollywood realism', which aims to create a seamless visual reality in which the audience is virtually unaware of the camera, lighting and other technical devices by which this 'reality' has been created. Nevertheless, our understanding of the interpersonal meanings – the ways in which the characters relate to each other and how we might respond to them, and of 'mood' – what attitude the characters have towards their own behaviour and that

Table 9.2: Technical devices.

	Signifier	Signified
Camera angle	High (looking up)	Power, authority
	Low (looking down)	Disempowerment
	Eye-level	Equality
Camera distance	Big close-up	Emotion, internal focalisation
	Close-up	Intimacy, internal focalisation
	Medium shot	Involvement, internal focalisation
	Long shot	Distance, context, external focalisation
Lens	Wide angle	Dramatic emphasis
	Normal	Diegetic reality
	Telephoto	Voyeurism
Camera movement	Pan (camera rotates on fixed point)	Context, external focalisation
	Tracking (camera runs on track parallel to action)	Involvement, pace, internal focalisation
	Tilt (following movement up and down)	Effect of movement – drama or humour
	Crane (high shot moving quickly to or from subject)	Entrance to or withdrawal from diegesis
	Handheld	Participation in diegesis, point of view
	Zoom in	Surveillance, external focalisation
	Zoom out	Relation of subject to context
Focus	Sharp focus	Diegetic reality; anticipation
	Soft focus	Interpersonal function; mood
	Selective focus	Significance; privileging
Lighting	High key	High modality; positive mood
	Low key	Low modality; uncertainty; negative mood
	Back lighting	Interpersonal function; high value
	Fill (closest to natural light)	Diegetic reality

of others – is produced through a range of technical signifiers whose meanings have become conventional within mainstream cinema.

I have summarised these meanings in table 9.2, using categories drawn from Selby and Cowdery (1995) and Lacey (1998). Some of these technical signifiers, such as camera angle and distance, are aspects of focalisation, indicating where the camera is located and how it is related to the participants in the shot. Others are related to modality. It should be remembered that the meanings signified by various types of shot and camera angle and so on can vary considerably, depending on aspects of the field, or context, and of the tenor or interpersonal relationship constructed between the characters in the film. In addition, many directors and editors consciously subvert the conventional meanings of technical signifiers to achieve a particular mood or set of attitudes between characters, and between the viewer and the characters. As Rosemary Huisman points out in chapter 12, equating a particular technical strategy with one specific meaning (high camera angle signifies power and so on) is essentially a structuralist manoeuvre.

Cohesion

The term 'cohesion' refers to the way in which a text is organised so that its various elements hang together to form a complete event. It is an aspect of 'mode', the way in which a text is delivered to its audience in terms of verbal and/or visual style, aesthetic, organisation and medium. Cohesion, among other aspects of mode, constructs textual meanings through which we understand what kind of text we are consuming, what conventions are governing it and how we should approach it.

Different kinds of texts can be distinguished by their levels of cohesion. 'Realistic' texts, such as narratives, or texts that present an argument, tend to be highly cohesive, organised as a seamless and complete sequence in which the logics of time and place are clearly explained. Non-realistic texts, such as some types of poetry or advertising, or those referred to as 'postmodern' texts, are often characterised by their lack of cohesion, so that the reader or viewer is forced to make connections, often without any authoritative voice or viewpoint to suggest the 'right' way to read the text. In advertisements, the use of logos, slogans, brand names and images draw on intertextual meanings that point us fairly directly to the 'right' meaning of the text, even if there are few cohesive devices in the language itself. Such a film as *Mulholland Drive*, on the other hand, offers very little cohesion between sequences, settings or characters, provoking the audience into piecing the film together in whatever way makes sense to them. Whereas a 'realistic' or highly cohesive text tends to direct the reader or viewer to a single dominant reading, a 'postmodern' text tends to produce multiple readings, none of which is necessarily 'wrong'. This is one of the reasons why postmodernism, as an aesthetic, is regarded by some as a democratic style that does not close off alternative readings but rather invites them.

Strategies of cohesion in written texts include repetition of words, replacement of one word by another (such as a noun with a pronoun, or one word with a synonymous word or phrase), conjunctive devices expressing time, causation and so on, deictics indicating time and place, collocations of words suggesting the same context or environment, and ellipses, where an absent item can be supplied by the reader. We can see some of these strategies operating in this extract from

Tolkien's *Lord of the Rings: The Fellowship of the Ring*, a novel written in a highly cohesive style that partly helps to explain its enormous popularity with readers:

> Soon after six o'clock the five hobbits were ready to start. Fatty Bolger was still yawning. They stole quietly out of the house. Merry went in front leading a laden pony, and took his way along a path that went through a spinney behind the house, and then cut across several fields. The leaves of trees were glistening, and every twig was dripping; the grass was grey with cold dew. Everything was still, and far-away noises seemed near and clear: fowls chattering in a yard, someone closing a door of a distant house.
>
> (Book 1, chapter 6)

Each sentence draws the reader on to the next one by a variety of cohesive links. The 'five hobbits' in the first sentence encompass 'Fatty Bolger', 'they' and 'Merry' in the subsequent sentences. The phrase 'and then cut across' contains the conjunction 'then' and an ellipsis, referring back to 'path', which unites both clauses. The noun phrases 'way', 'path', 'spinney', 'house' and 'fields' form a collocation that traces Merry's journey, enabling us to follow him as he goes. The landscape terms 'spinney' and 'fields' overlap with another collocation in the next sentence, 'leaves', 'trees', 'twig' and 'grass', creating a unified rural context through which the hobbits are travelling. References to 'glistening', 'dripping' and 'dew' suggest the watery nature of the landscape, enhancing its uniformity. The noun phrase 'everything' refers back to the entire landscape that has been described, while 'far-away noises' refer forward to the chattering fowls and the closing door. The final phrase, 'distant house', is linked semantically not only to 'far-away' but also to the word 'house' at the beginning of the paragraph, suggesting that the travellers have left their own house, and other houses, back in the distance as they move forward through the landscape.

The effect of this high level of cohesion is to locate the reader very securely in the diegesis of the story, to create a level of expectation that the narrative is logical and that, even if the actual events are magical and supernatural, the created world of the story is consistent and believable. Cohesion in Ondaatje's *English Patient* is, by contrast, less pronounced. Sequences of actions performed by a single character, such as Hana, provide moments of cohesive logic that are then interrupted or interspersed with non-cohesive references to other times, places, people. As a result of this mode of storytelling, the reader has to work a bit harder to maintain a sense of a logical and uniform fictional space, to balance the various times and locations and work out which world we are in from a minimum of verbal cues. Our sense of belonging in these fictional worlds is therefore as contingent and unstable as that of Hana, Kip and the English patient.

The film versions of both novels, however, are in the same mode of 'Hollywood realism', which specifically works to create a seamless and coherent fictional world. The strategies of visual cohesion include *mise en scène*, sound and camera techniques, which have been described above. The three narrative spaces of Minghella's *English Patient* – the villa, the desert and Cairo – are distinguished and identified by clear signifiers of colour, lighting and *mise en scène*, but we are drawn from one to the other almost imperceptibly through various technical devices. At one point, an outline of the mountain deserts dissolves into the contours of the sheets on the English patient's bed; a close-up shot of the orange-brown cover of Herodotus in the villa prepares us for the change to the orange-brown colours of the desert; the sound of Hana's feet playing hopscotch turns into the sound of drumbeats in the desert; the voices of Hana and Katharine alternate during the story of Candaules and Gyges; voice-overs by Almásy and Caravaggio carry us over from one location to another.

Editing

Perhaps the most significant strategy of visual cohesion in film is that of continuity editing. Whereas a novel operates on a number of levels and over a number of time periods, a film has to be structured as a series of shots, which are then edited into sequences. A shot is defined by a change in camera angle, or the length of time between the starting and stopping of the camera, which can be less than a minute or the length of an entire film (as in *The Russian Ark*, 2002). The point about shots is that each one represents 'real time', so that the length of each shot and the way in which they are edited into sequences determine the pacing and chronology of the film, the 'screen time'. The arrangement of shots and sequences creates the 'plot', shaping and controlling the way in which 'story' information (the field) is told.

According to David Cook, modern continuity editing began early in the twentieth century, 'when [film-makers] realised that action could be made to seem continuous from shot to shot and, conversely, that two or more shots could be made to express a single unit of meaning' (Cook 1996: 25). The practices of continuity editing work to create a coherent and stable visual space in which the viewer feels securely engaged and able to move easily from one *mise en scène* to another without any disorienting breaks in the diegesis. This style of editing, commonly used to achieve the mode of 'Hollywood realism', is only one of a number of editing styles and can be subverted in various ways – for example, by the use of very long shots, as in Robert Altman's movie, *The Player*, the use of high-speed pans in a number of comedy films or the intrusion of digital effects, as in *The Matrix* series – which often results in more stylised and technically effective films, but also in less 'realistic' narratives.

The conventional practices of continuity editing, described in detail by Bordwell and Thompson (1979: 23–39), can be summarised as follows.

Establishing shot

An establishing shot is normally a long shot that enables viewers to orient themselves at the beginning of a sequence, to observe the location of various characters and objects and get some sense of where the action is located: town or country, suburb or city, economically privileged or deprived, and so on. We then read subsequent shots in relation to the establishing shot and assume a spatial relationship between all the shots in the sequence, until a different establishing shot is used. Towards the beginning of the film of *The Lord of the Rings: The Fellowship of the Ring* we see an establishing shot of the Shire and of Bilbo's house; there is a shot of Gandalf outside the house, and then of him coming into the house. Exterior and interior locations, separate sets and technical creations, are made to appear as part of the same reality.

Re-establishing shot

A re-establishing shot tends to be another long or wide shot, reorienting the viewer to the broader context after a series of medium or close-up shots, for example during a dialogue. Re-establishing shots also make us aware of the movements of characters towards or away from each other.

The 180-degree rule

According to the convention of the 180-degree rule, the camera stays on one side of an imaginary axis of action running across the screen, from one side to the other. The axis is suggested in the establishing shot, and functions to prevent the audience becoming confused as to where exactly characters are located in relation to each other; crossing the axis can also create effects of drama or suspense. In *The Lord of the Rings*, Arwen is chased on horseback by a group of Riders, with the chase moving across the screen from left to right. We can see that Arwen is ahead, on the right of the screen, and the Riders are following her, to the left. But then the shot changes, and the axis has been crossed, so that Arwen is now on the left of the screen, apparently heading in the opposite direction, while the Riders are to her right. Because of skilful editing, we keep up with the action, and the breaking of the 'rule' serves to enhance the drama and confusion of the chase.

The thirty-degree rule

When the camera changes position between one shot and the next, the change will appear to the viewer as a sudden 'jump' unless the angle of movement is fairly large. The convention is that the camera must move by an angle of at least thirty degrees in relation to the subject in order to avoid a rupturing of the diegesis to the watching audience. So, for example, the camera might show a full-face close-up, followed by a shot of the same face in profile. If the angle of change were any less, the viewer would not be able to accommodate it but would perceive it as a staccato jump in the film.

Eye-line match

When we see Almásy watching something in the distance from his car, then see a shot of Katharine alighting from the plane, these two shots are held together by the assumed 'match' between Almásy's eye-line and the object of his gaze. In practice, these two shots might have been filmed at different times, perhaps on different days. But the effect of the editing is to imply simultaneity and a cause-and-effect relationship. Almásy is looking, and this is what he is seeing.

Shot/reverse shot

The camera cuts between each end of the 180-degree axis, showing first one end and then the other, while staying on the same side of the axis and at a similar angle to it. This effect is often used in dialogues, where first one interlocutor and then the other is shown. Again, the logistics of filming often require dialogue to be filmed in two halves, with each actor speaking all their lines separately, and the scene cut together into alternate shots of each speaker – shot and reverse shot – at the editing stage.

Cut on action

In one shot in *The English Patient*, we see Katharine in the middle distance, alighting from the plane. This action is then cut, and in another shot we see her in a medium shot standing in the shade of the tent among the group of explorers. The action that must have taken place between these two shots – of climbing down from the plane and walking across the runway into the shade – is not shown, has been elided, yet it is easily reconstructed in the minds of the audience, who do not pause to wonder how Katharine could have got to the tent so quickly. Just as readers can supply the elided word or phrase in a cohesive passage of writing, so the viewing audience can supply the missing action, assisted by the 180-degree rule and the continuity of the *mise en scène*.

We can see, then, that the way in which shots are edited together, creating juxtapositions suggestive of spatial and temporal consistency and of cause and effect, constitutes a mode of visual storytelling that is highly cohesive and therefore extremely persuasive. The functions of this kind of editing are:

- *to create visual continuity or contrast* among a range of visual signifiers, such as brightness, colour, patterns, shapes, volume, depth, movement, stillness and so on;
- *to create pace through combinations of shots of different lengths*, with long shots allowing for more 'real time', and shorter shots making time seem to pass more rapidly;
- *to create temporal relationships*, indicating how much time is supposed to have passed;

Table 9.3: Types of edit.

	Signifier	Signified
Cut	Clean break between one shot and the next	Pace, realism
Fade-out	Scene fades to black	Time passing; ending of sequence or film
Fade-in	Scene appears out of black	Beginning; coming to consciousness
Dissolve	First shot is briefly superimposted over a second shot	Mood; interpersonal relations; memory
Wipe	Second shot is pulled horizontally or vertically across the first like a blind	Abrupt change of location; parallel storylines; humour

- *to create spatial relationships*, indicating where characters are located in relation to each other and to specific contexts.

Different types of edit, from a technical perspective, also work to convey a range of interpersonal meanings that help the audience to take up an appropriate attitude or set of expectations in relation to the diegesis and the characters within it. The five major types of edit are described in table 9.3, with a reminder that these signifiers have a range of signifieds beyond those indicated.

Conclusion

Editorial conventions, along with camera techniques and sound, constitute the mode of filmic narrative, creating textual meanings, and contributing to the tenor of the filmic text: the range of interpersonal meanings that suggests mood, attitude and social relations. These conventions work to dematerialise the technical processes of film-making and to create a seamless visual diegesis that seems almost inseparable from reality. The essential artifice of film-making is naturalised into a viewing experience that draws the audience into a highly believable world. By these processes of naturalisation, the fantasy world of the Shire seems as real as Egypt and Italy during World War II. Yet both these fields of action are as fantastical as each other; both are the constructed products of a professional and highly technologised industry.

Part 3

Television: narratives and ideology

Chapter 10

The genres of television

Anne Dunn

Each medium develops its own ways of telling stories. These different ways of telling stories encompass the devices of the plot, the technical aspects of the medium, and the codes and conventions of types of stories. Another way of putting this, which employs terms you will have encountered in earlier chapters, is that different media allow different possibilities of diegesis (telling the story) and mimesis (performance) and the relation between the two. Whether as readers (audiences) of texts or as producers of them, we recognise these combinations and categorise them, in order to advise or predict what kind of story this is going to be.

These categories of story may be identified as **genres** (the French word for types or kinds). On the one hand, genres can be seen as offering an important way of framing texts that assists comprehension. Genre knowledge orientates competent readers towards appropriate attitudes, assumptions and expectations about a text, which are useful in making sense of it. On the other hand, genres may be seen ideologically, as constraining interpretation, as limiting the available meanings of the text. What is a genre? Texts concerned with the study of television, such as Williams (1990), Tulloch (2000) or Creeber (2001), offer genres (or forms, as Williams calls them) of television program, such as news, drama, 'variety', sport, advertising, 'cop series', soap opera, documentary, cartoons, situation comedy, children's television and 'popular entertainment'. Some of these are broken down still further by Creeber (2001). Documentary, for example, includes 'fly-on-the-wall' documentary, docusoaps and reality TV, while 'popular entertainment' encompasses debate, quiz show, the celebrity talk show, the confessional talk show and 'daytime TV'.

Lacey (2000: 133ff) suggests that a genre will have specific textual features, or is a way of organising the elements within the text, and that this is what enables us to recognise a text as falling into a particular genre or generic type. The elements organised by genre include narrative, setting, types of characters, style, visual and aural signs (or iconography), mode of address and even (especially in cinema) the stars, associated with the particular genre. Expanding each of these textual features or elements in turn, first, there are generic narrative structures in the sense that they identify a text (a novel, a film or a television program) as belonging to a particular genre. We recognise this in part through familiar plot structures or devices, predictable situations, conflicts and resolutions. Note that these are particular elements of the wider topic of narrative analysis (the topic of this book), which are applicable to genre study. Diverse genres can share the structure of the classic 'Hollywood narrative', and the narrative conventions of one genre might not be too dissimilar to that of another; but there will be variations identifiable as belonging in particular genres.

The geographical and historical setting of a film can be immediately indicative of genre: prohibition-era and Chicago together suggest the classic American gangster movie, for example. Across texts of the same genre, we will find similar characterisation. The types of characters (including stereotypes), their roles, behaviour, goals and problems will to some extent fit predictable patterns (which is not to say these predictions may not be confounded in the world of the text – indeed that may be part of the pleasure it gives us). Certain genres, such as *film noir*, are associated with an identifiable style; that is, conventional filmic techniques of lighting, sound, camera work and editing. This is not the same as the stock of visual and aural images or iconography used by a generic text. 'Iconography' is a term that can include elements of the *mise en scène*, such as objects in the scene, or costume, or even the performers themselves (who can become 'icons' or 'stars'). In the 1980s and 1990s, if a film starred Sylvester Stallone, for example, the audience would expect a particular type of action movie; if the star were Harrison Ford, however, audience expectations might be somewhat different.

The use of stars in television does not work quite the same way as in cinema, but makes a point true for both media: that genre is also a way of organising elements in order to market the film or program to an audience. One of the ways it does this is through generic modes of address (Livingstone 1994: 249). The 'mode of address' refers to the way a text positions the audience or constructs an 'ideal' audience, usually in terms of age, gender or ethnicity (factors known collectively as demographics). It is a key element of genre, especially when genre is considered as central to the industrial context of the media.

The discussion of genre so far in this chapter draws on definitions developed predominantly in relation to novel and cinema texts, and much of it is also relevant to the use of 'genre' in thinking about television. You might have noticed that the discussion used such terms as 'familiar', 'predictable' and 'identifiable'. There are two reasons for this: the first is that genre is used by the media industries as a way of identifying texts for audiences, as a marketing tool, and this important aspect of genre will be taken up later. The second is a philosophical question begged by defining genre in terms of what the audience already knows. The question is: which came first, the genre or the texts taken to identify the genre? It can be illustrated by asking how you would define, say, a television sitcom, without there already being programs (which you have seen) that are defined as sitcoms.

The difference is between genre as an ideal type, made up of certain elements against which we compare particular texts (for example, a film in which people burst into song in the middle of the story has one element that matches up with the group of elements that together identify the genre 'musical'), and genre empirically defined by examination of numbers of individual texts (all musicals examined have people bursting into song as one of a number of elements they have in common) (Lacey 2000: 111–12; Hansen et al. 1998: 166). The problem with ideal types is that they tend to specify what a genre should be rather than what is actually found in media texts, and this points to another question: where does one genre end and another begin? Are Dennis Potter's ground-breaking television serials *Pennies From Heaven* (1978) and *The Singing Detective* (1986) musicals? They offer such a mix of both narrative and generic references as to defy easy classification; they overlap the genres of comedy, musical and drama. Genre divisions cannot be too fixed but must accommodate developments; hence the recognition of so-called 'hybrid' genres, such as some 'reality TV' programs (whether 'reality TV' is itself a new genre is another question and not easy to answer since there is much diversity within the group of programs labelled this way).

A related question to that of genre definition is how useful is the concept of genre in the critical analysis of texts. If texts are classified into genres by elements such as those listed above – that is, defined by the differences in their genres – then where can we go from there, once we have said, 'They're different genres, therefore they are different'? It is a circular argument, which seems to be a critical dead end. Lacey (2000) and Hansen et al. (1998) have offered the consolation that genre is a commonsense concept, understood and used by both consumers and producers of media, who can generally agree on some shared assumptions as a starting point for classifying media texts (although of course not all audiences can be assumed to be equally familiar with all genres).

The extent to which this tendency to classify is 'a fundamental aspect' (Neale in Creeber 2001: 1) of the way we understand texts of all kinds should be reason enough for the academic study of genre. If it is to move beyond commonsense understanding, however, genre analysis must move beyond merely identifying and classifying media texts. One way it can do this is through deeper and more detailed considerations of the symbolic and technical elements of genres, the relationships between them and their history and development. Another approach – and both can be used together – is to look at the ways in which genre is situated in society and culture, paying attention to the relationships between audience, industry and genre. All the questions raised in this section serve to demonstrate 'the multi-dimensional nature of genre itself: its numerous aspects, the numerous meanings it can have, and the numerous analytic uses to which it can be put' (Neale in Creeber 2001: 3). It is particularly important to keep this polysemy and the plasticity of genre in mind, when it comes to the critical analysis of television, as a medium and as an industrial system. Before moving on to a more detailed consideration of the idea of genre in television, the next section of this chapter provides context through a brief consideration of how narrative works in television in relation to the idea of genre.

Television, narrative and genre

Television has to work harder than cinema to keep its audience. Movie audiences make the effort to go out of their homes to the theatre and buy their ticket. They sit in the darkened space, visually and aurally dominated by the screen and 'surround sound'. Their expectations are higher of film than of television, both of the production values and that they will have a more intense experience than when watching television. Television is literally 'part of the furniture' and is consumed in a domestic setting, subject to interruptions, some of which – the commercial breaks – are scheduled. Until very recently television has appeared to be 'free', and it's always available and easy to switch on or off or over (to another channel). The viewer can exercise control over such aspects of television reception as the audio, unlike cinema. All these things affect the ways genre and narrative have developed in television.

When the new medium of television began, the ways it could tell stories were not initially seen as deriving from film but from radio and theatre (and, in relation to news, from newspaper journalism). Television cameras were fixed and heavy, so there was a tendency to place them directly in front of the action; in other words, the point of view of an audience in a theatre. Like radio, television programs had to be broadcast live (there was no videotape until the 1960s). Producers quickly realised they could appropriate radio program formats and present them more compellingly on television, with the addition of the visual sense. Comedy, quizzes and drama, the soap opera in particular, rapidly began appearing on television and dwindled on radio. Established radio stars, such as Bob Dyer and his *Pick-a-Box* quiz show, which began in 1948 on Australian commercial radio, simply moved their program over to television, which *Pick-a-Box* did, moving to ATN7 in Sydney and Melbourne's GTV9 in 1957.

In radio, the primary code is talk; so generic programs, such as quiz shows or plays, can be introduced as such by an announcer telling the listener exactly how to classify what they are about to hear ('Good evening. Now it's time for the Tuesday play'). In television, there have to be visual as well as aural markers to identify each genre. Genre in television is complicated, moreover, by the concept of *format*. A format in television can refer both to the kind of program being made and to the medium in which it is made, such as film or videotape. In its former sense, a format is also a commodity, in that it can be bought and sold between one television network and another. Many popular programs such as quiz shows and reality TV shows are made to formats designed by one person or a team and sold to a number of production outlets who realise the format in a variety of ways, depending on local audiences and conditions.

The use of the word 'format' also alerts us to the routine and formulaic nature of much television output; something that genre analysis also illustrates. For example, *The Singing Detective*, referred to earlier as difficult to classify generically because of its mixture of textual features, can without ambiguity be put into the industry format – or narrative genre – of 'serial'; that is, it was broadcast as a six-part mini-series, with a storyline that continued from one week's episode to the next. The structural complexity of the narrative, it has been argued, could have made the serial form the 'perfect vehicle' to carry it (Creeber 2001: 37), because the audience was brought back each week hoping for further elucidation of its mysteries.

Once pre-recording on film or videotape, and therefore editing, were possible, television producers quickly realised that the narrative visual codes of Hollywood cinema editing – also known as continuity editing – could be applied in the new medium. The demands on the television industry to keep the audience's attention tend to produce certain kinds of narrative form, however, which were not necessarily of the classic Hollywood model. The classic Hollywood model emphasises cause and effect – that is, a series of incidents that will be presented as connected in some way – often by means of the *post hoc ergo propter hoc* fallacy (from the Latin phrase, meaning 'after this therefore because of this'), whereby actions that follow one another sequentially are perceived by viewers to be in a causal relationship. For example, if in one shot we see a man with a knife in his hand, then in the next shot we see another person with a knife wound, we are likely to read the sequence as that the wound was caused by the knife-wielding man.

Ideologically, the classic Hollywood narrative model emphasises individuality; that is, individuals – not nations or communities or systems – are responsible for what happens in the story. The narrative is centred on individual psychological causes: decisions, choices and personal traits of character. According to structural narrative theories, such as that of Todorov, often the story gets underway because the central character wants or needs something; in other words, they have a goal or series of goals. But then a disruption, problem or conflict arises, and so the character must change something in order to attain his or her goal. The Hollywood narrative model also emphasises **closure**. The film doesn't just stop – it ends – and ends in ways that either satisfy or cheat the viewer's expectations. At the end of a classic Hollywood narrative, however changed by his or her experiences, the character does reach the goal. Most such narratives display strong closure.

However, most of the television narrative fiction we see today does not use this classic Hollywood mode of narration – or, at least, not all of its elements. We have come to expect that television narrative will give us multiple story threads, temporary or partial resolutions, or none at all. John Ellis in *Visible Fictions* (1992) calls the 'basic unit' of narrative organisation on television the segment. A segment is 'a coherent group of sounds and images, of relatively short duration that needs to be accompanied by other similar such segments' (Ellis 1992: 116). A segment could thus be a single TV news story, a commercial, a title sequence or the story action in that part of a program that occurs between one commercial break and the next. Each segment demonstrates an internal coherence, but might not be connected directly to the next. The other characteristic of the television medium is that, even if pre-recorded, it appears to be happening in the here and now. Certain genres, especially news, use textual features that emphasise that they are live, and this is explored in chapter 11.

Ellis argues that 'the characteristic broadcast TV forms of the segment and the series, and the pervasive sense of the TV image as live' have created a particular, specific mode of narrative: that of the 'open-ended format' (Ellis 1992: 145). The open-ended format provides thesis and antithesis – but not necessarily synthesis. Instead the audience is offered 'a continuous refiguration of events' (Ellis 1992: 147). Ellis suggests that the fictional forms of narration on television have a strong relationship to the non-fictional forms, citing the news bulletin as 'the first true use of the open-ended series format . . . endlessly updating events and never synthesising them' (Ellis 1992: 145) – and this is something chapter 11 also takes up. The segmentation that characterises television narration arises in part from the domestic setting in which television is viewed, which makes it eminently interruptible. Commercial television is regularly interrupted by the ad breaks; public service television by program promotions and station identification. It can be argued therefore that the television narrative has developed its segmented, episodic nature in response to the institutional character of the medium and the cultural setting in which it is used.

Genres of television

If the economics, circumstances of reception and signifying system of television demand interruption they also demand continuation; what Raymond Williams calls the 'flow' (Williams 1990: 89) of images that appear to be in real time. Although there is some argument as to what exactly Williams meant by 'flow', like 'genre' it is a very useful commonsense term. Intuitively, we recognise that viewers experience television as a flow; that is, as a singular, continuous, live experience; Williams cites the way we still speak of 'watching television' as an activity in itself, without need to refer to the specific program(s) we have chosen to watch (or not chosen – the 'couch potato' phenomenon is well known and widespread).

He describes the conventional way television organises its segmented, loosely knit narratives, the combination of interruption and continuation, as combining flow and segmentation to create a sense of continuity, despite the actual discontinuity of its elements.

A brief description of a typical television sequence illustrates the combination. It might (to take an arbitrary starting point) begin with a 'commercial break' part way through a program. The individual advertisements (segments) may be of durations between fifteen seconds and almost a minute. The break will typically finish with a promotion for the forthcoming program, possibly even a short trailer of it (especially if it is a movie), then perhaps a station identification of some kind. The program resumes, to be interrupted again between seven and eleven minutes later (more or less, depending on country) by another commercial or promotional sequence of items. There is no obvious connection between these individual items, yet an experienced viewer follows the transitions without difficulty, because he or she immediately identifies the generic features of each segment, distinguishing between advertisement, program promotion, station identification and the program itself, yet also experiencing the whole sequence as the continuous audio-visual experience of watching television.

The process is made more coherent by skilful presentation; that is, by the deliberate selection (by television programmers) of advertisements that are thought to appeal to the kind of people seen as most likely to be watching the particular program. In recent years, advertisers have created television advertisements to look and sound like the program in which they're to be placed. An example is an episode of the British sitcom *Teachers* (broadcast on Channel 4, 28 October 2004), which featured advertisements for a Toyota car, the Rav4. The car is marketed in Britain to younger male adults, a demographic that also both appears in and watches the program. Each advertisement was very short, and in each the car was depicted as an unruly pupil in a school, being given orders by a teacher figure. The humour was very much in the style of the program's comedy, and even the look of the advertisements contrived to match the visual style of the program, using similar school sets and predominant blues and greys.

The original genres of television, from the 1950s, developed strong conventions, adopted and adapted from radio and other media, making it a relatively simple matter for new programs to be marketed in ways that identified them for viewers as of a type. The concept of genre thus serves both producers (standardisation for production and marketing purposes) and audiences (recognition and accessibility). The genres that developed initially were those that had proved popular with radio listeners and were responded to with pleasure by television audiences as well, such as the situation comedy (sitcom), soap opera, variety and quiz shows. The segmentation demanded by the new medium also suited a distinction that was not in itself novel, but which proved very suitable to television and which television developed, between the series and serial. The following section describes narrative distinctions between 'series' and 'serial', but in an 'ideal' way, since in relation to the television medium many programs today, especially but not exclusively fictional ones, show overlap between or a mix of the two formats.

In a series, each episode features the same characters and settings but is generally self-contained. There tends to be a greater emphasis on character than in film, but less on cause and effect as a means of progressing the narrative. In narrative terms, each program ends where it began, so that it can begin again from the same point of equilibrium the following week. After the first few episodes of a series there is usually no need to re-establish the initial situation at the beginning; the audience is assumed to be familiar with the equilibrium. At the end of each episode, characters and settings are restored, ready to face next week's episode, without any apparent memory of what has gone before. This is especially true of the classic television genre of the police series or cop show, which quickly became and has remained very popular.

A serial also features the same cast of characters in each episode and there might be multiple plotlines, but there is one continuous metanarrative, which progresses from each one of a finite number of episodes to the next, typically through a succession of cliffhanger endings in individual episodes, towards closure in the final episode. The serial is a long-established narrative form. Nineteenth-century novels – those of Charles Dickens, for example – were serialised in newspapers. Cinema serials, especially for children to watch on Saturday mornings, thus bringing an audience regularly to the cinema, were very popular in Britain and Australia by and throughout the 1950s (and 'killed' by television). The classic television serial as defined here appears only in limited guises today, generally as 'costume' or 'period drama', such as the BBC adaptations of novels, such as *Pride and Prejudice* and *Middlemarch*, or as a 'mini-series' (as the industry confusingly names it) of two to six episodes (as opposed to the standard television industry season, for a series or serial, of thirteen episodes).

Serials represent a risk to producers precisely because you must watch all the episodes in order to follow the story. The story demands audience loyalty to every episode. That can be both a strength and a weakness. Any drama is expensive to produce, so if the ratings are low, a lot of money is lost. This is one reason the mini-series (usually in fact a short serial of two to six parts) was developed, to reduce the risk. The advantage of the classic series (with its self-contained stories in each episode, as opposed to the continuing story in a serial) is that it can have both a loyal, watch-every-week audience and a floating audience, who only watches sometimes. Long-running serials have been overtaken by soap operas, which remain open-ended, with only a number of small endings within the larger situation but no resolution.

The television genres of series and serial, soap opera and sitcom, are the subject of chapters 12 and 13 so they will not be discussed in greater detail here. However, it could be argued that since the 1990s almost all of television's fictional genres (and some of its factual ones, in the case of the so-called 'reality' TV shows) have been affected by the soap opera form of the serial; hence the earlier claim that the generic distinction between series and serial is now largely a historical one.

A television genre example: the police series

An example of this transformation is the British television police series *The Bill*. In its early years (it began in 1984), *The Bill* depicted the work of a group of police officers at the fictional Sunhill police station in London. Although there was some attention to the private lives of the individual officers and the relationships between them, the emphasis each week was on one or more plotlines concerning a crime or crimes. In this respect, *The Bill* began by following a long tradition of British television drama based on police procedure, including *Dixon of Dock Green*, which began on BBC Television in 1955 and ran until 1976, *Z Cars* (BBC, 1962–78) and *Softly, Softly* (also made in the 1970s). Over time and as producers changed, *The Bill* featured more continuing stories, sometimes continued over months, about the individual characters. Eventually even the crimes involved Sunhill's officers, with the death of a young female officer at the hands of a serial killer and the kidnap of the chief inspector's daughter. This 'serialisation' of *The Bill* saw its generic conventions move closer to those of soap opera and away from those of the police procedural drama series. *The Bill* built its large audience in part by combining the 'mix of repetition and anticipation' (Dyer 1997: 14) that characterises seriality, with the conventions of the police series genre.

It also illustrates the way in which the genre divisions of television are more permeable than those of other media forms. Television programs from the late 1960s onwards appropriated conventions from other genres or made intertextual references in order to signify something about the program; to give it greater authority perhaps, by reference to the genres of factual programs, such as news, current affairs and documentary. It can be seen from this that there are ideological effects of television genre, to the extent that genre conventions naturalise or normalise certain ways of seeing the world, and provide limits to the interpretive context available to the audience and the 'meaning potential of a given text' (Hartley in O'Sullivan et al. 1994: 128). Changes over time to police dramas on television can illustrate the extent to which the ideology of television genre can change in response to social and cultural change. Lacey (2000: 229–34), Cooke (2001: 19–23) and, from a somewhat different position, Tulloch (2000: 33–55) have all traced this change with reference to British television police shows, showing how the genre has adapted to changing audience (and academic) knowledge about and attitudes towards the police in society. For example, as the public became aware of various wrongdoings by police, from racism to criminal corruption, so such shows as *The Sweeney* in the 1970s and subsequently – and much more disturbingly – *Law and Order* and *Cops* accommodated bad behaviour by the police characters in the programs.

There are two kinds of narrative structure in police series. The first is the kind that focuses on one central detective character or a small group, no more than three. Examples include *Morse* and *Taggart* and *The Sweeney* in the UK and, in the USA, *Kojak*, *Starsky and Hutch*, *Cagney and Lacey* – and so on. This kind of narrative structure is sometimes called 'centred biography' (Selby & Cowdery 1995: 83). The second narrative structure focuses on the team. Apart from *The Bill*, other examples include *Hill Street Blues* (USA), *Blue Heelers*, *Water Rats* (Australia) – and so on. The men and women who work at Sunhill Police Station are presented week after week in *The Bill* as a kind of extended family. This format is known as 'decentred biography'. Attention can focus on different individuals each week. There might be storylines that are not resolved within single episodes but, in a way that characterises the serial or the soap opera form of serial, are carried and progressed through several episodes.

Hurd (1981) has used the structuralist approach of Lévi-Strauss to identify seven binary oppositions that together (he argues) underlie all police shows:

1 police v. crime
2 law v. rule
3 professionalism v. organisation
4 authority v. bureaucracy
5 intuition v. technology
6 masses v. intellectuals
7 comradeship v. rank.

The next section uses Hurd's seven generic oppositions in relation to an episode of *The Bill* (see also Lacey 2000: 164–7, who does a similar analysis in relation to the American police series *NYPD Blue*). This is not by any means the only way to use the concept of genre to analyse television (see Tulloch 2000 for an approach that combines genre and audience analysis), and, as Rosemary Huisman has outlined in chapter 3, the structuralist notion of a pre-existing underlying model is theoretically problematic. Nevertheless, a structuralist approach can help to illuminate ways in which generic elements activate a narrative.

The episode of *The Bill* analysed here (dating from 2001) begins with Detective Sergeant Don Beech, then a regular cast member, apparently off duty, arriving at what turns out to be an illegal poker game. In the opening sequence the two apparently unrelated narrative strands open up simultaneously, run in parallel and then converge around a point of decision for Don Beech. The sequence ends with Don making what has been signalled to the audience as apparently the morally wrong decision, in a symbolic act of taking the card of a man we know to be a villain, Howard Fallon. From this point on, the narrative follows what happens to Don, rather than following the second narrative. Various twists appear in the story, and character-based tensions are re-established from earlier episodes, such as an antagonistic relationship between Don and another detective, Geoff. At the end of this episode Don has taken money from Howard Fallon, putting himself further into the villain's power.

This episode of a series also demonstrates elements of the serial; that is, there are continuing storylines from one episode to the next (but no overarching narrative heading for a final conclusion), and *The Bill* offers narrative development of these over time. Not every episode returns to all of these continuing storylines, and some are not resolved. In the episode that follows this one, Don Beech's mobile phone number is discovered in the notebook of a girl found murdered, providing an undercover detective, Claire Stanton, who has been investigating Beech, with evidence for the first time that he might be directly involved in something illegal. Claire's superiors in the undercover operation order her to get closer to another detective at Sunhill, John Boulton, because they believe he might also be involved. The complication is that Claire had earlier broken off an affair with Boulton; when she makes overtures to him, after her earlier rejection, he finds this very hard to deal with. If this seems to be verging on the 'soap opera', it is. As with all soap opera, knowledge of this back story can add immensely to the pleasure of watching *The Bill* for its fans; and the need to know the back story has become increasingly important to *The Bill*, emphasising its soap opera style of seriality. As the earlier discussion of series and serial made clear, a viewer does not have to know the back story to follow an individual episode of a series, whereas with a serial proper the viewer needs to come in at or near the first episode and return each week.

The episode just described can be analysed in terms of Hurd's (1981) seven oppositions, as follows:

1 Police v. crime

Police series tend to concentrate on the role of the police in catching criminals, not on their role in containing dissent – in political demonstrations, for example. *The Bill's* storyline about Don Beech, focusing on internal corruption in the police force, is an exception to this norm in some respects, yet will end – after many episodes – in the (apparent) death of Beech.

2 Law v. rule

Law v. rule is an ends-versus-means opposition. The law embodies justice and as such overrides the rules and regulations the police must operate under; so these rules get broken in order that justice can be done – the end justifies the means. Examples of this include searching a villain's premises without getting a warrant, extracting information in an interview without the tape being turned on, harassing or even assaulting someone in order to force them to admit to wrongdoing. Needless to say, it is not acceptable for a villain to do this – in the way that Howard Fallon blackmails Don Beech with his participation in the illegal poker game.

3   Professionalism v. organisation

The police at the 'sharp end' or front line of policing are presented as professionals who might be hampered by the 'organisation men' – usually desk-bound senior officers who are more preoccupied with maintaining their own position in the hierarchy. In the world of *The Bill*, Chief Superintendent Brownlow is regularly presented as concerned about his own reputation and his career position in ways that interfere with the professional police – be they detective or uniformed – 'getting on with the job'.

4   Authority v. bureaucracy

Related to the above, the opposition of authority v. bureaucracy gives authority to professionals. They earn it by doing the job of crime detection and solving crimes well. This kind of authority is opposed to bureaucratic authority, which is granted by the hierarchy but is not earned 'on the streets'.

5   Intuition v. technology

The opposition of intuition v. technology is about the role of the 'hunch' or intuitive and experiential knowledge in police series, as opposed to forensic evidence. In many episodes of such a series as *The Bill*, a character will 'just know' who the guilty party is, by virtue of accumulated experience and their instinctive knowledge, but will lack sufficient evidence for proof. This can produce a dramatic irony whereby a known villain nonetheless gets away with his or her crime (although in a police series the same character might be caught in a later episode).

6   Masses v. intellectuals

The working police officer is a man or woman of common sense, not an intellectual, but is often shown to be smarter than the so-called experts. This tension is present in many episodes of *The Bill*. In one example, which also relates to the previous opposition, a woman with expertise in listening devices is brought in to help solve a crime, but the new bugging device fails to work at the crucial moment and 'good old-fashioned policing' has to save the day. The detective series *Cracker*, which had a criminal psychologist as its hero, is an exception to this rule (the detective or crime series is identified by some theorists as a separate genre from the police series – see Cooke 2001: 22). This opposition is one that might be changing for police series like *The Bill* that try to reflect some of the reality of contemporary policing, which is that more and more police are recruited as university graduates.

7 Comradeship v. rank

Comradeship v. rank is a very strong opposition in *The Bill* and indeed most police series. Rank does not impress our heroes; the most important relationships are defined by mutual respect. In the episode of *The Bill* following the one described, Don Beech is shown to abuse this relationship between peers by lying to another detective and asking him to conceal evidence in a murder enquiry. This opposition can be used to set up tensions between characters within storylines.

These oppositions are useful both in identifying the genre and where a particular example might have innovated or broken the formula. As with narrative, if one side of the opposition is privileged, the effect is ideological. There is a relative lack of representation of the 'other side of the story': repressive policing, corrupt policing, wrongful arrest and conviction, deaths in custody, the effects on policing of poorly educated and prejudiced police officers, and indeed of the whole police culture of mateship, sexism, racism, antipathy to technology and anti-intellectualism. These things are seldom explored by TV police drama series. Some go part of the way, such as the *Prime Suspect* serials or *Between the Lines*, which was actually about the internal investigation of police. There is far less social consensus than there was in the decade following the end of World War II, when 'the parochial and reassuring' (Cooke 2001: 19) *Dixon of Dock Green* emerged. That era found it very difficult to deal with the idea of the 'bent' or dishonest copper. By now we are used to such depictions; nonetheless, the police are still framed as the heroes, protecting society from a descent into chaos. Police shows like *The Bill* purport to reflect 'reality'. In its early years at any rate, *The Bill* was reputedly popular viewing with serving members of the British police; just as in the USA, real New York city police officers were said to enjoy *NYPD Blue*, and in Australia the police series *Blue Heelers* is apparently regularly watched by many police officers. Police series have also been credited with boosting recruitment. Most such series are extensively researched before and during their production run; writers go out in police cars, and the production often retains the services of an adviser who is or recently has been a member of the police.

The series relies on combining repetition and innovation; we know that each week there will be a new problem confronting the characters – but it will be the same kind of problem, depending on the genre. In the police series, the problem is the fight against crime. And this problem is never-ending, even though each week 'society is protected and the status quo maintained by the forces of law and order' (Cooke 2001: 19). Narrative resolution takes place at the level of incident. This is quite different, as Ellis (1992) points out, from the use of repetition and innovation in film. For example, in a movie Western (a genre that has been completely replaced by the cop show on television), there will be a resolution to the problem of lawlessness, within the world of the story. The television form is much more open-ended. Because of this repetition and open-endedness, television, whether series or serial, has a different ideology from that of the cinematic film: it *normalises* the central problematic of the program. In the world of *The Bill*, racism, poverty and dysfunctional families are everyday phenomena, but crime is an intrusion, an upset. Although, for example, racism is presented, it is not offered as an explanation for crime, which is committed by individuals who must take responsibility for their actions.

In the relationship between genre and ideology it can be argued that genres adapt to hegemonic changes – the way a dominant ideology secures consent to its world view, but has to keep on securing it in the face of oppositional forces. So if the dominant representation of the police force gets out of step with the consensual view of it, then the genre must adapt. At the industry level this is called giving the viewing public what it wants or what will be popular with audiences. At the level of ideology it is interpreted as helping to create a new consensus or dominant ideology. In this way, genres act to articulate, in a very powerful way, what Roland Barthes calls the 'myths' of society.

Conclusion

There is no agreed list of television genres and, as we have seen, television plays fast and loose with genre boundaries, embracing the hybrid genre (the medico-legal series, for example, such as *MDA* in Australia) and self-reflexively referencing other genres. Nonetheless, genre is still a much-used concept in relation to television, by audiences and by the television industry, even if they might not use the word itself. In marketing terms, genre is a way of distinguishing between programs for audiences; it is also a way of 'branding' broadcast channels (in Australia, for example, the commercial Channel 10 sells itself to a younger demographic through its programming of reality TV shows, soap operas, comedy and satirical programs, all with youthful casts). It is a way of identifying whole TV channels, some of which are named by genre: the movie channel, the comedy channel, music television (MTV) and so on.

The overlapping and hybrid nature of genre on television has been entrenched by technological changes in the distribution of television and in its consumption. The multi-channel environment in combination with the remote control, enabling constant 'zapping' from channel to channel and program to program, has produced extensive and sophisticated genre-recognition skills in audiences. For example, the British program *Green Wing* (Channel 4, 2003–) is at one level a situation comedy set in a hospital. However, it plays with the genres of medical or hospital drama, soap opera and sketch comedy in ways that are very pleasurable for the audience, because it invites delighted recognition of its intertextual references. Equally, the referencing of the soap opera genre by a police series, in *The Bill*, can work to attract a new and younger viewing audience, augmenting the older, 'welded-on' viewers of the program. Turner (2001: 6) suggests that the direct response audiences make to television programs, through ratings or by contacting the stations, leads in turn to faster reactions by producers than is possible in other media, such as the novel or film. Television producers adjust programs in response to audience feedback in ways that might change the format, creating new or hybridised genres.

Chapter 11

Television news as narrative

Anne Dunn

> I think that the same process is involved in the construction of any event televisually . . . You constantly draw on the inventory of discourses which have been established over time. I think in that sense we make an absolutely too simple and false distinction between narratives about the real and the narratives of fiction.
>
> (Stuart Hall 1983)

Recognition of a text as belonging to a particular genre can help readers (listeners, viewers) make judgements about the 'reality status' of the text, most fundamentally whether it is fictional or non-fictional. News is a very recognisable non-fiction genre. That it is non-fiction does not mean it will not use narrative, however, despite the fact that we might associate narrative (storytelling) with the imagined and invented. Television news is not only a popular source of information but also it enjoys a high degree of credibility. Public opinion polls and ratings surveys have shown that since the 1990s television news has become both the primary and the most believed source of news for a majority of viewers, in countries such as the USA, the UK and Australia.

This reflects the phenomenon referred to in chapter 10, observed by Ellis (1992) and Williams (1990), that television images appear to be 'really happening' in the present moment. The characteristic visual and audio codes and narrative structures of television news work together to construct such news values as truth and balance, as well as to convey authority and immediacy. It is important to realise that news comprises a set of formal conventions of representation and narration that together shape a view of 'reality', and television news is one of the most conventionalised formats of the medium (that is what makes it so easy to recognise). Another way of putting this, in semiotic terms, is to say that TV news employs a 'restricted repertoire' of codes (Bignell 1997: 110). Television news is also privileged in the view of reality it offers, precisely because it is so strongly associated, both historically and formally, with truth-telling. As a result, it has been claimed that 'the form of news is inseparable from popular understandings of social reality' (Baym 2004: 280).

News, however, is not unmediated reality (although it is about the real), but is constructed through processes of editorial selection as well as through its visual and audio elements. This does not mean that it is invention, bias or falsehood; rather, that a particular reality, affected by cultural, historical and economic factors, is created and normalised by television news. In the process an ideology is inevitably manufactured and promulgated. Ideology is used here in the sense of culturally specific beliefs about the world that are seen as unremarkable and are taken for granted. The widespread acceptance of televised news as offering the only reality, however, is under challenge. Satellites, multiple channels and the Internet mean that audiences are no longer confined to their local TV news, but can choose from news services that might have originally been made for a very different audience with a very different ideology. Conflicting ideologies can produce – or offer the possibility of – multiple perspectives on a given news story. This has emerged very clearly in the 'war on terrorism' waged by the USA and its allies since September 11, 2001. Western television news audiences – and journalists – could not help but see stark differences between the ways in which the offensives in Afghanistan and then Iraq were reported by their national media and by the Arab-language channel Al Jazeera.

This chapter will examine the ways in which television news gives shape to narratives of the real. It does so not only through its textual features but also via what are called 'news values'; that is, the professional values that journalists employ in gathering, selecting, writing and presenting the news. In order for an occurrence to qualify as newsworthy, it must meet a number of journalistic criteria, such as timeliness (it is 'new') or currency (it is already in the news). It must be perceived as having impact or significance on people and their lives, and the greater the proximity to the intended audience, the more likely the occurrence is to be newsworthy. Bad news (conflict, tragedy, natural disaster) is always 'good' news, especially if it is unexpected or contains irony. Certain people are always 'news', either because they have a lot of power (presidents and prime ministers) or influence ('captains of industry') or simply celebrity. A final reason for a story being considered newsworthy is that it concerns matters of 'human interest'. This kind of news tends to be about particular individuals, families or groups, who are 'Unknowns', rather than the 'Knowns', who tend to dominate the top stories in any news bulletin (Gans 1979). The difference is that the Knowns make news just by being who they are and doing what they do, whereas the Unknowns make news by doing (or having done to them) something extraordinary.

The existence of news values pre-dates television, deriving from newspapers, but they still influence television journalism. The industrial and economic organisation of the television industry has also affected television news in particular ways. Television is a competitive industry, and its networks and production companies survive only if they can attract and hold viewers and advertisers (even publicly funded television services, such as the Australian or British broadcasting corporations – the ABC and BBC – must attract audiences to justify how they spend taxpayers' money). In addition, television – as we noted in the previous chapter – is usually watched in private, domestic space under circumstances subject to regular interruption.

These institutional factors have combined to make television itself essentially an entertainment medium. News has also come to have a particular role in the television schedule, managing audience patterns of viewing; the theory being that if the channel can attract a large audience for the early evening bulletin, most or many of these viewers will stay with the same channel for the programs that follow (although this is not as certain as it was, affected by the advent of the remote control and multi-channel television). The nature of television as a medium of relaxation and entertainment affects television news in a way that contrasts with newspapers, with the result that television news has been described as more eager to please its viewers than a newspaper such as the *Australian* or the *Washington Post* is to please its readers (Hallin 1993: 91).

One powerful way of keeping audience attention is to employ narrative techniques, to tell a good story. Just as in the 1940s the cinema newsreels borrowed the visual codes of the films they accompanied, so from the 1960s onwards commercial television news in particular borrowed the narrative structures of prime-time, entertainment programming. Between that era and the present day, there have been changes in society and culture, inevitably including changes in the form of news. A central change in television news since the 1970s is a marked emphasis on the visual codes of the television medium. This appreciation of the televisual includes a greater privileging of narrative and 'the journalist's work of narration' (Baym 2004: 284).

The inverted pyramid and the rise of objectivity in news journalism

The early days of broadcast news (on radio) relied on newspaper journalism, both as a source and as a structural technique; there is more about this in chapter 15, which deals specifically with radio news. The public service broadcasters in Australia and the UK, and the big national networks in the USA, inherited in their news journalism the professional values of objectivity and impartiality. To some extent these values are also a matter of regulation as, in some countries, there are rules specifying that broadcast news must be 'balanced' and 'objective'.

These values are considered of special importance in so-called 'hard' news. 'Hard' news reports on politics, economics, the doings of the powerful and international affairs – in other words, on those aspects of a nation's public life that are considered to have the greatest influence on the lives of its citizens. It is contrasted with 'soft' news, which is about 'human interest', about celebrity, crime, the small-scale and domestic. 'Soft' news has long been written in a style that uses narrative devices, but 'hard' news, in newspaper writing, developed something called the 'inverted pyramid'. This refers to a structure also called 'lead-and-body', in which the most important information in the story is summarised in the 'lead sentence'. Standard practice is to include in the lead sentence the answers to at least three or four classic news questions, the five Ws: who, what, when, where and why. The rest of the information follows in the 'body' of the story, in descending order of importance. The criteria that determine 'most important' reflect the news values described earlier, such as timeliness, prominence, consequence, proximity, conflict and so on, which readers are assumed to share with journalists, and are therefore held to be the most salient points of information.

A range of explanations has been offered for the development of this structure, which arose in US newspaper journalism in the nineteenth century and is still taught to journalism students today. It has the advantage that it can be quickly and easily cut from the bottom, making it easier for an editor if there is not enough room on the page or time in a broadcast bulletin to run the full story. Pöttker (2003) has suggested five explanations for the development and persistence of the inverted pyramid. The first is technological, holding that it developed in the early and unreliable days of telegraphy, and the inverted pyramid ensured that at least the most important information was more likely to get through. The second, political argument is that the inverted pyramid developed during the American Civil War in the early 1860s, and served to cloak government views in its apparently objective construction. By placing its most important messages in the summary lead, the government ensured that the public received those messages first and saw them as most important. Journalists today still rely heavily on government sources and, significantly, public relations organisations often emulate the inverted pyramid style in their media releases, so this political explanation might still be relevant.

In a third theory, the pyramid style is thought to have been spread by the expansion of education and decline in illiteracy in the late nineteenth-century USA. This in turn, goes the argument, produced a change in the expectations and skills of both journalists and the public that demanded a more concise and quickly comprehended style. The fourth explanation is economic. The rise of cheap newspapers, the so-called 'penny press', commercialised newspaper production and introduced greater competition. The succinctness of the inverted pyramid style saved expensive distribution costs (the electric telegraph charged by the word), and led to the rise of such news agencies as Associated Press, which was founded in 1848. The need to appeal to as wide a readership as possible, in order to maximise profits, also meant the news agencies used a deliberately 'objective' reporting of the news, in order not to alienate any particular political opinion. Pöttker's own theory is that the persistence of the pyramid form is owing to its communicative success; that is, the story is more easily and quickly grasped by readers. This might be true for newspapers but is not necessarily so in the very different medium of television.

This is illustrated by the work of another news theorist, Norwegian academic Espen Ytreberg (2001), who contrasts the inverted pyramid with the use of narrative structures in television news. He does so in the context of the controversy caused by the increased use of narrative techniques in the television newsroom of the Norwegian public service broadcaster, NRK. He describes a process that occurred in the late 1980s and early 1990s, based on technological and format changes to NRK TV news. Reporters began to use a technique that foregrounded television images, rather than the words of the voice-over report. Ytreberg classifies the old and the new approaches as the 'information tradition' and the 'communication tradition' respectively (Ytreberg 2001: 362–3).

The 'information tradition' placed more importance on the inverted pyramid construction of news writing, emphasising factual information and analysis based on the facts. The usurping 'communication tradition' had audience attention and comprehension as its primary goal, being 'more concerned with relating the news in a way that was engaging and easy to understand' (Ytreberg 2001: 363). The differences apparently caused open animosity in the NRK News Department between the adherents of the two approaches, with each attacking the journalistic integrity of the other. The old guard accused the image school of 'tampering with journalists' integrity and credibility', while the new approach criticised the 'word school' for promoting 'officiousness and a generally backward attitude'. At the heart of the difference, Ytreberg believes, was a move to replace the long-held journalistic ideals of detachment and objectivity with 'a notion of engaged journalism'. The reporter in this view is emphatically a storyteller, albeit not of fiction, and the engagement is with the audience, in ways that change the relationship between news and audiences.

The main reason the change caused such concern was that the development of the inverted pyramid construction of news stories is associated with the rise of objectivity as a primary value, accompanying the professionalisation of journalism, in the late nineteenth century (the first journalism handbook, published in the USA in 1894, mentions the inverted pyramid structure as an example of how to write a well-constructed news story). US television news, however, has favoured the narrative approach since at least the 1960s, without seeing it as necessarily a threat to news values. Former NBC executive Reuven Frank, in a 1963 memo to his staff (quoted in Epstein 2000: 4–5), wrote, 'Every news story should, without any sacrifice of probity or responsibility, display the attributes of fiction, of drama. It should have structure and conflict, problem and denouement, rising action and falling action, a beginning, a middle and an end. These are not only the essentials of drama; they are the essentials of narrative.'

News story and narrative theory

In the language of news journalism a 'story' is a factual account or report. Clearly, story in the journalistic sense is crucially different from story in its fictional senses. These 'true stories' of news are not classical narratives. Classical or 'Hollywood' narrative as it is applied to film and television is characterised by a number of features that are notably absent from traditionally constructed, inverted pyramid news stories; in particular, these are:
* sequential development
* cause-effect relationships
* a double chronology of narrated time and the time of the events narrated
* resolution
* closure.

At the least, narrative – to be so defined – must demonstrate what Ytreberg (after Branigan 1992) calls a 'focused chain' or connected sequence of events, linked together 'through a process of transformation' (Ytreberg 2001: 360).

Langer (1998) illustrates ways that certain stories found in television news have long included at least some elements of the classic narrative models of Propp and Todorov, summarised here by Lacey (2000: 48) as a circular process of stages in the story:
* equilibrium through
* disequilibrium and
* opposition
* a quest for help or attempt to repair the disruption and finally – the part most often missing from the news –
* the achievement of a new equilibrium, or closure.

Langer specifically addresses the human interest and 'other news' stories often classified as 'soft news'. The use of narrative structures and devices has been acceptable in the case of stories of that kind for longer than in the case of so-called hard news: the political and economic stories that tend to lead a bulletin. The pattern of the 'binary oppositions' identified by Lévi-Strauss as paradigmatic in narrative is very readily found in television and radio news stories, and not only those that fall into Langer's 'other news'. Binary oppositions can be seen in the routine use of conflict to frame stories and as part of the tendency of news to personalise issues, groups and events as heroes or villains. Such narrative oppositions as Left v. Right or East v. West continue to appear in news stories in all media.

It is argued, especially by those who are concerned by the use of a narrative model in 'hard news' stories, that a narrative approach has the effect of personalising and depoliticising them. Issues and processes are minimised and elided; individuals are located as the agents and recipients of actions. This, the argument goes, can result in what has been called the 'tabloidisation' of the news (Langer 1998). A narrative model also allows more 'attitude' to be expressed: evaluations of behaviour and outcomes are coded into the narrative structure. Using the narrative model for some items therefore can have the effect of positioning the information model as objective and neutral by comparison. The information model of 'hard news' journalism purports not to be concerned with emotional effect, moral judgement or how the story ends.

As was described in chapter 10, Ellis (1992) has argued that television has developed a specific narrative mode; what he calls the 'open-ended format'. Recall Ellis' argument that fictional forms of television have borrowed their narrative structure from the non-fictional forms, citing the television news bulletin as 'the first true use of the open-ended series format . . . endlessly updating events and never synthesising them' (Ellis 1992: 145). In this definition, the television news bulletin, as a program, has always used an open-ended narrative form. His other argument you might remember about television narrative is its segmented, episodic nature. In a television news bulletin, each story might be called a segment, and each normally demonstrates an internal coherence, but might not be connected at all to the next. As soon as a connection is constructed between stories, however, the news begins to demonstrate that form of simple narrative that Branigan calls a 'focused chain', provided some consideration of motives or intentions is part of the connection made. Even without explicit links between news items, their arrangement in a sequence within a single news bulletin constructs an implied connection that directs the way audiences read each item.

The television medium, with both images and sound, potentially contains both a video narrative structure and an audio narrative structure. Some genres of television might place more importance on one than the other. For example, in that part of a television news bulletin in which the newsreader talks to camera, the audio tells the story while the video shows a 'talking head'. However, the visual is obviously so central to television that this situation – audio carrying the dominant meaning – is both rare and usually brief. The news reports themselves, which the newsreader introduces, will carry elaborated video narratives but minimal audio narratives. Even in a studio-based discussion program, considerable thought will be given to the visual design of the set, and the director will change the shot frequently, making an effort to capture the changing expressions of the participants in order to enliven the visual structure of the program.

A recognisable feature of broadcast news has been present since the advent of the film newsreel: the voice-over narrator. The extradiegetic narrator of television and radio news reports – that is, the newsreader or reporter, who are not part of the story – may be described as a 'dramatised narrator', in the sense that he or she is 'a character through whom the narration passes' (Lacey 2000: 109). But in order to satisfy the claims of news to truth and objectivity, a newsreader must be a reliable narrator. This is especially important in television as 'the connection between the voice-over and the images is traditionally rather loose and associational' in television news (Ytreberg 2001: 360). The reporter in the news report continues to be represented as an authoritative and reliable narrator. The reporter is equally a dramatised narrator who, unlike the newsreader, could at times be diegetic (that is, part of the narrated story), more so than in the past but still relatively rarely (in reports from scenes of war or political demonstrations, for example). Nonetheless, in cases when this happens, the story is moving out of the objectivism of the inverted pyramid and into the narrative world.

While Ytreberg is writing about a case in television, the same transitions are observable across the mass media globally, in a climate of deregulation and increased competition for audiences. One example of narrative and genre change is the blurring of form and content between news and not-news. Newspapers have introduced more feature and human interest material on to the front page, the traditional site of 'hard news' stories, and 'lifestyle' supplements have proliferated.* Television news might so far have retained the traditional half-hour or one-hour early evening bulletin, but the content mix has altered, in some cases to the point where the traditional mainstays of federal politics and national economics are little more than passing references, or are presented as personalised into 'human interest' angles on government decisions, for example, where once the human interest angle would have been supplementary to the 'straight' news presentation of the story. Journalists and others have expressed concern about these changes to the nature of news, using terms such as 'tabloidisation' or 'dumbing down' of the news. According to this argument, the changes represent a decline in quality, owing to the neglect or ignorance of central 'news values', values that in turn, it is argued, are aspects of the maintenance of a healthy public sphere (Langer 1998; Baker 1999). Some media analysts contest this view in terms similar to the 'image school' journalists in the NRK newsroom. Lumby and O'Neil, for example, assert that 'these developments are part of a dissolution of a prescriptive, rigid, social and cultural hierarchy' of media values (Lumby & O'Neil 1994: 154).

Analysing narrative techniques in television news

The form of television news is characterised by conventional techniques for establishing the immediacy, the reality (as in, 'this is the way things are') and the objectivity of the news. From the opening sequence of the bulletin, we can observe and analyse these techniques. In most developed countries, a nightly television newscast will begin in a highly recognisable way. The opening sequence can be

---

* For a discussion of the transition from 'objective to interpretive reporting' on the *Sydney Morning Herald* newspaper, see David McKnight, 'Facts versus stories: From objective to interpretive reporting', *Media International Australia* 99 (May 2001), 49–58.

interpreted not only as a call to attention but also as an interruption to the 'flow' of entertainment programming. It will usually be characterised by computer-animated titles in bright colours and 'sharply ascending' fanfare-like theme music (trumpets are 'typical') (Allen 1999: 99). The music and colours serve to establish urgency and immediacy, as part of the authoritativeness of news. Opening sequences also use visual symbols, to situate the news in time and space. Symbols such as a revolving globe or a ticking clock are signs both of the comprehensiveness and immediacy of the news. Australia's Channel 9 6pm news bulletin uses an animated 'pan' (camera movement) over a world map, coming to rest over Australia and clearly recognisable features of the city skyline to situate it in the world, in the nation and in the city of Sydney. The choice of opening images can also signify authority more directly, as when the British *News at Ten* includes Big Ben, the symbol of the British Houses of Parliament, in its opening titles. Over these iconic images, and as the fanfare fades, we very often hear headlines: brief summaries or indications of the news to come, sometimes phrased to intrigue rather than give the story away, and always announced with breathless urgency. Typically the whole opening sequence ends in the professional space of the studio: 'a pristine place of hard, polished surfaces' with their 'connotations of efficiency and objectivity' (Allen 1999: 99).

In the studio we find the newsreader(s), usually behind desks, formally dressed and with a not unfriendly but essentially business-like manner. Using two newsreaders makes mood transitions easier to effect, between serious and lighter items, as one can hand over to the other. In Western nations, if there are two newsreaders, one will usually be an older, white male and the other a younger (but not too young) and attractive female; together they can both establish authority and credibility (through sobriety of appearance, manner and tone) and provide viewers with someone appealing to look at. The mode of address of the newsreader plays an important part in conveying that the news is bringing viewers what 'really happened' today. Newsreaders use direct and dialogic address, speaking straight to camera, apparently talking to each viewer, which is rare in non-factual forms of television. It creates the impression of a 'dialogue' with the viewer and might begin with a personalised form of address such as 'Good evening'. The effects are to reinforce the co-presence of the newsreaders with viewers and to create a 'fictive we' (Allen 1999: 100).

The dialogic relationship is not necessarily equal, in the sense that the newsreader (and reporters) are presented as having information that we, the viewers, do not have but which we should want, because it is important. This is signified by the professional manner and speech of the newsreaders; they rarely use the first person, their vocal delivery is studiedly neutral, and they do not gesture as one might in a conversation between peers. The mode of address, plus the relations of co-presence, encourage the audience's complicity. As a result the newsreader can be seen as speaking to us and for us, with the implication that 'we' are part of a consensus (and equally, not 'they', so there are inferred others). Sometimes the newsreaders have been introduced by name in the voice-over of the opening sequence; however it is conveyed, viewers know who they are, and television station advertising emphasises the authority and credibility of its news services by association with established newsreaders. In Australia in the late 1990s, the commercial Channel 9 used 'Brian told me' as the slogan to advertise its evening news bulletin, which was for a long time presented by veteran newsreader Brian Henderson. In sum, television news is structured and organised in ways that encourage viewers to reciprocate the news values of the bulletins. Headlines initiate this by using a strategy of visualising the scripted words to the effect of 'see for yourself', creating an 'obvious' significance for the events and an obviousness about how to understand them. This is an example, in semiotic terms, of the image as indexical truth.

Following the opening sequence, the bulletin normally consists of a sequence of news stories, which can take a number of forms. The simplest is a straight 'read' (also called a 'reader') with the newsreader talking to camera, usually with a graphic displayed behind his or her shoulder. Much more common, especially on smaller news services that do not have many of their own correspondents but rely on agency footage, is the 'live voice-over' or LVO. This consists of a filmed and edited news report, with a voice-over read by the newsreader (who might or might not have written the script). The most elaborated form of news story, and most highly developed as narrative form, is the package. Packages are stories introduced by a newsreader but then presented by a reporter. This is done mostly in voice-over; that is, with the reporter's voice heard over visual images selected to make sense with the words. Note that the intention is to create meaning through the combination of script and images, not to match words to pictures exactly. Thus, pictures that symbolise what is being talked about, and might have been chosen from the news library, not shot especially, are often used in television news stories. One effect of this kind of selection can be to perpetuate stereotypes. For example, examination of the use of library footage in Australian television news revealed the repeated use of images of Aboriginal people, showing them as sitting and drinking under trees or on pavements (Putnis 1994).

Packages also usually contain 'actuality' or 'sound bites', in which some significant actor in the story is shown talking; and a 'stand up' or 'piece to camera' (PTC) in which the reporter talks directly to camera and therefore to the viewer. When, as very often happens, the PTC is the final segment of the report, the journalist might either 'sign off' ('Peter Cave, ABC News) or 'throw' back to the newsreader in the studio with a phrase like 'Now, back to you Jim', talking to the newsreader rather than viewers, and linking his or her presence with that of the newsreaders. The latter is more often, but not necessarily, used when there has been a 'live cross' to the reporter at the scene, and the live cross is another form of news story. Once confined to genuinely 'breaking' and significant news events, the live cross has been more frequently and gratuitously used, as satellite links, mobile satellite up-linking vehicles and lightweight broadcast equipment have become available and affordable. This is because the live cross so powerfully signifies the key news values of immediacy, reality and authority.

Baym (2004) draws attention to the role of the package in television news in terms of a distinction between what he terms mimetic and diegetic images in television news. Mimetic stories 'appear as unmediated, directly apparent', whereas diegetic stories 'are overtly mediated, constructed for audience appreciation' (Baym 2004: 286). Research by Baym suggests that there has been a steady movement from the mimetic to the diegetic in the images employed by television news since the 1970s or 1980s. He studied the ways in which network news in the USA covered the crisis in the Nixon presidency brought about by Watergate in 1973–74 and the impeachment of President Bill Clinton in 1998. He found that, between the Watergate coverage of the mid-1970s and the Clinton story, although the average length of the news packages was much the same, the number of visual images in each nearly doubled while the length of each image halved. This illustrates a considerable change of pace between the older and the more recent bulletins. It also suggests much quicker cutting between shots. Overall, the effect in the later coverage is more cinematic and less traditionally journalistic; that is, there is a move away from the linear and chronological assemblage of words and pictures towards a more symbolic reliance on images to produce narrative meaning.

Baym's findings in relation to the use of images of each president illustrate the point very clearly. In the Watergate coverage, relatively few moving pictures of President Nixon were used (only nine out of 513 shots were of Nixon; Baym 2004: 285). But in the Clinton coverage there were five times as many images of the president. Moreover, the shots used of Nixon were all long or medium shots; none was in close-up. Clinton, however, was shown in close-up (his face filling the frame) or big close-up (from just below the hairline to the bottom of the chin) in 17 per cent of the presidential pictures. This reflects cultural changes in the boundaries between public and private, a breaking down of the kind of convention that prohibited journalists from showing leading public figures 'up close and personal'; that is, in an intimate, even invasive, way. The effect is also to make the coverage of Clinton much less dispassionate, much more judgemental, in visual terms than that of Nixon.

Baym also found other differences, in the use of camera motion and editing styles, which show that by the late 1990s television news was using more diegetic narrative techniques and symbolic representation, in contrast with the mimetic and indexical approaches of two decades earlier. These terms – indexical and symbolic – are derived from the work of Charles Peirce (the 'father' of modern semiotics), who identified three types of sign in terms of their perceived relationship to external referents: the icon, or a near approximation of an object (as in a photograph); the index, or a metonymic representation of a referent (such as broken glass on the road indicating a car accident); and the symbol, or an arbitrary and conventional indication of a referent (as in a linguistic sign).

The 'images of the real' produced by the mimetic mode of visual representation, in which news footage appears to reflect reality, offering us a 'window' on the world, are iconic and indexical. They provide direct evidence, through iconic signs, of what is actually there while also working as metonyms, or selected items that represent a bigger picture. The symbolic images used by diegetic stories, on the other hand, are not anchored to the real but produce meanings by the context in which they are seen and by their juxtapositions. Baym gives the example of one shot of Clinton beginning with a close-up of a portrait of George Washington, the US president credited with having said, 'I cannot tell a lie.' The camera then zooms out to reveal President Clinton, whose 'problem with the truth' was by then a central topic in the news, speaking at a podium (Baym 2004: 291). The meaning is obvious but is also clearly constructed; this is not 'just the facts', the claim of traditional journalism. It also makes a much more televisual use of the medium.

A similar process is at work in the use of 'actuality' or 'sound bites'. The two terms are used equivalently but suggest the difference that has emerged between television news techniques of the early 1970s and today. 'Actuality' suggests that viewers are hearing and seeing what 'actually' happened. 'Sound bite' suggests not the whole meal but an edited portion. Baym found that sound bites were longer in the Watergate coverage, and the decreasing length of sound bites has been well documented. He found too that the use of sound bites in the Clinton story was more likely to be characterised by the editing together, or linking, of several very short grabs of sound. Just as the use of montage has the effect of rendering time meaningless (the images might come from different times, and are assembled in a non-linear way), so the montage of sound bites 'reveal[s] a shift . . . away from the ideal of the stenographer and toward a narrative device more complex', because it takes bits of 'the actual from the whole and reassembles them within the narrative' (Baym 2004: 290).

Conclusion

Television news uses conventions of narration and representation to shape the real. Those conventions reflect the nature of television as an audio-visual medium, its institutional aspects, and the values and assumptions of journalism. From the 'typographic paradigm' (Baym 2004: 285) of newspaper journalism, with its emphasis on the pyramid structure and on language (words) to present evidence, contemporary television news has moved to a 'televisual' structure, which emphasises the visual and the assemblage of images and sound. Other techniques and codes work to authorise the news and its narratives, including the newsreader's manner, appearance and mode of address, and the professionalism of the studio environment. The televisual paradigm could undermine the credibility and authority of the news, because it moves from indexical representations to symbolic ones, from 'what is to what may be' (Baym 2004: 296).

While most news journalists remain committed to 'a model of journalism which . . . assigns to the journalist the relatively passive role of transmitting information to the public' (Hallin 1993: 47), the increasingly cinematic use of the television medium is problematic in news because it compromises its truth claims. Moreover, the growth of 'reality TV' and the use of news and documentary techniques in such programs further undermine the distinctiveness of the form of television news and therefore its authority. What this chapter has illustrated is the potential of narrative to work in different ways and take different forms. In the case of television news, changes to the narrative form of news might now be challenging its role in informing people about the world and its versions of the real.

Chapter 12

Aspects of narrative in series and serials

Rosemary Huisman

One understanding of postmodern style is that of fragmentation. What is fragmented, broken up, will depend on what is usually understood to have 'coherence' in a particular medium and discourse. In poetry a postmodern style can be read as a dispersal of the unified persona of the traditional lyric; in prose fiction, such as the novel, it could be an incoherence of character, event or setting. (Is that the same character? Has this event already happened? I don't understand!)

The Hollywood tradition of film narrative has on the whole pursued the tight coherence of the nineteenth-century classic realist novel (the American D. W. Griffith, producer and director of the much-studied 1915 film, *The Birth of a Nation*, was said to have been very influenced by Dickens' novel structure). In comparison, the smaller European markets have allowed more aesthetic freedom. European films offer examples of narrative disruption from the earliest period, from the surreal distortion of setting in the German film *The Cabinet of Dr Caligari* (1919) to the ambiguity of character and event in the French film, *Last Year at Marienbad* (1961). For film, greater aesthetic freedom, relative to economic constraints, can favour experimentation, including various types of fragmentation. But in contrast, for television, it is the very economic constraints within which it is produced that oblige the television product to be fragmented in particular ways. These ways have led to the series and the serial being the dominant modes of narration in television.

Series and serials

The following definitions are derived from the glossary of the Archival Moving Image Materials of the United States Library of Congress:

A television series is a group of programs created or adapted for television broad-cast with a common series title, usually related to one another in subject or otherwise. Often, television series appear once a week during a prescribed time slot; however, they may appear with more or less frequency. Television series are usually created to be open-ended, not with a predetermined number of episodes. In a fiction series, the programs typically share the same characters and basic theme.

> (www.itsmarc.com/crs/arch0391.htm; viewed 6 November 2004)

A series can be on any subject matter, fiction or non-fiction, such as the series *Walking with Dinosaurs*, or the various history series on Britain, World War II and so on. Fictional series typically introduce and complete a new story of events in one episode, although various threads or storylines, such as relationships between the regular characters, can develop from one episode to the next. Think of *Friends* or *Ally McBeal*, for example.

A television serial is 'a group of programs with a storyline continued from episode to episode' (www.itsmarc.com/crs/arch0946.htm; viewed 6 November 2004). The Archival Moving Image Materials resource tells us that film serials had been very popular ('The serial engaged audience interest in a hero or hero-ine whose exploits reached an unresolved crisis at the end of each episode'), but their production ceased in the early 1950s, just as television sets became more widely available. This suggests the role in popular entertainment that television was beginning to assume.

The film serial typically had a finite number of episodes, and featured television serials can similarly have a finite number; in any one of its three seasons, the serial *24* (2003–), in which each hourly episode was equated with an hour of real time for the characters, had – surprise! – twenty-four episodes. However, a feature of television serials, which derived from radio serials, is the development of the open-ended serial, which will go on for as long as audience interest and advertising support endure. This is characteristic of the genre of soap operas, discussed in chapter 13.

A program can change its nature over time. Early episodes of the British police drama, *The Bill*, belonged to a series. Each episode had a self-contained plot, often one serious storyline and one more humorous one (an element of the sitcom genre), and by the end of the episode each new storyline was complete: the crime solved, the kitten found. As Anne Dunn has shown (in chapter 10), the emphasis in these earlier episodes was on the actions of the police; the characterisation of individual police remained fairly static. More recent episodes have developed storylines concerning the personal lives of the police: romantic triangles, ani-mosity between individuals and so on (plot elements more associated with the soap opera genre). This focus led to more storyline continuity between episodes, with the romantic triangle storyline, continuing from one episode to the next, becoming as prominent as the solving crime storyline, complete in one episode. In a further development of *The Bill*, a limited number of episodes can become a full serial, with interwoven storylines (for example, a sequence of six episodes centred both on the pursuit of a serial rapist and on the place of a policewoman in a traditional male police culture).

Models of communication

An old-fashioned model of communication simply described a sender who sent a message to an addressee (listener or reader). Michael Reddy called this the 'conduit model' because it assumed that language is a kind of conduit, or container, through which information or meaning is passed from one person to another. In fact, all that is passed from one person to another is a signal (*the vehicle of a Peircean sign*) – a disturbance of air waves or marks on the page or digital dots on a screen – that signifies a meaning to the sender (*is understood as a sign that implies an interpretant that signifies a known object*) according to their particular context of production, and which might or might not signify a meaning to the addressee: have you travelled in a country where you do not speak the language? And if the signal is interpreted as meaningful, that interpretation might or might not be similar to that intended by the sender (Reddy 1979: 284–324).

The addressee interprets according to their context of reception; in personal encounters, to the extent that the social knowledge and experience of the sender and addressee overlap, communication is reasonably successful, although we can never be sure we have understood 'what's in the other person's mind' (as the conduit model assumed). But with mass media, such as television, the communication model becomes even more complex. The sender we might now call the **agency** – and that agency is itself complex, made up of a collaboration of many contributors, with varying degrees of power over the final 'product', the program. The addressee is now the **audience** – but this is a twofold concept. There is the audience that the agency projects, the one it would like to attract: I will call this the **illocutionary audience** (appropriating the term 'illocution' from speech act theory, where it denotes the intended meaning of the speaker). The other audience is the actual audience who chooses to watch the program: I will call this the **perlocutionary audience** (again, 'perlocution' is the term from speech act theory for the meaning that the listener 'takes up'). Members of the perlocutionary audience do not of course necessarily 'take up' the same or similar interpretation. Some film analysis would use the term 'speaking subject' for both agency and perlocutionary audience – those who produce meaning or those who interpret it – so media texts have a proliferation of 'speaking subjects'. (The term 'spoken subject' is then apt for the illocutionary audience – the position of interpretation prepared or projected by the producers of a media text.)

Finally there is the signal itself, the media text of a program, such as an episode of a series or serial, which is created and broadcast. Its producers will try to give it characteristics that satisfy economically proven criteria, but there is no guarantee of audience response. Remember, the meaning is understood by the viewer in their own context of reception – there is no meaning 'in' the signal itself. Moreover, as N. J. Lowe points out,

> when we watch a film or a television program, we are processing not one nar-rative track but two. There is the visual text on the screen, and there is the soundtrack separately assembled, often by different people, and lovingly pasted together to create the impression of unity, but it is our 'reading' of the film that actually connects and collates the two.
>
> (Lowe 2000: 25)

Agency: the contexts of production

'Agency' refers to one causing an action, here the production of a media text for television. But this agency is complex as it includes the collaboration of many individuals. It is impossible to identify 'an agent' in the way we are accustomed to do, for example, in the author of the traditional novel (although, even with the novel, the contribution of a good editor can be very important, even if not acknowledged). In all this variety, there are two dimensions of agency that must be taken into account: first, the agency as 'creative activity' and, second, the agency as a television company or organisation.

The agency as 'creative activity' includes the scriptwriter(s), director, photog-raphers, actors, editors and so on – all those concerned with directly producing the television program we eventually see. Most of the credits at the beginning or end of a program acknowledge people involved in creative agency. The agency as a television company or organisation is depicted by the very first and very last shots of a program, which identify the company in image and language – for example, for the series *Seinfeld*, the first credit is the familiar Columbia image of the woman holding a torch aloft, just as an MGM production has the roaring lion or a Paramount production the mountain with stars above. As the second-last credit for *Seinfeld* we see the words 'A West/Schapiro Production in association with', followed by the final credit, 'Castle Rock Entertainment', with the image associated with that company, a lighthouse and its sweeping beam. Presumably these are the smaller companies to which the larger Columbia company contracts the production of this particular program.

The agency of the television company encompasses both how it is organised internally and how it is governed externally by rules and laws, such as the reg-ulations of government bodies that control the media. This television company agency is the primary agency, in that the pressures, both internal and external, generated and experienced by the company will be the context within which the other agency, of creative activity, can take place. Thus it is no accident that the first and/or last credits of a program describe this agency – the position in the program sequence symbolises the company's dominant enclosure of the creative activity.

To repeat: agency in the production of television texts is complex. The list of credits on a television program shows how many individuals are involved in production decisions and actions. I noted the credits for an episode of the comedy series *Seinfeld* (that is, the credits for creative agency, in between the company identifiers previously mentioned). If you saw any episodes of this show, you'll know it was relatively simple – a good script, four regular actors, all very good comedians, and a few star guests – so if anything this is a more limited list than more complicated productions would require. Of course, the same person may perform more than one of these functions:

Credits at the beginning of the episode – one name for each function, unless otherwise indicated:
In separate sequence, the names of the four regular actors, then
Producer
Supervising producer
Executive producer
Created by (two)
Written by
Directed by

Credits at the end
Executive producer (not the same as the executive producer at the beginning)
Executive producers (two)
Producer (not the same as the producer at the beginning)
Co-producer
Story editor
Program consultant
Line producer
Associate producer
Guest starring (three)
Also starring (two)
Production designer
Unit production manager/first assistant director
Second assistant director
Casting by (a company/agency name)
Director of photography
Music by
Edited by

Production coordinator
Script supervisor
Production mixer
Set decorator
Property master
Costume supervisor
Key grip
Online editor
Colourist
Technical coordinator
Camera operators (three)
Production accountant
Assistant accountant
Make-up (two)
Hair stylists (two)
Writer's assistants (two)
Assistant to the producer
Production assistants (two)
Executive in charge of production

What this list demonstrates is that creative agency – by which meanings are made – is complex and multivocal in television texts, involving far more than the writers (or 'authors') themselves.

Here's one writer commenting on the experience of writing for a television series:

> The tube is death on writers. Especially television series work. It rots talent at an astounding rate . . . the real culprit is the demand for speed and repetition. You're writing as part of a team – often with five or six other writers. And you're labouring within strict formulas for the show's characters and plots. It's like making Pintos at the Ford plant; you stamp out the body [with lots of help] and somebody else puts in the headlight. And you're doing it fast: 14 days is luxury for about 45 pages of dialogue.
>
>   (www.pubinfo.vcu.edu/artweb/playwriting; viewed 6 September 2002)

This context of situation is very different from that assumed in a romantic understanding of the writer as an inspired novelist (or poet), where narrative coherence in the production of the text is assumed to derive from the author's individual identity. The coherence in production in a media text written in these circumstances will typically derive not from any individual, but from the collective agreement by the different writers in following conventions already established for this series or serial, for example in genre and characterisation.

The online Wikipedia entry for 'Television program' has an illuminating account of 'the standard procedure for shows on network television in the United States'. Here is a summary (the italics are in the entry):

- The show *creator* comes up with the idea for a series. The idea includes the concept, the characters, perhaps some crew, perhaps some 'big-name' actors.
- The creator *pitches* the idea to different television networks.
- An interested network *orders* a pilot (a prototype first episode of the series).
- The structure and team of the whole series is put together to create the pilot.
- The network likes the pilot, it *picks up* the show, it orders a *run* of episodes (the network doesn't like the pilot, it *passes*; the creator *shops the pilot around* to other networks).
- The show hires a *stable* of writers; they might write in parallel (one writer on the first episode, another on the second and so on) or they might work as a team (as in the disgruntled quote given above). 'Sometimes [writers] develop story ideas individually, and pitch them to the show's creator, who then folds them together into a script and rewrites them.'
- The executive producer (often the creator) picks crew and cast (subject to approval by the network), approves and often writes series plots, sometimes writes and directs major episodes. Other subordinate producers, variously named, ensure that the show works smoothly.
- The written script must be turned into film, with both language and image. This is the director's job: deciding how to stage scenes, where to place cameras, perhaps to coach actors. A director is appointed for each episode.
- A director of photography controls the lighting and 'takes care of making the show look good'.
- An editor cuts the different pieces of film together, adds music, puts the whole show together with titles and so on. (http://en.wikipedia.org/wiki/Television series; 12 October 2004)

Obviously, a media text produced through the interaction of so many people will be very expensive, as will a film. However, films sell seats to individuals, but commercial television sells viewers to advertisers. If the series can attract a large viewing audience, then advertisers will want to buy time during its episodes, and the television station showing it can charge a premium rate during its time slot. If the series is not successful, and therefore cancelled, the network has not only lost money in its development but also still has to gamble on bankrolling new 'pitches'. So narrative in television series and serials will be very different from that in texts of print culture and in film, as economic factors place three (at least) constraints on television narrative from the perspective of agency:

- the risk of investing leads to a conservative attitude to creative production, with great reliance on narrative conventions already established as successful; the latter also facilitates the preparation of scripts by teams, rather than individual authors;

- the structure of the narrative of the individual program episode has to accommodate the interpolation of advertising texts within the episode as it goes to air;
- television narratives will preferably be open-ended (resist closure) and repetitive so that, if successful, they can be continued.

The perlocutionary (actual) audience

As described above, the commercial television company must regularly interrupt a fictional narrative to broadcast advertisements. For example, for three half-hour episodes of the sitcom series *Seinfeld*, I noted that the sitcom content in fact took just over an hour; that is, about ten minutes of each half-hour episode – one-third of the viewing time – had been taken up with advertisements.

Viewers know – or at least feel – that the more popular the program, the more it is fragmented by advertisements and the more advertisements are in each advertising segment. In an episode of the popular action serial *24*, shown from 8.30pm to 9.30pm, I counted five sequences of advertisements between program segments, and in each sequence there were ten or eleven different advertisements for a diverse list of 'products'. This diversity reflects the network's assumption that mid-evening is a prime time for advertising to the widest demographic of viewers. For example, the 9pm advertisement segment contained advertisements for: *All Saints* (a television network series), Oz lotto (lottery), *Triple X* (film), Mitsubishi (car company), HCF (health insurance company), Claratyne (hay fever product), a job search agency, SPC baked beans, a home loan company, Optus mobile phones and *Marshall Law* (a network series).

Why does the television viewer tolerate this fragmented narrative? In fact, it is generally compatible with the context of reception in which television is usually experienced, that is, a private home. This is a very different context from the experience of film in the cinema, where the viewer has paid to sit (quietly! other patrons hope) in the dark in a public space. For television, viewing is likely to be interrupted by various domestic demands and behaviour: the phone call, the break for preparing food, the calls of nature. Viewers 'channel-surf', leave a program and perhaps return. More recently, viewers have had the capacity to tape programs and view them later, fast-forwarding over the advertising segments. Current developments in digital technology are increasingly empowering viewers to select when and how they watch programs.

Non-commercial stations, such as the ABC in Australia and the BBC in Britain, transmit a television narrative continuously (although increasingly, advertisements for the ABC's own programs and bookshop products are scheduled between completed programs or episodes). Noticeably, the non-commercial channels feature short, two- to six-part serials, whose scripts often originate in novels (typically historical or crime). This construction makes different demands on the viewer, who must 'commit' continuous time to viewing in a way more comparable to the reader's 'committing' continuous time to the reading of a novel.

The illocutionary (assumed or projected) audience

The principal concern of the television network or station is: how can we attract the audience which will attract advertisers to us? Television and advertising companies know there is not one homogeneous audience but the possibility of various audiences and various responses. Obviously advertising companies will do audience (market) research before doing the creative design for a particular consumer product. However, in commercial television (as for magazines, discussed in chapter 18), what is advertising and what is editorial seep into each other's area: in order to attract and maintain a high advertising revenue, a station needs to broadcast programs that appeal to an audience similar to that wanted by major advertising sponsors. To do this they need to ask, at least: what is the nature of the target audience, and what is the audience positioning strategy?

Studies of the target audience can be demographic or psychographic. The former is the familiar segmenting of the population primarily by occupation, which is assumed to relate to spending power; thus the highest category is senior managerial, administrative or professional, while the second lowest is semi-skilled and unskilled manual workers. In Australia, for example, the non-commercial ABC and the multilingual SBS are usually said to attract a demographic with higher levels of education and so in higher-level occupations, while the commercial stations appeal to a wider cross-section of the community, and have larger audiences overall.

The ABC's original charter with public funding was to provide news, current affairs, comment and 'culture'; every so often a new general manager tries to extend the demographic appeal and compete with the commercial channels for viewers. This socially admirable intent is a goal not necessarily compatible with the ABC's traditionally strong orientation to information as well as entertainment and its tendency to be more innovative in encouraging those with creative agency. The looser link with market pressures does help to explain the more variable spread of media texts, including series and serials, presented on the ABC and SBS, both those locally commissioned and those purchased from elsewhere. In a loose generalisation, one could say the ABC purchases more programs from the BBC in the UK, the commercial channels purchase more programs from the USA, while SBS shows programs, especially films, from many non-English-speaking countries, with English subtitles. (Commercial stations have a practical difficulty in buying BBC rather than American sitcoms; BBC sitcoms are made half an hour long, whereas a commercial sitcom is about twenty-two minutes long, allowing for the inclusion of advertising segments in the scheduled half hour.)

The second kind of audience analysis, the study of psychographic variables, has become more popular in recent years. Here the population is segmented by lifestyle aspirations. Theories of identity are important in this kind of analysis: the idea is that an individual with a dominant psychovariable of one kind will identify more readily with a television advertisement or program which represents or endorses that category. If you have watched episodes of the Australian soap opera *Home and Away*, you might decide, as I did, that its target audience is adolescents in secondary school, with experience principally limited to that of family and local community (as indeed its title declares). On the other hand, the American serial *24* was targeted at a wider range of audience identification, with principal characters who were young and middle-aged, white and black, with strong female roles, although centred on the traditional white male character, Jack Bauer. And finally, the series *Sex and the City*, with its focus on female sex and fashion, targeted the post-adolescent urban female consumer. The mode of address of each program is tailored to fit the illocutionary (assumed) audience: characters are given dialogue which is assumed to be that with which such an audience can identify (both in subject matter of interest and in 'realistic' interaction between characters).

The programming schedule of the three programs just mentioned, in 2002 in Sydney, Australia, indicates the target audience judgement of the television channel: 7 to 7.30pm every evening for *Home and Away* (a similar demographic can catch the soap *Neighbours* on a rival channel in the previous half hour), prime time 8.30pm to 9.30pm for *24* (twice a week in the early episodes to 'hook' viewers, once a week thereafter), and once a week, a two-hour slot from 9.30pm to 11.30pm for two episodes of *Sex and the City*, the first a new episode, the second a repeat for recent converts or addicts.

Another way to identify the likely target audience of a program is to take note of the advertisements filmed in its breaks – the advertisements and the program (the network hopes) are aimed at the same target audience. An example of the number and diversity of advertisements aimed at a wide demographic viewing in prime time was given above for the serial *24*.

In trying to position the audience, those with agency are most directly trying to act upon the perceptions of the viewer. Audience positioning can refer just to the physical construction of the media text by those with creative agency. In film studies, the term 'spoken subject' is sometimes used for the position of the camera, the viewing position prepared for the individual viewer. But by metaphorical extension, the term 'spoken subject' can also be used of the ideological position prepared for the viewer. (Typically, commercial agency favours the ideological status quo, since in a society that perceives itself as stable, commercial stability is more favoured.) 'Modes of address' can serve this ideological purpose. As Sonia M. Livingstone has written: 'texts attempt to position readers as particular kinds of subjects through particular modes of address' (Livingstone 1994: 249).

But a viewer can be compliant or resistant. I was a resistant viewer of the following: in the *Home and Away* episodes I watched, the mother appeared to me to be a classic 'pour-oil-on-troubled-waters' stereotype, trying to placate a troubled adolescent daughter and a belligerent and irrational father. To explore my response, I made a quick analysis of the mother's dialogue in two sequential scenes (the husband or daughter speak between the numbered utterances):

(With husband, in house)
1 Can't you go a bit easier on her? You know what she's going through.
2 The way you're acting, you're going to drive her further away.
3 *I know* she put us through hell in the last few weeks, but that doesn't mean she deserves to go through hell. Our daughter's in pain, Rhys. At least try to understand that.

(With daughter, in backyard)
1 Oh, sweetheart.
2 Your dad doesn't mean to be so hard on you – he's just – he's just finding it difficult seeing you this unhappy.
3 Oh, *I know* it doesn't feel like it now, but you will feel good about yourself again – without Kane. *I want* you to make a deal with me – OK? *I want* you to write down all the good things that happened to you during the day, and at the end of the day *I want* you to count them all up. Please, Kirsty. There are good things in your life right here and now. You just have to be on the lookout for them. *I bet* you won't be able to count them on one hand.

I've italicised each instance of the mother as grammatical subject. In each of the six examples the associated verb realises a mental process (two 'I know', three 'I want' and one 'I bet'; that is, 'I imagine'), but there are no verbs of material processes of action. So in the social world projected by her speech, the mother thinks but does not act at all. Her language choice is placatory: with her daughter she tactfully avoids the power role of direct commands – not 'Write down all the good things . . .', but 'I want you to write down . . .' – and her one direct command to her husband is that he attempt a mental process, 'try to understand'. The very script in these two scenes inscribes a particular ideology of 'family values': the mother as thinking of the needs of others but not effective in initiating her own actions.

Effective, efficient – such terms seem to be important in the ideology of power relations portrayed on television. George Gerbner made an interesting early analysis of violence in television narratives. (His studies, published in 1970, are described in Fiske and Hartley 2003: 15–21.) Gerbner concluded that heroes and villains were more or less equally violent, but that heroes were 'more efficiently violent'. (They were also more physically attractive.) 'Cool efficiency, and, to a lesser extent, manliness and youth, appear to be the chief correlates of success and virtue in a fairly impersonal self-seeking and specialised structure of violent action' (Fiske & Hartley 2003: 19).

The relevance of this to ideology is that Gerbner does not see violence on television as a direct representation of the extent and nature of violence itself in society, but rather as a symbolic representation of 'the value-structure of society':

> violence . . . is used in the pursuit of the socially validated ends of power, money or duty . . . So despite its obvious connection with power or dominance over others, it is not the dominance of one personality over another, but of one social role over another social role. It is linked to socio-centrality, in that the victims are likely to belong to less esteemed groups, defined in terms of age, class, gender and race, and the successful aggressors are likely to be young, white, male and middle-class or unclassifiable. Violence is not in itself seen as good or evil, but when correlated with efficiency it is esteemed, for efficiency is a key socio-central value in a competitive society.
>
> (Fiske & Hartley 2003: 19–20)

It is worth remembering that this study was carried out before 1970, and we need to consider whether its conclusions are still relevant.

The media text – series and serials

At the end of the section on agency, I described three characteristics of television narrative that economic constraints frequently would impose. These are:
- the risk of investing leads to a conservative attitude to creative production, with great reliance on narrative conventions already established as successful (narrative repetition within the episode);
- the structure of the narrative of the individual program episode has to accommodate the interpolation of advertising texts within the episode as it goes to air (narrative segmentation);
- series and serials will preferably resist closure and be open-ended; for budgetary reasons the company prefers to find a successful formula for a program, then repeat that formula (narrative repetition between episodes).

Given the circumscriptions described above, the production of narrative coherence in a television program is a conscious construction, and therefore explicit and established codes of television production are likely to be followed – and repeated. These codes will include:
- an ideology (an assumed understanding of social values)
- an established television genre or text type
- the typical field, tenor and mode of that genre (see below)
- conventional narrative deployment of character, action, dialogue, setting/location, *mise en scène*/iconography
- the use of technical conventions of televisual construction
- the use of recognised units of televisual text construction in editing.

The next chapter will make a more detailed study of ideology and narrative deployment in relation to the genre of sitcom (an example of a series) and the genre of soap opera (an example of a serial). Here we consider the analysis of genre in terms of field, tenor and mode and, more briefly, the codes of technical construction and the units of televisual text construction for television narrative.

Genre: field, tenor and mode

A genre is a recognised text type. The financial constraints within which television texts are produced promote a structuralist understanding of texts, including narrative texts, by producers. This refers to the attempt to define and reproduce the characteristics of previously successful texts. Whether or not producers have much insight into their own ideology of production (apart from a general sense of being conservative, not 'rocking the boat'), they will be very clear on the category of text – the genre, that they want to produce. Chapter 10 discussed genres of television. Here I elaborate on the description of genres in terms of field, tenor and mode as a way of structuring our analysis of genre. These terms are derived from a model of the context of situation, as used in systemic functional linguistics (Halliday & Hasan 1985: 12–14; Halliday 1978: 142–5).

Field can have two dimensions. The first is the field of social action. For narration in television, these are (in Aristotle's sense) the two social acts of telling (diegesis) and showing (mimesis). The viewer is shown characters doing actions, and shown interactions between characters, including conversations. But who 'shows'? Watching a game of football as you sit in the grandstand is not the same as watching a game of football being broadcast on television. The latter has camera angles chosen and is broken into the usual segments for advertisements; 'real time' is stopped for replays of highlights, even during the first transmission. The football game is being 'structured' to fit the exigencies of television production. All images seen on television are mediated, even if the agency of that mediation appears effaced. Even more patently, a fictional narrative, such as a sitcom or soap opera, is structured; the apparent showing of the characters and events effaces the narrator, who 'tells' what is 'shown'. The possible effects of this effacement will be discussed later.

The second dimension of field is that of subject matter. This is the one we readily understand, and is the usual content of television program guides. Here is an extract from a soap magazine section, 'Your complete guide to what's coming up', for the soap opera *Days of Our Lives*. It is headed 'Dream Cheater': 'Carrie gets emotional as she and Austin are about to make love. The next day Austin says they can wait until they're ready to try for a family. As he watches her sleep, she dreams of making love to Mike instead of her husband.' (*TV Soap* (Australia), 12 August 2002, p. 33.)

Tenor refers to social relations and social attitudes. We can describe a tenor in relation to each field. The first dimension of field, that of social action, for narrative media texts such as the sitcom and soap opera, was telling, including effaced telling. (In print culture narratives, such as the novel, this tenor is usually realised by a clause choice of the declarative mood in statements.) The tenor in relation to this field is the relation between the producer of the sitcom or soap opera and the audience. Complications multiply! I spoke of the illocutionary audience – the one the producers aim to attract using the results of market research. So the illocutionary tenor is the relationship the producers aim to achieve between the television network agency and the target viewing audience; it is a power relation of teller and projected compliant viewer. The perlocutionary tenor will of course refer to any relationship a viewer actually interprets.

Again, it is easier to describe the tenor of the second-order field, the subject matter of the fictional world (the diegesis in Genette's sense), since this refers to the social relations between the characters and their attitudes to what is going on, as revealed both in their dialogue and actions, and the social roles assigned to them. However, the postmodern stylistic features of television narrative (its segmented and non-linear features), together with its usual private context of reception, work to undermine (deconstruct) this nice opposition of tenor associated with the first-order field and tenor associated with the second-order field. Television has been described as having 'permeable diegetic boundaries': that is, the boundaries between the first-order world of the viewer and the second-order world depicted on the television screen (whether in a segment of narrative fiction or a segment of advertising) can become blurred. In the fiction, the characters address each other; in the advertising, the speakers usually appear directly to address the viewer (as newsreaders always appear to do).

This discussion of tenor highlights an important difference between television and film, which has been described as 'oral interaction versus gaze'. One online account of television narrative puts it like this:

> TV presents itself as discourse (acknowledging speaker and listener) rather than as story/history (which hides the source of enunciation so that it seems to happen all by itself), and all of its stories are framed by its 'superdiscourse' of scheduling. This discursivity mimics oral culture, yet structures it into a rigid form. It also works to draw us into the industry's presentation of social meanings and to present them as a consensus. Through the device of direct address, an illusion of actual contact is created which works in TV's interest and promotes certain ideologies. But just as cinema only presents the illusion of history (it does really have a source and is artificially created), TV gives only the illusion of discourse (we don't see the real source and it isn't real conversation).
>
> (www.brown.edu/Departments/MCM/courses/MC11/outline/
> TV_narrative_outline.htm; 14 October 2004)

This aspect of television, that much of it is scripted and produced to be presented as interactive conversation, is a feature of mode, the organisation of the message. The mode is designed to promote the conflation of viewer's world and viewed world and the identification of the viewer with the values assumed in the television product (both narrative and advertisement). The British sitcom, *The Royle Family*, depicting the family slumped on the sofa in front of the telly, commenting occasionally on the program as they munched or scratched, beautifully (or horribly) played with the mirroring of mimesis and the telling of diegesis – which world (viewer and viewed) was the reflection of which world?

So, finally, **mode**. 'Mode' refers to the organisation of the message so that it is coherent with its context. Here is an example from spoken language: if you and I had been talking about sitcoms in general, I might then say: 'Yes, one sitcom I guess everyone liked must be *Fawlty Towers*.' On the other hand, if we had already been talking about *Fawlty Towers*, and you asked what genre I thought it was, I might say, 'Oh, I think it's a sitcom.' In both examples what we were already talking about ('sitcom' in the first example, 'it' for '*Fawlty Towers*' in the second) comes earlier in my statement, whereas the words for the new information ('*Fawlty Towers*' in the first example, 'sitcom' in the second) comes at the end of my statement. The subject matter is similar in both my sentences, but they're differently organised so as to be coherent with our previous conversation. Given the fragmentation of the television text, the role of the editor is very important in organising the mode of the completed program – shots to scene, scenes to segment, then segment to episode (these are units of narrative editing, discussed later). The repetition of features from episode to episode of the same series also constitutes a feature of mode. (It is not the features themselves but the fact of their repetition that links the programs.)

Generic expectations

A genre can be defined in terms of different likely configurations of field, tenor and mode, sometimes through the dominance of one or more of these parameters. Fictional series can usually be differentiated by their subject matter or field: a police drama, hospital drama, the inhabitants of a country town, of an urban street. However, the genre of sitcom is primarily defined through its tenor in relation to the first-order field, the effect on the viewer – as its very name (short for 'situation comedy') tells us, it is designed to make its audience laugh, or at least amuse them. The sitcom can therefore have a wide variety of subject matter. (With a quite opposite emotional colour, the film genre of *film noir* is also understood primarily through its tenor.) And some genres are noticeably defined by their mode, the organisation of their structure: the musical is a traditional example.

The term 'categorisation' is sometimes used to refer to the prior experience of media texts a viewer is assumed to have. This previous experience, it is assumed, has led the viewer to have certain expectations about media texts, including that media texts fall into certain categories with fairly predictable characteristics. The usual term for a recognisable media text type is 'genre', for example, the soap opera genre. So if a viewer is told in pre-advertising that a particular new program is a 'soap opera' then the viewer will bring generic expectations to that program. They will, for example, be very surprised if the episodes turn out to be about a lone man's courageous battle to climb a lonely mountain: that is, about a single individual struggling with nature rather than a social group agonising about their relationships. Again, if the program does in fact turn out to have a soap opera subject matter (field) but its camera shots are mostly long shots, with very few close-ups of the face, the technical construction of the program will be generically unusual, and the new viewer will probably find it a rather unsatisfactory program in terms of usual generic expectations, because of the reduced visual intimacy with the characters (the expected tenor).

From the point of view of agency, you can see that the choice of genre will have been determined by the results of audience analysis in relation to the purpose of the television network – a genre that market research has shown is attractive to the demographic and/or psychographic profile of the desired audience. You can also see why the two agencies might pull in different directions here: the creative agency – scriptwriter, director, costume designer and so on – might push towards innovation and aesthetic originality, wanting to rework generic conventions, whereas the very predictability of the genre serves the agency of the television company. If all goes well, what worked last year will work this year. The company agency, you might say, is best served by a fixed or structuralist approach to narrative and genre: these are the narrative features of a soap, a sitcom, a cop show/police drama – now go off and produce another one to the structuralist formula. In contrast, the creative agency might incline more to a post-structuralist perspective: let us deconstruct the past narrative structure of the genre, confound the narrative expectations. In some ways, for example, the storyline of *24* tried occasionally to do that – shockingly unpredictable events have occurred – but at the same time the conventional ideology of the political thriller remains undisturbed, realised in a narrative in which the ultimate success of the hero brings closure. Compare the ideological subversion of the plot of one late Agatha Christie detective story, *Cat among the Pigeons*, in which the narrator of the novel turns out to be the murderer. At the time that novel appeared, critical response ranged from indignant to outraged!

Construction: technical codes

The technical conventions of televisual construction relate to the technology used in filming the program: conventions of camera work, of lighting and colour, of sound-recording. A list of the technical codes of visual construction could include shot size, camera angle, lens type, composition, focus, lighting codes and colour. Particular techniques are assumed to signify a particular meaning to the illocutionary (assumed) audience, but it is a structuralist assumption to relate a choice of technique directly to a particular interpretation. There is no guarantee that the viewer (a member of the perlocutionary audience) will take up this interpretation, although the more 'literate' (the more experienced) viewers are in televisual conventions, the more likely they are to 'read' the technical codes in a socially conventional way.

- The shot-size is associated with the continuum private/public – the close-up is more intimate or more emotional than the more distant shot.
- The camera angle is associated with the continuum authority/weakness – the camera looking up at the object gives the object a looming aspect.
- The lens type can give a dramatic effect (wide angle), an 'everyday effect' (normal) or a voyeuristic effect (telephoto).
- A symmetrical composition seems 'calm', a static composition seems to lack conflict, while a dynamic composition signifies (it is assumed) disturbance and disorientation.
- Soft focus is romantic.
- High key lighting signifies happiness, low key a sombre mood, high contrast in lighting is dramatic, low contrast is realistic, documentary.
- Colour signifies optimism, passion, agitation with 'warm' colours (yellow, red, orange, brown), pessimism, calmness, reason with 'cool' colours (blue, green, purple, grey). (I have taken many of these terms from table 3.1 in Selby and Cowdery 1995: 57, although I do not reproduce their Saussurean terminology.)

All the significations conventionally associated with the technical codes are realisations of tenor: that is, interpreted as interpersonal meanings of social relations and attitude. They do not tell us what the narrative is about, but they are intended to suggest an attitude to the narrative. Remember, we cannot at all assume that the perlocutionary audience will understand the technical construction in these ways, but such codes would be part of studying television camera techniques. And since particular genres might be characteristically realised by certain tenors, it is unsurprising that the camera techniques taken to signify those tenors might become associated with certain genres. At the same time, television genres are very permeable, so an action drama serial like *24* nevertheless includes sequences of soap-like emotional 'focus', produced through the technical close-ups on faces, which are thought to signify emotional intensity.

Construction: units of narrative editing

In descending order of temporal duration (viewing time), we can identify televisual units of text construction as

- the series or serial
- the episode
- the segment
- the scene
- the shot.

The shot is the time in which one camera angle is held on the object. The camera can zoom in or pull back (a zoom shot); the camera itself can move while focused on the object (a tracking shot) or it can move so as to follow a moving object or obtain a panoramic shot (a pan shot). Shots must be edited into a scene, and there are practical constraints on the number of shots. For example, the BBC *writersroom* guidelines say, 'If you are writing a comedy to be shot entirely on location, then try to avoid complicated set-ups. Studio shows use four or five cameras. Location shows use one, and every angle has to be covered. Look analytically at a sequence . . . and see how many shots go to make it up.' (www.bbc.co.uk/writersroom/writing/tvcomedy.shtml; 13 October 2004)

The scene is a sequence of shots in the same location. Conventionally, it signifies a continuous action; a change in space or time means a change of scene. Scenes must be edited into the segment. The segment is a sequence of scenes, which is delimited by advertisements, making the segment the quintessential unit for commercial television. For narratives produced for non-commercial television, the segment is not marked externally by advertisements. It is recognised, in production or reception, by the internal coherence of its field – staying with the same topic or same characters, for example, rather like a paragraph in a printed text. If there is a scheduled break in narrative transmission for some reason, the break will be after a segment. Segments are edited into an episode. The episode is a sequence of segments, into which the television network can interpose advertisements. The series or serial will repeat basic features in each episode.

You already see the work that the viewer has to do, in order to interpret a coherent narrative from this edited sequence, with its segmented transmission interrupted by advertisements. This narrative ability with television input is learned from experience, and is a skill comparable to the narrative literacy learned from reading novels.

Any analysis of television narrative should pay particular attention to the segment, since it is one of the important ways in which television differs from film. A segment does not need linear development. Each segment must be entertaining on its own, almost a mini-episode; otherwise the viewer might not bother to come back after the 'commercial break', or might have surfed to another channel with more interesting material. For series and serials this leads to a pastiche model of narration, a very postmodern characteristic, in which several storylines, centred on different characters and events, are juxtaposed, rather than one principal storyline followed. (In this television is noticeably different from film, in which a more linear development facilitates the focus on one 'hero's' progress.) In each segment each of these storylines will receive some but not a great deal of attention. The action serial *24* did this noticeably, moving several storylines forward a little in each segment.

Soap opera is generically concerned more with characters' reactions to events rather than with the events themselves, so it might not move any 'storyline' forward at all in any one segment. Each scene in the segment, typically the interaction of two characters, can reiterate (show again) the characters' feelings towards an already told event (or, in infinite regress, towards another character's attitude towards an already told event).

Conclusion

This chapter has defined series and serials in terms of producers, theorised as 'agents', and audiences, theorised as perlocutionary (actual) and illocutionary (assumed or brought into being by the text). Interactions of agents and audiences are closely related to the construction of genre, identified by aspects of field, tenor and mode. Deployed in various ways, these in turn produce the generic expectations that we use to categorise and decode new programs. The technical codes of television narrative not only structure programs in familiar ways but also work to naturalise or critique social relations and attitudes. Moving on from these general points about series and serials, the next chapter will explore the particular structures and techniques that define soap operas and sitcoms as generic types of television narration.

Chapter 13

Soap operas and sitcoms

Rosemary Huisman

Ideology

In chapter 2 I introduced the concept of the *Umwelt*, to describe human under-standing of reality, the objective world (in a Peircean sense) of experience and imagination. The term 'ideology' is variously used, but here it is used to mean the perspectives that a person takes up towards his or her *Umwelt*, the ethical values that seem unproblematic, unarguable, objectively 'natural' in her or his world. In 'A Policeman's Lot', chapter 12 of their book, *Reading Television*, John Fiske and John Hartley discuss the ideology of several police series of the 1970s: *A Man Called Ironside*, *The Sweeney*, *Starsky and Hutch*. I quote their specific comments on *Ironside* to exemplify the general concept of 'ideology' in the sense above:

> *Ironside*'s team is presented as a harmonious society – part hunting party out of American mythology, part microcosm of Western class structures. But in terms of the way this 'society' is presented in the series itself, *Ironside*'s team derive their satisfying meaning not only from their metonymic reference but also by binary opposition to each other:
> male: female
> white: black
> cerebral: physical
> age: youth.
> The left-hand set of terms show the 'esteemed' or dominant values of this series. It is interesting to notice how the integration of these values into a harmonious society is presented as natural, and this offers us a graphic example of what

Barthes terms the 'ex-nominating' process that operates in the ideology of our society. The structure of these relationships is never foregrounded for inspection or criticism, but appears as the natural order, and as such does not require any conscious statement – it does not need to be *named* (Barthes 1973, pp. 138–41). Hence any contradictions in this structure, as for instance between the subordinate characters' function (to relate to each other and to Ironside as a harmonious society) and their jobs (to do menial, unpleasant or delegated tasks), are simply never shown as contradictions. Only an aberrant decoding by the audience will bring them out, if the audience's view of social relations does not fit that of the series.

> (Fiske & Hartley 2003: 142–3)

By 'metonymic reference', the authors mean that a feature assigned to a character could remind the audience of a more general social role, function, relationship or status. Note the possibility of 'aberrant decoding' – this is aberrant from the producer's point of view, of course. Members of the perlocutionary (actual) audience might interpret their *Umwelt* from the perspective of an ideology different from that encouraged by the producers.

The binary oppositions that Fiske and Hartley read in *Ironside* are a classic 'structuralist' way of understanding interpretation; compare Lévi-Strauss' analysis of myth, discussed in chapter 3. Nevertheless, such reductive accounts can be particularly helpful for analysing television series and serials, given the template of repeated narrative features that is explicitly used for scripting individual episodes. Different members of the audience could be 'aberrant' from each other, differing in their 'view of social relations' and so diverging in their responses to a media text. In 'What makes viewers diverge when interpreting narrative?', Daniel Chandler adapts information from Sonia M. Livingstone's book (1990a, chapter 7) and article (1990b) on television audience interpretation (www.aber.ac.uk/media/Modules/TF33120; 4 September 2002: lecture topic 8). Sixty-six regular viewers (forty-two female, twenty-four male) of the British soap opera, *Coronation Street*, completed a questionnaire about a storyline that had developed over several months. I quote the storyline summary:

> Susan Barlow, the 21-year-old daughter of Ken Barlow by his first marriage, returned to 'the Street' to live with her father and his new wife, Deirdre Barlow. Susan began a romance with Mike Baldwin, a local factory owner much older than her [*sic*]. Ken opposed the marriage of Susan and Mike because of Mike's adulterous affair with Deirdre a few years before (of which Susan was initially ignorant). Ken was persuaded to attend the wedding at the last minute, thus atoning for his neglect of Susan when she was a child.

The questionnaire included attitude statements for agreement or disagreement; the responses were analysed by cluster analysis, which identifies groups of similar responses. This gave four clusters, which Livingstone labelled 'Cynics', 'Negotiated cynics', 'Romantics' and 'Negotiated romantics'. I paraphrase the gloss for each of these interpretative positions:

- *Cynics*: were most strongly on Ken's side and against the couple; felt that Ken had acted reasonably and had been right to oppose the marriage. Didn't think Susan and Mike's marriage would last. Were particularly critical of Susan; she wanted Mike for his money and success and as a father figure.
- *Negotiated cynics*: were similar to the cynics, broadly favouring Ken and disliking Susan and Mike. However, did not agree that Ken should have been so strongly opposed to the marriage. Were less inclined to question the strength of feelings between Mike and Susan, and were less critical of Susan.
- *Romantics*: were the ones most strongly against Ken and in favour of the couple. Saw Ken as unreasonable, vindictive and possessive. Believed that Susan and Mike were right for each other and that the marriage would last.
- *Negotiated romantics*: basically agreed with the romantics, but also believed that Susan and Mike might not really be in love, that there might be some truth in the 'father figure' explanation, and that the couple would be likely to face some problems.

Livingstone's research on 'sociological and demographic factors' suggested that 'Identification' was very significant in 'Character Evaluation' and 'Perspective-Taking/Sympathy', and hence to interpretation. 'Identification' refers to whether viewers identified with/saw themselves as similar to a character. 'Character Evaluation' refers to a viewer's positive or negative evaluation of a character. 'Perspective-Taking/Sympathy' refers to the extent to which viewers perceived the narrative sympathetically from a particular character's viewpoint. So those in the cynical clusters saw themselves as more like Ken (than those in the romantic clusters) and liked Ken more (those in the romantic clusters didn't like Ken at all!). The cynics sympathised with Ken more whereas the negotiated cynics could also see Susan's point of view, 'possibly because they are mainly women'. However, Livingstone noted that overall, gender and interpretation were not clearly related: 'women did not especially side with Susan'. What has been labelled 'identification', I suggest, could also be called ideological recognition as it correlates with the value judgements and interpretative orientation of the viewer.

The sitcom genre: ideology

The Wikipedia definition is as follows: 'a sitcom or situation comedy is a genre of comedy performance devised for radio but today typically found on television. Sitcoms usually consist of recurring characters in a format in which there are one or more humorous story lines centred around a common environment, such as a family home or workplace' (http://en.wikipedia.org.wiki/Situation_comedy; viewed 12 September 2004).

The situation comedy is the most numerous narrative genre on television. The situation is the regular situation in which the permanent characters find themselves; it provides the context in each episode for fresh storylines with visiting characters. As the word 'comedy' implies, the sitcom should contain humour, should make us laugh (canned laughter is sometimes used, to give the impression of a performance in front of a live audience). However, the characterisation and setting can vary from cheerfully superficial to a more complex and darker social setting.

Richard F. Taflinger has written a book-length study of the (American) sitcom and made it available on the web (www.wsu.edu:8080/~taflinge/sitcom.html; viewed 19 October 2004). Taflinger divides this large genre into three distinct types or subgenres of sitcom: what he calls the action comedy, the domestic comedy and the dramatic comedy. The action comedy is the most numerous; its emphasis is on verbal and physical action. He cites *I Love Lucy, Bewitched, Gilligan's Island* and *McHale's Navy*. The domestic comedy has a wider variety of events and involves more people. He cites *The Brady Bunch, Roseanne* and *The Cosby Show*. Its emphasis is more on the characters and their growth and development, and 'almost invariably set in and around a family unit'. This subject matter easily lends itself to soap-type treatment, later discussed. The dramatic comedy is the least common. *M*A*S*H* would be a good example: the series on a medical unit treating American soldiers in the Korean War of the 1950s. The narrative theme – such as the horrors of war – of a dramatic comedy is not humorous but the 'comic intensification' in the portrayal of characters provides a kind of black humour.

Taflinger published his online book in 1996. We can already chart some developments in sitcom subject matter that extend beyond that time. The sitcom *Seinfeld* (the series was actually entitled *The Seinfield Chronicles*) was one of the most successful series of the 1990s. Its pilot episode ran in July 1989, in its first season in 1990 there were four episodes, in its second season (January to June 1991) twelve episodes – then its third through to ninth seasons each ran the full American television season from August/September to May, with twenty-one to twenty-four episodes. The last episode was broadcast in May 1998. (These dates are for its scheduling in the USA.) *Seinfield* actually ceased when its creator and principal character, Jerry Seinfeld, decided to stop producing it, not because audiences or sponsors had fallen away. Of Taflinger's three subgenres, the term 'domestic comedy' seems most relevant, but the domestic situation was that of three friends and a neighbour (Kramer), all much the same age. It wasn't the mother, father and children of the nuclear family. The cramped apartment of single urban dwellers, rather than the family home with gatherings in the spacious kitchen, was the domestic setting. (You can find a great deal of information on popular sitcoms on the web; for an interesting paper on *Seinfeld* see http://web.mit.edu/mr_mole/www/seinfeld.pdf; viewed 19 October 2004, unattributed.)

The other most successful American sitcom of recent years must be *Friends*. The pilot ran in September 1994, and the series began its first season immediately a week later, running the full season of twenty-four episodes. The tenth and final season aired the last episode in June 2004. Again, *Friends* was a 'domestic' comedy in that the characters lived together or close by, and incessantly talked about each other's everyday successes and failures but, like *Seinfeld*, the characters were of the same generation, not members of a nuclear family, like *The Brady Bunch*. Although each episode began in the local coffee shop, the urban apartments of young singles were the usual location.

Sex and the City took this transition a step further: again, there was a group of friends sharing each other's lives, but the 'comedy' scarcely derived from traditionally 'domestic' situations. (This series first aired in the USA in June 1998; in its sixth and final season its last episodes went to air in February 2004.) Moreover, in this sitcom the location itself, New York, almost becomes a 'character' in the sitcom (it is after all in the title) as the friends meet in named restaurants, go to specific art gallery openings and buy clothes or wedding presents in well-known fashionable stores. The James Bond novels by Ian Fleming were noted for their 'naming' of consumer goods – a prestigious brand of drink, of car. Similarly, in *Sex and the City*, the choice of shoes, for example, went beyond the usual iconography of 'signifying a social type' to an identifiable brand, a narrative existent in its own presence. Whether the viewer identified with a capitalist consumer ideology or took the series as a parody of such a value system is up to her (the target audience member is presumably a 'her').

Television is a conservative medium, but changes in society inevitably produce ideological changes in television production. We can certainly see such changes in the US domestic sitcom since the 1990s, as the domestic situation of many of its targeted audience moved outside the traditional nuclear family of husband, wife and children, out of the large family home into the small urban apartment, and out of the anxieties and pleasures experienced through the different power relations between those of different ages in the family into the anxieties and pleasures experienced in interacting with one's contemporaries.

What new pleasures await us (and do they tell us anything about changes in contemporary society)? Many new shows introduced in the 2004 US season have crashed and burnt, but the two most successful, shown on American ABC, are *Desperate Housewives* and *Lost*. The former takes a 'campy comedic look at the secret lives of sexually frustrated wives' (it sounds soapy but is described as a 'series'). *Lost* is about '48 strangers who survive a horrific plane crash only to be stranded on a desert island with some gnarly creatures'. It sounds like a fictional version of reality TV survivor programs. Perhaps *Housewives* is *Friends* and *Sex and the City* now married and suburban (from Josh Grossberg at http://primetimetv.about.com; viewed 26 October 2004).

The sitcom appears to have begun in the USA (the first perhaps in 1947), but a large number of sitcoms have been produced in Britain and have a more varied selection of basic situations than are covered by Taflinger's three-part analysis of US subgenres. An excellent web facility is at www.british-sitcom.co.uk/list.shtml (viewed 17 October 2004), which has an alphabetical listing of more than 800 British sitcoms, together with a shorter list of the 'top 50 shows' and access from the lists to many specific program details. A glance down the lists reveals the variety and originality of many of these series. The British sitcom differs from the US sitcom in its deployment of narrative features: as the Wikipedia comments, 'The British sitcom tends to rely less on quick-fire jokes and quirky characters than plots, the analysis of the British individual and exaggerated caricatures of everyday stereotypes.' Perhaps there is more inclination towards the *M*A*S*H* style of humour than in the USA; that is, black humour found in a seriously painful situation. The Wikipedia comments on the British sitcom *Steptoe and Son*, the rag-and-bone father and son (a dark reversal of the family 'domestic sitcom'): '[It] can be heart-breaking as the ambitions of Harry are quashed by his needy, manipulative father.' (For further comparative comments on the British sitcom, see www.wordiq.com/definition/Britcom; viewed 19 October 2004.)

The sitcom genre: narrative deployment

The group of characters, rather than the individual character, is usually the narrative focus in the sitcom. It is from the interaction of these characters, rather than the action of one character, that the comedy develops. (In tragic drama, on the other hand, the focus is more typically on the individual character, especially the 'tragic hero'.) This gives a social rather than an individual emphasis to the storyline(s) and a static rather than a dynamic effect to the narrative sequencing of events. In the sitcom, it is the group of characters and the possibilities of their interaction that drive the actions in the plot. The sitcom begins with the characters. (Propp's Russian fairy tale, on the other hand, begins with the events; characters are merely devices to carry out those events.)

This observation is borne out by BBC online instructions to writers wanting to submit comedy scripts for possible production. The BBC web site *writersroom* gives guidelines for 'Writing Narrative Comedy' for television. Unlike the panoramic outdoor vistas that film can pan across so well, the more intimate reception context of television favours the close-up on facial expressions or the mid-distance shot of two or three people talking together. It is not surprising therefore that the BBC guidelines centre their suggestions on the characters:

> When planning a new idea, the characters should come first and if they are the right characters they will arrive with their world attached . . . Think about the people first, give them histories, test them out in different situations where they are under pressure and see how they react, think about what makes them happy

or scared or angry, write monologues for each character in that character's tone of voice . . . Make the people authentic, put them in an authentic world and then find their comic tone.

> (www.bbc.co.uk/writersroom/writing/tvcomedy.shtml; 13 October 2004)

In these instructions you note the difference between the synthesis of narrative asked for from writers and the analysis of narrative that the critical viewer might offer. The BBC guidelines emphasise 'authenticity', the 'right characters' bringing 'their world' (their human *Umwelt*) with them. A critical stance, on the other hand, emphasises the mediation of the television experience and the constructedness of the world (the diegesis) presented in the drama, the artfully chosen *mise en scène* and mode of address. What seems 'authentic' to the scriptwriter, and to the BBC producers if they accept the script – and to you or me as compliant viewers – derives from shared ideological perspectives and generic expectations.

Given that each episode in a sitcom series is in some way a repetition of the previous episodes, and given that the narrative of the sitcom is usually generated by the nature of the characters (and hence the nature of their interaction), it is not surprising that the characters in the sitcom usually change little over time. This also facilitates reruns and repeats in any order. Critics of the sitcom have focused on this static nature, and linked it to a conservative ideology. For example, '[TV's] repetitive structures/formulas offer ritualistic reassurance but inscribe a static view: the lack of development (particularly in the series) reinforces the status quo and, in particular, presents the family as unchanging' (www. brown.edu//Departments/MCM/courses/MC11/outline/TV_narrative_outline.htm; 14 October 2004). However, a long-lasting sitcom like *Friends* might show developments in individual characters and changes in their interrelation, so that the storyline acquires a direction, a more serial-like sequence, and, in consequence, more soap opera-like potential. (The British crime series *The Bill* has suffered a notable transformation of this type, as mentioned in chapter 12.)

The soap opera genre: ideology

The soap opera remains a more conservative television genre. Its origins mark it as the 'domestic' genre par excellence. In 1932 the detergent manufacturers Procter & Gamble sponsored a program, a daytime serial domestic comedy, to advertise Oxydol, a washing powder. The serial's name was *The Puddle Family*. Hence the term 'soap', and hence also the typical emphasis on family, or at least a group, in these serials. The term 'opera' was added in the late 1930s or early 1940s – and is usually 'taken to be a reference to the fact that most soap dramas had a marked tendency to be rather larger than life and often prone to indulge in melodramatic excess' (Kilborn 1992: 141). Soaps, unlike sitcoms, are always serials, but unlike the film serial of a set number of episodes they are never-ending – or at least they continue as long as audience interest, and sponsorship finance, lasts.

Helena Sheehan, a lecturer in media studies in Ireland, has recorded her own experiences as a viewer of soap operas:

> Television soap operas came into the world and into my own life in America in the 1950s. It was my mother and not me who was their target audience, but I saw as much of them as school holidays and parental indulgence would allow. They were utterly addictive and I have been hooked since then. Women would organise their days around their 'stories' and they became an essential ritual of everyday life. These stories were meant to be about ordinary lives of ordinary people in ordinary towns of the time, although it was extraordinary how many affairs, surprise appearances and disappearances, exotic diseases, afflictions of amnesia, murders, kidnappings and frauds befell such a small number of characters in such small towns.
>
> (www.comms.dcu.ie/sheehanh/itvsoap.htm; viewed 2 September 2002)

Perhaps you recognise some of these storylines from your own viewing. Note the use of 'their' to signify ownership or identification: 'women would organise their days around their stories'. We will see that identification with some stories, but not others, in the accounts of Australian schoolgirls given by Patricia Palmer Gillard, to be discussed shortly.

Looking back into her own past, Sheehan can see the conservative ideological audience positioning that she and others then took for granted as natural:

> These daytime dramas did take up matters rarely permitted on primetime television then, such as marital breakdown, frigidity, extramarital sex, alcoholism, professional malpractice. They did so, however, within tightly circumscribed boundaries. Although these serials featured many transgressions of traditional values, it was unthinkable to question those values. Whatever problems and pitfalls characters encountered in their pursuit of the American Dream, they never ceased to believe in it. Their tragedies were due to natural disasters or human failings, but there was nothing wrong with God, marriage, motherhood, apple pie or the American way.
>
> That was by and large what most people in this society naively believed. It was certainly what everyone I knew believed. However, for those who did see beyond it and would have raised further questions, there was always the black list to prevent them. It was a conservative form produced by an extremely conservative and confident society.

The 'black list' referred to is that associated with McCarthyism in the USA during the 1950s, when suspected 'unAmerican activities' in the motion picture and broadcasting industries were rigorously investigated. This Cold War period of intense scrutiny coincides with the decade of initial growth of the television industry so it is not surprising that the most successful and hence most common narrative genres developed specifically for television, the sitcom and the soap opera, should be conservative in ideology. Although television was first used commercially in 1941, its rapid expansion came after the end of World War II. From 1948 to 1950 in the USA, there was an especially rapid increase in the number of television sets owned: 350,000 by July 1948, 2,000,000 by August 1949 and more than five million by April 1950 (www.tvhistory.tv; 12 October 2004).

Moving forward to the early 1980s, Patricia Palmer Gillard, a teacher who did postgraduate work at that time, interviewed Australian schoolgirls between the ages of thirteen and a half and fourteen and a half (Cranny-Francis & Gillard 1990). The aim of her research was 'to understand how girls of this age defined their experience of television viewing: the meaning it had in relationships with friends and family and its significance to the way they thought about themselves in the present and the future' (p. 172). The following is part-summary and part-quotation of her major findings.

The girls' favourite television programs were soaps, and '. . . the reasons they gave for loyalty to favourite programs were strikingly similar. Girls enjoyed programs which they felt were "true to life", "realistic", "down to earth", and which usually concerned people their age and older . . .' (p. 172). They usually didn't like documentaries, the news and nature shows. These were 'boring' (p. 173) – although in the sense of being true to actual experience, these programs could be described as more 'realistic'. For the girls, 'real' meant 'real' on a personal level, an experience they could identify with, not real in the sense of factual. Gillard noted:

> Whatever the kinds of interests the girls described, the striking finding throughout the interviews was the association of 'realistic' with an ability to be involved with the situations and the people in a particular programme. There was not one girl whose television viewing showed an undifferentiated enjoyment of a wide range of programmes. Girls were very definite about favourite programmes and their reasons for choosing them. However, their definition of 'realistic' and 'true to life' was not that of an outsider making a judgement about 'the way life is', but was more an intuitive response to the authenticity of the characters and events portrayed.
>
> (p. 178)

For example, one girl commented on the portrayal of a marriage in the soap, *The Sullivans*: 'Her wedding wasn't like weddings now, it was different. They looked like they were really, truly in love. It was more emotional – people really felt about it. Now, people just get married because everyone expects it' (p. 175).

However, Gillard's comment 'more an intuitive response' (a 'natural' response?) might efface the girls' 'learning of ideology'. Cranny-Francis (the co-author) comments:

. . . an alternative reading might be that the girls are learning the conventions of the soap opera genre, the genre characterised as 'women's television' (in the same way that romantic novels are characterised as 'women's fiction') . . . [Perhaps] what the girls are concerned with is not so much 'realism' as 'consistency', that characters and events are consistent – not by reference to 'reality', but to the conventions of the genre in which they are operating.

(pp. 177–8)

Robyn Warhol, discussed later in this chapter, offers a particularly subtle reading of 'learning to be feminine'.

When a new soap began, girls in a particular group of friends decided whether it would be one of 'their' shows to watch (remember Sheehan's comments on women's ownership of and identification with specific soaps). Friends liked to compare each other with the soap characters, although this comparison might be put together with traits from different soap characters, even male characters. However, this applied to talking about themselves in the present. I quote Gillard's important observations and conclusions:

. . . when it came to using television characters to predict their own future, to represent themselves as adults, the picture was quite different. Diversity and complexity gave way to uniformity. The girls used a narrow range of qualities repeatedly to represent their future selves: they aspired to be friendly, under-standing, and to live in a happy home, married and with children. The models for this future self-representation were provided by sisters, mothers and female, not male television characters . . . when it came to representing their adult selves, the girls were apparently channelled into a narrow range of options which empha-sised interpersonal skills, homemaker, mother. And they felt unable to appropri-ate qualities from male characters.

(p. 174)

Since the male characters still typically had the more authoritative occupational roles in the soaps, this limited the range of imagined futures. The girls' responses give an insight into the effects of ideology – what seems culturally natural – on audience positioning, in reinforcing conservative and established values (see also Fiske & Hartley 2003: 11–14, 157–8).

The origin of the 'soap' as a daytime serial for women is supposed to per-sist in the storylines – centred on domestic crises, and focusing on the relations and emotions of characters rather than action. When the soap was transferred to the evening, the first being *Peyton Place* in 1964, more action and varied locations were introduced to cater for the assumed interests of a 'wider' audi-ence: that is, men. These expanded soaps were sometimes given the genre 'super-soap'.

The soap opera: narrative deployment

First a caveat (a warning), which is relevant to all the chapters in this book, but which especially needs to be remembered when studying soap opera. In studying narrative in a media text we must initially note two features: first, the medium in which the media text is realised; second, the social practices associated with the production and reception of that media text. The kind of narrative analysis that has proved helpful for the study of one medium will not necessarily translate readily to the study of another. Modern literary theories of narrative typically derived from the study of prose fiction, especially the novel, with the assumption of a single author and a private context of reception (reading). The study of film introduced the necessity to study a media text of image as well as language, with the contribution of many agencies, commercial and creative, and a public context of reception (viewing in a cinema). And then television: chapter 12 pointed out some of the effects that the social practices of production and reception had on narrative produced for television. Nowhere are these effects more pronounced than in the genre of soap opera. The caveat reminds us that we must suit the kind of narrative analysis we do to the genre in its media context, rather than assume that narrative theories derived from the study of other media can be uncritically applied.

Two comments are invariably made on the narrative of the soap opera: one, it is non-linear and, two, it is open-ended. These are statements made about what is traditionally called 'plot', the narrative ordering of events. 'Non-linear sequence of events' can describe any kind of disordering or repetition. 'Open-ended sequence of events' describes a lack of closure or dénouement. What implications do these observations have for the study of 'plot' in the soap opera? 'Plot', the causal relation of a sequence of actions, was the central concern of Aristotle's analysis; character was a secondary concern, although for Aristotle the better plot developed from the appropriate character traits (such as virtue for a hero). But here in the soap opera the concept of 'plot' is better replaced by the concept of 'storyline'. What emerges instead as the central concept for studying the soap opera is 'character' and the interaction of characters.

In the soap opera genre, what is usually first planned is the setting, the social context: a small town, a country district, a hospital. This remains relatively constant from episode to episode. It provides continuity for viewers, and the limited number of sets (typically indoor) reduces production costs. In an analysis of television programs, it is always worth noting the proportion of 'in-studio' to 'outdoor' shooting, since it is usually related to the available budget; for example, in episodes of the soap opera *Days of Our Lives*, a story of families in the town of Salem, characters frequently encounter each other in an 'outdoor' shopping mall, Salem Place, which is patently fake, an indoor set. A serial that airs a one-hour episode every day obviously has to have relatively low production values (the amount of time and money spent on the way the show looks on screen).

This setting is populated with characters, typically in groups, such as one or more extended families or the medical staff, who interact in the various (familiar) sets. Some accounts of soaps speak of 'social realism', but I consider this a misnomer. In all soaps, the crises and dramas of 'everyday life' are unrealistically exaggerated in number, although there are cultural differences in the 'realistic' social identification of the characters. In US soaps, characters are usually handsome, beautiful, rich and generally enviable, by materialist values. In the UK, soaps have more typically focused on working-class communities, with specific geographical settings, and with more 'realistic' social concerns. (Robert C. Allen attributes this to the origin of British soaps in the regional locations of commercial broadcasting in the UK, in contrast to the centralised and non-commercial BBC. *Coronation Street* began in Manchester in 1960. www.museum.tv/archives/etv/ S/htmlS/soapopera/soapopera.htm; viewed 19 October 2004.) In contrast, US soaps float more freely in an undifferentiated environment of wealth, while the Australian soaps (that is, their characters) interact in a lifestyle of middle-class suburban comfort and good weather.

The field (subject matter) of soap opera is overwhelmingly that of interactions between characters, but the 'storyline' developed in those interactions is subjectively interpreted. In an illuminating article, 'Feminine intensities: Soap opera viewing as a technology of gender' (1998), Robyn R. Warhol contrasts the 'naive' viewer, the one who tunes into a soap opera episode for the first time, with the 'experienced' viewer, a long-term viewer of the serial, who therefore has a knowledge of the 'back story'; that is, what has happened in previous episodes. She writes, 'Occupying the reading position of the experienced viewer means being able to interpret the unspoken aspects of the soap opera narrative: the long looks and enigmatic remarks exchanged between characters, the double-takes, the pauses in dialogue, and the seemingly arbitrary cutting off of scenes upon certain characters' entrances.' (www.genders.org/g28/g28_intensities.html; viewed 18 October 2004.)

Warhol speculates explicitly on the different readings of a particular storyline in *As the World Turns* that differently experienced viewers might make. (She describes the storyline as 'Emily's desperate attempts to interfere with Samantha's affair with Craig so that she might become romantically involved with Craig herself' – a summary that suits the purpose of, for example, a television program schedule.) These are viewers for six days, for six months, for six years, for sixteen years, for twenty-six years, for thirty-six years (!), and 'the plot' that these viewers understand differs considerably according to their knowledge of the back story. (The television soap *As the World Turns* began in 1956; it was sponsored by Procter & Gamble, the same detergent manufacturers who sponsored the first radio soap in 1932. Obviously at that time the advertiser was satisfied that the genre appealed to its target demographic.)

Warhol concludes, 'The current text sometimes drops allusions to details of back story, so that the more initiated can put together the basics of the long-term plot, but the experienced viewer who has gone through the "feelings" of all those years of story will have a different relation to what is happening on the soap today.' She points out the difficulties this gives the academic who wants to analyse 'soap opera plots' (over and above the difficulties described by Hernstein Smith, discussed in chapter 3). In effect there is no single 'objectively' closed plot (whether as summary or as full narrative), only an open-ended weaving of storylines. Viewers will subjectively interpret 'the plot' according to their background knowledge of the characters and their previous interactions, potentially gained not only from their period of viewing but also from the reading of soap magazines, from interaction on soap fan web sites and so on.

Chapter 12 described the agency involved in the sequence of production steps of a television narrative, but it is helpful to reconsider these matters with particular reference to the writing of soap opera. In the following paragraph I summarise these notes from the online article of Robert C. Allen, who writes of 'the genre's unique mode of production' (he uses 'plot line' rather than 'storyline').

First, the head writer (more usually female than for other television genres) 'charts the narrative course for the soap opera over a six-month period and in doing so determines the immediate (and sometimes permanent) fates of each character, the nature of each intersecting plot line, and the speed with which each plot line moves toward some (however tentative) resolution'. Second, 'she supervises the segmentation of this overall plot outline into weekly and then daily portions, usually assigning the actual writing of each episode to one of a team of scriptwriters ("dialoguers" as they are called in the business)'. Third, the scripts return to the head writer for her approval. They then become the basis for the production of each episode. Fourth, 'the long-term narrative trajectory of a soap opera is subject to adjustment as feedback is received from viewers by way of fan letters, market research, and . . . the weekly Nielsen ratings figures'. (www.museum.tv/archives/etv/S/htmlS/soapopera/soapopera.htm; 19 October 2004.)

The head writer thus has considerable power over the 'creation and maintenance of each soap opera narrative world' (its diegesis), but the storylines she charts must develop the 'lives' of the existing characters acceptably. 'Any head writer brought in to improve the flagging ratings of an ongoing soap is constrained in her exercise of these options by the fact that many of the show's viewers have a better sense of who the show's characters are and what is plausible to happen to them than she does.' Again we see the primacy of character over storyline, or the development of 'plot', in the soap opera narrative.

The narrative open-endedness of the soap opera means that storylines proliferate – and to do this, characters must also proliferate. This means interactions between characters proliferate. As dialogue, rather than action, is the usual nature of interaction in the soap opera genre (compare the usual 'interaction' of violence in the genre of action drama), this means that talk between characters is the main vehicle of the soap opera narrative. (Note above that scriptwriters 'are called dialoguers in the business'.) On the pragmatic side, this structure facilitates the context of reception: the same 'event' is repeatedly discussed between different characters so that a viewer can leave the room or miss a complete episode and still 'catch up' on the lives of the characters when 'she' (producers assume) returns. On the theoretical side, feminist analysis has studied the proliferation of talk in relation to 'women's culture' and socially assumed understandings of 'the feminine'. For example, in 'Fables and endless genealogies: Soap opera and women's culture', Mary Ellen Brown and Linda Barwick write:

> Soap opera characters talk in clichés, they talk to themselves, they talk on the telephone, they lie, they dissemble, they encourage others to get it off their chests, to confess, to tell it like it is. Whereas the ideal woman in patriarchal discourse is silent or silenced through her construction in dominant or masculine discourse as unproblematic – the 'fulfilled' housewife, the selfless mother, the innocent virgin, the happy whore – the woman in the soaps embodies the contradictions inherent in women's lives. In the soaps no one 'truth' is ever allowed to predominate in the multiple story lines that refuse to tie things into neat, unified happy endings. 'And they all lived happily ever after' is one of the basic masculine myths challenged by soap operas.
>
> (*Continuum: The Australian Journal of Media & Culture*, vol. 1, no. 2 (1987), at wwwmcc.murdoch.edu.au/ReadingRoom/1.2/Brown.html; 19 October 2004)

Taking a feminist analysis further to consider 'gender' rather than 'woman', Robyn R. Warhol's article, 'Feminine intensities', analyses the 'ebb and flow' of soap opera storylines and viewer response. I quote, selectively:

> . . . it had been my impression that particular episodes [of *As the World Turns*] tend to be unified around the representation of certain sets of emotions . . . anxious days, angry days, erotic days, joyous days . . . My analysis of all the scenes in [six weeks of] episodes indicates this is generally true . . . [However] the 26 episodes are dominated by the expression of *Angst*, in the forms of worry, concern, tension, anxiety, dread, suspense, depression, and unsatisfied sexual desire, except for those episodes that function as the crisis point in a particular storyline, where the dominant emotions are anger, terror, and erotic gratification. [A footnote here indicates that 'this particular configuration of dominant emotions, especially the emphasis on worry and anxiety', may be 'peculiar to *As the World Turns*'.] The emotional wave pattern cuts across the familiar five-day pattern of a 'miniclimax' on Wednesday and a 'cliffhanger' on Friday . . . After 10 days or two weeks of tension/worry/suspense/anxiety, one or more of the subplots will culminate in a crisis day of rage/terror/eros.
>
> (www.genders.org/g28/g28_intensities.html; viewed 18 October 2004)

At the same time, other storylines continue. Warhol adds that 'some brief scenes' from other storylines (which she calls 'subplots') 'reflecting happiness, warmth or affection' will always be present in the crisis episode and in the 'build-up' and 'recovery' episodes before and after the crisis.

The 'crisis' episode is not a resolution, since the open-endedness of soap opera narrative does not permit 'plot closure'. Rather, the narrative of soap opera, described above, tends to a 'wave pattern'. In Warhol's words, 'This wave pattern contributes to the rhythm of suspense in the serial form, and results from the form's radical resistance of closure: no subplot is ever really resolved, as the undertow of emotional repercussion after the crisis keeps the pattern of affect constantly moving.' (The pattern of affect is here the viewer's emotional response to the viewing.) Warhol's insight, from studying the comments of long-term viewers (and being one herself) is that, although viewers' responses are certainly not identical to each other (viewers don't simply take up the emotion evinced by a character), and are sometimes quite negative (disapproving of the storyline), these responses nonetheless 'follow the pattern of intensities set by the soap's plotline: even the viewers' ironic outrage (a negative response) ebbs and flows with the climaxes of the story'. Her subtle conclusion is that '"Feminine" emotional experience, in this view, does not emanate from the female body or even from any given woman's psychology. It is a process structured by culturally produced and received intensities.' This understanding of 'feminine gender', as a subject position, can be taken up by a viewer of any sex. 'Any long-term soap opera viewer whose daily mood tracks with the structure of the series is submitting, therefore, to a technology of gender, a process that patterns and reinforces what the culture assumes feminine emotion ought to be.'

This 'feminine' wave pattern, with its ebb and flow of affect, stands in marked contrast to the Aristotelian plot of closure, resolution, dénouement ('well-constructed plots must conform to the pattern' of 'a whole . . . which has a beginning, a middle and an end'; McQuillan 2000: 41). Certainly, in the conclusion of his book-length study, N. J. Lowe's characterisation of the classical plot could be called 'masculine', in Warhol's terms: '. . . above all, classical plotting is teleological: it asserts the deep causality and intelligibility of its world even where it denies human access to direct apprehension or control. As such, it is a uniquely powerful system for the narrative articulation of claims about the order of the world' (Lowe 2000: 260).

Conclusion

This chapter has focused on the different narrative structures of sitcoms and soap operas in order to examine their different ideological operations. In chapter 2, the term 'metanarratives' was used to refer to 'the stories or myths, through which a culture tells itself its ideology, its idea of what is natural in its social order'. In the light of this understanding, we could paraphrase Lowe's statement above: classical plotting has been a uniquely powerful system for telling metanarratives; that is, for articulating the dominant ideology. From this perspective, the 'feminine' narratives of the soap opera can be read as subversive, undermining the 'masculine' assumptions of an intelligible and objective world order.

Part 4

Radio and print journalism

Chapter 14

Structures of radio drama

Anne Dunn

The history of radio drama is to a large extent a history of theorising the radio medium; it charts the discovery of the nature of radio and its relationship to the listener. Radio plays began as plays on radio. In the early days of radio, few writers thought to write specifically for radio. It was considered a good medium on which to broadcast plays written for the theatre; its distinguishing feature, the absence of the visual dimension, was not considered a problem. Plays are, after all, a literary form, and the canon of classical drama was prized for its language, its use of words, rather than for what you could see happening on stage. Andrew Crisell, who has written extensively about radio (1994, 1997, 2000), has pointed out that until the sixteenth century at least people spoke of 'hearing' a play rather than seeing it, reflecting the relationship of drama to poetry in rhythm and rhyme. There are examples of this usage in Shakespeare's plays: Hamlet says, 'Follow him friends; we'll hear a play tomorrow.' The word 'audience' is derived from the Latin 'audire', to hear.

Crisell (2000) attributes an increased concentration on visual effects in theatre to the development over time of new staging technology – such as perspective in scenery at the end of the seventeenth century – and artistic innovations, such as the elaborate machinery, spectacular sets and costumes of the Paris Opera of the early eighteenth century. The result was that, by the time of Dryden and Pepys, people were speaking of going to 'see' plays. In the eighteenth century the term 'spectators' from the Latin 'spectare', to see, became an acceptable synonym for 'audience'. The eighteenth and nineteenth centuries saw improvements in stage lighting, making a range of innovative visual effects possible; and of course the twentieth century saw the introduction of those quintessentially visual mass media, film and television, completing our association of drama with spectacle.

Yet through the twentieth and into the twenty-first century, drama in the 'blind medium' of radio has developed. It prospered before television and has survived since, reasonably securely in Europe, more tentatively in Australia and the USA. In the 1920s drama on radio made no concessions to its lack of vision; in fact, the BBC behaved as though listeners could somehow tell if the performers were not appropriately costumed, and when producing variety shows even included dancers. Until theatre managers were able to prevent their productions being recorded without authorisation, the BBC simply used to broadcast plays, variety shows and music hall live, as outside broadcasts directly from the theatres. During music hall acts such as jugglers or dancers, listeners had to infer what was happening from the reactions of the audience in the theatre.

By the end of 1925 the BBC had a revue program called *Radio Radiance* that consisted entirely of light entertainment material written specifically for radio, and this program produced the first entertainer whose celebrity was created by radio, comedian Tommy Handley. In 1933 producers who feared radio would steal their livelihood excluded the BBC from theatres, so it was forced to set up its own variety department. It still continued to make few concessions to the medium, putting actors in costume and make-up and using a live studio audience.

Over the 1920s and 1930s, as the medium became established and audiences grew, a growing number of dramatists felt radio was worth writing for – among them J. B. Priestley, Tyrone Guthrie and Dorothy L. Sayers. But the distinctiveness of the medium in these very early days of radio was thought to lie not in its blindness but in a sort of clairvoyance: its ability to enable listeners to visualise dramas of a kind that would not be possible within the confines of a stage. The result of this belief was a number of dramatic productions so ambitious in scope that listeners would have had the greatest difficulty in following them. For example, the program notes for a 'stageless drama' called *Speed* expressed a rather tentative confidence that the events of the drama would be self-evident: 'There is . . . no occasion to give details of scenes for the play is self-contained and demands no introduction nor any "stage directions". If the author has been successful, this fantasy of the gods on high Olympus and the speed-mad, self-destructive mortals below will tell its own story in its own way' (quoted in Crisell 2000, from Briggs 1981: 120).

By the mid 1930s it was realised that there were limits to the visualising faculty of listeners. Theorists returned to the centrality of the voice on radio and the ability of radio to create 'an autonomous yet intelligible world of pure sound that required no visualisation at all' (Crisell 2000: 467). In other words, the emphasis was again placed on the ear not the eye.

Radio comedy

Comedy on radio had also to make a transition from stage to sound. Many vaudeville comedians saw great opportunities in radio. The lack of an audience was, however, a major problem. Radio required projecting a personality through a box and not via a live audience. These former stage comedians based their humour and timing on the response of their audience. Now they could not hear their audience and had to judge how best to deliver their lines. Some succeeded, but others, despite stage and film successes, failed miserably. One way early radio producers solved the problem was to bring a live audience into the radio studio. This worked well on the whole, but the problem again was always that the inevitable visual elements of an act – a shrug, a wink, a grimace – might cause gales of studio audience laughter but leave a listening audience at home completely out of the joke, an alienating experience for them.

Early radio comedy was nonetheless very much like vaudeville, relying on songs and banter between comedy teams such as Billy Jones and Ernie Hare in the USA. Gradually, stand-up routines developed into comedic narratives and continued to become more sophisticated as radio moved into the 1930s. It was at the beginning of this decade that two of US radio's greatest comedians made their broadcast debuts. Jack Benny and Fred Allen were actually friends, but radio created an on-air feud between them, effectively making them characters in a story. Early radio personalities appeared as 'themselves'. Later narrative series contained actors portraying characters unlike themselves. Jack Benny was not an actor, but a complex and detailed 'life' was built up around him and his cast involving not only his professional life but also an on-air version of his 'personal' life, with cast members going over to his house, going shopping or on trips, taking the show on the road and getting into various scrapes. This has a direct contemporary equivalent in the TV show *Seinfeld* (hailed as highly innovative for precisely its integration of the 'real' Jerry Seinfeld with a fictional life).

The epistemological unreliability of sound

The reason people had such trouble knowing how to use radio is that understanding radio is problematic, because sound is epistemologically unreliable; that is, we cannot know the true nature of things as reliably through our hearing as we can through sight. Of course our eyes can deceive us too, but not quite to the same degree as our ears, when we are listening via the electronic medium of radio. Erving Goffman used semiotics to identify the sound signification in the conventions of radio drama and how they are meaningful (Goffman 1974). Radio – the sound – exists in time, not space, as visual signs do. Because of this, radio signs are constantly threatened by silence, because silence portends non-existence. Moreover, without vision, sounds can be misleading as to what they represent.

The easiest way to make this clear is to describe sound effects. Sound effects were originally simulations of actual sound. Before the availability of recorded 'real' sound effects on CD, studio technicians used to do things like open and close an umbrella rapidly to evoke the flight of a pigeon, crumple cellophane to suggest the sound of a fire, bang coconut shells together to create the clop of a horse's hooves, or shake a cardboard box with gravel in it to convey the sound of marching troops. The fact that these sound effects work so well on radio and yet are not what we think they are – an umbrella is not a pigeon, nor a coconut shell a horse – points up this untrustworthiness of radio sound.

On the other hand, this same unreliability, which can be seen as a disadvantage, is also a great strength of radio, a dramatic strength. And this was demonstrated by the very first play ever written for radio, by Richard Hughes in 1924. Called *A Comedy of Danger*, it was set in a coal mine in which the lights have failed; in other words, in total darkness. For the first time in its history, theatre had become something that could be presented in the dark; or, to put it another way, something that could portray the invisible. It is partly for this reason that radio has been called 'the invisible medium' (Lewis & Booth 1989). Another famous play written for radio in 1954 is Dylan Thomas' *Under Milkwood*, and it too begins in darkness. The play opens with a single soft voice: 'To begin at the beginning. It is spring, moonless night in the small town, starless and bible black, the cobblestreets silent and the hunched courters'-and-rabbiters' wood limping invisible down to the sloe-black, slow, black, crowblack fishing-boat-bobbing sea . . .'

The narrator's voice breaks the silence and enables the listener to see with the mind's eye the dark and sleeping village. Radio allows us to see in the dark. So radio's unreliability as a means of getting the audience to visualise accurately led to the creation of wholly original forms of drama, in which much is evoked but there is nothing to see. These forms of drama consisted not only of plays set in literal darkness, like *A Comedy of Danger* or the opening of *Under Milkwood*, but also of plays with abstract themes. In such a play, the 'action' might be all internal to a single character, a debate or crisis in which the mind of a single character is split into different 'voices'.

The limitations of sound can also be exploited for comedic or psychological ends. For example, in Harold Pinter's *A Slight Ache*, written in 1959, an elderly couple take into their home a third character who was selling matches outside their garden gate. Because they discuss this character and talk to him, we readily assume he exists. But then we realise that the character never speaks, we never hear from him, and so – because silence on radio suggests non-existence – we begin to wonder whether this character might in fact be a figment of the elderly couple's imagination, a means by which they can communicate to each other thoughts and feelings that they might find too painful to express directly. But the point is we don't know – and this ontological uncertainty is central to the meaning of the play. It is an uncertainty that of course would be immediately and damagingly resolved if the play were to be performed on a conventional stage.

The Pinter play also exemplifies the way in which silence can be powerful on radio. Correctly used, prepared for, it can be as expressive as words. There is an important distinction between the use of dramatic silence and 'dead air'. Dead air is just that – the absence of any sound at all. The fade to dead air, the 'fade out', is the audio equivalent of cinema or television's fade to black: it signifies the end of a scene and heralds a shift forward in time or to another space. There are lots of such short silences in radio; but if they go on too long they are disturbing. We look at the radio and wonder: what's happened? Has the station gone off air? Dead air can cause concern to listeners if it goes on too long; and they tend to tune to another station to check the problem isn't with their radio. Dead air must exist only for less time than it takes a listener to reach for the dial or button.

But the other kind of silence, dramatic silence, is not absolute silence. It is the silence of a pause for thought, of reaction, of an action that interrupts the flow of sound. It can be filled with anticipation, expectation, wonder. During this kind of silence, things happen invisibly, in our minds. When sound – speech – is abruptly halted, listeners are immediately alerted to the fact that something has happened. And while they wait to find out what it is, the mind is filled with possibilities: is it a kiss, a blow, a gun, a monstrous apparition? In order for the difference between dead air and dramatic silence to work on radio, it must be not only structural but also technological. These moments of dramatic silence are technically not silence at all; they are atmospheric or ambient noise – what broadcasters refer to as 'atmos'. Unless recorded in a space that has been specially built to create an absence of sound, all spaces and places carry their own audio atmosphere. 'Atmos' refers to whatever sound is left in the recording environment when people stop talking: traffic, air conditioning, a computer motor hum, distant sounds of children playing, the barely perceptible buzz of a fluorescent light or rustle of clothing. It might be no more than the slightest movement of air across the microphone, as someone breathes. Atmos is potentially the most subtle noise we hear on radio.

Acoustics and perspective

Through sound, radio can take us to other places and other times. This flexibility in the handling of time and space is a distinctive characteristic of radio drama. As earlier chapters have described, the manipulation of time and space in cinema required the gradual development of specific visual codes, such as continuity editing, and the development of audience competence in reading those codes.

Compared to radio, flexibility with time and space is difficult and expensive for film or television and quite beyond the limitations of the conventional theatre. On radio, the elements of sound effects, speech and music can move the audience about in both space and time, not just in the way these audio codes are arranged; that is, edited and mixed together – as cinema and television do with the visual – but also in terms of the technical qualities of the sounds.

In addition, we can distinguish between sound acoustics and sound perspective. The acoustics of sound refers to the way it is treated technically, such as the distortion of it for effect. The term 'perspective' refers to the spatial qualities of sounds, such as whether they are heard close up or as if from a distance. Experienced radio actors and producers learned to create perspective just by how close to or far from the microphone the speaker stood. Sound is actually the movement of air – or rather the vibrations in air caused by moving objects, be it the coil or diaphragm of a microphone or the delicate movements inside the human ear. But we can 'hear' space, either through the reverberation of sound on walls and other objects (the bouncing of sound waves off surfaces, with an effect on the listener similar to an echo) or by the distances between different sound sources. If there is reverberation, the sense of a large enclosed space, like a hall or church, is created. If there is no echo, if sound is deadened, then the sense of a small or open space can be created. In both cases, space is created acoustically.

What kind of space it is can be created not only by whether there is reverberation but also by how much reverberation there is and how long that reverberation lasts. A lot of reverberation over a long duration creates the effect of a large empty space, whereas no reverberation produces the sense of outdoor space. A large, furnished interior – a living room, say – is produced by using a little reverberation for a long duration; that is, longer than the normal reverberation time of 0.2 seconds. The opposite effect – a small but echoey room like a bathroom – is created by using a lot of reverberation for a short duration. Meanwhile, if all the sounds emanate from the same point, a lack of space is created. But if one sound is foregrounded against a background of other sounds, more distant ones, then a sense of a larger or extensive space is created. This is what is meant by audio perspective.

Together, acoustics and perspective indicate the spatial dimension of the environment occupied by the sounds. The radio drama studios of the BBC or the Australian Broadcasting Corporation (ABC) contain different acoustic environments built into them. The ABC, for example, has a small 'dead air' space inside the larger one of the studio proper and different floor surfaces, to simulate steps on pavement or wood. The acoustic properties of sound can convey information that on screen or stage we could see at a glance (but which might be very expensive or impossible to create, especially on stage). When radio producers add to the use of acoustics and perspective additional noises, in the form of sound effects and music, they can create specific environments that are immediately recognisable by a listener, such as a busy street, a restaurant or a farm.

Styles of radio drama

Thanks therefore both to the limitations and the evocations of this sound-only medium, radio has added new dimensions to what drama is. Crisell (2000) argues that these new dimensions of radio drama have in turn influenced the conventional stage, particularly the theatre of the absurd. He identifies these dimensions or characteristics as:

1 the substitution of an inner landscape for an exterior one, and the adoption of a flexible attitude towards time and space, which can expand or contract according to the requirements of the characters;
2 the creation of a fluid, indeterminate environment in which the distinctions between fact and fantasy can be and often are blurred;
3 the use of precise, succinct language 'as a kind of weapon against the overwhelmingly problematic and disorderly nature of experience' (Crisell 2000: 472).

Such British writers as Harold Pinter and Tom Stoppard, as well as John Mortimer and Samuel Beckett, have been very committed to radio, employing it as an ideal medium for their considerable skills with the ambiguities and nuances of the spoken word.

By the 1970s advances in radio technology such as FM stereo led to what is called 'acoustic art' in radio drama and features. This arouses fierce argument, with its proponents describing it as a new art form in its own right, and its critics using such phrases as 'a well-puffed curiosity', the product of technicians and producers rather than of writers. At its most extreme, in almost a return to the very first radio productions, these programs do not use words or recognisable speech at all but attempt to construct a narrative with a sequence of realistic recognisable sound effects; not the symbolic evocations of the coconut shells and cellophane but replications of the everyday sounds of the world around us, what radio writer Jonathan Raban calls 'iconic' representations, because of their concern with sounding real.

It can be argued that radio which privileges non-verbal sound – sound effects, music and silence – is much more confusing to the listener than radio drama that acknowledges the fundamental nature of words if communication via the radio medium is to be successful. In this view, noise, music and silence need to play an essentially secondary and supportive role in relation to speech. Too many sound effects can be extremely confusing and seem cluttered to the ear of the listener.

By way of illustration the second part of this chapter examines two excerpts from different examples of radio drama. The first is from a series on the Radio National network of the ABC, called *Airplay*, described as a program of new Australian radio writing and performance. Weekly half-hour dramatic fiction experiments with form and explores a wide range of subjects, genres and styles, aiming to offer innovative and engaging programs. This particular drama was called *Slowianska Street*, by Noelle Janaczewska, and was first broadcast in

September 2001. It is described as 'a requiem for voices and other sounds'. The play 'explores identity and disappearance across the history of 20th-century Europe, from the cities of the 1930s and 1940s to the post-Glasnost era' (ABC 2004).

The writer was apparently inspired by music from Polish composer Gorecki's *Symphony of Sorrowful Songs*, which is used throughout the play. The piece relies heavily on the use of acoustics and perspective as well as the integration of speech and sound effects. This kind of work is characterised by 'multi-tracking'; that is, the use of layers of sound, at differing acoustics and perspectives, built up to create particular effects of complexity and, sometimes, obscurity. It is impossible in a book chapter to convey fully the effects of what is described below, but some description and analysis might help to create a sense of how this kind of 'acoustic art' works, as well as what is possible on radio.

Slowianska Street begins with sound that establishes an exterior perspective, perhaps a street, almost certainly in a town or city, although not one busy with motor traffic. We hear a mix of a church bell in the distance, the murmur of conversation, walking feet on pavement. Gradually, sound that is unclear yet menacing grows in volume, then as it becomes quite loud it gives way to a babble of unintelligible voices with reverberation, speaking Polish. This is supplanted in turn by the tramp of marching feet, in time, suggesting we are hearing soldiers. This fades out and we hear the tolling of bells, mixed with low music (the Gorecki symphony), over which a number of adult voices, men and women, recite people's names and dates (which sound like their birth and death dates so we must assume they are dead), sometimes with anecdotal descriptions. At intervals, the recitation and the music are abruptly interrupted by a chorus that chants 'Slowianska Street'.

Since we have heard street sounds at the start of the play, and know (if we heard the beginning) it is called *Slowianska Street*, we can deduce we are hearing the stories of people from the street. We could go further and infer a temporal and causal sequence, from normal life to military invasion (the interruption of street sounds by the tramp of marching feet and funereal tolling of the church bell) to the death of the individuals. The narrative requires concentration and interpretation on the part of a listener, and far less certainty is possible than if one were watching a conventional Hollywood film, for example. This is the 'fluid, indeterminate environment' Crisell speaks of. Indeed, at this point it is impossible to know whose voice we are hearing. These sounds could as easily represent the memories of an individual as the documentary evocation of historical events. Whichever might be the case, the emotional effect of the sequence is moving and absorbing, an example of the direct appeal of radio to the heart, which is one of the reasons why Marshall McLuhan (1964) called radio a 'hot' medium.

Compare this now with a play that is abstract, in the sense of its being interior, about what is happening in the mind of a character. The play is called *The Mermaid's Tail*, by Lucy Gough, and it was commissioned and broadcast by BBC Radio 4 in 1999. This production used multi-tracking (more than one source of sound) in a less complex way, but the meanings and emotional effect created are no less complex than those of the first example. It begins with a long monologue, mixed with sound effects, of music and water. The other elements it uses are the BBC shipping forecast and documentary material on the mythology of mermaids, written and narrated by Marina Warner. The 'stage directions', which appear in the script, have been removed, since a listener would not have the benefit of them. 'SFX' is a shorthand term for 'sound effects'.

GIRL: (SFX RADIO PLAYING AND WATER RUNNING.) Stupid scales.

(REASSURING HERSELF)

It'd be less with me clothes off.

(DESPAIR)

It should be less than that with all this off!

SFX RADIO ON IN THE BACKGROUND. THE GIRL SINGS TUNELESSLY 'BOBBY SHAFTOE'. SFX GIRL BRUSHING TEETH, WATER SPLOSHING AND RUNNING.

Ouch!

SFX RUNNING WATER

GIRL (INT.):

I float.

Float,

Flesh,

Bone,

Hair,

I float.

Lighter than air.

Float in the bath.

Hair draped around me.

I float.

Like the Lady of Shallot.

(SFX: SHE DISTURBS THE WATER)

Or a fish.

(SILENCE)

Skin stretched silver.

Ridged over bone.

I float.

A pale white corpse.

Mountain ranges breaking surface at their tips.

As an underbelly of coral leads to a dark triangle of submerged forest.

(SHE MOVES IN THE WATER)

Sometimes . . .

Suddenly revealed by the tide pull.

Folds and ridges fall either side,

As the sea erodes the edge.

Carving it.

Shaping it.

A long Atlantic ridge merges . . .

Skin turning bone . . .

(SILENCE)

I could disappear,

Float away.

(SFX: THE GIRL SLOSHES SOME WATER OUT OF THE BATH)

Dissolve in the water,

Sink without trace,

Be swallowed up.

Who'd care?

(SFX REVERBERATION – OF GIRL HOLDING BREATH UNDER THE
    WATER, THEN SWOOSH OF WATER AND CHANGE OF ACOUSTIC AS SHE
    RESURFACES)

A pale naked corpse . . .

Carving my shape . . .

(UNDER THE WATER SFX AND COMING UP AGAIN)

You think you know who I am.

What I want to be.

What I want to do with my life.

But you're wrong,

completely wrong.

(SILENCE)

I swallow words . . .

Skinning each one as it rises,

Gutting it.

Boning it.

Holding words down,

down deep in my belly.

Sustaining myself on a feast of silence.

On the flesh of unspoken words.

Having to be different.

If I try, if I try and hawk up the words, they lodge in my throat like shells.

Only silence can truly express the hugeness of this.

You don't understand me,

understand what it's like, all this changing.

Your words shoal like mackerel,

Darting through the water.

Changing . . .

Changing.

Silently.

Shapeshifting . . .

(DEFIANTLY)

I swim caverns. (Gough 2000)

Later in the play we hear the voice of a mature woman, clearly the young woman's mother, who complains about how long she is being in the bathroom. The play begins with a well-known pop song. Since music can locate us in time and space, a listener can infer the time is now or very recent and the place likely to be Western. That it is England is confirmed almost immediately by the young English-accented female voice over the sound effects of water running into a bath. A distant siren of the kind heard on police cars or ambulances suggests we're in a city. The girl's words: 'Stupid scales . . . it'd be less with me clothes off', tell us she's in a bathroom and is running a bath, if we haven't already realised that.

The title is not announced until two minutes into the play. The title and the talk by Marina Warner tell us that the subject is somehow related to mermaids. However, it is not clear where the commentary is coming from, where it is in the world of the play. Is it the radio (we have heard the sounds of a radio being tuned before Warner starts speaking) and therefore diegetic; that is, in the world of the play, or is it non-diegetic; that is, sound that only the audience, not the characters, can hear? Despite this ambiguity, listeners might have a pretty good idea what is happening. For example, the changes in the acoustics convey that the girl has gone under the water. Words and other sounds work together to create meaning for the listener, but there is room for more than one interpretation of events and the play. It might just be about a young woman who wants to be a mermaid, or it might be about the experience of the eating disorder anorexia nervosa. In fact, in the script, Gough describes the character as 'slightly anorexic' (Gough 2000). The difficulty of knowing exactly what we are hearing remains despite the use of dialogue (between the young woman and her mother); yet we can interpret the audio codes of sound effects, music and talk to set up and follow the narrative more easily than is the case with *Slowianska Street*, which uses few words and no dialogue. This is highly imaginative use of the radio medium that moves us as listeners between worlds, exterior and interior.

The great majority of radio drama today, especially on the various BBC networks, is more conventionally play-like (that is, using a mode of realism) than either of these two examples. In listening to these, we draw upon our knowledge not only of radio but also of theatre and even television; we can 'visualise' what is happening. Radio plays of this kind privilege words, particularly dialogue, while using layers of sound to situate listeners in space and time. All – words, music, sound effects – are narrative elements and serve to construct and develop the story.

Conclusion

In an age of multi-channel digital and interactive television, as well as many other sources of visual mass entertainment and the Internet, it is perhaps remarkable that radio drama has survived at all. In Australia, original commissioned work is heard only on ABC Radio National, which has very small ratings, and there it is constantly at the mercy of budget cuts because, compared to radio talk or music in flow formats, drama is expensive to produce. Similarly, in the USA, except on public radio, drama has all but disappeared. In Britain, radio drama is a more securely established tradition; the radio serial *The Archers* has been going since the 1930s and is still regularly listened to by a loyal audience of a respectable size. The 'quality' UK daily newspapers (such as the *Independent* or the *Guardian*) offer previews and reviews of radio drama, albeit in the context of much more television coverage. In other parts of Europe – Germany and Scandinavia, for example – it is also still a vigorous radio form, although it does not attract large audiences.

Radio drama requires harder work for contemporary audiences accustomed to the ubiquitously visual, which is so much easier to 'read'. Yet radio offers unique dramatic strengths, in its power to create spectacle of the mind and transport the listener to other worlds.

Chapter 15

Radio news and interviews

Anne Dunn

No matter what the radio station, 'the news' is a distinctive form of radio sound. It is obviously not music, and it differs from other radio 'talk' in a number of identifiable ways. News is usually at the 'top of the clock'; that is, the main bulletins occur on the hour. The fact that news usually starts at the top of the hour is an important part of the way radio structures time throughout the radio day. News on the hour is usually announced with an audio 'call to attention'. This could be as simple as a voice cue from an announcer or the 'pips' of a time signal, or it could be as elaborate as the appropriately named 'Majestic Fanfare' that heralds the radio bulletins on the Australian Broadcasting Corporation (ABC), the most widely recognised news theme in Australia. Whatever it might be, nearly all radio stations have some kind of aural cue to the listener that the news is about to begin.

Most radio is live to air; part of establishing the credibility and authenticity of news is that it comes to listeners in the here and now, even though the voice reports of the journalists might have been pre-recorded. In its distinguishing structure and sound, news can be called a genre of radio programming. And just as media theorists and news practitioners distinguish between tabloid and broadsheet newspapers, so we can distinguish subgenres and discourses of radio news. News on radio has a particular, specific mode of speech and register of address. News writing is sufficiently recognisable as a genre for it to be satirisable. The way newsreaders speak is also different from the way other announcers on radio address their audience; it is more formal and less conversational.

The news on commercial music radio, such as the DMG-owned Nova FM in Australia or on Virgin Radio in London (UK), sounds very different from the news on Classic FM (there are stations of this name both in Australia, where it is an

ABC – that is, public service – station, and in Britain, where it is commercial). Listeners recognise all of them as news, and at the same time the differences in sound are part of the marketing of each station, its positioning. News on radio is an event within a usually formulaic structure of repetition and rotation of events, arranged in a sequence in such a way as to disguise the 'seams' or transitions from one to the next. The aim is a seamless flow of sound, within which there are recognisable punctuation marks, of which news is a regular and important structuring one. The news is a part of a radio station's credibility with its listeners. As is reiterated throughout this book whenever news is mentioned, what is selected to be in the news is an attempt to interpret the world and its events to listeners. While it is possible to generalise about what journalists will define as news, the bulletins are also tailored in content and in style to the assumed or desired audience (the **illocutionary audience**, to use Rosemary Huisman's term from chapter 12).

Stories in the news and news values

Journalists refer to episodes in the news as 'stories'; in that sense, narrative can be seen as the professional norm. The professional concept of a news story has both content and form: the reasons for its being identified as a news story – that is, as newsworthy – and the way it is constructed.

The values that identify a person, an event or an issue as newsworthy were set out in chapter 11. They include:

- Consequence or impact: what effects will this story have on the audience? The greater and more direct the effects, the more likely it is to be selected as newsworthy.
- Prominence: important, known people and institutions are more likely to be heard in the news. 'Celebrities' are more likely to make news because being considered newsworthy is part of the phenomenon of celebrity.
- Proximity: may be cultural or geographical, and is an aspect of relevance to the audience. Events 'close to home' are considered more important than ones that occur far away, unless they happen to people or in places culturally close.
- Unambiguity: stories are more likely to be selected if they can be reduced to simple levels, in pursuit of clarity and because broadcast news stories are so short.
- Predictability: stories about or related to known events such as anniversaries, release of statistics, award presentations or launches.
- Unpredictability: an event's rarity or unexpectedness will give it news value.
- Conflict: events are often represented in terms of conflict or oppositions, as an aspect of unambiguity or for dramatic value.
- Human interest: the tragic, the ironic, the cute and so on.
- Timeliness: freshness, newness, immediacy – an overriding concern is to capture the story as close to the moment of its happening as possible. This

is particularly important in radio, which is characterised by its immediacy, its 'liveness' (Conley 2002: 42).

These 'news values' are some of the reasons why some events, issues or people are identified as newsworthy and not others.

Radio news structures

Radio news bulletins typically follow a structure that begins with an audio signal that the news is about to start (the 'call to attention'), sometimes followed by headlines indicating what stories are to come. Next there is a series of individual news stories, beginning with a 'lead' or most important story and often ending with a lighter, so-called 'colour' story and perhaps sports news and weather. This order varies from station to station, affected by the presumed audience for each. Stories in radio news normally take one of three forms, the names of which vary slightly from place to place. The simplest is a 'straight read', 'reader' or 'copy read' story; as the titles imply, this is a written typescript read by a newsreader, without any other sound. The second kind is an 'intro plus voicer', or 'voice story/report'. In this, the newsreader has only one or two sentences of introduction to the story, which conclude with a phrase that introduces the reporter, such as 'More from . . .'. The journalist is then heard reading the second part of the story, occasionally live but more often pre-recorded, and the journalist's voice is the only one we hear. A variation on this form is an introduction by the newsreader followed by a 'grab' (a short piece of audio, usually edited from a longer interview) from a narrator who is not a reporter, but identified as a significant figure in the story ('intro plus grab').

The final form is the 'package' or 'intro plus package'. It includes a newsreader's introduction, again usually quite short and concluding with a spoken 'throw' to the name of the reporter. The second part is a pre-recorded and 'packaged' item, consisting both of the reporter's voice and of the voice or voices ('grabs', 'sound bites' or 'actuality') of relevant people, speaking for themselves, albeit in edited versions. An example of a package is given a little later in this chapter, in the story from the reporter called Luke Lawler about pay television, using a 'grab' of the Opposition communications spokesman. The length of such grabs, as in television news, has become shorter and shorter, as little as four or five seconds, which is really only enough to provide convincing evidence that the person has been spoken to by a journalist. Sometimes, if the event being reported suggests it, there will be other 'actuality'; that is, sound recorded at the scene and mixed with the reporter's and any other voices. An example would be a report of a protest or demonstration, which might begin with the sound of protestors chanting, then the reporter would come in, describing the scene and usually then linking to 'grabs' of such people as the relevant government minister and perhaps someone speaking on behalf of the protestors.

The length of each story type varies but is generally only between fifteen and twenty seconds for a read and fifty seconds for the longest package. The number and type of stories in any bulletin varies according to the length of the bulletin and the particular radio station. Radio stations that play music, especially popular music for a target audience of younger people, tend to run fewer and shorter bulletins than weightier talk-based stations such as ABC Radio National, BBC Radio 4 or National Public Radio (NPR) in the USA. Commercial stations that are music-based tend not to put resources into news (it is relatively expensive to produce), so they rely on news agencies (the 'wires') or syndicated network news reports and have few reporters of their own. This means that the form of their news is likely to feature more read-only stories and fewer 'voicers' and 'packages'.

Radio news and the inverted pyramid

As described in chapter 11, the classic structure for news stories is referred to as an 'inverted pyramid'. Traditionally, journalists have been (and still are) taught to begin each story with a 'lead' or introductory paragraph that contains the most important pieces of information in the story and answers at least two or three key journalistic questions (the 'five Ws and the H'): Who and What, sometimes also Where and When; more rarely, Why and How.

Here is an example from an ABC radio news bulletin: 'Insurance giant AMP has struck an enterprise deal with its staff where family issues are taken into account . . . in return for greater flexibility.' This opening par gives us the Who and the What, and summarises the most important information in the story. Subsequent paragraphs give more information and background.

The inverted pyramid is a newspaper structure, designed to be read by its 'audience' (see chapter 11 for the history of the inverted pyramid and theories about why it developed and has persisted). But radio news is written to be heard. In the same ABC radio bulletin is another story that demonstrates a different structure; one considered more appropriate to radio news. It begins with what is sometimes referred to as the 'tease lead'; that is, a lead or introduction that tells listeners what kind of story they are going to hear. The lead is: 'Pay TV is causing more embarrassment for the Federal Government.' This lead only gives the Who and a bit of the What, by means of a metaphor: pay TV and the Federal Government are personalised and individualised, as if they were able to cause or be caused embarrassment. But listeners do not find out what the source of embarrassment is until the second and subsequent paragraphs; the story unfolds in a narrative structure. There is a disruption to equilibrium, and a character faces change; in this case, the head of the Transport and Communications Department takes the 'blame' and offers to resign over a bungled tender process. The story then introduces a second narrator – in addition to the newsreader, that is – in the form of a reporter, whose voice report tells the story chronologically.

The newsreader goes on to say: 'Luke Lawler reports the government has been forced to abort the tender process for new microwave pay TV licences.' And Lawler is then heard, telling us quite a complicated little saga:

> In January this year, when microwave licence holder Steve Cosser threatened to upstage satellite delivered Pay TV, the Government said it would legislate to block him until satellite Pay TV was on air. That legislation is now in place. But back in January, the government also decided to stop issuing any new microwave licences, terminating the tender process at the last minute. That decision was overturned in the courts, and the tender process went ahead. Now, due to a bureaucratic bungle, the process has again been scrapped.

This story moves in time, between what happened in the past ('In January this year', 'back in January') and the consequences in the present ('that legislation is now in place', 'Now . . . the process has again been scrapped'), but it is essentially a linear chronology, bringing the listener up to date with the story so far. The narrative has no resolution, however, no closure. Moreover, it is an episode that is presented adjacent to another episode in the same overarching story of the introduction of pay TV. The story that immediately follows this one is a copy read, with a 'grab'. It refers not only to what it calls 'the pay TV saga' but also to the department head's offer of resignation:

> The Federal Opposition is renewing its push for a Senate inquiry into the pay TV saga, and is calling for senior Communications Minister Bob Collins to stand aside.
>   Opposition Communications spokesman Richard Alston plans to hold talks with the Democrats today when the Senate resumes sitting.
>   Senator Alston claims the Prime Minister's refused to accept the Department Head's offer to stand aside, to protect Senator Collins.

And then we hear Alston's voice, saying that if the department head's resignation is accepted, then the minister will also have to resign. There is an understood 'meanwhile' at the start of this story; coming as it does straight after the Luke Lawler report, we are effectively being told what else is going on at the same time in another part of the narrative. In its open-ended and fragmentary structure, this story is not unlike that of soap opera.

The second news item about pay TV does not provide a resolution to the story but another episode, which is connected to the first by topic, time (it is also in the present) and conflict. Conflict is a key news value, as is the journalistic require-ment, especially strong in public service broadcasters such as the ABC, to present 'both sides of the story', which is defined as 'balance' and is one of the ways broadcast news constructs news as not only real but also true and fair.

Narrative structures and functions in radio news

The examples above illustrate the application of Todorov's circular narrative process in news, from equilibrium through disruption (Todorov 1977); but in this case there is no possibility of a newly restored equilibrium, at least within the one news story. Lévi-Strauss' narrative theory of binary oppositions and Propp's narrative 'functions' or character roles (discussed by Rosemary Huisman in chapter 3) can also be applied to the use of conflict in news narratives, in the context of stories constructed around heroes and villains and around 'us' and 'them'. It has long been recognised that not everyone has a voice in the news; some people are represented without being able to speak for themselves – they are 'talked about' – whereas others are able to speak. In the example just used, a senior federal politician, Senator Alston, is heard speaking. It is typical to hear from such people in the news; it is not typical to hear from members of the general public or members of minorities, those characterised as deviant or otherwise marginalised. So the cast of characters is quite restricted in news as a form, and this is apparent in radio news in terms of whose voices listeners hear. It is not difficult to find examples of news depicting people, nations or organisations as 'heroes' or 'villains'. News stories about dramatic events, such as accidents or natural disasters, as well as those about salient political issues, such as asylum seekers or acts of violence ('terrorism'), provide a rich source of such oppositions.

Notice how the first of the two stories under discussion began: 'Pay TV is causing more embarrassment for the Federal Government.' This opening sentence assumes knowledge of a context on the part of the listener; otherwise to use the word 'more' is meaningless (a listener who has not heard previous stories, or is unaware of the 'story so far', can infer from the word 'more' that there is a continuing story). These two items are part of what journalists call a 'running story', one the impact of which lasts for several days or even weeks. Often such a story will give rise to other, related ones. 'Currency' is the value whereby something is selected as news because similar issues or events are already in the news.

Because there are so many radio bulletins compared to television news or editions of newspapers, radio stories usually are updates; they are episodes in a continuing story. Because each radio news story is so short – less than a minute, sometimes less than thirty seconds – and bulletins themselves are short, typically five minutes or less (with exceptions, especially in public service radio), radio news has no time to provide a context or background to any story except in the briefest terms. And the open-ended format of radio news stories means that there is no end to them either; they both start and finish in the middle of some larger story. This is also true of radio news bulletins as a whole; they are a collection of stories, usually without any connection between one and the next, and this does not constitute a classic narrative in structural terms. In recent years, however, an increasing use of narrative structures has emerged, and this is taken up in the section headed 'Radio news and narrative' towards the end of the chapter.

Modes of speech on radio and broadcast news writing

The mode of address of radio is uniquely direct. Radio works hard to address each of us personally. Radio presenters talk as if they are talking to one person, and this is the way they are trained. Radio speech strives to create the illusion of personal and verbal interaction, the illusion of participation and response, even though it is essentially a one-way medium, talkback or phone-in radio aside. The way someone talks to an audience in a hall or conference room, where they are addressing people as a group they can see in front of them, is quite different from the way a late-night radio DJ talks to his or her audience. Speakers in a meeting or at a public talk tend to raise their voice slightly, even if amplified (and amplification itself is a clearly artificial device), and to speak carefully and clearly. Very often they will speak from notes.

Radio speech, on the other hand, is intended to sound natural, conversational and spontaneous, even if it is in fact scripted. The challenge of much writing for radio is that it must be written in a way that can be read aloud and sound like spontaneous speech. There is a wide variety of speech forms on radio – including radio drama, considered in chapter 14 – and no single one of them could be said to typify radio talk. But news is quite distinctive, in part because it makes little or no attempt to disguise that this talk is being read from a script. The reason is to stress that this is objective speech, not the opinions of the newsreader. It is part of the claim to truth, which news makes. But even within news bulletins there will be different kinds of speech that are less formal and institutional, in reports from the scene, actuality of participants in and eye-witnesses to events.

Talk is one of the codes of radio; the others are music, sound effects and silence, but words, speech and language constitute the most fundamental code. Even on a music station, the music is organised around speech events, such as news bulletins, but including commercials, weather and announcer talk. Talk is part of the way radio stations market themselves, part of their branding (Potts 1989: 101). If you turn on the radio and use the tuner, not presets, to move from station to station, you'll find that not just the music but especially the way each station 'talks' to you will tell you something about it. There are certainly differences between stations that might play the same kind of music but are in different sectors of the industry. The 'sound', the way the announcers talk to listeners and link the different items, is quite different on a community station, where the announcers are volunteers, from the sound of a network that is part of the national public

Table 15.1: Triple J news opening.

Audio and comments	News script
News begins with a recognisable but electronically distorted version of the well-known ABC Radio News theme. Newsreader has a youthful male Australian voice. Headlines come before station identification, greeting and self-identification. Mixture of formal structures and informal greeting. Speaks much more slowly than commercial counterparts. Content of headline stories selected to interest target audience.	'Justice for the family of murdered backpacker David Wilson and green groups fearful of big changes to environment laws.' 'Triple J News. Hi, I'm Tony Connolly.'

broadcasting organisation whose announcers have been trained within that structure. Popular music stations try hard to distinguish the music they play from their competition; but the importance of the presenters and how they sound can be gauged by the way a new station will set about 'poaching' successful personalities from other stations.

The style of language, the vocabulary and the accent of radio talk are all vital parts of radio programming and positioning; and this has become more the case as radio stations have come to target particular segments or niches of the audience. Obviously, different ways of speaking are called for in different kinds of program as well as on different kinds of radio station. Radio news tends to have a very distinct mode of speech. Even on music radio stations aimed at people aged, say, 14 to 29, news will be written and spoken generally more formally and be more carefully enunciated than other kinds of talk on that station, although this is changing. The manner of the newsreader might be friendly and relaxed compared to a newsreader on the public service radio stations, but he or she will usually still try to project the authority and factuality listeners expect of news.

The examples in tables 15.1 and 15.2 are taken from Sydney radio stations, but have their equivalents in most mature metropolitan radio markets. The first comparison is between the introduction to the morning news bulletin on two youth music stations, one run by the ABC (public service), Triple J (table 15.1); the other commercial (Triple M; table 15.2).

The comments reflect the target audience and what is deemed to interest it. This young audience, primarily interested in popular music and not in news, does not want the length and formality of the kind of bulletin presented on serious talk-based stations. Another network that aims for a young (aged 14 to 29) audience, the Nova FM network, has taken the process of 'embedding' news in the overall sound of the station one step further than Triple M. An instrumental

Table 15.2: Triple M news opening.

Audio and comments	News script
Triple M station 'sting' and music that suggests Morse-code like beeps. Youthful female voice, standard Australian accent. Notice it begins with the weather.	'Sixteen degrees on Triple M. Kylie Baxter checking the triple headlines at 12 . . .
The newsreader introduces herself but does not use the word 'news' or any greeting words. Layered sound (reader speaks over the introductory music) and the speed of the speaker's delivery create a sense of urgency and immediacy. The reader does not really draw breath until the first full stop (inserted in transcript).	(1) 'Low-income workers are in for a twelve-dollar a week pay rise . . . more than a million workers in New South Wales will get the extra cash approved by the State Industrial Relations Commission. It follows a similar Federal decision a few months back, but the Employers' Federation is not happy about it, saying it'll stop companies putting on extra staff and force them to lay people off if costs get too high.
Compare story construction and vocabulary with 2UE bulletin below: more colloquial.	
Second story: another episode in a 'never-ending . . . saga'.	(2) 'The never-ending Phil Coles saga has taken another turn with the embattled IOC member struggling to keep his head above water . . . New allegations have surfaced with a report by Atlanta Olympics organisers saying that Coles was one of six IOC members who took two or more companions on trips to Atlanta in 1996.
Importance of sport to listeners: 'the Triple M sports net'.	(3) 'Updating the Triple M sports net and ultra-marathon runner Pat Farmer's due to arrive in Sydney around 1.15 this afternoon on the fourth leg of his seven-month historic run . . .'

music track with a fast, insistent rhythm plays continuously under the bulletins, which are very short (two to three minutes), consist almost entirely of copy reads and always begin with a weather and (if at breakfast or drive time) traffic update.

The Triple M bulletin repeats the station name twice in quick succession just after the identifying 'sting' (a brief and distinctive sound that is used repeatedly to identify the station). It is important that listeners not be allowed to forget which station they are listening to because they have to identify it if and when they fill out a ratings booklet.

Table 15.3: 2UE news opening.

Audio and comments	News script
Time pips. Burst of fanfare-like music over urgent-sounding, Morse-code-like beeps . . .	'2UE 954 News . . .
Station identification is delivered by authoritative, deep male voice over beeps and music . . .	
Morse-code-like beeps continue under female reader with mature, educated Australian voice. Gives the time (aspect of structure) and greets listener (direct address) fairly formally.	'It's nine o'clock. Good morning, I'm Sandy Alhouisie . . .
Throw to male reporter. He speaks his voice report at a fast pace. It begins with attribution – who is responsible – as evidence of its truthful and factual status.	'More than a million of the State's lowest-paid workers have been awarded wage increases of between ten and twelve dollars a week. The details from Ian Craven.
[Craven's voice]	'The NSW Industrial Relations Commission has granted the twelve-dollar pay rise for workers earning less than 510 dollars a week . . .'

The Triple J bulletin sound reflects a mix of commercial and public service imperatives, perhaps signalled by the distorted but recognisable reworking of the ABC's 'Majestic Fanfare' news theme. It is a very traditional bulletin in its structure, beginning with headlines, before the reader identifies the station and himself, but then he greets us by saying 'Hi', a markedly more casual greeting than any other station uses and one that acts to undercut the 'stuffiness' the audience might associate with 'news'. The stories chosen to head the bulletin clearly reflect the assumed priorities of the Triple J audience. The headline for the first story suggests the end of a story, or closure: a perpetrator brought to justice – almost the only kind of closure ever heard in broadcast news.

A second comparison between a commercial talk station, 2UE (table 15.3), and an ABC talk station, 2BL 702 (now called ABC Sydney 702; table 15.4), illustrates that both have a much older audience than the first two stations (aged 45 and older) and show more formal characteristics.

The commercial station chooses a local story as its lead whereas the public service station chooses international news, and this is a typical example of the way news is prioritised differently in different industry sectors. News values and beliefs about the audience drive such decisions, in that so-called 'hip-pocket' stories

Table 15.4: 2BL 702 news opening.

Audio and comments	News script
Music and station identification, including frequency on AM band. Educated, mature Australian female voice . . . Music segues to Morse-code-like signal over time code pips . . . then ABC News theme, the 'Majestic Fanfare'.	'Up-to-the-minute news and information . . . Your 2BL 702.
Educated Australian male voice comes in on the back of theme (but not over it). Begins with headlines before greeting, identification of ABC News and introduction of reader. No time call.	'The collapse of peace talks on Kosovo . . . A peaceful start to polling day in Indonesia . . . and a court sequel to the murder of a two-year-old boy. 'Good morning. ABC News with John Hall. 'Talks between NATO and Yugoslav military commanders in northern Macedonia have broken down, prompting the Alliance to announce it will intensify its bombing campaign until Belgrade gives in.'

and local ones both demonstrate the 'consequence' and 'proximity' news values. Public service broadcasters such as the ABC or BBC, on the other hand, will adopt different news priorities according to which of the networks or stations the news is to be broadcast on (compare the 2BL 702 with the Triple J bulletin; both are ABC stations).

This 2BL 702 bulletin shows a traditionally 'serious' approach. It and Triple J are the only ones to begin with headlines before the newsreader introduces himself. The newsreader identifies the news service ('ABC News'), not the individual station, in contrast to the commercial stations. The headlines serve to advise listeners what is of importance in the bulletin and to keep listeners interested. The priority given to overseas news is characteristic of national public broadcasting and is in direct contrast with the priorities of commercial radio, which takes the view that listeners want to hear stories about themselves (about 'us'), not about what is happening a long way away (about 'them'). The public service broadcasters, on the other hand, have it as part of their remit or duty to contribute to an informed and educated citizenry. The ABC News theme, the 'Majestic Fanfare', is one of the best-known pieces of music in Australia. As such, it makes a very important contribution to the 'branding' of ABC Radio news; it has come to signify the authority, impartiality and accuracy associated with ABC news.

Among the four bulletins, differences in story construction are apparent, even from the short excerpts provided. The 2UE story is much closer to the inverted pyramid. It begins with a summary lead sentence, given to the newsreader, and the reporter then provides the detail and the background. The Triple M bulletin uses a headline-like tease line to introduce each of its stories ('Low-income workers are in for a twelve-dollar a week pay rise'), rather than a summary sentence. But each of the Triple M stories is like a mini-narrative, with conflict at the heart of it. In the first it is the Employers' Federation threatening the loss of jobs; the second is introduced as another episode in a 'never-ending . . . saga', while the third is an update, another continuing story. 'Never-ending' is the key term: none of these stories has a resolution. The ABC news has a different structure, providing both summary and narrative in the opening sentence of the story. It not only summarises what has happened (talks have broken down and the Alliance says it will intensify its bombing campaign) but also provides a causal link between the two events ('prompting the Alliance to announce'), thus setting up a narrative chain.

Radio news and narrative

I have previously argued (see chapter 11) that one reason for the development of the inverted pyramid construction of news stories was the rise of objectivity and neutrality as primary values in the professional ideology of journalism. The lead identifies the people, events and places essential to an understanding of the story. It emphasises factuality; that is, there is an emphasis on what are presented as 'the facts', and these are in turn supported by attribution: who did and who said what.

Narratives in fiction do not insist on identification and attribution in this way, and this is a key difference between fictional radio (or television) forms and the news genre. Another difference is the role of the speakers of the stories: the newsreader and the 'actuality'; that is, the audio of the reporter and participants in the story. For a long time (until the early 1960s in the case of the ABC) public service broadcasters resisted the use of any voice other than that of a (usually anonymous) newsreader in news. The threat to the objectivity of news that actuality represents is the admission of what in narrative terms are diegetic narrators, the voices of people who are a part of the story.

The use of the package or 'wrap', also used in television news, is an aspect of the use of narrative in radio news. Giving listeners an incentive to keep listening by means of a tease lead, one that sets up an enigma, is another. The term 'package' has already been defined as containing different audio elements: the journalist, 'grabs' of other speakers, and 'actuality': other speakers or sound from the scene or story (diegetic sound). The package or wrap are also terms used for the technique of 'packaging' different stories together as related to one another, or presenting different aspects of the same story as a 'wrap', indicating the definitive version of the story to date (Ericson, Baranek & Chan 1987: 198–9). This narrative mode can come much closer to the classical narrative, offering cause-effect relationships or even a form of resolution. And this is more problematic for news, because it introduces explanatory readings of the story, something the audience is not supposed to be offered but to construct for themselves, based on the 'true facts'.

Radio interviews

It is hard to believe that the interview as a journalistic technique is relatively recent, yet it appeared in newspapers only in the mid-nineteenth century. It was met with suspicion in part because it inevitably employs a second narrator, the interviewee, in addition to the interviewer, the journalist (Schudson 1978). Its vividness and directness in the right hands, however, produced an irresistible sense of reality and truth, of hearing from the source, unmediated. This impression is deceptive. As Bell and van Leeuwen (1994) point out, in most media interviews, the interviewer retains power and control over the duration and structure of the interview, and the audience is provided with the interviewer's perspective on the story. Media interviews have been divided according to the power relationships that characterise them (Bell & van Leeuwen 1994) or to the purpose for which they're undertaken (Phillips & Lindgren 2002).

Phillips and Lindgren suggest that there are four main reasons for doing an interview: to elicit information (get the facts); to comment, justify or interpret (explain the facts); to recount a personal experience (react to an event); or to explore (and/or enjoy) a personality. The first two purposes are more often associated with 'hard news' stories, the latter two with 'soft' news or with the extended feature interview. The analysis offered by Bell and van Leeuwen begins by considering all the different ways in which interviews are used by a range of professions, from lawyers and police (interrogation) to priests and counsellors (confession) and teachers and employers (test). In the media versions of these interviews, however, there are rarely material consequences: a journalist cannot fail an interviewee's examination paper, offer expert advice or send someone to jail (although a journalists' actions might ultimately lead to such consequences for an individual).

Whatever the purpose or the power relationship set up by the interview, it creates a perspective from which the listener understands the events and significance of the story. Media interviewers establish which answers are valid, interesting or entertaining, and which are irrelevant, marginal or even deviant. The radio interviewer can establish this by the kinds of questions asked (and not asked) and by his or her reactions to answers. If the interview is pre-recorded, the intended meanings of the interviewee can be changed through editing. Moreover, in any media interview, both interviewee and interviewer adopt narrative roles or functions. To go back to Bell and van Leeuwen's typology, the interviewer can adopt the role of interrogator, counsellor, teacher (or student), interpellator or colleague.

The problem with the interview as a narrative technique is that neither the interviewee nor the interviewer might be reliable narrators. Interviewees sometimes lie. Interviewers might adopt roles for which they are not qualified, such as claiming expertise they do not have. A very common role in commercial talk radio (usually in weekday breakfast or morning talkback programs, the nearest that commercial radio comes to 'current affairs' programs) is that of 'interpellator'. This means that the interviewer claims to speak for listeners, acting as a voice, usually for such unproblematised and stereotypical groupings as 'the battler', 'consumers' or 'the general public'. The difficulty that can arise is that the interviewer might not be disinterested but actually self-serving, representing vested interests. This happened in Sydney in the late 1990s, in a case that came to be known as 'cash for comment', in which two high-profile radio presenters were found to be receiving large and undisclosed financial retainers to convey positive messages about certain companies and commercial interests (for an account, see www.aba.gov.au, web site of the regulatory body the Australian Broadcasting Authority). Despite these difficulties for journalism with the narrative power of the interview, radio would certainly be the poorer without it.

Conclusion

Narrative modes of storytelling in the classic 'Hollywood' sense are still relatively rare in radio news, partly because of the constraints on time. In the more extended reports of radio current affairs programs, they are more commonly found, both in the form of the reports and through the use of interviews. The advent of 'infotainment' in news media has touched radio news bulletins only in such ways as we have seen in the examples: by leading a bulletin with weather or traffic news in the breakfast shift on commercial stations with a younger target demographic. Yet, in terms of the way radio is used by audiences, comprehension and interest might be better served by such narrative techniques as the 'tease' lead and the use of diegetic narrators, at least in actuality reports, if not in the character of the reporter.

The priority assigned to audience retention and interest by commercial radio helps to explain the greater emphasis in commercial radio news on narrative techniques and structures. The linking of episodes in a package or wrap can be more problematic, however. The danger is in creating pseudo or spurious narratives. This is because of the tendency of the package to frame explanations and conclusions more explicitly than standard thematic news narratives. They remain open-ended and episodic, without beginning and without end. Nor do they necessarily overcome the criticism levelled at the inverted pyramid, that it cannot convey 'the weight of emotion or subtlety' (Ricketson 2000: 152). This is an irony for radio, the most intimate of media, one still unparalleled among mass media in the sense of closeness it is able to engender between speaker and hearer, one reason the interview can be so powerful in this medium. Ricketson describes the price of 'the freedom to borrow fictional techniques' as 'keeping faith' with the audience; that is, being faithful to the truth. The problem, as he acknowledges, is that when the narrative modes of fiction are borrowed, the audience cannot know for sure they are being told the truth; trust is all there is.

Shingler and Wieringa (1998: 95) have argued that for largely historic and cultural reasons, radio enjoys audience trust to an extent that film and television do not (although this is not necessarily so of news, as opposed to other genres). News as a radio genre needs to employ at least some of the techniques of storytelling in order to keep the audience. Retaining not only the audience but also their trust in having reliable narrators is the challenge for radio journalism.

Chapter 16

Print news as narrative

Helen Fulton

In his book on American television culture, *Amusing Ourselves to Death* (1985), Neil Postman argued that 'television speaks in only one persistent voice – the voice of entertainment' (Postman 1985, chap. 5). In its lack of contextualisation, analysis and seriousness, he says, television news has become pure entertainment. This kind of 'tabloid television', deplored by many commentators (Smith 1992; Langer 1998), is the visual reflex of a type of narrative news first popularised in tabloid newspapers and now a staple item of most mainstream newspapers. The increasing narrativisation of news, both in print and on television and radio, is seen as an inevitable result of market forces exerting pressure on news outlets to become substantially more focused on profits and audience size.

This chapter begins by accounting for some of the ways in which news is structured and circulated as 'stories' at an institutional level. It will then examine and critique a conventional division between 'information' and 'narrative' models of print news, suggesting that this division needs to be collapsed and restated as a generic distinction between (non-narrative) 'information' and (narrative) 'news'. In setting out the narrative strategies of news stories, I argue that these strategies undermine journalistic ideals of objectivity. Finally, I review some of the ideological consequences of constructing and reading print news as narrative.

News as construct

Although it has become a truism of media studies to assert that news is a construct, it is worth explaining this idea in terms of how 'news' circulates in the form of deliberately structured stories that people tell to each other. The methodologies of news-gathering, which rest on professional and institutional values and standards, work not only to construct the news but also to create it. News is brought into being by the practices of making the news. Whatever appears in a newspaper or TV bulletin is, by definition, the news; 'news' does not exist somewhere outside the media organisations, waiting to be found and brought inside. Nor do journalists, by and large, go out looking for it. Events come to their attention, from sources and from other media, which can then be turned into 'news' by the application of various linguistic and professional practices. I look in more detail at the discursive construction of news in chapter 17; here I briefly outline the most significant professional practices in terms of producing and defining 'news', especially print news (although much of what follows can equally be applied to television and radio news). These practices can be defined as:

• use of sources
• application of news values
• gate-keeping
• agenda-setting
• economic determinants.

Use of sources

The management of news through the interaction of journalists and sources, whether as individuals, organisations or agencies, is one of the major factors in the construction of news as the activities of the powerful (Whitaker 1981: 31–2). Journalists' 'contacts' are indicators of their professional standing: the more prestigious and highly placed their contacts, the more status they have in the workplace. With the rise of digital media, especially the mobile phone, fax and Internet, journalism has become an office job, with information pouring in by phone and fax, and research to confirm or flesh out a story largely being carried out on the phone or the Internet.

The various sources that supply information to news organisations can be described under the following headings:

• *Sources that are routinely monitored* by the media themselves, who assign journalists to particular 'rounds' where information might be gathered. These sources are located at the institutional level of society, such as chambers of government, local councils, police, law courts and emergency services.
• *Organisations that have their own press offices* or employ public relations (PR) companies to issue regular bulletins about their activities. These include government departments, public services such as transport and electricity, large companies, trade unions, political parties, hospitality and entertainment organisations.

- *Research organisations* that undertake and publish the results of various polls and studies. These include medical and educational research, political polls and sociological research, much of it published in standard professional journals that news journalists access online in order to find 'stories'.
- *Elite individuals* seeking media attention, such as celebrities or corporate executives. Such individuals send press releases to the major news organisations, usually through a press office or PR company.
- *Regular events*, such as religious festivals, street parades, sporting fixtures and so on, can be managed in advance, often through a PR company.
- *Other media*. Increasingly, journalists rely on other media for their information, picking up the latest developments from the Internet pages of other major news outlets, both local and international.

If we consider the news stories reprinted in this chapter (figures 16.1, 16.2, 16.3 and 16.4), we can determine fairly easily where these stories came from. The first, 'Media will pay for trial collapse', comes from a government department responsible for constitutional affairs, whose workings are routinely monitored by journalists specialising in legal issues. The second item, '*Garçon*! You're slow, surly and at last you've admitted it', is based on a report published by France's main hotel and catering trade association, UMH. The third, 'Town living in fear over mining deal', does not specify a source, and although the reporter quite possibly visited the town to collect information and interview the people concerned, he might well have been alerted to the story in the first instance by another media representative or by the police. The fourth story, 'Roosters claim NRL minor premiership', represents the work of a specialist journalist, the sports reporter, whose specific job is to cover important sporting events and to liaise with appropriate sources of information, such as professional sporting associations and other sports journalists.

News-gathering is therefore a routine task associated with the regular monitoring of specific sources and the reworking of press releases and other information supplied by various individuals and organisations. One result of this reliance on sources is a lack of diversity in the news made available to us as readers or viewers. The same kinds of people and events crop up in the news all the time, arranged into predictable templates or storylines. At the same time, the tradition of investigative journalism, involving the expense of reporters doing time-consuming interviews, research and fact-checking, has declined because of the greater availability of ready-made stories supplied by communications agencies.

Inevitably, those individuals and organisations with access to public relations agencies, or who are positioned within the same institutional structure as the media themselves, are more likely to get their 'story', or their side of the story, into the newspaper than those left to lobby on their own. The result is a skewing of 'news' towards those in positions of institutional or economic power and a reinforcement of existing power relations as the 'natural' order.

Application of news values

A number of studies have shown that stories or events are recognised as 'news' on the basis of a common set of professional values regarding what is newsworthy. The most famous of these studies, by Johan Galtung and Mari Ruge, identified twelve factors by which an item may be judged as suitable to be included in a newspaper or TV news bulletin (Cohen & Young 1973; Watson 2003: 135). These include unambiguity, familiarity, predictability, surprise, negativity, eliteness of people or nations, continuing interest and magnitude.

These 'news values' are often invoked as if they exist outside and before news texts themselves and can be referred to as an impartial and professionally expert method of selecting one news item rather than another to be included in the daily paper or TV bulletin. If we think about 'news' in terms of discourse, however, it is clear that virtually any utterance on any topic can be restated in the discourse of 'news' and therefore turned into a news item which demonstrates one or more of the 'news values' that are supposed to define it.

Information that is restated in a way that foregrounds one or more of these values is more likely to end up on the news pages of the paper than information presented according to different priorities. This means that public relations agents, and journalists themselves, can turn virtually any event into 'news' by writing it according to the established news values. In figure 16.1, 'Media will pay for trial collapse', the news values of unambiguity, surprise (a change from current practice), continuing interest (in the role of the media) and magnitude (in the amount of money that might be paid) are invoked to turn a rather dry legal decision into a news 'story' about the media and the reporting of crime.

Our expectations of what 'news' is and how we can recognise it are therefore constantly reinforced by what we read in the paper, a process of naturalisation that elides the constructedness of news as manufactured stories. The use of conventional story templates based on news values constantly reproduced in the media determines what can be presented as 'news' and therefore how the 'real world' is defined. Newspaper readers are unlikely to be surprised by such a headline as 'Mother of three awarded honorary doctorate' but might well find a similar statement, 'Father of three awarded honorary doctorate', a little odd. In the world of the news media, which is supposed to be the 'real world', women are more likely to be defined by their domestic relationships whereas men are defined by their occupations. These are among the narrative templates that characterise the discourse of news.

Gate-keeping

The term 'gate-keeping' refers to the process by which some items of information become news; that is, they are let through the 'gate' into the newspaper or bulletin

Media will pay for trial collapse

Clare Dyer

Legal correspondent

Newspapers and broadcasters who cause a criminal trial to collapse through prejudicial reporting could face a bill for millions of pounds under rules outlined yesterday by ministers.

Jurors, witnesses, news organisations and anyone else whose 'serious misconduct' derails a criminal trial could be ordered by a judge or magistrate to pay prosecution and defence costs.

. . . The constitutional affairs secretary Lord Falconer said: 'The move fires a warning shot to anyone who risks causing criminal proceedings to collapse through serious misconduct, such as witness intimidation, juror impropriety or prejudicial reporting. A huge amount of time, money and effort is wasted when a case collapses.'

In long and complex cases, the prosecution and defence bill can be millions of pounds.

The lord chief justice, Lord Woolf, said the power would not be used in an indiscriminate manner; only a judge could make an order, after hearing the parties and knowing all the circumstances. There would also be a right of appeal.

Figure 16.1: 'Media will pay for trial collapse' (*Guardian* (UK), 16 September 2004, p. 8.) Columns altered, punctuation and spelling retained.

while others are kept out. Gate-keeping practices, although part of a generalised culture of professional journalistic practice, vary from one news organisation to another and help to explain why different newspapers and bulletins run a different selection of stories on the same day. Each news outlet tells its own stories in its own way.

The status of sources and the presentation of recognised news values are two criteria by which an item makes it through the gates. Others are less easy to define or identify, and are connected to the daily routines of news-gathering, the availability of material before deadlines, the availability of images to support written or spoken text, professional standards of technical achievement, and the institutional and personal preferences of individual owners and editors. Local cultural factors also determine what kinds of information will be let in through the news gate. It is unlikely that the story in figure 16.1, 'Media will pay', would have made it through the gates of an Australian newspaper because of its specifically British application, although it would almost certainly have come to the attention of the Australian media via British media sources.

Whether overtly acknowledged or taken for granted, workplace practices of this kind result in a 'news' that is highly selective and only partially representative of the stories that might have been available on any given day.

Agenda-setting

The selection of certain kinds of events as 'news' presupposes an implicit agenda on the part of a news institution. Stories about national politics are likely to feature in the front pages of wide-circulation daily papers such as the *Australian*, the *Guardian* or the *New York Times*, whereas popular tabloid papers are more likely to lead with human interest stories involving high-profile public figures. Choices of this kind suggest an agenda of newsworthy events, ranked in order of importance from the front page to the middle of the newspaper. Each paper itself constructs a narrative of the day's events.

More significantly, it can be argued that the selection of news constructs for readers or viewers an agenda of what is happening in the world that needs to be noticed. By covering some events or issues (and omitting others), the news media put these events on the public agenda, drawing them to our attention as issues of importance that need to be debated (O'Shaughnessy & Stadler 2002: 15; Schulz 1998: 154–5). Reportage of national politics as conducted in the chamber of government constructs an agenda in which the democratic process is taken seriously as a matter of concern to all citizens, and should therefore be constantly under review by a scrutinising media. Reportage of allegations of sexual misdemeanours by national politicians, on the other hand, constructs an agenda in which the personal behaviour of individuals needs to be scrutinised and monitored more assiduously than their public role in managing the democratic process.

In the news items included in this chapter, a number of agendas are implicitly set. In figure 16.1, 'Media will pay', the focus is not on the ruling itself, which applies to anyone who causes a trial to collapse, but on the implied restriction of the media's 'freedom of speech' to report the 'facts' about criminal trials. The agenda here is to assert that media freedom, a taken-for-granted value to which we are all assumed to subscribe, must not be compromised by government pressure. In figure 16.2, '*Garçon!*', a number of prejudices about the French hospitality industry, including its supposedly poor service and lack of hygiene, are stated more or less without comment or qualification, suggesting that these ideas are part of a 'commonsense' British attitude towards the French – certainly one that has an ancient and venerable position on the British news agenda. In figure 16.3, 'Town living in fear', a number of concerns to do with rural instability, Aboriginal populations, land ownership and mining rights form an uneasy background to the story. It suggests an agenda of confirming the 'uncivilised' nature of Aboriginal culture, compared to white culture, which works to justify white Australia's continued exploitation of Aboriginal people.

The news agenda, then, sets out the issues for debate and concern, but also confirms the myths and stories that we already believe to be true or obvious. Clearly, different newspapers will have different agendas, largely implicit, often controlled by owners and senior editors. News consumers will not only be attracted to those news products whose agendas align with theirs but are also likely to model their personal agendas of significant issues on those of the papers they read. If some newspapers and TV bulletins regularly feature agenda items such as terrorism, refugees, football violence, drug-related crime and youth suicide, these are likely to be salient issues in public debate, however far removed from the personal experience of most readers or viewers. A spate of fatal car accidents involving very young drivers, or the potential dangers of poorly maintained public roads or railways, might feature on the news agenda only briefly but long enough to cultivate a general sense that 'something needs to be done'. In this way, the news media 'set the agenda' of what is important, an agenda that is sometimes very different from those of such decision-makers as politicians, local government, the police or the judiciary, leading to further media claims of incompetence or indifference on the part of those in public office.

Economic determinants

Since the largest sector of the news media in most Western countries is commercial and profit-driven, economic factors are among the most significant determinants in the collection, construction and presentation of news. Even in the non-commercial sector, such as the state-owned ABC in Australia or the BBC in Britain, where expenditure has to be fully justified to government and taxpayers (and licence-holders in the case of the BBC), economic imperatives tend to drive the selection and presentation of news. Both the ABC and BBC regard themselves as exemplars of 'public service broadcasting' (Garnham 1990: 128–30), with a commitment to socially responsible news journalism that includes a diversity of viewpoints, an attention to minority issues and the fostering of citizenship and nationhood.

Commercial media organisations commodify their news services in order to attract the advertisers who support them. Television news bulletins are less about 'news' as a public service than about attracting and retaining a diverse demographic that can be 'sold' to advertisers. Similarly, newspapers arrange their stories in the 'news hole' left after all the advertisements have been arranged on the page (Turow 2003: 303). In an effort to retain readership and advertising in the face of increased competition from television and the Internet, newspapers have moved to a higher ratio of 'lifestyle' journalism, often in the form of lift-outs and magazines whose content largely comprises advertisements, 'advertorials' and product-oriented reports. Topic-specific lift-outs, featuring careers, property, information technology, home decorating, food and wine, and so on, target specific demographics and provide opportunities for advertisers to reach receptive audiences.

It can be argued, then, that the core business of newspapers is less about providing news than about attracting advertising (both commercial and classified) via a promised mass market of demographically diverse readers. In order to bring this mass market into being, newspapers need to provide news that has salience for the largest possible readership, is couched in language understood by the majority of the population, is politically uncontroversial and which promotes hegemonic consensus through a shared recognition of 'the way things are'. This kind of mass-market and market-driven news characteristically conforms to existing conventions of news values and agendas, with the result that minority issues and alternative viewpoints are marginalised, and the public interest is subordinated to commercial imperatives.

Economic factors also account for the heavy reliance on readily available inexpensive sources of news, such as agencies, press releases and published research studies, as opposed to the more expensive option of investigative journalism. The privileging of some news values, such as 'elite' persons or places, depends on their economic connection with the newspaper itself, with the corporate and institutional structure to which the newspaper also belongs, or with the region in which it is published. The selection and reporting of news and sport is arranged to fit the economic agenda of the newspaper in terms of the kinds of audiences and advertisers being addressed. Just as one-day cricket was invented to suit commercial television's demand for self-contained events, the predominance of mass-appeal male-dominated sports in newspaper coverage, such as football, golf and racing, guarantees a regular audience of people who might not read the front sections of the paper at all but can be targeted by the advertising in the sports section.

Such strategies as the selection of stories, the organisation and layout of the newspaper, the inclusion of specialist and lifestyle features, and the provision of service information, for example, television schedules and weather forecasts, all help to maximise audiences and therefore to attract advertising. The promotion of 'celebrity' columnists and reporters helps to establish a regular readership, while references to other media, through book and film reviews, stories about media celebrities, and references to relevant web sites, work to suggest the relevance of newspapers to audiences engaged with a wide range of media products.

In their pursuit of mass audiences, newspapers therefore have similar preoccupations to those of commercial television channels. As with television programs, newspapers rely on standardised products that audiences can immediately recognise from a headline or photograph, and know at once if they are being presented with a political story, a human interest story, a celebrity feature, an opinion column and so on. The economic imperative of the mass market has determined that formulaic stories packaged into recognisable genres are the easiest to sell to both audiences and advertisers.

Information and narrative

What kinds of 'stories' are preferred by newspapers, and how are they packaged into standardised formats? Is it even viable to claim that a news story is also a narrative? We can all perceive a difference between the kind of news item that provides factual information, such as figure 16.1, and the kind that tells us a story about specific individuals caught up in a human drama, such as figure 16.3. Are both types of story narratives? Critical opinion is divided on this issue, with some arguing for a clear distinction between 'information' and 'narrative' as types of news, and others claiming that narrative is a basic structuring principle found in all news stories.

The distinction between news as information and news as narrative was first made in 1926 by George Herbert Mead, who was claiming for professional journalists a clear divide between facts and 'story' (Mead 1926). Since then, the validity of this distinction has been upheld by text-type theorists, who argue that narrative is one way, but not the only way, of organising facts into a coherent text (Ytreberg 2001: 359), and by media professionals themselves whose credibility depends in part on being able to demonstrate a difference between factual information and opinion-based reporting (Turow 2003: 45–50).

There is some overlap between the information and narrative models of news and the concepts of 'hard' and 'soft' news, and with the overarching journalistic ideal of 'objectivity' (see Anne Dunn's discussion of this in chapter 11). John Hartley has defined six major topics of news – politics, the economy, foreign affairs, domestic news, occasional stories and sport – and separates 'hard' news, characterised by conflict, from 'soft' news, including humorous and human interest stories, within the category of 'domestic news' (Hartley 1982: 38–9). However, this distinction prevails across all six topics. 'Hard' news is the most recent news, involving politics, economics, industrial relations, public-sector organisations and private-sector corporations, events that have just happened and therefore need to be reported at once. 'Hard' news is the newspaper's idea of what the public needs to know in order to continue to act as effective and well-informed citizens; it conventionally appears in the first few pages of the newspaper and has the largest amount of column inches devoted to it. Figures 16.1 and 16.3 both qualify as domestic hard news stories, although their respective positions towards the back of the news section indicates their relatively low priority in the news agenda for those particular days. The journalists who cover 'hard' news stories tend to have a higher professional status than other journalists, because they are seen as doing a more cutting-edge and demanding job (Tunstall 1971).

'Soft' news, on the other hand, refers to news items that are not necessarily specific to a particular day, but provide background or a 'human interest' angle relating to current events, including political and economic issues. The item in figure 16.2 is a classic soft news story, not tied to events of that particular day, but useful to fill up a 'news hole' on the front page, providing some light relief to counterbalance the more sober political happenings of the previous day. Soft news stories appear to be more obviously structured as narratives, with many of the features of fictional narratives. Individuals are represented as 'characters', often stereotyped and brought into being by direct speech. A specific setting or

Garçon! You're slow, surly and at last you've admitted it

Jon Henley in Paris

In a mea culpa as welcome as it was unexpected, the owners of France's 60,000 bars, brasseries and cafés admitted yesterday that all too often their staff are surly, service slow and hygiene horrendous.

'Customers are right to complain of a poor or non-existent welcome, an excessively long wait and a lack of basic courtesy and reactivity,' said André Daguin, president of the French hotel and catering industry's main trade association, UMH.

. . . The neighbourhood café, with its trademark counter of zinc and assortment of variously voluble or lugubrious Gallic drinkers, is suffering from social change. The French today have less time, do not drink as much and are increasingly inclined to favour cheap chain restaurants, fast-food joints and sandwich bars.

But the legendary (if largely exaggerated) rudeness of French waiters, particularly in Paris, has not done much to help the café's cause. Nor has an at times limited grasp of the concept of cleanliness, most often evident in the toilets.

In Le Firmament near the Place de l'Opéra in central Paris yesterday, customers were naturally reluctant to condemn their regular watering hole. 'This place is fine,' said Jean-Pierre Mangin, a printer. 'It's spotless, and the staff are genuinely pleasant. But it's true many places make you feel like you've got a disease.'

. . . The industry plans to draw up 100 criteria by which bars and cafés should be judged, and to hire independent inspectors to visit thousands of establishments a year. Those that comply – a targeted 2,000 within three years – will be awarded a 'seal of French café quality', Mr Daguin said. The project will be presented to the tourism minister next month.

Figure 16.2: *'Garçon!* You're slow, surly and at last you've admitted it' (*Guardian* (UK), 16 September 2004, p. 1.) Columns altered, punctuation and spelling retained.

location is invoked, recognisable even to readers who have never been there from existing intertextual references ('central Paris', 'the Hollywood Hills', 'the West Bank', 'Sydney's western suburbs'). There is a development of events over time, marked by deictics such as 'yesterday', 'then', 'back at home' and so on. Finally, there is some kind of conflict, which might or might not be resolved but which serves as a parable illustrating a moral position.

It would seem that a distinction can be made between 'hard' news stories constructed according to an 'information' model and 'soft' news stories constructed as narratives. Contemporary work in discourse and cultural theory, however, starts from the assumption that both hard and soft news stories are types of narrative, although they are likely to be structured in different ways (Hartley 1982; Sperry 1981). As Allan Bell says, 'Journalists do not write articles, they write stories – with structure, order, viewpoint and values' (Bell & Garrett 1998: 64). The apparently factual and objective 'hard' news story that reports information without overt commentary exemplifies a specific kind of narrative in which the narrative voice is deliberately elided.

Objectivity in the news

The distinctive structure of 'hard' news stories is that of the inverted pyramid, in which the most relevant information – who, what, where, when – is placed first, followed by supporting detail, quotations from involved parties, alternative viewpoints and additional comments. The inverted pyramid therefore moves from the most general account of the event to a limited number of specific details, and it also implies a ranking of details in descending order of importance. Selection of the opening sentence, which is normally the first paragraph of a news story, directs readers to the 'angle' of the story, the aspect of it that the reporter deems to be the most newsworthy in terms of the conventional news values of unusualness, conflict, proximity, unambiguity, elite persons and so on. The opening sentence of figure 16.1, 'Newspapers and broadcasters who cause a criminal trial to collapse through prejudicial reporting could face a bill for millions of pounds under rules outlined yesterday by ministers', draws our attention to the centrality of the media to the issue being reported and implicitly asks us to think about how the new ruling will affect the way the media do their job.

This structure of the inverted pyramid is usually assumed to be a characteristic of 'objective' news reporting (Turow 2003: 46), whereby objectivity is privileged as a defining aspect of a 'hard' news story, as opposed to the evaluative nature of most 'soft' news stories. Ideals of objectivity in news reporting, particularly in print news, are among the most pervasive of journalistic professional values, and form the standard by which the performance of news journalism is judged (McQuail 1992: 183–7). If readers cannot trust newspapers to give factual information, the unwritten contract between them – that the media are a credible source of knowledge about the world – is broken.

The concept of objectivity as an achievable ideal has taken a battering under the onslaught of post-structuralist theories in philosophy and semiotics. If objectivity is defined as the extra-ideological reporting of absolute or universal truths, then it is clearly unachievable, since external reality can be accessed only through practices of visual or linguistic representation that are 'always already' ideologically positioned. Yet, as Judith Lichtenberg has argued, even the critics of objectivity on theoretical grounds cannot quite bring themselves to abandon the idea of it, and she herself concludes that 'we cannot get along without assuming both the possibility and value of objectivity' (Lichtenberg 2000: 252).

In his consideration of objectivity as a professional value and a normative measure of performance, McQuail cites a research report on those aspects of reporting that many journalists identify as hallmarks of objectivity (McQuail 1992: 184–5). They can be restated as:

- *balance*, presenting different sides of an issue;
- *accuracy*, ensuring a report corresponds to verifiable reality;
- *completeness*, the presentation of all main relevant points;
- *factuality*, distinguishing fact from opinion or comment;
- *neutrality*, or impartiality, suppressing the writer's own attitude or opinion.

This list could just as well serve as a description of the mode of hard news reporting as it is conventionally recognised by both journalists and readers. But, as Kevin Williams has observed, 'each of these attempts to operationalise objectivity is problematic' (Williams 2003: 125). *Balance* appears to be a straightforward matter of giving both sides of an issue and allowing them equal space. The problems here are: how to identify the 'sides' in the first place; deciding how many and which viewpoints should be represented; and the context and evaluation framed for each viewpoint. Most news stories focus on two sides, with quotes from representatives of both sides, but this approach tends to set up a simple binary conflict, often represented as a conflict between two individuals, which elides complexity and institutional structuring of problems. Moreover, as Stuart Hall has argued, 'the setting up of a topic in terms of a debate within which there are oppositions and conflicts is also one way of *dramatising* an event so as to enhance its newsworthiness' (Hall et al. 1978: 59).

The goal of *accuracy* implies that factually correct information is reported, that facts should be checked with sources, and that information received should be compared with other reliable versions of the same information. However, the 'sources' of particular 'facts' are often other media, public relations agencies or people with a particular agenda or social positioning, such as heads of companies or government departments. Checking information against external evidence is time-consuming and expensive, and reliable evidence is not always available. There is also the perennial difficulty of matching perceptions of accuracy: a report might have been verified by a journalist but could still strike someone involved in the event as a misrepresentation of what 'really' happened.

Attempts to achieve *completeness* in the coverage of a specific event are usually aligned to the 'inverted pyramid' structure as a way of alluding, in rank order of importance, to as many aspects of the story as possible within a limited space. The movement from the general to the particular works to orient the reader within the 'world' of the story and implies that we are in possession of all that we need to know to make sense of the story. Other aspects of completeness include giving a full coverage of all the significant events of the day within one newspaper or TV bulletin, and giving an adequate cumulative coverage of continuing stories that develop over days or weeks. All these attempts to achieve completeness are constrained by news-gathering routines, what is available on any given day, the selection and gate-keeping practices of particular media organisations, the amount of space available after the paid advertisements are included in the page layout, and the economic constraints on how much news can actually be fitted into the paper or bulletin.

Establishing the *factuality* of a news report, and separating fact from opinion, is achieved through references to named sources with direct quotes and references to the 'real world' of places, countries, historical events and so on. Most newspapers distinguish between the 'news' section at the front of the paper and the 'op-ed' (opinion and editorial) section towards the middle, where regular columnists, often promoted as 'celebrities', write first-person opinion-based accounts of topical events. The spatial separation of the two kinds of journalism, 'hard' news reporting and opinion columns, suggests that there is a measurable difference between them in terms of factuality and objectivity. However, separating fact from opinion is by no means a simple matter. Physical 'facts' about the external world can be retrieved only through linguistic or iconic signs that are themselves wholly connotative and open to interpretation.

Similarly, in figure 16.1, the 'hard news' story, the claim that 'in long and complex cases, the prosecution and defence bill can be millions of pounds' appears to be factual, whereas the statement in figure 16.2 that 'the neighbourhood café, with its trademark counter of zinc and assortment of variously voluble or lugubrious Gallic drinkers, is suffering from social change' suggests the writer's own opinion. Neither statement is verifiably factual; the difference in their status as truth claims is an effect of their different registers: formal in the first, informal and slightly humorous in the second. The confident separation of fact from opinion, normalised in journalistic practice, is an example of hegemony at work, whereby the opinion of the hegemonic order becomes the 'fact', which is presented as natural, absolute and unchanging.

Finally, the goal of *neutrality* or impartiality, in which all opinion or evaluation is elided from a piece of reportage, is as hard to achieve as the others. A third-person perspective, sticking to the 'facts' of names, dates, places and other empirical data, a lack of accompanying commentary or evaluation, can all contribute to an impression of impartiality. Once again, however, we come back to the issues of news-gathering routines, which privilege the selection of some information and sources over others, thereby positioning the news story within an ideological framework, and of language itself as entirely connotative, since what appears to be denotative or neutral to one user of the language might well appear connotative to another. Even the omission of information or comment can reveal a discursive positioning: an 'objective' account tends to leave out any material that directly challenges the dominant view of 'the way things [really] are'.

The impartiality of the news media is seriously compromised by their relationship with other areas of institutional power. The prevailing viewpoint of this sector is the result of what Stuart Hall has termed a 'structured preference given in the media to the opinions of the powerful', who then become the 'primary definers' of news topics and issues:

The important point about the structured relationship between the media and the primary institutional definers is that it permits the institutional definers to establish the initial definition or *primary interpretation* of the topic in question. This interpretation then 'commands the field' in all subsequent treatment and sets the terms of reference within which all further coverage or debate takes place . . . [T]he media are frequently not the 'primary definers' of news events at all; but their structured relationship to power has the effect of making them play a crucial but secondary role in reproducing the definitions of those who have privileged access, as of right, to the media.

(Hall et al. 1978: 58–60)

The problems with objectivity in news reporting are conventionally grouped under the headings of *impossibility* and *undesirability* (McQuail 1992: 187–8; Williams 2003: 127–8). While Lichtenberg finds an essential contradiction between these two claims (Lichtenberg 2000: 238), they in fact presuppose slightly different meanings of the term 'objectivity'. If we accept that a totally objective (that is, extra-ideological) view of the world cannot be retrieved through representation, we can then argue that attempting to construct a simulacrum of objective reality, which is the aim of 'objective' reporting, is in itself an undesirable goal for news journalists. These sets of objections can be summarised as follows.

Objectivity (as the retrieval of reality) is *impossible* because:

- no account of reality is outside ideology; all accounts of real-world events must be structured through sign systems, such as language, which are inseparable from ideology;
- no account of reality is complete or completely correct on its own; we all have different impressions and interpretations of what we experience;
- factuality is always subjective – determining what the facts are, and what they mean, is not an absolute process;
- all events have to be contextualised, or placed in a wider frame of reference, which immediately imposes evaluative meanings on them;
- news is produced within a system of internal and external determinants – economic, organisational, technical, professional – that structures and commodifies news stories;
- the institutional practices of news-gathering, gate-keeping, selection and agenda-setting involve subjective judgements and evaluations, however unconscious;
- omissions and elisions, as much as selection and inclusion, construct implicit value judgements about social 'reality', 'commonsense' and 'the way things are'.

Objectivity (as a discursive practice of journalism) is *undesirable* because:

- the 'objective' view of events is the dominant or 'commonsense' view, promoting a version of reality that elides and naturalises systems of power;

- the lack of an overt critical perspective allows truth claims to be presented without challenge, so that ideology becomes normalised as fact;
- objective reporting discourages journalists from taking responsibility for what is reported, and encourages them to focus on high-prestige sources;
- the role of investigative, issue-based and 'advocacy' journalism is reduced;
- the association between objectivity and fact works to privilege 'objective' reporting over other kinds of news stories, such as human interest and socially responsible journalism, which can be equally valuable sources of information.

If there are so many objections to 'objectivity' as a goal of news reporting, are there any reasons to support it? I think it can be supported on the grounds of diversity. What we think of as 'objective' reporting in 'hard' news stories – changes in the law, election results in another country, the outcomes of a trade summit, movements in the stock market – is in fact an effect of discourse. Objectivity is a style, a set of linguistic practices that we have learned to recognise as signifiers of factuality and impartiality. As such, it provides an alternative to other styles of reporting in newspapers or TV bulletins, including opinion columns, advocacy journalism, editorials, human interest, entertainment and advertising. Among these varieties of journalism, many of them explicitly positioned in evaluation and ideology, objective news reporting offers a different kind of voice and access to a different kind of information, which helps us to interpret and rank other styles of journalism. As long as the ideological role of language and of other social and professional practices that produce 'hard' news is not overlooked, this style of reporting helps to maintain a much-needed diversity in the range of news and current affairs offered to us.

News as narrative

'Hard' news is marked as 'objective' through a number of discursive practices. These include a third-person narration, in which the narrative voice is externalised and elided from the account; a high proportion of empirical information regarding dates, places, times, amounts of money and so on; and a lack of modality, that is, an absence of adjectives, adverbs and phrases indicating evaluation or opinion, and a preponderance of declarative (that is, not conditional) verbs indicating certainty. This low level of modality tends to result in a bland and rather dry account, as in figure 16.1, although the use of modal verbs in that news item, such as 'could', 'can' and 'would', indicates that the writer has a contingent attitude towards the truth claims she is making. Similarly, the use of metaphor to describe trials that 'collapse' or are 'derailed' introduces an element of modality or appraisal that enlivens (and ideologically positions) an otherwise bald account. 'Soft' news, on the other hand, is marked by its more engaged narration, informal register, foregrounding of individuals and their personal experiences, and interpersonal approach to the reader that implicitly asks us to respond emotively to the story.

These modes of news discourse, both 'hard' and 'soft', are realised through the same set of narrative strategies. Information and events are turned into 'news' by means of a standardised set of professional practices and procedures that have the effect of sorting stories into different types on the basis of discourse rather than content. 'Hard' news is therefore distinguished from 'soft' news not by content or by the nature of the event itself, but by the format and discourse in which the content is reported. An earthquake occurring the day before might be reported in the format of the front-page 'hard news' story in the newspaper, but it might also (or only) be reported in the format of a 'soft news' background piece (the increasing number of earthquakes in certain parts of the world; the 'heroes' who saved lives) in the inner pages of the paper. The same event could be the lead story in one paper and not be reported at all in another. There is nothing intrinsic to an event that predetermines its quality as news, either 'hard' or 'soft. How it is reported, and whether it is reported at all, is a matter of professional process, selection, availability, space and so on.

The narrative strategies of journalism work to turn information into news. All news is narrative, I would argue, but information is not necessarily structured as narrative, although it can be. Mead's early distinction between an 'information model' and a 'narrative model' of news therefore works only to support an argument for the special place of 'objective' news reporting, and as a means of claiming a generic distinction between 'hard' and 'soft' news. The privileging of some types of news over others is part of a larger scheme of institutional privilege directed towards perceived standards of 'objectivity'.

There are a number of narrative strategies typical of news discourse in its broadest form, which can be discussed under the following headings:
- angle
- point of closure
- individualisation
- focalisation
- chronology.

Angle

The various modes of news discourse are realised through a number of 'angles' that determine the narrative template. These templates can be compared to narrative plots in fictional works. They seem to be generic, almost universal, ways of ordering our world and yet are distinctive to specific media, in this case the news media, where they enable seamless transitions between news, information, entertainment and advertising. The headline or first paragraph of a story – the 'lead' that comes before the body of the story in the inverted pyramid structure – establishes the angle and therefore the general outline of the 'plot' or format, cueing us in to expect a particular type of narrative. I have already mentioned the headline and opening sentence of the news story in figure 16.1, which alerts us to the 'plot' of this particular story, as a narrative about media performance and their position as a 'fourth estate' outside legal or government sanctions.

One format or angle that has been the subject of considerable research is the 'moral panic', in which an event is reported as a perceived threat to the social and/or moral order, with a view to invoking public concern (Cohen 1972; Goode et al. 1994; Thompson 1998). The narrative structure of the moral panic is that the social fabric is under stress in some way, implying that this threat needs to be resolved by various 'rescues' or official interventions, such as higher levels of policing, lower levels of migration, more regulation of young people and so on. The news item in figure 16.3 is a typical example of the 'moral panic', starting with the headline 'Town living in fear'. The article constructs a view of Condobolin, in rural New South Wales, Australia, as a frontier town where competing interests of whites, Aboriginals and large mining companies constantly threaten to provoke serious violence. Fears of Aboriginals as the 'other', marked by 'tribal lore' and 'traditional garb', are also invoked to assign blame for the social instability of the town, implying that the 'solution' lies with restricting Aboriginal access to land claims and to corporate work structures.

Other narrative formats are based on different propositions and outcomes, which can be negative or positive. Information about the education sector, particularly primary and secondary education, has a high news value (since most newspaper readers have first-hand experience and many have children at school) and is easily sourced from professional bodies and research teams. To turn this information into news, journalists might make use of the moral panic ('One in ten teenagers unable to read'), the industrial relations angle ('Teachers – underpaid and underperforming'), the scare story ('Literacy rates plummet'), the piece of folk wisdom ('Early reading damages under-fives'), the research-led discovery ('New hope for dyslexics'), the political or policy issue ('Education minister under fire') or the eccentric event ('Robot dolls used to teach sex education'). The news story in figure 16.2 combines existing British folk myths about the French (as rude, dirty, inefficient and so on) with a report on a new policy initiative to reinvigorate the French café industy, surprising us with a new twist on what seems to be an old story.

Point of closure

The various angles, selected by journalists as a way of presenting different kinds of information, are like plot summaries, telling us what the story is about. Unlike most fictional narratives, however, the point of closure in a news story generally comes right at the beginning, either in the headline or in the 'lead' paragraph, at the top of the inverted pyramid. The 'lead' is in fact the point of closure in the

Town living in fear over mining deal

By RHETT WATSON

TWO houses have been attacked with spears and death threats delivered in a dispute over a gold mine in western NSW.

The town of Condobolin has been divided by the construction of the mine, at Lake Cowal, on land that was the subject of a two-year court dispute over native title.

Spears were thrown at the doors of the homes of two directors of the Wiradjuri Condobolin Corporation, which won the native title claim – which has led to more jobs, training and money.

The left leg of a kangaroo was left on the porch of each house, signifying a death threat in Aboriginal lore. Police suspect the incidents may be linked to one earlier in the evening at the Condobolin Hotel – made famous as *Australian Idol* contestant Shannon Noll's local – when men briefly entered the pub wearing traditional garb and armed with spears.

The door of the corporation's office was also smeared with kangaroo intestines.

The attacks have frightened many in the town's Aboriginal community but it has also stirred talk of violent reprisals.

'If they come back here, they won't walk out,' corporation chairman Dawn Johnson, whose front door was pierced, said.

'We thought someone might attack our office, but this has gone too far.'

Christie Brandy and Shae Smyth, both 16, had left the home they share with their uncle, John Daley, and his wife, Valerie – both corporation directors – a few minutes before their front door was pierced at 10.30pm.

. . . Talk has spread it was the work of a tribe called the Feather Feet, who, so the rumour goes, enforce tribal lore and warned the corporation to pull out of the Native Title agreement signed with Barrick Gold in 2002.

There is no evidence that the rumours are true. However, locals from both sides of the court battle and the police say it is the work of outsiders trying to stir trouble. Three of the people police suspect live in Sydney or on the central coast [of NSW].

Betty Atkinson, one of the five people fighting the claim through the courts, said the 'out-of-towners' should be ashamed of themselves. 'They're making a mockery of our culture,' she said.

Figure 16.3: 'Town living in fear over mining deal' (*Sunday Telegraph* (Sydney), 29 August 2004, p. 31.) Columns altered, punctuation and spelling retained.

narrative of the news story. The whole point of the 'lead' is to tell us everything we need to know about the story, including its outcome. In a fictional narrative, this information is normally withheld until near the end of the text. In a news story we are given the information up front, and can then choose whether or not to read the details of how this point of closure was reached.

Roosters Claim NRL Minor Premiership
All hail Freddy

For years Sydney Roosters fans have chanted 'Freddy Fittler walks on water.'

Yesterday, conditions were right for a miracle but Fittler settled for an outstanding farewell performance instead.

Lightning, driving rain and hail combined to make the last regular season match of Fittler's career a dramatic occasion at Aussie Stadium.

The Roosters' thumping 48–10 defeat of the Parramatta Eels ensured the club won the minor premiership for the first time in 23 years.

And, after a 333-match career, Freddy now has plans for a bigger farewell – Grand Final day.

Figure 16.4: 'Roosters Claim NRL Minor Premiership' (*Daily Telegraph* (Sydney), 6 September 2004, p. 1.) Columns altered, punctuation and spelling retained.

It is conventional for news stories to be structured as 'inverted pyramids', opening with a point of closure, or a 'lead', which enables us to reconstruct most of the narrative, or at least to place the narrative within a recognisable format. Figures 16.1 and 16.3 use the language and narrative structure of the hard news story, reporting events of the immediate past from an external viewpoint. In figure 16.2, the lead paragraph, 'In a mea culpa as welcome as it was unexpected, the owners of France's 60,000 bars, brasseries and cafés admitted yesterday that all too often their staff are surly, service slow and hygiene horrendous', cues us in to expect a funny story about how strange the French are, and this is more or less what we get. The structure of the inverted pyramid, the empirical data ('60,000 bars, brasseries and cafés'), and the deictic reference to immediate time ('yesterday') discursively construct a hard news story, something that is relevant to that day's news. Yet the informal register ('you're slow, surly and at last you've admitted it'), the internal narrator ('the neighbourhood café . . . is suffering from social change') and high levels of modality ('variously voluble or lugubrious Gallic drinkers') are all characteristic of soft news reporting, indicating that the boundary between the two is merely discursive.

Generally speaking, the nearer the point of closure is located to the end of the news item, the 'softer' the story. In other words, a news item in which the point of closure comes virtually at the end of the story, as in a fictional narration, is barely 'news' at all, but rather an opinion piece or a profile, review or commentary. The brief front-page sports story in Sydney's *Daily Telegraph* (figure 16.4) cannot claim to be 'news' since few readers would be unaware of the outcome of the game, so instead it situates the Roosters' win in a familiar sporting template of dramatic conflict, individual heroism and the triumph of the underdog. There is no 'lead' at the beginning but rather a narrative hook, which leaves us expecting further elucidation. The 'angle' suggested by this opening, focusing on one of the players, Freddy Fittler, foreshadows the plot of a heroic narrative. The point of closure, in the paragraph beginning 'The Roosters' thumping 48–10 defeat', comes almost at the end of the piece, followed by the footnote that returns us to the main subject of the article, the hero Freddy Fittler. If this paragraph had been placed at the beginning, as the 'lead', the story would have been constructed as an 'inverted pyramid' news story about the Roosters' surprise win rather than as a post-game profile of a single player.

Individualisation

News stories typically associate events with specific individuals. In the sports story in figure 16.4, an unexpected win is attributed not to a whole team, or to their corporate aspirations and tactics, but to a named individual who is constructed as a hero within a conventional story template of triumph over adversity. The player becomes a leading character in a larger narrative.

Even news items composed in an objective style, such as the item in figure 16.1, make use of individuals as reference points and spokespeople, and in so doing attribute qualities, actions and words to them, effectively creating them as fictional characters. The 'constitutional affairs secretary Lord Falconer' and 'the lord chief justice, Lord Woolf', speak directly or indirectly about their role as upholders of justice, arbitrators on matters of national significance and exercisers of extraordinary power and judgement. They are constructed as powerful agents in the continuing drama of the criminal justice system and its articulation with other layers of society.

Real individuals who form part of news stories therefore have their 'characters' constituted from the same kinds of discursive material as fictional characters. We can compare these two law lords, for example, with the character of the judge in Brian Friel's play, *The Freedom of the City* (1973). In this play, loosely based on the events of 'Bloody Sunday' in Derry, Northern Ireland, on 30 January 1972, when a number of civil rights marchers were shot dead by British troops, a judge presides over an enquiry into a similar tragedy played out on the stage. His measured language – 'Our only function is to form an objective view of the events which occurred in the City of Londonderry' (Friel 1984: 109) – and repeated references to 'facts' and to aspects of the law and legal practice are drawn from a discourse of professionalism that Friel has imitated from the 'real world' of the law as reported in court documents and in the media. Although it is part of the fiction of the play that Friel's judge is not impartial in his handling of the enquiry, a flaw that certainly does not apply to judges in general, his discourse as a character nonetheless marks him out as belonging to much the same kind of professional context as Lords Falconer and Woolf in the news story. Just as Friel borrowed from the language of the media, so the news media model their 'characters' on those of fiction.

More informal news stories come even closer to fiction in their construction of real individuals as characters, such as the 'voluble or lugubrious Gallic drinkers' in figure 16.2 or 'corporation chairman Dawn Johnson whose front door was pierced' in figure 16.3. These individuals are attributed with social roles, personal qualities and actual utterances that convey their feelings and intentions, and with grammatical functions of agency or goal (being acted upon by others) that affect the way we perceive them – as representatives of a particular class or gender, as more or less empowered and capable of effective action. The reductive nature of news reporting encourages the shorthand of stereotyping, so that a brief phrase or reference, such as 'tribal lore' or 'Freddy Fittler walks on water', can suggest an entire social and cultural context. Stereotyping is itself an effect of intertextuality, whereby signifiers are constantly cross-referenced from one text to another, and the stereotypes of news reporting become meaningful with reference not only to other news stories but to fiction and film as well, each mode in dialogue with the others.

News reporting does not merely incorporate 'characters' into a story but also actively aims to associate events with individuals rather than with institutions. The story in figure 16.2 is not simply about the French hospitality industry but about the consumers of that industry, represented by the views of 'Jean-Pierre Mangin, a printer'. This strategy of individualisation has a significant ideological consequence, which is to affirm the view that the social order is actively enabled and determined by individuals, rather than by corporate or institutional structures. In the story of the 'town living in fear' (figure 16.3), the events are narrated as a series of transactions between groups of individual 'characters': the corporate directors, their children, the locals, the 'out-of-towners'. Problems are caused by one or more of these individuals, and solutions have to be found by other individuals. Presenting the story in this way not only oversimplifies the issues to the point where the dispute is almost incomprehensible, it also elides those political and economic factors – the relationship between Aboriginals and white Australians, the impact of mining on rural Australia – that would enable us to contextualise the events and therefore to analyse them separately from the people involved.

The strategy of individualisation is therefore a marker of news discourse, particularly 'soft' news and human interest stories, which invites us to understand events in the news through the perspective of individuals affected by those events. But this strategy also works to assert the ideology of the individual as self-determining actor, ultimately responsible for problems and their solutions, while eliding the role of institutions, government and big business in social transactions.

Focalisation

The narrative concept of focalisation, referring to the viewpoint from which events are described or shown to the audience, has been discussed in earlier chapters in relation to film (see chapters 7 and 8). Fictional narratives employ a variety of perspectives, including first-person and third-person narrators, located internally or externally to the story, and the viewpoints of individual characters expressed through direct speech.

A similar range of focalising positions is available to news reporters, and the choice of focalisation is one of the ways in which different genres of journalism can be distinguished. The objective style of 'hard news' reporting typically relies on an external third-person narrator who claims no privileged knowledge of how events came about, what motivated individual participants or what the various 'characters' might be thinking or feeling. Individual responses are made accessible to the reader only via the actual words of the people concerned, either quoted directly or given to us indirectly, as in figure 16.1 ('Lord Falconer said: "The move fires a warning shot . . ."' – direct speech; 'Lord Woolf said the power would not be used . . .' – indirect speech). During direct or indirect speech, the focalisation appears to shift from the narrator to the speaker, further distancing the journalist from the events being recounted. This use of external focalisation is therefore one of the key strategies for creating the effect of objectivity, in the sense of an impartial account of what happened, uninfluenced by the personal views of the journalist.

However, the point of view constructed by the external narrative voice, representing an assumed 'commonsense' position, is inevitably that of the dominant ideologies and institutional interests within the social order. The 'legal correspondent' in figure 16.1 speaks not only on behalf of the legal profession, tacitly supporting the power of judges within a court of law, but also to and about the institution of the media and how its interests are potentially threatened by the ruling. Other sectors of the community who are similarly affected by the change, such as witnesses and jurors, do not have their interests represented in the story or their views canvassed. The choice of quotes is also confined to members of the political elite. This selectivity of information and authority reminds us that an apparently 'commonsense' account is already positioned within ideology and therefore directs us to dominant or preferred meanings.

Human interest and soft news stories tend to be focalised by an internal third-person narrator, one who seems to be present within the event and directs our understanding of the event by means of evaluative statements. The narrator of the French story in figure 16.2 writes from a viewpoint located where the story is happening ('in central Paris yesterday') and positions us within his own perspective ('an at times limited grasp of the concept of cleanliness'), as if writing a travel guide. Similarly, the sports writer in figure 16.4 'shows' us the match from within 'Aussie Stadium', directing us to share his view of it, and of Fittler's performance, as 'dramatic', 'outstanding' and a 'thumping 48–10 defeat'. This type of internal focalisation is a powerful way of creating an audience of 'us', a community of readers who are assumed to share the same opinions and commonsense view of 'the way things are' with the journalist.

Taking the range of possible focalisations found in fictional narratives, the most striking omission in the discourse of hard news is that of the 'omniscient' voice that characterises many third-person narratives. The journalist, as focaliser, is like the camera in a film, showing us what 'actually' happened without overt commentary or opinion except via other characters acting as focalisers. Even the internal narrators in figures 16.2 and 16.4, who make evaluations, do not presume to have privileged knowledge of what the other characters (the printer, the footballer) might be thinking or feeling. This lack of any claim to narrative omniscience is another aspect of journalistic 'objectivity' as a discursive construct. Whether positioned outside or inside the narrative event, the journalist focaliser appears to be merely acting on our behalf by reporting what happened.

Chronology

The time frame within which reported events occur is one of the main structural elements of narrative. In chapter 2, Rosemary Huisman identified three temporalities governing our experience of the world and how it is represented: sociotemporality (a culture's understanding of its history and being over time); human mental temporality (the personal present, which includes memory of the past and a prediction of what will happen next), which includes the 'plot' or temporal order in a narrative; and organic (living) temporality of the real world, which corresponds to the structuralist concept of 'story'. In many fictional narratives, the linear chronology of 'story', the order of events in real time, is subverted by the technical and aesthetic demands of 'plot', which use such strategies as flashback and multiple focalisation for the purposes of drama, suspense and other effects.

In the discourse of news reporting, the linear chronology of events is typically obscured in order to emphasise the immediacy of what has happened – to make it seem more like 'news as it happens'. The story reported in figure 16.3 gives us very little sense of the actual order of events. Were the spears thrown before or after the kangaroo leg was left on the porch and the intestines spread on the office door? Temporal phrases, such as 'earlier in the evening', give us some orientation, but the general impression is of a number of events happening in random order over a relatively short period of time. The range of verbal tenses, from present perfect ('two houses have been attacked') to present ('police suspect', 'so the rumour goes') to past ('said'), work to avoid a statement of completed actions in the past, apart from what people actually said, creating an endless time of continuing actions that never reach a resolution.

The lack of a specific temporal order also results in a minimising of causation. Because one action or event is not specifically linked to another temporally, there is very little sense that one action has caused a particular reaction or resulted in another event occurring. In the story reported in figure 16.2, there is no direct causative relationship between the admission made in the opening paragraph – that French bar staff are often surly and slow – and the plans announced by the industry body to draw up a hundred criteria by which bar performance will be judged. We might assume a connection, but it is not clear which event preceded the other or whether one caused the other. Similarly, in figure 16.1, no causative event is explicitly identified, although we can assume it lies in the statement: 'In long and complex cases, the prosecution and defence bill can be millions of pounds', hence the perceived need to fine anyone who disrupts the judicial process. The causative statement, coming towards the end of the story, inverts the chronology of the event, so that the 'lead' paragraph recounts a consequence rather than an initiating action.

Obscuring the temporal order and the nature of causation is a characteristic feature of modern news reporting, since it enables stories to be edited down to a specific length without impairing the meaning to any great extent. Since the nub of the story, the 'lead', is given in the opening paragraph, all subsequent paragraphs are to some extent redundant, a mere restating or glossing of what has already been told. News stories are subedited from the bottom upwards, with one or more paragraphs trimmed off if the story is too long to fit the space available. This explains why news stories often seem to end rather abruptly (as in figures 16.1 and 16.3) and why journalists tend to refrain from making one event dependent on another that might be subedited out of the story.

The effect of this kind of obscured chronology is to support the veracity of a news story as a 'slice of life'. As in 'real life', events are presented as they occur, with no overt massaging of the story into a 'plot' of choreographed actions forming a cause-and-effect chain that leads to an inevitable resolution. News stories tell us that in 'real life', there is no resolution – events continue to unfold in such a way that one ending merely becomes another beginning. Such a world view has the effect of decontextualising agency. Individuals appear to act completely independently of the sociotemporality, which is itself obscured by news discourse. The events recounted in figure 16.3 appear to belong to a time period no longer than two years, the longest period specified in the story, and the actions of the individuals therefore belong only to this time frame. The sociotemporal context of the relations between Aboriginal and white Australians, a context stretching back well before 1788, is rendered invisible, and is therefore unavailable as a means of explaining the events of 'yesterday'.

Where temporality and causation are foregrounded in news stories, the purpose is normally to apportion individual blame or responsibility. Political or corporate 'scandals' are often documented in minute detail by media analysts, who provide moment-by-moment accounts of individual actions and how these precipitated further disasters and cover-ups. This temporal detail, typically including specific times and dates, not only helps us to follow the course of events as they unfolded but also works to assure us of their factuality. In terms of ideology, the emphasis on organic temporality, at the expense of sociotemporality, positions individuals as sole agents working to an immutable timetable, with exclusive responsibility for their own actions.

Finally, it is worth remembering that contemporary news discourse, and its handling of temporality, is itself positioned in the sociotemporal context of modern Anglo-American cultures. Allan Bell, noting that 'perceived news value overturns temporal sequence and imposes an order completely at odds with linear narrative' (Bell & Garrett 1998: 96), points out that this style of reporting is quite at odds with most nineteenth-century news journalism, in which events were related in strict chronological order. The economics of sensationalist and issue-driven reporting dictate that a news story should lead not with the chronologically prior event but with the news value that effectively determines the angle.

Consequences of news as narrative

Information comes to journalists in a variety of ways, usually by means of institutionalised pathways, such as press offices and public relations companies. The journalist's job is to spin information into narrative, and I have been arguing that both 'hard' and 'soft' news are forms of narratives, although with different discursive techniques. News narratives also differ from fictional narratives in a number of ways, such as the typically disordered or disconnected chronological structure and comparative lack of causation, but they are distinctively narratives in the sense of being shaped into stories or myths about the 'way things are'.

What is seen as a growing trend towards the narrativisation (or 'tabloidisation') of news is in fact an increasing tendency to present information about current events in the form of 'soft' news, particularly human interest stories. Although the story in figure 16.2 about the French café industry might have been represented in the discourse of industrial relations, it has instead been 'spun' into a humorous story about national stereotypes, tourism and individual perceptions of French cafés. The genre of 'infotainment', produced by the economic imperatives of media advertising and realised in the commodification of news stories, is marked by the use of popular narrative formats that foreground conflictual and dramatic plots involving characters representative of media-specific categories. The more the newspapers are filled with 'infotainment', the less actual information and overview of world events are made available to us.

There are a number of other consequences of presenting news as narrative, all with ideological implications. The first is individualisation, which I have already discussed as an aspect of news narrative. By presenting events as the work of individual people, constructed as 'characters' by reference to their names, ages, occupations and often stereotyped or conventional attributes, news stories suggest that most events are the result of individual human agency and that their impact is to be perceived mainly through individual experience. At the same time, institutional factors, political relations or environmental consequences are often elided or minimised as social 'actors', except where blame or responsibility needs to be diverted from particular individuals and spread across an organisation or institution. In figure 16.1, the article expresses concerns about newspapers, broadcasters and news organisations as potential disrupters of court trials, terms referring to organisations rather than to individual journalists; on the other hand, the other possible sources of disruption – jurors and witnesses – are represented as groups of individuals, members of the public who might behave inappropriately. Members of the media are therefore protected by their institutional affiliation: their individuality, and therefore their personal responsibility, is subordinated to a broader corporate identity.

Another consequence of framing news as narrative is that it enables complex material to be conveyed in the form of accessible and comprehensible formats. Rather than spend time explaining the political, historical and cultural factors that have led to war, journalists tend to write about individual battles and the people involved in them as examples of heroic endeavour, tragic outcomes and triumph over adversity. The drama of military ritual, acted out in a thousand war movies, provides an accessible template for war reporting in the news. For some critics, this accessibility of news by means of narrative templates is an important aspect of the democratisation of information in the public arena.

While the media undoubtedly play a crucial role in informing the public and helping them to understand the workings of the world around them, the formulaic narrativisation of news inevitably leads to a diminution of the information function of news. The public might be informed in a mode that is easily comprehended, but it is also routinely denied access to the complexities of political, economic and cultural negotiation that generate many news events. This in turn leads to public perceptions that politicians are not doing their job, that poor outcomes in terms of economic success or job rates can be attributed to the incompetence of single individuals (whether government ministers or job-seekers), and that social issues identified as 'problems', such as immigration or unemployment, could easily be solved if only the relevant people would change their behaviour or could be voted out of office.

Narrativisation of news also works against the unfolding of continuing stories over time or the analysis of the longer-term consequences of particular events. None of the examples of news stories in this chapter is likely to be followed up with specific reference to these events and their outcomes or consequences. Other stories might appear that relate to these events – perhaps an account of a fine imposed under the new regulations, or another outbreak of violence in Condobolin or some other rural town – but the chances of a long-term consideration of the effects of these events are slim. Because the narratives of news are focused on what has happened just recently and on the immediate outcomes of a single chain of events, audiences perceive events as disjointed and seemingly random occurrences appear to be almost devoid of context or explanation. In some cases, comforting if short-term resolutions are offered, such as the 'right of appeal' in figure 16.1 or the '100 criteria' in figure 16.2, giving the impression that the matter is under control and the problem will be fixed. In other cases, however, such as the violence described in figure 16.3, there appears to be no solution but only a sense of inevitability that the same story will be repeated on future occasions. Very rarely are readers provided with any kind of social or historical context within which events can be located and assessed.

The ultimate consequence of narrativisation of the news is that audiences are often left feeling helpless and disempowered. The stories they read in the newspapers, or hear on the news bulletins, seem to have no easy resolutions, no answers to intractable problems, but instead repeat the same stories over and over again, stories of unnecessary bureaucracy, political incompetence or corruption, sudden violence, social breakdown and medical breakthroughs that never seem to cure anyone they know. Only the human interest stories – of love rediscovered, unexpected wealth from the lottery or triumph after disaster – provide some 'closure' which reassures us that 'happy endings' are possible and indeed desirable. This limited range of news templates, of stories that are defined as 'news', operates to erode our sense of citizenship, our sense that we are socially empowered to influence the world around us, not simply by one-off events such as winning the lottery, but through the slower and less newsworthy processes of political democracy, economic moderation and socially responsible behaviour.

Conclusion

The operations of print news production as both professional and industrial practices tend to work against any stated aims of objectivity and impartiality. In turning information into news, a specialised kind of narrative with its own recognisable genres, the news industry translates the world of experience into a very specific set of impressions presented as universal truths. News stories constantly reconfirm the ideology of randomness, of the inexplicability of events and of the need for charismatic individuals – politicians, movie stars, 'ordinary heroes' or military leaders – to restore order in an otherwise chaotic world. It is possible to tell other kinds of stories and construct other kinds of ideologies about the world – but such stories are not generally told in the newspapers that we read.

Chapter 17

Analysing the discourse of news

Helen Fulton

In the last chapter, I described some of the main features of print news construction that work to bring the genre of news into the broader textual category of narrative. The chapter also raised some of the ideological consequences of the production and consumption of news as narrative.

In this chapter, I outline some strategies for analysing the discourse of print news. Like any kind of critical text analysis, interpretation of news discourse needs to be grounded in an understanding of how language choices in a given context construct particular meanings. This is in fact what **discourse** means: language choices related to a specific social context, or, as Norman Fairclough defines it, 'language as a form of social practice' (Fairclough 1989: 20).

Although most of us can describe in general terms the difference between an 'objective' news story and a sensationalised human interest story, accounting for those differences requires a reasonably sophisticated toolbox of linguistic and interpretive concepts that can be applied to different kinds of texts. A semiotic methodology of critical analysis enables us to show how meanings are made and ideologies are reiterated. Systematically identifying specific linguistic choices and their semiotic potential is also effective for calibrating the differences between various genres of news narratives.

Some basic tools for text analysis, based on the work of Michael Halliday and his theory of language as a 'social semiotic', have already been introduced and applied in this book (see especially chapters 8 and 12). To start with the 'big picture' view of texts, we can regard a piece of text, such as a news story, as becoming meaningful because of the various functions performed by the language choices. Words, phrases and clauses can perform one or more of the following semantic functions:

- *ideational*: expressing the field or content of what the text is about;
- *interpersonal*: expressing the tenor of the social relationships between the participants in the text, and the relationship between narrator and audience;
- *textual*: expressing the mode or style of the text, how it is put together and the medium by which it is conveyed to an audience.

The discourse of news can be analysed in more detail using these three meta-functions of language as starting points for a closer look at the linguistic choices that characterise news as a social practice. I have reprinted two examples of news texts in this chapter, figures 17.1 and 17.2, and my discussion draws mainly on these examples. I also consider some aspects of image analysis, using figure 17.3 as an example.

Public idiom

Daily newspapers published in the same country or city invariably speak in different voices, addressing a range of imagined audiences distinguished by location, socioeconomic groupings, political viewpoints and other factors. In the UK the *Guardian* addresses urbanised professionals in the public service, educational, creative and media sectors, who share a high level of interest in and knowledge of contemporary politics viewed from a centre-left perspective. The *Daily Telegraph* in the UK, on the other hand, addresses the business sector, including corporate professionals, small-business owners and the self-employed, whose interest in current affairs, from a largely right-of-centre viewpoint, is shaped by financial concerns ahead of party-political issues.

In Sydney, the *Sydney Morning Herald* and its sister Sunday paper, the *Sun-Herald*, address a politically centrist middle-class audience with a wide age demographic, drawn from the public service (especially health and education sectors), small business and the rural sector, as well as urban professionals. Both papers are committed to 'watchdog' journalism, providing elements of public education while informing readers of what is going on in their city, region and state. The *Australian* newspaper is more akin to the British *Daily Telegraph*, constructing a nationwide conservative audience focused on business-related issues and economic power-broking placed in the context of national and international movements of share markets and business fluctuations. In Sydney and London, tabloid newspapers such as the British *Sun* and the Sydney-based *Daily Telegraph* (both owned by Rupert Murdoch, as are *The Times* (London) and the *Australian*) target a range of demographics, focusing mainly on non-professional workers and marginal groups such as the unemployed, students and home-based workers.

Aligned to a greater or lesser extent with their actual readers (the **perlocutionary audience**) in terms of class, occupation and demographic, newspapers (like TV channels and magazines) have a broad understanding of their intended or **illocutionary audience**, the one constructed by the language of the text. The discourse of news calls these illocutionary audiences into being by addressing them, or 'interpellating' them, to use Althusser's term, in a language that they are assumed to recognise as their own (Easthope & McGowan 1992: 55). The news does not seem to speak to them in a special voice, like a teacher or actor, but in more or less the same voice as their families, their friends and themselves. By invoking this shared discourse, and along with it a set of shared values and beliefs about the world, a news outlet attempts to secure the kind of perlocutionary audience it needs to sell to advertisers.

This concept of a shared discourse is what Stuart Hall has called a public idiom, and which Roger Fowler describes as 'a discursive norm . . . a sense of a "neutral" language embodying "normal" values' (Fowler 1991: 47). What this means is that news products address their audiences in a language that seems familiar to them, something they can recognise as belonging to their own world of everyday interaction and experience, and which therefore helps to define them and their sense of reality. A public idiom not only creates a comforting sense of identity and belonging, a sense that the newspaper (or newsreader) is speaking directly to oneself, but is also an affirmation of the 'rightness' of shared opinions and values. The stories told in the newspaper are the stories that its audience recognise as fundamentally meaningful to them.

In using a range of public idioms to inform the public of current events, newspapers work to reinforce ideological consensus, a general agreement that the status quo is, if not perfect, the way things should be. Economic and power relations between different sectors of society are implicitly confirmed as part of the 'natural' order of things. The story in figure 17.1, from the *Weekly Telegraph*, the weekly version of the British *Daily Telegraph* available to international readers, conveys the results of a poll in judicious terms which still manage to suggest that George W. Bush, despite a resounding election win, is in trouble with his electorate. The headline and the lead paragraph provide the point of closure that sums up the plot, leaving little room for disagreement or alternative interpretations of the poll results. Written as if to contribute to dinner-party conversations about the future of Bush's administration, the article asks our consent to marginalise the war in Iraq and regard it merely as a test of Bush's authority.

The language of different news outlets – whether newspapers, TV bulletins, radio news or web sites – therefore constructs a particular kind of subject position, inviting us to respond to the text as credible, common sense and more or less 'true' in the sense that it conforms to our understanding of reality. The various public idioms of news media exert a powerful ideological pressure that reinforces the consumer's sense of identity and continuously rebuilds consensus to the prevailing social order.

Americans see war as mistake

By Alec Russell

President Bush's post-election honeymoon came to an abrupt end last week when it emerged that, for the first time since last year's invasion of Iraq, a clear majority of Americans believe the war is a mistake.

Before the news broke of the devastating attack on a US military base in Mosul, a Washington Post/ABC News opinion poll found that 56 per cent thought that, given the cost in American lives, the war was 'not worth fighting.'

A slender majority think the invasion of Iraq has contributed to the future security of the USA but 70 per cent believe that the 1,300 dead soldiers are an 'unacceptable price.'

The growing disillusionment is not leading to pressure to pull out the 150,000 troops in Iraq. Nearly 60 per cent of Americans support keeping them there until 'civil order is restored.'

But the findings puncture the mood of invulnerability and triumphalism in Republican circles since Mr Bush's election victory last month . . .

Figure 17.1: 'Americans see war as mistake' (*Weekly Telegraph* (UK), 29 December–4 January 2005, p. 18, headed 'Iraq'.) First five paragraphs of a longer story; columns altered, spelling and punctuation retained.

Constructing a public idiom

Ideational function – defining the field

Linguistic choices that perform a primarily ideational function construct the field of discourse, telling us what the story is about. This headline, for example, from a tabloid newspaper article reporting on a book about George W. Bush, contains all the main ideational references: 'New Book claims Bush took drugs' (*Daily Telegraph* (Sydney), 6 September 2004: 7). Each nominal item in the headline – book, Bush, drugs – could potentially attract to itself a collocation of related items that would expand its field to provide more detail and information. Phrases occurring in the body of the article, such as 'took cocaine', 'experimented with drugs' and 'coke-taking', form a collocational set that expands the field suggested by 'drugs' in the headline. However, the largest collocation is connected not to Bush or his alleged drug-taking but to the 'new book': 'the book, to be published next week . . .', 'the 700-page biography', 'huge and controversial bestseller'. The main point of the article, then, is to advertise the forthcoming book by creating interest in its contents, author, subject and the controversy it is likely to create. This kind of field suggests an audience more interested in consumerism and celebrity rather than in global politics and the future of nations.

Field is also defined by the participants, the kinds of people involved in the action and how they are described or categorised. Categories of people are ideologically significant and culturally produced groupings that reveal authorial positioning and assumptions of consensus or 'normality' in relation to such social structures as gender, class and power (Fowler 1991: 92; Fairclough 1995: 113–14). In figure 17.2, the category of 'pregnant women' is set against the official might of the Royal Australasian College of Obstetricians and Gynaecologists and the World Health Organisation. The only spokesperson is given a full list of titles: 'Australian Centre for the Control of Iodine Deficiency Disorders chairman Professor Creswell Eastman', locating this person as part of a category of medical professionals. 'Pregnant and lactating women', however, are defined entirely in terms of their fertility, with no mention of their possible professional roles, creating an imbalance of gender and power that is naturalised in the article under the guise of public information and education.

News reporting makes a distinction between the categories associated with hard news (politicians, experts, government representatives, business leaders) and those with soft news (celebrities, 'ordinary' people, occupational groups, minority groups), implying a hierarchy of social positioning. At the same time, some categories are overrepresented in the news compared to others. Groups associated with political, economic and cultural power tend to be overrepresented as significant participants in and producers of the events of the day; groups defined as marginal or minority in terms of age, gender, class or ethnicity barely appear in hard news except as victims or criminals, but are overrepresented in human interest stories of 'ordinary life'. Categorisation is therefore a powerful way of naturalising social divisions and hierarchies that are the effects of cultural and economic factors, including the institutional conventions of media reporting.

This article also illustrates the grammatical roles played by different participants in clauses, a phenomenon known as **transitivity**. In the clause 'Iodine deficiency can damage the developing brain of a foetus', the verbal part, or process, 'can damage', functions as a transitive material process that links the active participant (actor) with the receiving participant (goal). The medical condition of iodine deficiency is therefore positioned powerfully in this clause as one that has material consequences. In figure 17.1, the phrase 'the news broke' is intransitive since there is an actor ('news') but no goal. Furthermore, in this combination of actor and process, the two are not functionally linked – as in the phrase 'the cup broke', the process appears to have no agent at all but to have come about spontaneously. (This grammatical feature is known as 'ergativity'. See Thompson 1996: 112–15.) Such a construction is very useful in journalistic writing as a means of conveying events while eliding the agency of those events.

Returning to figure 17.2, the article (like the headline) begins with a passive construction, 'Pregnant women will be instructed to boost their intake of iodine', which positions 'pregnant women' as the goal but elides the actor (they will be instructed by whom?). Already disempowered grammatically, the goal is further objectified by the absence of an explicit actor. In the next paragraph, the actor is revealed as the 'Royal Australasian College', a depersonalised institutional authority acting upon a group of individuals, which articulates a very unequal relationship between actor and goal. 'Pregnant and lactating women', regardless of their state of health, are grammatically and semantically constructed as 'patients' under

Pregnant women urged to take iodine

By Miranda Wood

Pregnant women will be instructed to boost their intake of iodine to reduce the risk of miscarriage and foetal abnormalities.

The Royal Australasian College of Obstetricians and Gynaecologists will recommend early next year that women consume more iodine when planning to have a baby or as soon [as] they become pregnant.

Iodine deficiency can damage the developing brain of a foetus and lower a child's IQ by 10 to 15 points.

The World Health Organisation, which recognises iodine deficiency as the world's most common cause of brain damage, will also meet in January to discuss the poor intake of iodine.

Australian Centre for the Control of Iodine Deficiency Disorders chairman Professor Creswell Eastman said Australia's consumption of iodine was very low and had created a significant health problem.

'It's a serious concern, particularly for pregnant women and lactating women,' he said.

'They should be supplementing their diet with iodine.'

Figure 17.2: 'Pregnant women urged to take iodine' (*Sun-Herald* (Sydney), 5 December 2004, p. 4. Columns altered, spelling and punctuation retained.)

instruction from the medical profession. The transitivity patterns therefore exert a very persuasive ideological pressure on 'women', categorised as a single homogeneous group, to see themselves as 'patients' when they become pregnant and to obey without question the commands of medical authorities. In addition, the transitivity patterns of actor and goal inscribe our consent to the commonsense idea that 'women', pregnant or otherwise, should be treated as the passive objects of institutional decision-making.

This commonsense idea (or ideology) is reinforced by the 'angle' chosen by the journalist, which focuses on 'pregnant women' even though iodine deficiency affects both men and women and 'Australia's consumption of iodine [is] very low'. Calling on the common category of 'pregnant women', with its intertextual connotations of helplessness, vulnerability, health problems and unpredictable behaviour, the article reinforces a familiar ideological message that women, not men, are entirely responsible for the health and well-being of embryos, babies, children and the 'family' in general, including men. Terms such as 'urged', 'instructed', 'recommend' and 'should be supplementing', belonging to a category of didactic verbal processes, signify that it is a pregnant woman's duty and obligation to take iodine supplements and that she needs to be 'instructed' to do so.

Faced with this barrage of ideological pressure from all sides, individual women reading this article would have to be made of strong stuff indeed to ignore its message – quite apart from the accuracy or otherwise of the report, the advice of their own doctors or indeed their own preferences. The 'public idiom' of the article is that of the concerned journalist engaged in socially responsible reporting with the primary aim of informing – but also instructing – the public regarding such matters of importance as health and the welfare of babies.

Categorisation and transitivity construct not only the field of discourse but also the ideological significance of the message. A further aspect of field that also has ideological meaning is **nominalisation**, whereby actions are expressed not by verbal processes but by noun phrases. In figure 17.1, the nominals 'invasion of Iraq', 'devastating attack on a US military base', 'the cost in American lives' and 'the growing disillusionment' have been selected instead of corresponding verbal forms: 'America invaded Iraq', 'Iraqi soldiers attacked a military base', 'American lives have been spent' and 'Americans are disillusioned'. One of the most striking effects of nominalisation, as we can see in the above examples, is to remove agency. References to 'invasion' and 'attack' omit the people or nation responsible, while the semantic difference between these two concepts ('invasion' suggesting something inevitable and liberationist, 'attack' suggesting something aggressive and unprovoked), together with the addition of the modal adjective 'devastating' in relation to the Iraqi 'attack', implies a qualitative difference between the 'good' Americans and the 'bad' Iraqis.

The lack of actors helps to suggest that events are in some way inevitable, such as 'the cost in American lives', as if this is an expense for which nobody budgeted but it occurred anyway. Another effect of nominalisation is to remove or minimise the causal relationship between events. Nominalised events, such as 'invasion', 'attack', 'disillusionment', 'pressure', 'election victory' and so on, express completed actions that can then be positioned in time as part of a constructed reality: 'last year's invasion', 'Bush's election victory last month'. These events seem to have happened inevitably and ahistorically, as milestones simply occurring as time goes past rather than as the products and consequences of a whole series of choices, happenings and human agency. They are effects with no apparent causes.

Finally, nominalisation is one of the main stylistic features of the 'objective' form of news reporting, which, as I described in the previous chapter, is an effect of discourse rather than a retrieval of 'facts'. In both stories, figure 17.1 and figure 17.2, nominalised forms help to construct the mode of objectivity and factuality. 'The mood of invulnerability and triumphalism' (figure 17.1), although highly evaluative in its assessment of post-election Republican USA, suggests a proper distance between narrator and the events being narrated. References to 'poor intake of iodine' and 'consumption of iodine' in figure 17.2, eliding the individuals who might or might not take it, help to medicalise the problem by identifying behavioural phenomena associated with health. The medical discourse of the article not only constructs us as actual or potential patients who need urgent treatment but also works to distance the journalist from the content. Using nominalisation rather than assigning agency assures us that the story is factual and objective and that it comes from a reputable professional source.

The field of discourse locates us within a particular construct of the real world, with its boundaries and contours mapped out, together with the roads along which we may travel, and those that are closed to us because of our gender, class or other kind of social determination. Relations of power, concepts of appropriate behaviour and a consensus as to what are 'facts' and what are 'opinions' are naturalised as 'common sense' through the ideologies articulated in the ideational metafunction of journalistic discourse.

Interpersonal function – defining the tenor

The 'tenor' of discourse refers to the social relations between participants in the text, including the narrator and audience. It includes the idea of **voice**: whether we are addressed in the third or first person, and the idea of **register**: how formally or informally the participants speak to each other. One of the simplest ways to assess the tenor of a text is to look at the forms of address, or the ways in which participants name each other. In figure 17.1 George Bush is referred to as 'President Bush', and later as 'Mr Bush', using his titles rather than his first and second names, as I have done. This creates a more formal tenor than such titles as 'George W. Bush' or 'the President', which both imply a popular media-led familiarity. These two forms of address are frequently used in tabloid newspaper stories, such as the *Daily Telegraph* (Sydney) article reporting on a book about the 'Bush dynasty' (6 September 2004: 7). Headlined 'New book claims Bush took drugs', the article reports on 'allegations about Mr Bush's coke-taking . . . from his former sister-in-law Sharon Bush, who divorced his brother Neil Bush'. The opening reference to 'George W. Bush' serves to distinguish the son from his father, a former US President also called George Bush, and therefore to locate us in the world of family dynamics that is the subject of the book, called *The Family: The Real Story of the Bush Dynasty*. We are reminded that 'the President' is just one of us really, part of a big family ('the Bush dynasty', 'former sister-in-law Sharon Bush', 'his brother Neil Bush') that has its own dysfunctional aspects like our own. This domestication of George Bush provides the context for the 'plug' for Kitty Kelley's book about the Bush family, but it also expresses the ambivalence of the disempowered towards those in power – the desire to reduce them to ordinary levels, so that we can understand them – coupled with a desire that they should be positioned beyond our sphere of experience and therefore unknowable.

The kinds of colloquialisms and metaphors used in journalistic discourse also help to construct tenor, particularly the relationship between narrator and reader. The reference to 'coke-taking' in the tabloid article belongs to the same register of popular speech as 'the President did coke at Camp David', an actual quotation from a speaking subject. This juxtaposition unites us all – narrator, interviewees and readers – in an informal register of popular colloquial speech, creating a

Table 17.1: Constructing a 'public idiom' in news journalism

Field (Ideational function)	*Tenor* (Interpersonal function)	*Mode* (Textual function)
collocations	voice	thematisation
categories	register	cohesion
transitivity	metaphor	– repetition
nominalisation	modality	– ellipsis
	appraisal	– conjunction
		graphology

public idiom that we are assumed to recognise as our own kind of language. It also normalises drug use as a recreational pastime among the public at large, not an activity confined to the criminal underworld. This further confirms the ambivalence towards George Bush who is supposed to be 'one of us' and therefore at liberty to indulge in recreational drug use, but who is also supposed to be an exemplar of morally correct behaviour, powerful enough to resist the temptations of illegal activities.

The range of metaphors used in figure 17.1 constructs a somewhat patronising and superior tenor between the narrator and the main participant, 'Americans'. Starting with 'post-election honeymoon' and finishing with 'the findings puncture the mood of invulnerability and triumphalism', the article suggests a certain amount of satisfaction at the outcome of the poll, an expression of attitude that undermines the empirical factuality of the report. The reader is invited to share the narrator's attitude, drawing us all into a language of British superiority to American folly, a public idiom redolent of the competitive corporate marketplace. The poll is interpreted (and was perhaps originally worded) as if the war in Iraq is a failed business venture: 'Americans see war as mistake', 'cost in American lives', 'not worth fighting', 'unacceptable price' and 'future security of the USA'. We are positioned as the subjects of a global capitalist discourse in which economic outcomes are the primary standard by which events are judged and in which Britain and the USA compete for economic and political power.

One of the most significant ways of constructing tenor is the use of **modality**. Modal forms – processes, adjuncts and some phrases or clauses – enable the narrator to convey varying levels of commitment to the truth, desirability, necessity or likelihood of particular events. Whereas figure 17.1 uses mainly declarative statements – 'came to an end', 'a majority of Americans believe' – that enable us to attach a high truth value to what is being said, modal verbs such as 'can' or 'may' (as in 'can damage' in figure 17.2) qualify the truth claim and make it more contingent. Modal adjuncts such as 'perhaps', 'possibly' and 'almost certainly' similarly express a low modality, or a relative lack of faith in a truth claim, which is why they are not often used in journalism, where the aim is to convey truth and factuality. We can compare a different kind of modal adjunct used in figure 17.1, 'for the first time', which signifies a high modality, a complete commitment to the truth of the statement, adding to the assertive tenor of the whole piece. Modality is therefore one of the main discursive strategies for making a distinction between fact and opinion in journalistic writing.

Modal forms can also distinguish between different viewpoints or focalisations in the narration. When the narration in figure 17.2 changes from the high modality of declarative verbs, such as 'will recommend', to the lower modality of 'can damage', this indicates a shift in the viewpoint of the narrator to that of her source. The whole paragraph beginning 'Iodine deficiency' echoes the 'voice' of the report or press release issued by the medical college that clearly formed the source for this article. The quoted spokesperson also uses a modal form – 'They should be supplementing their diet' – indicating a strong opinion regarding desirability or necessity, and this provides yet another focalisation, explicitly positioned. Although this opinion is clearly marked off as separate from that of the newspaper, the voice of the college is merely implied through the change from a higher to lower modality, so that the medical information is appropriated by the newspaper rather than attributed to its source. By suppressing this alternative focalisation, the newspaper can support its image as one committed to public education.

Closely related to modality, as another aspect of tenor, is evaluation or **appraisal** (Butt et al. 2000: 120). Serious journalism written in an objective style is marked by its relative lack of both modality and appraisal, with evaluative comment clearly assigned to named sources or marked off as opinion pieces (Thompson 1996: 64). This creates a public idiom marked by impartiality, detachment and a concern with facts rather than opinions. Such a discourse implicitly realises the ideology that the world is amenable to this kind of objective study, as in figure 17.2, where the relative lack of appraisal, or subjective comment, helps to assert the factuality of what is reported and the authority and credibility of the source.

High levels of appraisal are a feature of the public idiom associated with tabloid journalism, based on conversational speech patterns and the rhetoric of marketing and consumption. People, objects and events are appraised in relation to levels of graduation (on a scale of negative to positive) and force (on a scale of 'hardly' to 'very', or low-impact to high-impact), which associate them with the language of advertising and therefore commodify them. Terms expressing force, such as 'sensational allegations', 'controversial new book' and 'huge and controversial bestseller' (where 'bestseller' is also an example of graduation), construct the tenor of marketing, where the relationship between narrator and reader is that of advertiser and consumer. Highly evaluative journalism constructs an informal register in which the narrator appears to be engaging us in animated conversation while assuming that we all share the same appraisal about the topics under discussion.

At the same time, any level of appraisal introduces an element of persuasion and positioning, evidenced particularly in the rhetoric of urgency, outrage, mockery, drama or triumph that inevitably accompanies tabloid journalism. With this style of highly evaluative narrative, we are rhetorically coerced by the force of the appraisal into the confrontational subject position of advertising, where our only options are to submit to the overdetermined narration of need and desire – 'hotly disputed', 'eagerly awaited' – or to resist with equal force our subjection to commodification.

Appraisal is not always explicitly realised through adjectives, adverbial expressions and metaphors, but can be implicitly coded in lexical items, such as verbs and noun phrases. The series of verbs at the beginning of figure 17.2 – 'urged', 'instructed', 'will recommend' – suggests a graduation of appraisal of the risks from highly urgent to not immediately pressing. The low-risk appraisal continues during the body of the article, rising again towards the end, with the quoted comments of 'serious concern' and 'should be supplementing'. This shifting in the terms of appraisal actually makes it quite difficult for the reader to assess the situation, undermining the newspaper's implied aim of informing and educating its readers on matters of public health and safety.

Forms and levels of appraisal are therefore an important part of the public idiom of newspapers, positioning us to view people and events as more or less important, significant, urgent, threatening, humorous, quirky or typical of particular social and cultural groups. Implicit discrimination against some groups, and the privileging of others, can be conveyed by terms suggesting a scale of evaluations. In figure 17.1 Bush's 'post-election honeymoon' not only came to an end, it also came to an 'abrupt' end, and the majority of Americans who believe the war is a mistake, according to the poll, are a 'clear majority', while those who support the war are merely a 'slender majority'. This careful calibration of graduating appraisal works to emphasise the extent and significance of Bush's apparent decline in popularity.

There is of course a variety of public idioms available within the discourse of journalism, and most newspapers regularly employ more than one, while maintaining a dominant idiom throughout, much as radio channels cultivate their own distinctive 'sound' (see Anne Dunn in chapter 15). The idiom of objective hard news reporting suggests an impartial narrator, authorised by institutional affiliations, whose function is to inform and educate a diverse but willing community in order to encourage citizenship and socially responsible behaviour (as in figure 17.2). A more informal idiom, conveying the opinions of a single reporter (institutionally positioned) through an evaluation of the facts, addresses us as participants in a conversation of the informed electorate, weighing up together the significance of the latest events (as in figure 17.1). The clamorous and emotionally charged idiom of tabloid journalism subordinates information to the demands of commodification and interpellates us into the text as subjects of the marketplace.

Variations of tenor and interpersonal meanings distinguish most clearly between different versions of the public idiom. How we are addressed, who is hailing us and in what register position us in relation to the narrator in such a way that we are ready to receive the message being sent to us, whether it contains information, opinion, education, a moral lesson or advertising.

Textual function – defining the mode

The mode of a news text is closely related to the narrative aspect of news since it refers to the way in which a text is assembled and delivered as a meaningful whole. Such words and phrases as 'yesterday', 'before', 'because' and 'also' perform a textual function by indicating the relationship between one clause and another and the way each clause fits in with the others to convey a complete event. Among the most significant aspects of mode distinctively realised in news journalism are thematisation, cohesion and graphology.

'Thematisation' refers to the choice of theme in each clause; that is, the part of the clause (participant, process or circumstance) that occurs first (Thompson 1996: 118). Whatever is mentioned first positions us to receive the rest of the clause in a particular order and with more or less emphasis on particular elements. An unmarked or unemphasised theme is normally the grammatical subject, which regularly occurs first in most English declarative sentences. In the tabloid article about the Kitty Kelley book, the themes include 'George W. Bush', 'the book', 'Laura Bush, the president's wife', 'the claims', 'the allegations', 'the President' and 'Kelley'. These themes, along with the headline and lead paragraph, indicate those parts of the story considered to be the most significant and cue us in to what the article is really about: promoting a book based on 'sensational allegations'. The pattern of thematisation throughout the article isolates the book and the people connected with it as the main news event, with the issue of drug-taking grammatically and semantically moved into second place.

Thematic patterns also highlight differences of power and hierarchies of significance. In figure 17.2 the themes of the headline and opening sentence are the same, 'pregnant women', while many of the subsequent themes refer to institutional organisations ('Royal Australasian College', 'World Health Organisation') or nominalised abstractions ('iodine deficiency', 'Australia's consumption of iodine'). These themes indicate the national and international importance of the issue and the role of Australia in world affairs, while identifying a single group of people as the ones most affected by the issue. This group is therefore ranked thematically as less empowered since they are excluded from any comparable institutional structure and are positioned at the level of local and personal conditions rather than at the level of international policy debate.

A particular feature of journalistic writing is the very long nominal groups that most often form the grammatical subject, and therefore the theme, of many clauses. This example from figure 17.2, 'Australian Centre for the Control of Iodine Deficiency Disorders chairman Professor Creswell Eastman', forms a single nominal group standing as the subject (or, in functional terms, the sayer) of the verbal process 'said'. Such extended themes facilitate the incorporation of several layers of information (status, title, institutional affiliation, occupation, often age, gender and family role as well) into a single constituent of the clause, saving space in the news story and creating a unit that cannot easily be edited out by a subeditor. They also contribute to the factuality of the story by positioning individuals in a recognisable and verifiable social order. But they also work ideologically by categorising individuals according to conventional descriptors that, by being frequently thematised, become naturalised. Thus 'chairman' or 'professor' function as 'normal' designations for a man, whereas 'full-time parent of three young children' is more likely to occur as a 'normal' way to describe a woman.

Thematisation therefore draws our attention to the main topic of a news item and helps us to identify the 'angle', including the plot and characters. In addition, the opening section of a clause or sentence contributes to the **cohesion** of a continuous piece of text by indicating how each clause is linked to the one before. This is usually achieved by various kinds of repetition, either of a complete word or phrase, or by substituting one item for a similar or synonymous item, as in this clause from figure 17.2, 'they should be supplementing their diet with iodine', where the pronoun 'they' clearly refers to 'pregnant and lactating women' in the previous clause. Similarly, in figure 17.1, the use of the adverb 'there' in the clause '60 per cent of Americans support keeping them there' provides a deictic reference to Iraq in the previous clause. Clearly marked linguistic repetitions such as these help us to work our way through a text and understand what is going on.

Cohesion can also be achieved by ellipsis, or by omitting an item that has already occurred earlier in the text, requiring the reader to make the connection. In figure 17.1, the theme 'a slender majority' refers to the respondents of the poll that forms the main topic of the news item, linking this new paragraph with the one before and reassuring us that we are still reading within the same semantic context. It also forms part of a collocational set referring to opinion polls: 'majority', '56 per cent thought that', 'nearly 60 per cent of Americans' and so on. The regular distribution of such terms throughout the article reminds us that the main topic is not the war itself but the results of a poll about US attitudes to the war. In addition, the repeated use of 'Americans' rather than 'respondents' works not only cohesively but also ideologically, moving us from the discourse of opinion polling to the discourse of nationalism in a context of nations at war.

Whereas repetition, ellipsis and collocations signal to us that clauses are related semantically, conjunction indicates the ways in which they are related temporally or causally. Figure 17.1 contains two significant conjunctive forms, 'before' and 'but', both positioned as marked themes at the beginning of clauses. The first explains the chronology of the poll and provides an opportunity to mention and appraise the 'devastating attack on a US military base'. The second indicates a dependent and contrastive link on the pattern of 'not one thing but another', implying that the 'findings' of the poll are a 'growing disillusionment' that is directly causing Bush's popularity to decline. Other common conjunctive prepositions and adjuncts include 'after', 'because', 'so', 'nevertheless' and 'although'.

We can also include deictics – words or phrases indicating relations of time and place – among conjunctive devices since they link one event to another temporally or spatially. The first few lines of figure 17.1 contain a succession of temporal deictics and conjunctions that locate us fairly precisely in a specific time frame, relating the poll results of 'last week' to the invasion of 'last year' and 'before' the news of an attack. Conjunction and deixis are working here to overdetermine the significance of the poll results. The poll is positioned as a definitive turning point in a continuing chain of events, one that marks a major shift in Bush's popularity and Republican confidence. Yet there is no real evidence for such a causative connection, which has been constructed by cohesive strategies of the discourse. The results of the poll have been inflated into a hard news story, given urgency and drama, by being grammatically and semantically linked to the large-scale events of the war in Iraq and the recent presidential elections in the USA.

The mode of a text – the way in which it is unfolded step by step – creates a textual logic that enables us to recognise generic styles and narratives and understand what is going on in a text. The choice of mode, however, also precludes and elides other possible ways of presenting events. By looking at textual meanings, realised in choices of cohesive strategies, theme and conjunction, we can see how information has been turned into a narrative, given a particular sequence, set of major players, location and causation, in such a way as to appear natural and seamless.

What is striking about the mode of news reporting as a form of narrative is the relative lack of cohesion. Apart from a few locating deictics such as 'yesterday', 'early next week' and 'last year', which are necessary to define the immediacy of news, most news stories represent events without clear causative or conjunctive links, although these are sometimes implied. In figure 17.2, pregnant women are being urged to take iodine *because* Australia's consumption of iodine is low and *because* iodine deficiency has serious health consequences. But these causative links are not made explicit in the text. The information rolls out as a series of unconnected utterances as if this is the way reality 'really' happens.

In general, news stories proceed from one paragraph to the next as a series of statements whose logical connections are suggested by a certain amount of repetition and ellipsis, but are otherwise implicit. Abbreviated headlines and one-sentence paragraphs, highly typical of the mode of journalism, enable nuggets of information to be released one at a time in easily digestible portions. This mode not only promotes oversimplification of the issues being reported, it also assists the subediting process, which lops off one paragraph at a time, starting at the bottom of the column. The fewer causative or logical links expressed between the paragraphs, the easier it is to lose a few of them without compromising the meaning of the story. Here again, we can see how the institutional practices of journalism – the need to carve up text into specific sizes and shapes to fit the page – determine the way in which news is presented to us.

Most significantly, however, journalism's lack of cohesion helps to construct a style of objectivity and detachment. Without conjunctions, such as 'because', 'so that', 'since', 'on the other hand' and so on, the story appears to be told to us as a series of factual happenings unmediated by the writer's own interpretation or gloss. The narrative voice is elided, and only the time frame is important, as part of the factuality of the report. The thematised conjunction 'but' in figure 17.1 not only performs a textual function in linking two paragraphs, it also performs an interpersonal function in suggesting the narrator's evaluation of the relative significance of events. Journalistic writing that displays the highest levels of explicit cohesion tends to be opinion pieces or commentary articles in which a specific line is being argued, evaluations are being made and the narrative voice deliberately identifies itself, claims our attention and assumes our agreement.

Finally, the physical appearance and layout of news stories form part of its distinctive mode. The graphology of text, the way it looks visually on the page, contributes to its textual meaning by setting up expectations of genre, function and content. Print advertisements typically announce themselves graphologically by their ***mise en page***, their distinctive mixture of image and text, use of colour, range of fonts and font sizes, and prominent placement of a distinctive logo or brand name. The aim of their graphological devices is both to separate advertising material from the editorial content of the newspaper and magazine and to imitate the appearance and public idiom of the particular publication in which it appears, so that the reader's movement from editorial to advertisement and back again is as seamless as possible.

Similarly, print news as a genre is instantly recognisable by its distinctive graphological signs, including headlines in large bold font, small-font text arranged in columns with justified margins, broadsheet or tabloid page-size, and a variety of text, image, news and advertisements combined on each page. Our attention is drawn to particularly significant news items by variations in the standard graphology, such as banner-sized headlines or break-out boxes containing quotes or background information, or graphics, such as maps and diagrams. This graphological variety serves a textual function by presenting the news text in a conventional way and giving us the same information in a variety of forms, such as words and graphics. We are also given visual prompts about how to manage the different items on the page and whether they are related or separated. In addition, graphology serves an ideological function in presenting information multimodally, through both text and image, and an interpersonal function by 'speaking' to us loudly or softly (through larger or smaller fonts) or positioning us to respond emotively to a photographic image or boxed quotation.

Analysing visual images in the news

Although early newspapers contained very few images, the availability of relatively cheap photography and rapid processing in the 1950s and 1960s encouraged the emergence of photojournalism as an essential component of newspapers (Hartley 1996: 196). With the rise of a heavily image-based advertising industry, and as television news became more widely accessible to mass audiences, offering the iconic veracity of film footage and 'actuality', newspapers had to compete for authority and credibility by providing more images to support written text. Since the development of digital technology, newspaper layout has made even greater use of photographic images, in colour as well as black and white, exchanging graphological formats with its newest competitor, the Internet.

Changes in technology have been accompanied by a change in the relationship between written text and printed image. Until the latter part of the twentieth century, written text commanded an authority of meaning. Important messages were (and to some extent still are) printed in books or journals without any pictures, or accompanied by images whose function was clearly subordinate to that of the written text. The use of predominant images was associated with children's books, comics or simplified information, such as instruction manuals. According to this 'old' model of visual literacy, images were subservient to language and not the other way round (Kress & van Leeuwen 1996: 21).

Spurred on by the rise of visual technology, particularly the Internet, the balance of authority has shifted in favour of images. Although written text is still important, it is images that often drive or dominate a printed message and mark it out as important. In news journalism, the front-page lead story is selected not only on the basis of news values but also on the basis of having an arresting image that can be placed centrally on the page. Single colour images, supported only by a brief line of explanatory text, regularly form complete news items on their own, devoid of any other text. Truth and factuality, once encoded primarily in written language, are increasingly associated with pictures rather than words, even as we all become more familiar with the processes by which pictures can be digitally created and altered. The prestige of technology, in which images and multimodal messages outrank written text on its own, comprises an ideology that increasingly locates authority of meaning and the power to communicate with the producers and manipulators of image.

Analysing images in newspapers is therefore an important aspect of media literacy, enabling us to explain how news narratives are constructed in image as well as text, and how both modes of delivery are often in dialogue with each other. While printed text uses the semiotic signs of language, punctuation and graphology, images become meaningful through a combination of technical and visual codes (in the sense of sign systems). Most of these signifiers have a narrative function, directing us to the setting, participants and basic plot of what is

Figure 17.3: 'Moving forward . . . riot police charge pro-independence demonstrators outside the Basque parliament' (*Sydney Morning Herald*, 1–2 January 2005).

happening while also indicating the narrative point of view. Using the example of a newspaper photograph that appeared in the *Sydney Morning Herald* in January 2005 (figure 17.3), we can see how these semiotic codes work together to produce visual meaning.

Technical code

Signifiers operating within the technical code are those produced by the photographic hardware – camera, lenses, lighting, processing – and by the processes of production and editing. They can be summarised as follows:

* *Content*: what is actually shown in the shot, the combination of participants and locations. Collocations such as the riot gear shown in figure 17.3 construct a specific context within which we 'read' the event. The appearance of two photographers in the shot introduces another field of activity, which suggests the ritualistic nature of the demonstration, as a public spectacle to be watched by others.
* *Composition*: how participants are arranged in the frame and where the focal point of the camera is located. In figure 17.3 the demonstrator is clearly the focal point, occupying the central spot where the camera is pointing while other participants are arranged around him.

- *Perspective*: the spatial relationship between the participants, with some located closer to the camera than others. Constructed by effects of lighting and focus, perspective can create an image that appears either two-dimensional (where the participants appear to occupy the same plane of action) or three-dimensional, as in figure 17.3, where the ground slopes away towards the back of the shot, giving some depth, and there are additional figures in both the foreground and the background. Typically in sports photos, the perspective is particularly deep, demarcating the different areas of activity occupied by players and spectators, so that the players appear to loom large against the background of a vast stadium packed with tiny people. Perspective also enhances or minimises the significance of foreground and background and the relationship between them. An image that is mostly foreground, with an obscured or indiscernible background, as in figure 17.3, conveys a sense of the importance and seriousness of what is occurring by decontextualising it and therefore removing it from a larger series of events.
- *Point of view*, or focalisation, the relationship between the camera and its subject. I have already summarised the conventional meanings associated with camera angles and distance (see chapter 9), which work to motivate the way in which the viewer perceives the subject. Seen only in the distance, a participant appears insignificant and disempowered; a big close-up, on the other hand, encourages empathy and recognition of a shared humanity.
- *Colour*, on a scale from black and white to full colour saturation. Shades of colour can be used to draw attention to specific items in the frame, to create a perspective and to rank participants as of greater or lesser importance in the 'story' of the image.
- *Focus*, from sharp to blurred. Advertising and film tend to use soft focus to convey mood, but news images use focus primarily to distinguish between foreground and background, and therefore to indicate who are the main protagonists or what is the main point of interest in the shot.
- *Lighting*, from bright to shadowy. In outdoor shots, lighting simply indicates when the shot was taken, by daylight or at night. A well-lit shot constructs factuality and objectivity, whereas contrasts of light and shadow suggest authorial evaluation of participants. The fairly high-key lighting in figure 17.3 creates a flat, unemphatic look that reduces the modality, as if we are merely being offered a snapshot of what 'really' happened without any mediation by the camera.
- *Body language*: the gestures, posture and clothing of the participants all have a semiotic salience that invokes conventional codes of meaning. In figure 17.3 the raised arm of the demonstrator and outstretched arms of the police officer behind him suggest aggression, while the pose of the photographers shown in the photo, in the act of filming, indicates their detachment from the main scene and engagement in a completely different field of activity. All the police depicted have some kind of weapon, while the demonstrator is clearly unarmed,

problematising the implied validation of the police as authority figures applying the force of law.

* *Framing and editing*: the way in which the image is cropped or edited to fit the space available, and how it is framed, whether by a box, caption, columns of text, advertisement or other kind of text. In figure 17.3 there are signs of other participants in the outer edges of the photo who have been almost edited out of the shot, creating more emphasis on the demonstrator and his interaction with the riot police as the main event of the image. The accompanying headline, 'Basque nationalists issue challenge to Madrid', runs across both the story on the left-hand half of the page and the image on the right, visually joining them together and directing us to 'read' them as part of the same story. In addition, the single-line caption under the photo directs us to the dominant reading, limiting the potentially polysemous nature of the image.

Visual code

Most of the technical signifiers listed above contribute to the visual semiotic of photography in terms of how we 'read' images and make meanings from them. In other words, they contribute to the three Hallidayan metafunctions – ideational, interpersonal and textual – that visual signs perform in order to realise various meanings. The narrative elements of still photos, such as character, location, plot and causation, are all conveyed through these metafunctions, as they are in verbal texts.

The signifiers of visual image can be distinguished from those of written text by reference to Peirce's typology of signs as iconic, indexical and symbolic (see Rosemary Huisman, chapter 2). While linguistic signifiers are largely symbolic, because the link between a sign and the object to which it refers is entirely arbitrary, visual signifiers can be all three: iconic because they look like the objects they represent, indexical because they can stand metonymically for something else, and symbolic because they can represent an idea or association that is arbitrary rather than literal. However, it is the iconic role of visual images – their direct likeness to reality – that makes them appear more 'truthful' than written text and enables them to play a formidable role in constructing the factuality of news (Cottle 1998: 201)

Kress and van Leeuwen (1996) have provided a detailed reading of images in terms of Halliday's three metafunctions, and much of what follows is derived from their analysis. The work of the art historian Michael O'Toole (1994), who has reconfigured Halliday's metafunctions as the representational (field), modal (tenor) and compositional (mode) functions, provides an analytical approach to still images from the context of the creative arts that also has relevance for news photos.

Looking first at the field, ideational meaning in images is constructed by the participants and the setting conveyed in the composition and content of the shot.

As in written text, collocations and categories help to define the field. Clothing and 'props' (such as the rifle and the cameras in figure 17.3) indicate different fields of activity as well as the categories to which participants can be assigned. We do not need the caption in figure 17.3 to tell us who are the riot police and who are the demonstrators. The clothing and props are not merely iconic but have also taken on a symbolic value as signifiers by virtue of frequent repetition in media stories about social disturbance. The helmets, rifles and batons of the riot police symbolise state violence legitimated as the only appropriate response to the serious threat posed by civil disorder. The only visible face is that of the demonstrator, making him appear more vulnerable compared to the masked faces of both the police and the photographers, obscured by their cameras. His lack of any symbols of authority – like the weapons, uniforms and cameras – also marks him out as standing outside the authorised social order, without an identifiable social role or occupation other than that of 'demonstrator'.

More significantly, the composition of an image can also indicate the transitivity roles played by the various participants. Where material processes are shown, as in figure 17.3, we can literally see which participant is the actor and which is the goal: the riot police are acting on the demonstrator, and so are the photographers. Similarly, in a photo showing people talking, we can usually see who is the sayer and who is the receiver (of the message). Kress and van Leeuwen suggest that actor and goal are invariably linked by some kind of visual or implied line, called a **vector**, which is always present in narrative (as opposed to conceptual) images (Kress & van Leeuwen 1996: 57). There are two such vectors in figure 17.3: the baton pointed towards the demonstrator and the outstretched arms touching him, so that the demonstrator is caught between these two actions as the goal of both of them. At the same time, invisible vector lines connect the demonstrator with the two cameras pointing at him, objectifying him as a media construct. His subordination to the forces of authority is therefore doubly imposed.

Turning next to the tenor of an image, interpersonal meanings involving the participants, the producer of the image and the consumer of the image can all be in play. Body language and facial expressions form iconic signs that indicate attitude or emotion. Symbolic relationships can also be indicated by eye-line vectors, the line of sight between two participants who are looking at each other or at something else. Participants who look out of the photo straight at the viewer are soliciting a response from us, whether compassion, empathy, admiration, revulsion (as in the 'mug shots' of alleged criminals) or merely indifference. In figure 17.3 there is an eye-line vector between the photographers, behind their cameras, and the demonstrator, who is looking not at the cameras but ahead at the riot police. The vector from the stills photographer on the right continues through and beyond the demonstrator, forming a single line from photographer to policeman. Such a link emphasises the professional role of both photographers, who are there at the scene but apparently not part of it, capturing both demonstrator and police with equal detachment. This vector gives the viewer permission to regard the demonstrator in the same way, as a media event rather than as a person. Positioned as voyeurs, we dispassionately regard an objectified person who cannot see us and whose needs or thoughts are unaccounted for.

The modality of an image – the attitude towards truth and certainty expressed by the participants and producer of the image – is conveyed through such technical signs as colour, focus, lighting and the position of the camera (focalisation). Variations in these elements can indicate a higher or lower modality, which is connected to the effect of naturalism – the more naturalistic the shot, the more it looks as if the camera caught the action just as it happened, without any coding or mediation, the higher the certainty that we are seeing 'reality'. Naturalism, like objectivity, is a semiotic effect constructed by conventional signs of discourse or visuality. A high modality of truth and factuality is constructed by evenly lit colour shots which suggest some depth of perspective, and which convey a naturalistic view of reality (Kress & van Leeuwen 1996: 135). Black-and-white photos tend to have a lower modality: as obviously stylised representations of reality, using the codes of black-and-white photography, particularly light and shadow, they suggest a more contingent relationship to reality, an acknowledgment that one version of events rather than another has been chosen.

Point of view – where and how the camera is placed – also serves an interpersonal function since it brings us in to the narrative at a specific point and positions us relative to the participants so that we can evaluate their behaviour. The distance between the viewer and the participants is a measure of both social and emotional distance, while camera angles construct power relations. A camera held up high, as in figure 17.3, reduces the height of the portrayed subject, suggesting disempowerment. We are placed among the spectators and positioned so that we can see the unarmed demonstrator subdued by the heavily armed authorities.

Shades of light and focus also suggest shades of opinion and appraisal, often by adding a symbolic or indexical aspect to the sign: the demonstrator is very sharply focused and therefore picked out for scrutiny as the index of a more widespread civil disorder. The equally sharp focus of the figure of the photographer on the right implicates him in the action, despite his apparent detachment, and therefore implicates us since we are also looking at the action through the lens of another (invisible) camera positioned on the other side of the scene. The use of black and white emphasises the uneasy juxtaposition of state-sanctioned violence and an apparently detached media, which, by its very presence in the scene, fails to provide the objective and unmediated view of reality that it promises.

Finally, the mode of a photographic image is determined partly by its composition – the way the information is organised into a visually coherent reality. Photography textbooks refer to the 'rule of thirds', by which a shot is divided into three roughly equal sections within the frame, either from left to right, or from top to bottom, with the focal point directed at one or other of these sectors. Such a division serves a textual function of helping us to make sense of several layers of information at once, organised into distinctive areas of the shot. Figure 17.3 can be divided into thirds both horizontally and vertically to show that the police and demonstrators occupy separate sections of the frame and are connected mainly by weapons. The figure of the photographer on the right cuts across these imaginary lines of division, intruding into the space occupied by the demonstrator and the space occupied by one of the police officers, suggesting his ambivalent position in relation to the two 'sides' of the conflict. Moreover, the presence of the two photographers suggests a ring of people surrounding the demonstrator on all sides, containing the potential threat posed to social stability.

Textual meaning in images can also be produced by the thematisation of particular elements, usually placed on the left of the image, or in the top half of the image, since in Western cultures texts are read from left to right and top to bottom. In advertising images, a shot of the product is normally prominently thematised by its position in the frame. The theme, normally on the left of the frame, presents something familiar and already known or agreed on by the viewer, while the rest of the shot contains something new or not yet fully understood that has to be made sense of and incorporated into a commonsense world view. With its circular composition contained within the square of the frame, figure 17.3 is not clearly divided into left and right, but rather problematises the distinction between what is 'given' (the theme) and what is 'new' (the rest) (Kress & van Leeuwen 1996: 186). The image contains only a theme, only what is already known, understood and accepted as unproblematic; namely the submission of social protest to the force of law and the economic imperatives of the media.

This image itself appeared on the right-hand side of a broadsheet page, with the left-hand side occupied by three columns of print about Basque nationalist activities. Its framing, by headline above, story at the side and caption below, is part of its mode – the way in which it is presented to us and how we make it meaningful. In terms of thematisation, the written story is the theme while the image is the 'new' information that has to be assimilated in relation to what has already been given. Since the angle of the story focuses on agreement and cooperation among rival factions of Basque nationalists, the photo seems to be telling a different version of the story that has to be reconciled with the first. This is done by adding a combative headline running across the top of both written text and image, 'Basque nationalists issue challenge to Madrid', and by placing a caption under the photo that 'anchors' its meaning: 'Moving forward . . . riot police charge pro-independence demonstrators outside the Basque parliament.' The 'new' information of the photo, supported by the caption, enables us to get a fuller or 'complete' version of the story: there was some agreement among rival groups but there was also protest from others.

The way in which images are framed by text, headlines, captions and other parts of the newspaper page, including advertisements, therefore constructs textual meaning that enables us to assimilate new information into an existing understanding of how the world works. Dominant ideologies are naturalised through the processes of thematisation and anchorage that link events and ideas into a seamless whole. The caption in figure 17.3 mentions the riot police and the 'pro-independence demonstrators' but fails to include the photographers in the list of participants in the photo, naturalising our view of the scene as a 'typical' violent encounter between 'good' authorities and 'bad' demonstrators. Yet it is the presence of the photographers which destabilises that reading of the image, adding a problematic element that is reinforced by the binary opposition of armed police and unarmed demonstrator. Within an apparently conventional iconography, symbolic of fears about social disorder, an uneasiness prevails that suggests our fears are at least in part connected to the 'riot police' whom we have delegated to act on our behalf and the ethical role of the media.

Conclusion

It is impossible to analyse media texts in any meaningful way without recourse to some kind of linguistic terminology. Semiotics, a term often bandied about by media studies commentators but seldom applied systematically, is in essence a theory of language and signification that becomes an effective analytical tool only when combined with a detailed articulation of linguistic structures and choices. The system offered here, based on Michael Halliday's concepts of ideational, interpersonal and textual metafunctions of language, has the advantage of being a self-contained system that can be applied to texts in any medium, whether written, visual or multimodal. Using this approach, such ideas as Stuart Hall's concept of 'public idiom' in news journalism can be systematically explored and defined, while claims of ideological positioning, of one kind or another, can be matched against the range of linguistic choices and their socially constructed meanings.

Part 5

Popular print culture

Chapter 18

Magazine genres

Rosemary Huisman

'Print culture' is a term used to describe the social practices associated with the use of print. The printing press was invented in the late fifteenth century, but 'print culture' did not develop overnight. Early practitioners understood the value of the printing press as a reproductive tool, compared to the laborious and inaccurate practices of copying manuscripts by hand. However, they did not immediately change their practices of layout and text organisation; that is, the earliest printed books look like manuscripts. But over time, from the new possibilities that print offered – a new authorial control of the physical appearance of the text, a new mode of economic organisation for the distribution of large print runs – an early 'print culture' began to emerge.

This culture continues to change and develop in changing social contexts. It meant – and means – the social recognition of new textual objects, associated with new modes of production and interpretation of meaning. The study of narrative in print culture has in most cases focused on the textual object, 'the novel', as part of the study of 'literature', or literary discourse, which typically includes those uses of language classified as having a 'high' social value. In contrast, the study of 'the media' has focused attention on the phenomenon of the mass audience, and hence pointed to those textual objects that are 'popular'; that is, have wide distribution and consumption. In this and the next chapter we will look at two aspects of popular print culture: the popular text object known as the 'magazine', and the discourse of advertising, as it is realised in print.

General definitions

What is this known object, the magazine, generally understood to be? Here is one dictionary definition (Collins 1979): 'a periodic paperback publication containing articles, fiction, photographs etc.'

The words 'paperback publication' confirm that the magazine is a known object (the Peircean term) within print culture. The prefix 'e' has come to signify computer use of terms derived from print culture; thus we note the recent 'e-magazine' for online publications.

The word 'paperback' tells us that this publication is given a less formal status, in its physical materiality, than the book. Although today many books are initially issued in paperback, because of the high production cost of hard cover books, originally in print culture the more ephemeral publications, intended for immediate consumption rather than long-term conservation, were issued in paperback.

The word 'periodic' tells us that the magazine is both a single known object and the collective series of similar objects, issued over time. Thus I can say, 'Have you seen the *Women's Weekly*?' and mean, 'Have you seen this month's single issue?', or I can say, 'Do you read the *Women's Weekly*?' and mean, 'Do you read any of the issues of that magazine?' (The *Women's Weekly* – more accurately referred to as the *Australian Women's Weekly* – is a long-lasting magazine. It is a paradox, derived from its publication history, that this magazine retains its original title of 'weekly' but is actually published monthly.)

Several words of print culture circle around this notion of 'periodic'. The noun 'periodical' is given a dictionary meaning similar to that of 'magazine' (a periodical – meaning 1: a publication issued at regular intervals, usually monthly or weekly), but often keeps more formal or less frequent company, say as an academic publication four times a year rather than a 'popular' weekly or monthly issue. Similarly, the word 'journal' appears in the title of many academic periodicals (dictionary definition: 'a newspaper or periodical'). Different libraries have different habits of cataloguing a text object depending on whether it is known to them as a 'periodical' or a 'magazine', or even a 'journal'. If you are doing any research into magazines in library catalogues, you are likely to find yourself searching for material under any of these words.

The definition for 'magazine', already quoted ('a periodic paperback publication containing articles, fiction, photographs etc.') is given as the first of seven meanings. The other six meanings listed are to do with various containers for weapons (for example, a magazine that holds cartridges) and then with the extension of the container meanings to photography. What is common to all the meanings of magazine is the notion of 'container'. Its etymology is illuminating. The word 'magazine' came into English in the sixteenth century via French from Italian; the Italians derived it from Arabic; and in Arabic it was a noun, meaning 'storehouse', which was derived from the verb meaning 'to store away'. The semantic extension is plain. A magazine as a known object of print culture is a storehouse of articles, fiction, photographs and so on; that is, a collection of such items brought together. This immediately tells us that we will not expect to make one generic generalisation about a magazine, because it is of its nature to store together items of various genres: that is, to store together different types of texts, such as editorials, factual articles, fiction, letters to the editor and so on.

Now, laboriously, we have a general understanding of the word 'magazine' in popular culture: it signifies a known object in the institutional discursive context of print culture, which stores together texts of different genres and is issued periodically in paperback format.

Classification categories of magazines

Rather than try to go on making generalisations about magazines – such as what types of genre are possible – I think it is more helpful to make some basic empirical observations. There are a lot of different kinds of magazines. These 'different kinds of' will be the labels used in different social contexts because they are useful in that context. These labels are the 'classification categories' for a particular social purpose, so that magazines will be classified differently depending on the context and purpose of the classification.

Two of the different social contexts that I have investigated are, first, the magazine stands in a general newsagency (in the Holme Building, which houses student union facilities at the University of Sydney), and, second, the AustLit Database, accessed through the University of Sydney Library, on which publications relevant to Australian literature are listed. Each place classifies magazines in ways relevant to its social purposes.

First, the Holme Building. At the time of investigation, magazines were arranged on a parallel pair of facing shelves (referred to here as east and west) and a shorter display on the southern end of the shop. The classification categories listed in bold italics are the written labels actually fixed to the shelves.

Holme Building south end display

Comics

Business and current affairs

West side display, from left

Gardening

Home living

Architecture and the arts

History and literature

Politics, essays and philosophy

Lifestyle and music

Cooking

Children and pregnancy
New age
Fitness and health
Sport
East side display, from left
Unlabelled: *Who* magazine box display
East side centre display
Top shelves, unlabelled mixed: *Woman's Day, NW, Australian Women's Weekly, Reader's Digest* (these appear to be the highest circulation items) plus *SMH Good Food Guide* and *Good Schools Guide* (annual publications)
Lower shelves, unlabelled: football magazines (relevant to a recent event, a football final)
Lowest shelf: newspapers
East side display, shelves on right
Travel
Fashion male, female and mixed (many; includes 'glossies' like *Vogue*)
Queer press
Animals and nature
Computer (many)
Science
Camera, hi-fi, technology and electronics
Motor

It is evident that the Holme newsagency classification has been made by two criteria. The first is the field of the magazine: that is, the primary subject matter of its content. This classification derives from the internal contents of the magazine. The second criterion is external: the circulation figures of the magazine. This derives from its institutional context in print culture, in studies of consumption. The display above the newspapers, on the east side centre display, appears to group the most popular magazines, the ones with the highest circulation. No doubt marketing studies have suggested two principal types of magazine consumer (the one person may be either at different times). First, there is the actual consumer who dashes in, grabs a well-known item (newspaper and/or magazine), and dashes out again. Second, there is the potential consumer who likes to browse, spending more time looking through the magazines of his or her personal interest, before deciding whether to buy. The dashing-in consumer can look quickly at the central shelves of most popular items, while the browser can idle through the magazines in the favoured classification categories.

We can contrast the general newsagency's classification of magazines with that in the AustLit Database. A search on the word 'magazines' yielded 520 entries. In the first hundred of those entries, the following classification categories, using the word 'magazines', appeared (this list is in the order in which the terms first appear):

- magazines
- literary magazines
- Canberra literary magazines
- little magazines
- Australian literary magazines
- poetry magazines
- fashion magazines
- women's magazines.

The first category, magazines, is obviously the broadest classification. The next five terms, down to poetry magazines, all refer to literary magazines; this is a more refined subdivision of the category appearing in the newsagency as 'history and literature'. The criteria for subclassification vary, however. The geographical subclassification of place of publication is clear enough: Australian, Canberra (the capital city of Australia). The discursive subclassification is also clear: the discourse of poetry is a subcategory of the discourse of literature.

However, the term 'little magazines' is not so clearly distinguished. 'Little magazines' typically refers to those hopeful but often brief efforts at private or university publication in the literary sphere: a few issues, and the money or the energy or both run out. Yet some publications, initially 'little magazines', go on to survive as mainstream 'literary periodicals', as, for example, the Australian literary magazine *Meanjin*, initially published in 1939. (Unsurprisingly, the term 'little magazines' is sometimes used as if synonymous with 'literary magazines'.)

The last two categories are unremarkable at the newsagency but somewhat anomalous in the database. Given the 'Australian Literature' focus of this database, the last two classifications, 'fashion magazines' and 'women's magazines', enter the database only because some item in a particular magazine issue has been judged a literary text object – perhaps a poem or short story – or has been judged relevant to literary subject matter, for example, an article on an Australian author. 'Fashion magazines' corresponds to one of the newsagent's content categories, 'fashion male, female and mixed'. The last category, 'women's magazines', is not found among the newsagent's categories.

Considering why this is so reminds us of ideological changes in society, reproduced in marketing, since the 1980s or longer. Once, for example, the Thursday *Sydney Morning Herald* (a daily newspaper) had a regular section entitled the 'Women's Pages'. This was on the assumption that 'women' could be grouped together as a homogeneous cluster of readers, who shared an interest in certain subjects that were outside the matters of general (male?) interest (there was no part of the paper headed 'Men's Pages'!). Feminist critiques had a lot to say about this marginalisation of issues regarded as 'of interest only to women', and so modern newspapers have dropped such labelling. While the physical grouping together of categories at the newsagency might suggest some related areas of interest that have traditionally been regarded as 'female' or 'male' – 'cooking' next to 'children and pregnancy', or 'camera, hi-fi, technology and electronics' next to 'motor' – the categories label the subject matter, not the reader. However, as we can see, the AustLit Database preserves here the ideological mode of classification of an earlier period. (The reference, incidentally, is to the topic of a satirical verse in the magazine, the *Bulletin*, on horoscopes in 'women's magazines'.)

These details, contrasting the classification categories of the newsagency and the academic database, illustrate a basic point: the way types of magazines (what are sometimes referred to inaccurately as 'genres' of magazines) are differentiated (that is, classified) will depend on the purposes of the classifier. It is important to identify the subjective basis of classification in any study of the media: who has promulgated the criteria of classification? What social purpose does the classification serve? What ideological commitment do you infer? In answering such questions, we can begin to describe our understanding of the social practices that characterise media culture.

To continue such study, once the classification criteria have been identified, we can then turn to the genres in magazines. If we were to look at magazines classified as 'the same', we would then need to ask what types of text (that is, what genres) are characteristic of those magazines in that classification. Similarly, we could compare the types of text, the genres, in magazines classified as different to see whether they also have genres in common. From such work it would be possible to draw general conclusions about genres in magazines. But here, to begin the identification of genres, I will look at one issue of a particular magazine – the *Australian Women's Weekly*, October 2001 – in order to describe its contents. I have chosen this particular magazine because it has a long history in Australian print culture and, as a well-established, widely distributed publication, its generic features are likely to be comparable with those of other mainstream magazines.

Narration through language and image

The first generalisation we can make is that, as the *Australian Women's Weekly* is a known object (a magazine) of print culture, and hence a text we interpret visually, it can offer texts realised in both graphic language and image. Its pages are designed to appeal to the sense of sight. (Occasionally you might find an appeal to the sense of smell, as in an advertisement for scent with a folded margin infused with the advertised perfume, or even of touch, as in raised or embossed lettering.) Thus it is a rare page that is all language – there is at least one small image. In fact, in this particular issue I did not find one page that is exclusively language. (The continuation pages of Barry Humphries aka Dame Edna's story, 'Hook, Line and Sinker', from page 302, are anomalous in having no illustrations related to the text, but half of each of those continuation pages has an advertisement with its own images.) This immediately means that earlier theories of narration, typically in structuralist narratology produced to explain traditional fiction (the oral fairy tale, like Propp, the oral myth, like Lévi-Strauss, or the printed short story or novel, like Todorov), are inadequate. Any narratives we read in magazines are being told through both language and image, and it will be up to us to decide on the possible relations between the two for any one text type, or genre.

For example, the genre of 'authorised column', as for three regulars on page 307, 308 and 310, has the authority of its named author indicated both by the verbal byline ('with Lee Tulloch in New York', 'with William McInnes', 'with Pat McDermott') and in a small image of the face of each author above the byline. The three texts, being the same genre of 'authorised column', are unified in both visual layout (each has three columns on the one page) and font choice (the same fonts are used for the main text heading and subheadings for each columnist). Similarly, the whimsical idiosyncrasy permitted an individual who is a 'named columnist' (a possible feature of the 'authorised column') is emphasised in the same way for each author, with a mildly witty or colloquial title, and a cartoon illustration for each page.

So before we read the language of the text, the images have already oriented our generic expectations. When we read the language of the texts, we find our expectations confirmed: the pronoun 'I' is used frequently, there is an informal emphasis on personal history and experience in everyday life, along with the occasional sententious pronouncement. Thus McInnes ends his column with a little piece of autobiography worthy of an eighteenth-century novelist, the kind whose narration came to be dominated by the specific time and social space of the individual's experience, leading to the moment of universal reflection:

> Tonight, as the current ring announcer calls for the fireworks to begin, I remember so many things from all the Redcliffe shows I have attended. I feel sad, because I'm afraid that nobody thinks the show is important any more.
>
> I wander over to join the crowd. We watch the fireworks soar and dazzle in the sky. A brilliant flare explodes and, as one, the crowd sighs. The show has always been about community, joy, fun and being together. Surely, as long as people feel the need to come together and share those moments, there will always be a place for the Redcliffe Show.
>
> (*Australian Women's Weekly*, October 2001, p. 308)

Because magazines can offer texts realised in both graphic language and image, it is appropriate for a text analysis to comment on every detail, to whatever degree of delicacy seems relevant. For example, magazines can differ in the level of self-conscious coherence between image and language. From my investigation, the *Australian Women's Weekly* appears tightly edited, constructing high levels of cohesion. The use of colour for the three 'authorised columns' links them visually: each byline uses shades of pale green, each text begins with a small square of pale green. As in the other repeated visual details, already described, the generic identity of the three texts has been visually emphasised.

Agency: editorial and advertising

Before continuing to identify different text types or genres, we need to make a major division of texts in the magazine in terms of their origin of production, their agency. Is a text, in its composition of language and image, produced by advertising staff, or is it produced by the editorial team of the magazine? An advertising company (the creative agency) produces an advertisement for a client (the corporate agency), who pays the advertising company and pays the magazine company for the placement of the advertisement in the magazine. The editorial agency is also complex: the publishers, employers of the editorial team of journalists, have at least the social purpose of marketing the magazine. The owners of the magazine might also have other ideological purposes, such as a greater support for one political party or system over another, or a concern with promoting particular social values. These last are not necessarily sectarian: they might include maintaining a reputation of credibility through social responsibility.

This distinction between the advertising and editorial origin of texts is initially useful, yet no sooner does one hypothesise a dichotomy, a two-part division, than empirical data suggests its limitations, its deconstruction. The purposes of the advertisers and editors might overlap to such an extent that it can be difficult to distinguish between texts presented as editorial and texts presented as advertisement.

For example, the October 2001 issue of the *Australian Women's Weekly* contains an editorial article entitled 'Susie O'Neill, new horizons'. (Susie O'Neill, an Australian, won a gold medal for swimming at the 2000 Olympics.) Page 96 has a full-page picture. The facing page (p. 97) is divided into two columns, the left being one-third of a page width containing the language text and the remaining two-thirds to the right showing another picture. Both pictures are of O'Neill in different swimsuits. The article tells the story of O'Neill's post-Olympics life, foregrounding in the opening paragraphs her new venture into 'her own fashion label'. The full-page picture of the swimmer in a swimsuit (p. 96) has the small caption, 'The Susie swimwear range, priced from around $50, is available from selected Target stores nationally from October'. On these two pages, the editorial text on page 97 purports to belong to the editorial genre 'magazine article', but the photo caption clearly belongs to the genre 'advertising image caption'. Thus the marketing aims of advertising and editorial content converge into the 'advertorial'.

The opposite convergence is also possible; that is, an advertisement might appropriate the discourse of editorial text. This can be seen in the advertisement for 'Prescription Medicines THE FACTS' (*Australian Women's Weekly*, October 2001, pp. 94–5). The text appears to be motivated by an ideology of social responsibility, albeit allied with a positive positioning of certain products: it is full of information, apparently for the public good. In general, editorial text has more language than contemporary advertising, and in this respect this particular advertisement is more editorial-like. On page 94, the lower half of the page has a large image of finger and thumb holding a capsule, the upper half language. Page 95, facing, is almost entirely language, printed in three columns. The first sentence (p. 94) has the subject 'we' – 'Earlier this year we commissioned independent research to discover what Australians knew about prescription medicines' – but it is not at all clear who this 'we' refers to. The first two columns of page 95 are structured as a series of questions and answers, derived from the commissioned research, on 'generic prescription medicines'. This structure mirrors the question/ answer interview in which an authority figure gives information 'objectively' (for example, patient and doctor), although accumulatively, so that the 'generic prescription medicine' is given a positive 'spin'. (The last answer concludes with the comment: 'Of course, you can pay a premium and ask for the "originator" drug to be dispensed if you prefer.' Of course a customer always likes to pay more!)

At last, at the top of column 3, we read a trademark (the name of a company) and, at the bottom of that column, we see a trade logo and address and discover these two pages have been inserted by a company that is 'proud to be a major sponsor of National Braille Week'. And finally, at the very bottom of column 3, in minute letters barely legible to the naked eye, we see that this trademark is one of 'Faulding Healthcare Pty Ltd'. Overall the corporate agency (the company client) appears to have instructed the creative agency (the advertising company) to produce an advertisement that looks like an editorial article. At the same time, without advertising any specific product, the advertisement has a more general marketing function: promoting a positive attitude to a class of products associated with the client (that is, the client as a producer of generic – or unbranded – prescription drugs).

Certainly the editorial staff of the *Australian Women's Weekly* want to represent themselves as having an ideology committed to social values, one that is not subservient to the demands of advertisers. The outcome of any ideological difference between editors and advertisers is that editorial comment might tell a different story, a narrative with different social values, from that told by particular advertisers. This is explicit in a response to a letter to the editor in the October 2001 issue, on a page of editorially chosen content (p. 13), most texts being of the genre 'letters to the editor'. Each letter has an editorially chosen heading, in the same colour and font, creating a cohesive and recognisable space in which readers' letters are clearly marked off from editorial material while implicitly being subject to editorial decision-making. This letter indicates reader awareness of the intertextual meanings that inevitably cross the conventional boundaries between editorial and advertising:

Poor placement
I have just reread your latest magazine and would like to say it is a very informative and fabulous read. However, one thing concerning me is the article entitled 'Survival of the thinnest' (AWW Sept). I am one of the women who thinks

this body image is very damaging to our younger generation. After an article like this, how can your magazine condone turning the page for a Jenny Craig advertisement and on the next page a Roche promotion for weight loss? Seems hypocritical to me!

Concerned Reader etc.

This is the only letter to which the editor makes a response in the October issue. She (or they) replies: 'The *Weekly* apologises for any insensitivity in the placement of these advertisements. There was a breakdown in communication between our editorial and advertising staff. However, it does reinforce that we are a magazine that will not be compromised by advertisers.'

So there you have it. A clear division between the editorial and advertising staff, which needs to communicate about the appropriate social values for 'place-ment' in the magazine. The first two sentences make a pragmatic admission: there should have been more pages between the editorial criticism of the ideal of thin-ness and the advertising promotion of the ideal of thinness. So the magazine will tolerate ideological contradictions, at an appropriately paginated distance. The last sentence then makes a virtue of its misplacement: if we were a magazine whose editorial values had to be subservient to the values of our advertisers (says the editorial team), then we would take care not to juxtapose such a contradiction of values, for fear of alienating our advertisers – which proves that editorially we are independent!

Narration in contemporary magazines

How would we go about looking at narration in the magazine? The magazines of the 1950s and 1960s, like the UK *Ladies Home Journal* (its first issue was in 1932), contained many fictional stories, both short stories and extracts from soon-to-be-published books, often by famous authors. Obviously the narrative structure of these stories could be studied with all the terminology of structuralist narra-tology, while a post-structuralist concern would remind you to consider cultural metanarratives and their possible influence both on the author and the editor of the journal (who chose to include the narrative) and on your own interpretation. But contemporary magazines?

Recent magazines have very little overt fiction, but are filled with stories of 'real people'. The 'cult of celebrity', or the commodification of the individual (such that the name of a person becomes instead a recognised sign, 'the brand', whose interpretant of 'celebrity status' can be associated with any product, including the product 'a magazine') gives our society the characters – the 'narrative exis-tents' – through whom dominant social myths can be told: stories of individual success, failure, romance, feud, tragedy (although rarely comedy). The stories remain much the same, but the characters are now understood to be 'real'. What kind of reality is that?

For example, the cover of the Australian *Who* magazine, 8 October 2001 (see figure 18.1), has a head-and-shoulders picture of Victoria Beckham (a singer formerly known as Posh Spice, currently married to an international football player, David Beckham). Her face is centred on the page, her head slightly inclined down, looking straight up at you, the magazine reader, as if you were looking into a mirror – an identity of you as speaking subject (who interprets) and Beckham as subject of 'speech' (the first-person pronoun in the language text, but here the iconic image), if you are a compliant reader who values 'celebrity'. Above her head, in large upper-case letters, is '**POSH: MY STORY**'. 'Posh' is of course the 'brand' here, and 'my' signifies that this story has a first-person narrator. To the left of her head are third-person summaries of individual storylines in the story: 'Victoria Beckham on those food problems, Geri's shock Spice Girls exit and the secret romance that led to marriage.' As in Propp's fairy tale (and in the nineteenth-century novel), marriage realises the final 'plot function'.

'Posh' refers to a real person, but in this narration she is like a character in a first-person narrative. How factual are such stories? To what extent have they been moulded, by the teller or the editorial staff, to conform to narrative expectations of prose fiction centred on the individual, but given a familiar subject positioning in traditional storylines?

A second example: on the cover of the Australian *New Idea*, 6 October 2001 (see figure 18.2), the upper two-thirds of the page is devoted to Nicole Kidman (an Australian actress with a high profile in the Hollywood movie industry). On the left side, we see a waist-length image of Nicole, looking to the right (like a third-person pronoun in language, she is not directly engaged with us, the reader, but is already – as the result of the editorial *mise en page* (layout) – in some relation with others in an observed scene). On the right side, to which she is looking, four lines of large type read: 'Nicole V Penelope/The quest for/revenge/begins', with 'revenge' in noticeably larger type. And below this, we see a smaller picture of the actors Tom Cruise and Penelope Cruz, with the rubric: 'The court battle starts this week – and Penelope is caught in the middle.'

First, note that these people are such 'brands' that there is no need for surnames. Like the orally transmitted stories of traditional Germanic culture ('Cinderella', 'Snow-White and Rose-Red'), or the televisually transmitted stories of contemporary soap operas, the magazine story traverses a shared field, or subject matter, in which characters are already established and recognised. Second, note the venerable storyline into which these modern characters have been written: the revenge story. The archaic language – intertextually, 'quest' is a word that collocates with 'knight', 'oath', 'vigil' and so on – signifies the traditional nature of this (hyperbolic) storyline, updated with more recent intertextual references to fantasy films such as *Lord of the Rings* and *Van Helsing*, which also draw on the narrative of

Figure 18.1: Cover of *Who Weekly*, 8 October 2001.

Figure 18.2: Cover of *New Idea*, 6 October 2001.

'quest'. The 'Hollywood' characters are placed in the same discursive context as the movie plots from which they make their living.

H. Porter Abbott raises interesting questions about 'types' of characters and the inevitable 'flattening' that takes place in narrative, fictional or 'real':

> All cultures and subcultures include numerous types that circulate through all the various narrative modes: the hypocrite, the flirt, the evil child, the Pollyanna, the strong mother, the stern father, the cheat, the shrew, the good Samaritan, the wimp, the nerd, the vixen, the stud, the schlemiel, the prostitute with a heart of gold, the guy with a chip on his shoulder, the orphan, the yuppie, the Uncle Tom, the rebel. These are just a tiny selection of a vast multitude of current types in western English-speaking culture that migrate freely back and forth across the line between fiction and non-fiction and between literary art and other narrative venues.
>
> (Abbott 2002: 129)

And after pointing out the real dangers of stereotyping ('the terrible consequences of branding (the word is apt) human beings as types – Gypsies, Jews . . .') he asks, 'But . . . are human beings capable of characterizing without the use of types?' This is a question that we all need to think about for ourselves.

Conclusion

This chapter has raised some general issues about magazines in terms of their classifications and genres, the concept of agency and the relation between editorial and advertising content. The last of these, in particular, is a complex interaction common to all forms of commercial media that rely on advertising for their main or sole source of income. Narrative 'stories' that form the bulk of editorial content in magazines are deeply implicated in the presentation of advertising, providing not only the framework for the ads but also a carefully constructed cast of 'characters' who function to reinforce the consumer ideology of the imagined audience.

Chapter 19

Advertising narratives

Rosemary Huisman

In chapter 3 of this book it was pointed out that structuralist studies of narration typically study the text as object, looking for structures and relations within the text. In contrast, post-structuralist studies of narration typically focus on the text in relation to the subject, the subjectivity of the one who is interpreting or producing the text. Thus post-structuralist studies are usually concerned with ideology, with the assumptions of what is 'natural' and 'normal' to the subject in producing meaning. Post-structuralist studies of narration, then, focus on the ideological orientation of narrative. What stories are told? What stories are repressed? In whose interests is it to tell particular stories, or to repress them? And so on.

In this chapter I bring a post-structuralist perspective to bear on narration in print-culture advertising. Again, I illustrate my general remarks with examples from the October 2001 issue of *Australian Women's Weekly*.

Magic and information

The collection *Media Studies: A Reader*, edited by Paul Marris and Sue Thornham, includes seven extracts in the section 'Advertising'. The first extract is by Raymond Williams, 'Advertising: The magic system', written in 1960 but published in 1980 in his book, *Problems in Materialism and Culture* (Marris & Thornham 1996: 461–5). This is a much-quoted article. For example, it is one of only two articles included under the heading 'Consumption and the market' in *The Cultural Studies Reader*, edited by Simon During (1993: 320–36). I will first describe Williams' account in some detail, then suggest some modifications.

Williams begins with a paradoxical statement:

> It is often said that our society is too materialist, and that advertising reflects this. We are in the phase of a relatively rapid distribution of what are called 'consumer goods', and advertising, with its emphasis on 'bringing the good things of life', is taken as central for this reason. But it seems to me that in this respect *our society is quite evidently not materialist enough*, and that this, paradoxically, is the result of a failure in social meanings, values and ideals.
>
> (Marris & Thornham 1996: 461; my italics)

Williams' point here is that 'the material object being sold is never enough'. He writes that, if we were sensibly materialist, 'beer would be enough for us, without the additional promise that in drinking it we would show ourselves to be manly, young in heart, or neighbourly. A washing machine would be a useful machine to wash clothes, rather than an indication that we are forward-looking or an object of envy to our neighbours.' Here is the relevance of narrative: you can see Williams is suggesting that advertising writes stories which link products or objects with subject positions of desired attributes, such as those of being manly, neighbourly, adventurous and so on. The purchaser, by associating him- or herself with the beer or washing machine, takes up the subject position in the story, thus gaining access to the desired attributes.

Williams calls this need for narrative excess in our culture *magic*. He writes, as a sort of paraphrase of Marx's concepts of use value and exchange value,

> if these associations sell beer and washing-machines, as some of the evidence suggests, it is clear that we have a cultural pattern in which the objects are not enough but must be validated, if only in fantasy, by association with social and personal meanings which in a different cultural pattern might be more directly available. The short description of the pattern we have is magic, *a highly organised and professional system of magical inducements and satisfactions*, functionally very similar to magical systems in simpler societies, but rather strangely coexistent with a highly developed scientific technology.

To reiterate, Williams calls modern advertising a 'system of organised magic' and claims its primary importance is that of obscuring a 'fundamental choice' in Western industrial society: that between 'man as consumer and man as user'. This is a choice between two metaphors for the human subject in relation to objects, and concurrently a choice between two metaphors for the object, as that which is consumed or that which is used. The subject as user and the object as used will be written into different stories from the subject as consumer and the object as consumed.

Users, writes Williams, ask for more than consumers: 'Users ask for the satisfaction of human needs which consumption, as such, can never really supply. Since many of these needs are social – roads, hospitals, schools, quiet – they are not only not covered by the consumer ideal: they are even denied by it, because consumption tends always to materialize as individual activity . . .' Note the contrast Williams draws between the individual needs of the consumer and the social needs of the user.

Williams goes on to suggest how this magic works: we know our social needs, our real sources of general satisfaction, from experience, yet advertising encourages us to believe that satisfaction is possible as consuming individuals. He writes:

> Advertising, in its modern forms, then operates to preserve the consumption ideal from the criticism inexorably made of it by experience. [This is similar to Lévi-Strauss's 'explanation' of myth: that it enables the contradictions of experience and belief to be reconciled. See chapter 3.] If the consumption of individual goods leaves that whole area of human need unsatisfied, the attempt is made, by magic, to associate this consumption with human desires to which it has no real reference. You do not only buy an object: you buy social respect, discrimination, health, beauty, success, power to control your environment. The magic obscures the real sources of general satisfaction because their discovery would involve radical change in the whole common way of life.

Overall, Williams' view of advertising is a pessimistic one of individual manipulation and social loss. It suggests an earlier view of ideology as 'false consciousness' in its dichotomy of consumer and user, whereby the consumer has a false understanding of self-gratification, the user a true understanding. But in a post-structuralist understanding, the individual is not a constant: subjectivity is always performed or, in other words, the subject is always interpreting or producing meaning from one ideological perspective or another (this perspective not necessarily remaining constant for any one person), always taking up or performing in some social story. Discrimination, rather than rejection, is a more helpful response to advertising.

Still, Williams' notion of 'magic' is very useful. I would argue that what Williams is describing as 'magic' is the extreme node, the more sophisticated node, at one end of a continuum that we can use to describe the communicative intent of advertising. The other extreme node is that of information. The minimal social function of advertising is that of information – think of those ill-lettered notices, stuck to telegraph poles, that one sees in suburbs: 'Garage Sale, 36 Hereford St, Sat. 10–4'.

All advertisements, in one way or another, share the social purpose of promoting a product, an event, a policy or idea, but an advertisement can be described as situated anywhere on the continuum from information to magic. The information node is associated with an object-oriented story; that is, one with information about the product, event, policy, itself. The magic node is associated with a subject-oriented story, one telling a story of attributes, like 'manly' or 'neighbourly'. A particular advertisement, situated somewhere between these two extremes, enables the telling both of an object-oriented story with information about the product *and* the telling of a subject-oriented story of attributes. The latter story, the subject-oriented story, merely by juxtaposition with the object-information story becomes part of the complex narrative of the object, a complex weaving of the two threads ('storylines' seems appropriate) of information and magic, a narrative in which the compliant reader could become the subject by associating themselves with the object.

Figure 19.1 offers an extreme and self-consciously over-the-top example: the object is the perfume in the lower right side; the subject-centred story includes the stretch limo and chauffeur and the words 'Glam it up at Giorgio's 20th anniversary in Beverly Hills'. The imperative mood of this clause offers a subject position (the spoken subject) of 'you' to the reader, and directly connects the 'you' to the object mentioned, 'Giorgio'. The last line of the ad spells out the fantasy story explicitly: 'spray on some Giorgio and imagine yourself in the back of the stretch limo' (p. 93). (It must be admitted that this advertisement, also offering a competition, allowed the faint possibility of fantasy becoming reality!)

For any student of modernism in twentieth-century literature, this model of advertising is reminiscent of one particular theory of poetry. This account of juxtaposition in advertising, of placing subject-desired situation or attributes adjacent to consumer object, sounds rather like Ezra Pound's theory of the ideogram. Pound's ideogramic theory is one of juxtaposition: the poet puts two verbal images adjacent to each other in a poem, and the reader synthesises a related meaning. The theory assumes that what the eye sees together, the brain relates in meaning. This theory is still one of the foundation insights of contemporary poetry.

It is not gratuitous to mention Pound, since many of the techniques of modern advertising have been transferred from the institutional practices of high culture, both literature and art – and indeed transference takes place in the opposite direction too, from advertising to poetry. The American literary critic Marjorie Perloff has particularly specialised in these areas, for example, in her book *Radical Artifice: Writing Poetry in the Age of Media*. One detail Perloff has tracked is that, during the twentieth century, there was a considerable reduction in language text in advertisements – what we could refer to as explicit verbal narrative – and there was a corresponding increase in the role of the image in advertisements (Perloff 1991). In short, modern advertisements tend to have fewer words than they did in the early twentieth century.

From my own consideration of magazines I suggest a hypothesis here: that the more significance an advertisement gives to the image, in comparison to the words, the more the advertisement moves towards the 'magic' end of the continuum. ('Magic' is almost an anagram of 'image'!) Some story books designed for very young children, before they can read, have pictures only, so that the child can tell a story from the pictures, or the parent can make one up to tell the child. Similarly, in an advertisement that consists primarily of an image, the things pictured in the ad (the *mise en scène*, the iconography) and the setting (the physical

Figure 19.1: Advertisement: Giorgio perfume (*Australian Women's Weekly,* October 2001, p. 93).

and social location, if any, in which the things are placed) more readily allow the subject-oriented story to be read. This subject-oriented story is the story in which the values of the reader associated with that iconography and that setting become dominant over the object-oriented story, the one in which the advertisement gives more specific information about the object. Of course language can also be used to tell a subject-oriented story but, in general, I suggest that the verbally sparse story allows a more open reader-oriented space for narratives of personal desire and wishful thinking.

A second generalisation to bear in mind here is the typical reading direction for English language: from left to right of page, and from top to bottom. In the examples that follow, we will see that the arrangement of magic and information in an advertisement typically makes use of one or both of these dynamic vectors of reading. (Arrangement on the page is sometimes called 'layout' or sometimes referred to by the French term *mise en page*.) The general rule is that the hook of the 'magic' story is encountered before that of the 'information'. In the Giorgio advertisement, the movement is from top to bottom. In the other examples below, we see a left to right movement. It is no accident that this layout repeats the written or printed appearance of the English clause, which is structured with already known 'themes' at the beginning of the clause and, usually, new information positioned towards the end of the clause: that is, to the right when written or printed. The 'magic' subject-oriented story attempts to invoke the desires and fantasies the reader is assumed already to have, or at least ready to accept, in contrast to the new information of the object-oriented story. Thus, the established habits of interpreting when reading any printed English language can be activated for interpreting the advertising text of image and language. (Not every advertisement will follow this conventional layout; when one does not, it is worth considering the effect.)

Examples of the 'magic/information' continuum

In the October 2001 issue of the *Australian Women's Weekly* (320 pages in all), the following objects are the most extensively advertised in terms of numbers of pages. (The classification of subject matter is devised by me; one advertisement might take up two facing pages, one whole page or part of a page.)

- food (thirty pages)
- health (twenty-one pages)
- skincare (fifteen pages)
- clothes (ten pages)
- hair care (ten pages)
- cosmetics (ten pages)
- cars (eight pages)
- other (four pages or fewer).

The advertisements in which image is noticeably dominant are those for hair care, cosmetics and cars. All three categories feature some two-page spreads, which suggests a large advertising budget for those products. An online site for Magazine Publishers of Australia claims that 'double page spreads perform better than single pages'; that is, double-page spreads 'achieve consistently higher readership scores' than single-page units (www.magazines.org.au, link **MPA QuickFacts** viewed 5 October 2004. The research was carried out for the *Australian Women's Weekly*.) Whether or not this is necessarily true, it is clear the advertising agency given the creative task of designing these advertisements will give them considerable professional attention.

The designers of the double-page hair care and cosmetics advertisements knowingly exploit the usual English reading direction in the layout. Typically, on the left page, the reader sees a large perfect female face and hair, with no background of social location. Thus the 'magic', the possible subject identification in a story with the already desired attribute of beauty, is encountered first, as the 'theme'. Now, looking from the left page to the facing page on the right, the reader meets an image of the object (the product) and some language about it. So in the layout of the advertisement, the reader encounters the object-oriented (possibly new) information *after* he/she has seen the subject-oriented 'magic'. The advertiser hopes that the more object-oriented information is communicated to a reader already 'magically' positioned to respond. The same left/magic: right/information layout can be seen on single-page advertisements – see figure 19.2.

I mentioned that there is usually no social setting or location on the left page image in the typical hair/cosmetic advertisement. The beautiful faces swim in space – any setting, with its associated iconography, has been blocked out. Thus the image focuses on the individual, with the associations (the iconography) that inevitably accompany the setting quite repressed. I interpret the magic of these advertising texts as telling a story of the encompassing availability and satisfaction of the possession of beauty: it doesn't matter where you are or what your social role is, beauty is available to you for the price of a product; your world will be centred on your own wonderful presence, a being fully satisfied in its attribute of beauty.

In contrast, the advertisements for cars typically place the object in a specific setting. This setting is often a wild landscape, which facilitates stories of escape or adventure, with a subject position of one with a free spirit, an adventurer. The image of the car can be read in both the 'magical' and the 'informative' story (I desire freedom of movement/this is what I could buy), so the car might be the only object in the location, as in figure 19.3. Three of the car advertisements in this issue of the *Australian Women's Weekly* are two-page spreads, and this extra space and the inclusion of 'location' allows them to tell more varied and socially imaginative stories than the static 'floating heads' of the hair/cosmetics advertisements, and to elaborate on the 'freedom' stories of the one-page car advertisements.

Figure 19.2: Advertisement: Schwarzkopf Extra Care (*Australian Women's Weekly*, October 2001, p. 75).

Figure 19.3: Advertisement: Chrysler car (*Australian Women's Weekly*, October 2001, p. 9).

Two of these three conform, in varying degrees, to the magic/information pattern of layout already established, but differ in their 'position' on the magic/information continuum. In one, that closer to the magic node (pp. 76–7), an urban streetscape (shot in Australia, but vaguely European) runs across both pages. On the left, a young man in a (very wet) dinner suit (it is light, so presumably the 'next morning') climbs out of a fountain (vaguely reminiscent of *La Dolce Vita*, a famous film of Italian café society); on the right page, we see a gleaming image of a lengthy red car. In the second advertisement (pp. 110–11), on the top half of the left page a young woman styled as a newsreader or 'successful female executive' (white trouser-suit, blonde hair, discreet jewellery, professional smile towards the reader) leans against a small grey car, with a background of night-lit city skyscrapers. On the top half of the right page, six small images show another young woman (or two almost identical young women) doing practical things to her (or their) car (changing a wheel, inspecting a tool kit and so on). These capable women (on the 'information' right side) contrast with the glamorous female on the left: they have long dark hair and wear casual, mostly dark, clothes.

I describe this advertisement as located more towards the information node, as the bottom half of both pages is filled with language text that 'explains' the narrative of the images. Women are afraid of their cars breaking down at night: hence the city nightscape on the left. Under the headline 'Maintaining your independence', the language text exhorts women to learn some basic car-maintenance: hence the six images on the right. The name, logo and (at that time) advertising slogan of the car manufacturer appear in the dominant information position, the bottom right of the right-hand page. As in the 'generic prescription medicine' advertisement (discussed in chapter 18), this text (images and language) advertises the company's ethics (social responsibility and reliability) rather than a particular product of the company.

It is also possible to reverse the 'magic': minus (–) magic, if you like. In the third double-page car advertisement (pp. 2–3), on the left page a man slumps (on a sofa?) while a young boy bounces above his head. On the right page we see a car-escape image, the car on an isolated country road, characteristic of one-page advertisements. The subject-oriented story that this minus-magic image invites is one of the reader's 'real' social situation: tied to one place with a family. Contrast it with the subject-oriented story that the first plus-magic image invited (the young man in the fountain): the fantasy of wild late-night partying in a wealthy social milieu. However, in comparison to the female-centred advertisement, both these male-centred advertisements are similar in giving comparatively little information in language. These advertisements are placed well towards the 'magic' end of the advertising continuum, designed primarily to arouse desire rather than give information.

These observations are always context dependent; that is, they depend on the magazine context in which the advertisement is placed. In a magazine of the field 'Motor', as classified by a general newsagency (outlined in chapter 18), you would expect to find car advertisements that gave more object information, since a reader subject with more specific interest in the field (subject matter) could be assumed. At the same time, the *Australian Women's Weekly* is divided into two editorial sections. The first section, approximately a third of the total (say to page 113), appears to assume a reader with general interests; the second, to assume a reader with more domestic concerns (subheadings like 'Food' are used). The placement of advertisements correlates with this editorial division. Thus all the advertisements for cars appear in the early pages of the magazine (although the female-oriented one appears just before the more domestic section) while all but three of the thirty pages of food advertisements are in the second section.

'Editorial' and 'advertising'

In chapter 18 I made the point that, although we can theorise a dichotomy in the magazine between those parts originating from the editorial team and those parts originating from advertising staff, a clear division between the two in terms of their ideological goals is not always possible. I used the examples of the editorial article on Susie O'Neill and the advertisement for 'generic prescription medicines'. This means that studies and theories of advertising could offer insights that are as relevant to editorial copy as to advertising copy, so that the concerns of this chapter might be extended more generally.

James Curran's discussion in his article, 'The impact of advertising on the British mass media' (Marris & Thornham 1996: 266–79), is relevant to this issue: that it is an artificial distinction to keep editorial copy and advertising copy in the one magazine strictly apart in any analysis. His comments also give more insight into the demographic and psychographic study of audiences, mentioned in chapter 18.

Curran points out that advertisers do not generally want to communicate about their object with all members of the public; rather they want to reach particular segments of the market, and they will pay more to those media outlets which give them greater access to that segment. Conversely, he points out, media outlets like popular magazines do not cover production costs with sales of the magazine, but must rely on advertising revenue to subsidise those costs. The implication is clear: to ensure adequate funds, there is pressure on the editorial staff to produce editorial material aimed at market segments to which advertisers want to appeal. Just as in commercial television, where program-makers are selling audiences to advertisers, there is a symbiotic relationship between editors and advertisers in magazine publishing, whereby each needs the other to be effective.

The whole business discipline of 'marketing' has developed the identification and analysis of 'market segments' for effective targeting in advertising. The results of such market research might then be displaced from advertising staff to editorial staff so that, driven by the perceived 'market segments', the magazine as a whole tends towards a homogeneous ideology: that is, one which will be read as 'natural' by the subject readers in that market segment. In her article, 'Understanding advertisers', Kathy Myers describes this convergence of editorial and advertising copy as particularly noticeable in 'women's magazines', because of their considerable financial reliance on advertising (Marris & Thornham 1996: 480–8).

One result of these attempts to appeal to one specific market segment is what Curran calls 'inequalities of cultural provision'. Women's magazines, he says, tend to be oriented towards the middle class: 'This is a consequence of the much higher advertising subsidies that middle-class women readers generate by comparison with working-class readers.' Most women's magazines sell at cover prices that do not cover costs. Therefore, revenue must be made up from advertisers, who will place their advertisements in magazines that are oriented towards the most likely consumers of their products. So, as already pointed out, the editorial staff are under pressure to produce advertising-friendly copy that draws on the same discursive practices as the advertisements themselves, creating a magazine apparently seamless in its textual cohesion.

Curran comments, '. . . this gravitational pull towards the middle class, exerted by advertising, has contributed to the remarkable conservatism of much women's journalism.' Curran's article was originally published in 1981, and he was writing about the British media and reading public. There have certainly been changes in the magazine industry since then, but his remarks still seem relevant to some publications, both in the UK and in Australia. A content survey of the October 2001 issue of the *Australian Women's Weekly* suggests the kind of audience targeted by advertisers and brought together by the editorial content.

As mentioned previously, the first general section (that is, not a specific section like 'Food' or 'Health') runs until page 113, approximately a third of the magazine. By page 104, twelve feature articles are completed. Ten of those articles are centred on celebrities from various fields, mostly Australian:

- John and Janette Howard (Australian politics; the prime minister and his wife)
- Elle Macpherson (Australian; beauty and business)
- Barry Humphries, aka Dame Edna (Australian; theatre)
- John Eales (Australian; sport)
- Princesses Caroline and Stephanie of Monaco (foreign royalty)
- Gai Waterhouse (Australian; horse racing)
- Prince William (British – and still Australian – royalty)
- Tom Cruise (American; films)
- Susie O'Neill (Australian; sport and business).

This list seems 'remarkably conservative' in terms of the areas of social activity represented compared to what is absent. Consider for example the absence of serious cultural, intellectual and professional achievement (there are no scientists, novelists, doctors, musicians, engineers, artists . . .). The areas of social activity that are represented particularly foreground those social worlds that, in contemporary society, are more compatible with an advertising ideology of 'aspirational' consumerism: the worlds of celebrity, fashion, movies, sport, business initiative and political success.

Raymond Williams commented that 'consumerism tends always to material-ize as an individual activity'; that is, the metaphor of people as consumers, as in the discourse of advertising, places an emphasis on individual gratification. The editorial articles in the magazine conform very closely to this ideology of individ-ualism: they focus on achievement or experience as an individual activity, centred on the named person. The eleventh feature article, of the twelve, is on the late Gianni Versace's grand mansion. The mansion story is still centred on an indi-vidual's possession, and in that sense it could be included with the previous ten, centred on celebrity. Only the twelfth feature article resists such inclusion. It is on the terrorist attack in New York on September 11, 2001, the month before this issue of the *Weekly*. This last item corresponds with what is judged high by news values, such as are used by newspapers, and it is the only item in the magazine centred more generally on social experience. The sheer scale of this awful event has forced its way into the otherwise bland sequence of individual achievement.

Demographic and psychographic variables

I have already outlined some of the issues relating to these variables in chapter 12, but they now need to be considered in the context of advertising. It is not inevitable that all readers will read the same narrative as that promoted in the 'magic' text, the image and language created by the advertising company from the instructions of the client company. Social associations will vary with different ideological positionings in society; the marketing section of business corporations tries to identify large groups of people with similar positionings as 'market seg-ments' so that advertisers can choose images and language that are likely to be read with the advertisers' intended story.

A comparatively structuralist account of the study of advertising, which yet acknowledges the inevitable post-structuralist, or ideological, aspects of its prac-tice, is given in chapter 2 of Selby and Cowdery's book, *How to Study Television* (1995). That chapter describes a billboard advertisement, using concepts or cate-gories that they call construction, audience, narrative, categorisation and agency. The questions and terminology they include for discussing the category 'Audience' (pp. 22–30) are particularly pertinent to understanding the theoretical ambiguities in studying advertising. Initially they gloss the category 'Audience' from a post-structuralist perspective: it is necessary to include this category because of 'the idea that a media text cannot be reduced to a single, fixed and coherent"meaning", but will instead be open to various interpretations by its various audiences'. How-ever, they then go on to describe the 'objective' structuralist categories through which advertisers try to categorise and segment their target audience, even though the identification of and discrimination between these categories is necessarily a subjective activity.

These include the paradigms of demographic or psychographic types. Demographic categories are differentiated by factors externally perceived, both objective (assumed income of occupation) and social (the status assumed given to an occupation); this English publication describes the external criterion as 'class'. Psychographic categories, in contrast, describe the internal perceptions of the audience. They attempt to 'divide audiences in terms of their needs, aspirations, attitudes, motivations and lifestyle'. A dozen such categories are given for 'the younger audience', such as 'Trendies, those who crave the admiration of their peers' and 'Egoists, those who seek pleasure'. (The advertising researchers perhaps admit defeat with the category of 'Drifters, Those who are not sure what they want'!) A psychographic approach assumes that consumers will want a 'product' (which could be a thing, service or even idea, as in political or religious advertising) that confirms or enables their own sense of identity. In other words, the story promoted by the magic of the advertisement should require a subject position confirming such an identity. Thus advertisers will try to give their product a meaning, a 'brand identity', that conforms to the 'psychographic' target audience. (The term 'brand' has now moved into more general parlance as a synonym for 'recognised identity', such that a university or a political party can refer to itself as 'a brand'. A brand with no strongly recognised identity has 'no pulling power', as one politician remarked of one political party in 2004.)

Of course one can always have resistant readers: in 'Discriminating or duped? Young people as consumers of advertising/art', Mica and Orson Nava claim that young people are now more 'media savvy' than previous generations, that items of popular culture, including advertisements, can be enjoyed, just as 'high culture', such as 'art', was enjoyed by previous generations, but that 'young people' don't necessarily rush out and buy the object – so the 'good' (that is, entertaining) advertisement can be appreciated as an art object, a story external to the viewer's own subjectivity (Marris & Thornham 1996: 503–9).

Others are less convinced. Alan Tomlinson, in 'Consumer culture and the aura of the commodity' (Marris & Thornham 1996: 510–14) remains more sceptical of claims of individual resistance to advertising (since individuals are socially produced by their environment). He reinforces Raymond Williams' observations in a more pessimistic way, concluding: 'Our personal identity is created by others and marketed aggressively and seductively.'

Conclusion

Raymond Williams' concept of 'magic' in advertising refers to the transformative powers attributed to material objects by advertisers: the 'magic' power of a particular product to make us more beautiful, manly, successful, rich and so on. Products are sold to us not merely as useful or desirable items but on the basis of these magic powers that they seem to possess. While acknowledging the usefulness of Williams' concept, this chapter also critiques, from a post-structuralist viewpoint, the notion of a coherent and consistent subjectivity, which is implied by the idea of 'magic' and its effect on an individual consumer.

Instead, we can posit a continuum of signification in advertising, from 'magic' at one end, where the attributes of the product are transferred to the consumer, to 'information' at the other end, focusing on the object product itself, more or less detached from a consumer. We can go further and suggest that advertisements in which image is more dominant than written text are closer to the 'magic' end of the continuum, since image creates a more dynamic space in which individual desires and fantasies can be located.

Finally, the chapter argues that industry categorisations of target audience into specific socioeconomic groupings determine the format and content of the advertisements themselves. Market segments are first defined, then targeted by advertisements that offer the 'magic powers' desired by particular segments. Given the unstable nature of subjectivity, the result is an uneasy balance between consumer willingness to adopt the subject position constructed by the advertisement (and therefore to buy the product) and consumer resistance to a subject position carefully crafted on the basis of market research and an imagined demographic. The extent to which individual consumers can step outside socially constructed subjectivities remains debatable.

Chapter 20

Conclusion: postmodern narrative and media

Helen Fulton

At the beginning of Tom Tykwer's film *Run, Lola, Run* (1999), the voice-over says: 'Countless questions in search of an answer . . . an answer that will give rise to a new question, and the next question will give rise to a second question, and so on.'

This announcement calls attention to the instability of meaning, which is a central concept of post-structuralist theory and lies at the heart of postmodern representation. The content and structure of the film challenge the conventions of causality, temporality, motivation and closure that characterise realist narrative and offer instead something closer to a postmodern narrative based on uncertainty, repetition with variation, multimodalism and a constant disruption of the movement from signifier to signified that stabilises meaning. Yet the idea of a 'postmodern narrative' appears to be something of an oxymoron, since postmodernism explicitly rejects totalising narratives with their neat explanations and carefully signposted points of closure. Is such a concept possible?

There is no doubt that contemporary media texts, and their narrative modes, continue to locate themselves comfortably in the aesthetic of classic realism. Emerging at the same time as the rise of industrial capitalism, in the late nineteenth century, the mode of realism enacts a specific ideological agenda, 'not only in its representation of a world of consistent subjects who are the origin of meaning, knowledge and action, but also in offering the reader, as the position from which the text is most readily intelligible, the position of subject as the origin both of understanding and of action in accordance with that understanding' (Belsey 1980: 67). So empowered are we as the subjects of media texts that it is no wonder we continue to consume them in ever-increasing quantities.

The most significant methodology for analysing realist texts in the last half century has undoubtedly been structuralism. Born from what seemed like a brilliant alliance between linguistics and anthropology, structuralist theory and its application to text (in all modes and genres) has dominated the study of narrative. With its strategies of identifying key elements interrelated as a complete system, such as binary oppositions and syntagmatic combinations, the goal of structuralism is effectively to identify the shape of an underlying model (the *langue*), which pre-existed and accounted for each semiotic realisation of it (the *parole*). As post-structuralist approaches have subsequently demonstrated, the apparent distinction between model and text, *langue* and *parole*, is no more sustainable than that between denotation and connotation. Models are reconstituted from existing texts or signifying practices, and not the other way about. Moreover, identifying the key structural elements that comprise an underlying model is itself an ideological and discursive practice (see chapter 3 by Rosemary Huisman). Despite Propp's heroic efforts, there is no single inevitable model to be discovered from a group of texts any more than there are single absolute meanings.

Eschewing linguistic analysis, and in default of any other systematic strategy of textual analysis, many media critics have found it hard to let go of structuralism. Textbooks on media studies regularly begin their accounts of narrative with Vladimir Propp and end with Roland Barthes, still in his structuralist phase, as if there is no other kind of narrative theory. Structuralist analysis can be useful in identifying sites of signification, but the limitations of its methodologies are rarely examined. Propp's system of 'functions', for example, provides a framework for comparing character roles, stereotypes and gender roles, but without a theory of discourse or of representation it cannot account for specific relations between characters or for narrative voice.

There is another reason why structuralist approaches to media as narrative continue to prevail, and that is because media texts exemplify the modes of realism and modernism that are most conducive to structuralist analysis. Divided into well-marked genres in order to maximise their commercial potential, most media texts can easily be reduced to an essential model or template, which the text itself then appears to embody. When we identify the binary oppositions common to action movies, or the basic 'story' of romantic comedies, realised in different 'plots', we are performing a satisfying game of matching the pieces in a puzzle, oblivious of our own ideological positioning and the partiality with which we recognise some structural elements and ignore others. Already positioned as the empowered and coherent subjects of realist texts, we remain in the same subject position as structuralist analysts of those texts.

The winds of post-structuralism, blowing most strongly in the 1970s and 1980s, revealed the theoretical problems inherent in structuralism. The impossibility of distinguishing in any practical way between *langue* and *parole*, denotation and connotation, model and text, story and plot, dismantled the certainties of structuralist analysis and led to a greater concern with signification and subjectivity as aspects of discourse. More than structuralism, post-structuralism is closely concerned with language, and such critics as Althusser, Foucault and Derrida based their theories on the discursive construction of subjectivity and power (Poster 1989: 109).

In particular, analytical approaches based on post-structural theories of meaning concern themselves with ways in which the stable subjectivity of most realist texts, including media texts, can be destabilised and decentred. When a text makes us aware that we need to do some work to interpret it, when it fails to offer a transparent window into a coherent reality, our subjectivity is exposed as fragile and contingent. We are no longer coherent and stable subjects, moving effortlessly from text to meaning, from sign to referent. Our sense of 'who we are', or what Angela McRobbie calls 'the real me', is threatened by our inability to process and respond to the text without conscious effort. This inability itself lays bare 'the fictive unity of the self and the essentialism entailed in the search for such a person' (McRobbie 1985: 62).

This type of unstable subjectivity is constructed by 'difficult' or non-commercial texts, such as James Joyce's *Ulysses* (1922). Most readers of this text need some kind of external assistance, from a teacher or critical handbook, in order to make any sense of it, and are therefore produced by the text as incomplete subjects, needy rather than self-contained. Similarly, texts that demand a conscious act of interpretation split the subject into 'reader' and 'interpreter'. By challenging the conventions of realist narrative, such films as *Pierrot le Fou* (1965) (Lacey 2000: 122–6) and *Mulholland Drive* (2001) disturb the unconscious movement from sign to referent. The reading position is destabilised, and the viewer has to supply his or her own meanings without authorial or authoritative direction towards a single 'right' meaning. The possibility of multiple meanings threatens the stability and coherence of the subject. This partly explains why news images, in newspapers and on television, are so clearly captioned and explained, to direct us to a single 'obvious' meaning and therefore to avoid the fragmentation of the subject-as-consumer. Concealing the contingent and fragile nature of our identities in order to position us as freely choosing consumers is the main function of media texts.

Post-structuralism is a significant theory in relation to the study of media narrative since it offers a way of understanding subjectivity, and because it dismantles the boundaries between the 'object' of study and the 'subject' who studies it. In its emphasis on language and discourse, it provides a platform for the analysis of power relations, the construction of genres and the interplay of different narrative modes. Its relationship to postmodernism is understood differently by various critics. For Angela McRobbie, postmodernism is 'a concept for understanding social change' (McRobbie 1985: 62). Steven Best and Douglas Kellner argue that postmodernism is a 'matrix' that includes post-structuralism within its brief: 'postmodern theory appropriates the post-structuralist critique of modern theory, radicalises it, and extends it to new theoretical fields' (Best & Kellner 1991: 25–6).

Although the term 'post-structuralism' has undeniably been appropriated, and subsequently ignored, by many postmodern critics, it has its own functional identity, which resists assimilation into the postmodern matrix of ideas. Post-structuralism is a theory of meaning. Postmodernism is, in terms of representation, a type of aesthetic or style, as modernism is, and therefore a legitimate object of study based on post-structuralist understandings of discourse and signification.

The term 'postmodernism' has two major inflections, signifying both a form of representation and a complete cultural system. Fredric Jameson identifies it as a cultural dominant that is inseparable from, and symptomatic of, the 'economic system of late capital' (Jameson 1984: 56). Terry Eagleton distinguishes between *postmodernism* as 'a form of contemporary culture' and *postmodernity* as 'a specific historical period', which he also calls 'a style of thought', returning to the essential idea of postmodernism as an aesthetic of representation (Eagleton 1996: vii). This distinction helps to explain why the postmodern aesthetic seems to appear in the past (as in James Joyce's *Ulysses*, for example) yet is also specific to our own period.

Post-structuralism is a way of talking about how postmodernist texts (including those of the plastic and visual arts) signify and how they position the reading or viewing subject. Baudrillard's concept of hyperreality, as the distinctive mode of postmodern culture (Baudrillard 1983: 2), depends on a post-structuralist understanding of the relationship between sign and referent, text and reality. As part of popular culture, the media work at the level of hyperreality, constantly reproducing not the 'real' but simulations of the real. When Baudrillard says: 'It is no longer a question of a false representation of reality (ideology), but of concealing the fact that the real is no longer real' (Baudrillard 1983: 23), he is drawing on the post-structuralist theory that reality is available to us only through the mediation of discourse, whether linguistic, visual, auditory or multimodal. It follows that postmodern texts (like all texts) are not precisely a symptom of postmodernity but are representations of an idea of a cultural condition that is itself available only through textual mediations.

Similarly, Lyotard's claim that the postmodern condition is characterised by 'an incredulity towards metanarratives' depends on post-structuralist theories relating to truth claims and how these are ideologically validated (Lyotard 1984: xxiv). The concept of a metanarrative as a totalising and homogenising force is given substance by Foucault's post-structuralist approach to the relationship between discourse and power and Lacan's theory of the subject emerging at the symbolic level of language. Slavoj Žižek asserts, somewhat hyperbolically, 'It is only with Lacan that the "postmodernist" break occurs . . . the only "poststructuralist" is Lacan' (Žižek 1999: 41).

The postmodern aesthetic and its political and semantic interpretations are unknowable without the analytical strategies made possible by post-structuralist thought. To return to the example of the film, *Run, Lola, Run*, its temporal confusions, parallel stories and juxtapositions of the modes of realism, surrealism and animation, proclaim it to be a notable example of a postmodernist text. Yet its opening voice-over, telling us in effect that every decoding is another encoding, that meaning exists only in an endless chain of signifiers, directs us to a post-structuralist reading of the film. The fashionable label of 'postmodernism' tends to eclipse the film's self-awareness of a post-structuralist reading of its textuality.

To say that we live in a period of postmodernity, then, is to say little more than that we live in a time when postmodern modes of representation are dominant. This period might well be associated with the economics of global capitalism, as Jameson has argued, but there is nothing postmodern about global capitalism except its success in promoting the postmodern aesthetic. 'Postmodern politics', the politics of this so-called postmodern age, remain conservatively capitalistic. When cultural historians try to describe the characteristics of postmodernism as a period of history – one marked by pluralism, absence of metanarratives, denaturalisation, rejection of authorised meanings and so on – they tend to accept the economic structures of capitalism as authoritative 'givens', the 'real' that cannot be simulated, the 'natural' that automatically resists denaturalisation. Postmodernism is offered as a radical break with past cultures but is in fact as politically conservative as most of them.

This conservatism is replicated in the analysis of postmodern texts, which is invariably structuralist in its orientation. The postmodern aesthetic is defined in terms of a model, or a set of defining characteristics, such as fragmentation, pastiche, juxtaposition, absence of closure and so on, all structural features that can be identified by a process of empirical observation and content analysis. Roland Barthes introduced the idea of a *simulacrum* as the model or underlying structure that comprises the rules of a text and 'brings out something that remained invisible, or, if you like, unintelligible in the natural object' (Barthes 1964: 213). This concept effectively prefigures Baudrillard's *simulation* in which 'models and codes become the primary determinants of social experience' (Best & Kellner 1991: 119).

A postmodernist text, then, is one that displays certain features typical of the aesthetic, and which can be interpreted using structuralist analysis and/or post-structuralist theories of signification. It represents an alternative aesthetic of representation, coexisting with realist, naturalist, modernist and other styles of textual representation. Most media texts rely on realist narratives; the question is whether postmodern narratives exist in the media, or indeed at all. If we accept that postmodernity is our current cultural condition, all texts produced in this period can be called postmodern. But in the sense of conforming to a particular aesthetic or model of expected stylistic norms, we can distinguish between postmodern norms of representation and other norms that utilise different logics of representation.

Some critics argue that postmodern texts, in this latter sense, are innately non-narrative, such as Ihab Hassan's binary opposition between modernist 'narrative' and postmodernist 'anti-narrative' (Swingewood 1998: 164). Such an opposition assumes, however, that 'narrative' automatically means realist narrative, the kind that has a cause-and-effect progression, a consistency of space and time, and an identifiable point of closure. If that is taken as the normative definition of narrative, then postmodern texts tell a different kind of story. Within the postmodern mode of representation, the linguistic signifiers of realist narrative are typically replaced with image, eroding the boundaries between high and popular cultures. Yet image is also a powerful mode of representation and a fertile source of narrative of all kinds.

Television sitcoms such as *Seinfeld* and *The Simpsons* can be regarded as postmodern representations of a postmodern condition, fetishising consumption and the commodification of popular culture, including celebrity. Episodes of *Seinfeld* seem to emerge as part of a continuum of lived experience, lacking resolution or closure, resisting progression or character development, returning again and again to consumption, commodity fetishism and exchange value. Some of the major trademarks of *The Simpsons* are associated with postmodernist style, such as its playful pastiche of different genres, its high levels of intertextuality and self-referencing, its self-conscious embrace of celebrity as both risible and seductive. Yet each episode of both these sitcoms is highly structured using the framework of realist narrative, featuring actions that later have consequences, characters who are stereotypical in their consistency of performance and resolutions that might be no more than the intervention of theme music and credits but still serve to mark off a narrative event.

Much vaunted for its innovation as a television genre, 'reality' TV can also be regarded as postmodern in terms of its status as simulation or hyperreality. The participants or 'contestants' in reality TV shows enact not reality but a simulation of reality determined by intertextual readings of other TV shows, media-generated concepts of celebrity, and the professional practices of producers and editors involved in making the shows. Even here, however, framing the statements of both postmodernism – pastiche, lack of closure, elision of authorial voices – and postmodernity – commodity capitalism, product placement, consumption of celebrity – the principles of realist narrative organise this simulated reality into the manufactured peaks and troughs of television fiction. The Internet, with its postmodern array of hyperlinks and infinite pathways, invites us to construct a coherent narrative in which we are the hero and our point of closure is the end of a quest, marked by the consumption of knowledge or the actual purchase of a commodity.

Postmodern media narratives, then, have their own structuring principles, a normative array of narrative strategies that overlap with those of realism. In the process of subverting the principles of realism, by rejecting closure or authority of genre, postmodernism still invokes a palimpsest of that which it subverts.

Narrative itself is the mode of representation; realism and postmodernism are different voices within it. Despite being heavily implicated in postmodernity as a cultural condition, the media tend not to generate many postmodern narratives. Apart from self-conscious realisations of postmodern style in film or television drama, the media tend to move entirely in the direction of realist narrative. Even the news is shaped into 'stories', which are provided with a logic of time and space and a resolution manufactured from the materials to hand. The role of the media is to produce the subjects of consumerism. We have to be continually reproduced as single coherent subjects through our consumption of media texts, and this subject position is most efficiently reinforced by narrative in its realist aesthetic.

The postmodernist style of narrative, on the other hand, draws attention to commodification. It strips away the illusions of advertising and threatens the power of advertisers to 'interpellate' us as subjects of capitalism. It can be confronting and destabilising and, like many episodes of *Seinfeld*, can disturb the consuming subject by parodying its commodity fetishism. Watching television, with its combination of genres, we engage in a constant cycle of fragmentation followed by the reintegration of the self through the familiar narrative models of sitcoms, police dramas and soap operas. Themselves the inventions of modernity, the popular media remain committed to the modernist project of narrative while constructing the hyperreality of the postmodern condition.

Processing reality and experience through the narrative strategies of consumer capitalism, the media seem to represent a site of struggle between postmodernity and postmodernism. As fast as postmodernism attempts to collapse the generic boundaries of media narrative, the economic logic of the media demands that they be re-erected, since they are needed for marketing and audience segmentation. Such television programs as *Big Brother* and *The Simpsons*, innovative in terms of genre and narrative when they first appeared, have been assimilated into the kind of totalising genres – reality TV and animated sitcom – from which they had sought to escape. Imagined as a democracy of information liberated from the metanarratives of modernism, the Internet has instead become incorporated into the postmodernist metanarrative of commodification and the illusion of choice.

Yet this apparent struggle between the economics of postmodern culture and the aesthetics of postmodernism, enacted on the terrain of the mass media, is itself a narrative construct. The aesthetics of postmodernism, whether articulated in art, architecture, literature or the media, are powerfully entwined with the economics of commodity capitalism, shaping themselves into the very commodities that postmodern texts claim to deconstruct. Media texts that might be described as postmodern in their narrative strategies are in the end complicit in the media agenda of positioning audiences as sovereign consumers, the coherent subjects of capitalism.

Glossary

agency At the level of text, *agency* refers to the sender(s) of a communicative message, who control its form and content and who project an interpretive position into the text. Most media texts have a complex system of agency, since they are normally produced by more than one person, including writers, editors, producers and other media professionals. Agency is responsible for the subject positions constructed by a text; that is, the way subjects are positioned in relation to the text. In accepting or resisting these subject positions, readers or viewers are engaging with the agency of the text. At the level of individual clauses within a larger text, *agency* can also refer to the participant who carries out or controls the action of the clause.

appraisal See *modality*.

audience The audience for media texts can be theorised as comprising both an *illocutionary* and a *perlocutionary* audience. The illocutionary or '*virtual*' audience is projected by the producers of a text or 'interpellated' by the text. It is a discursive construct brought into being by the language of the text, and is more or less the same as the 'target' or 'assumed' audience that underlies commercial media production and which is sold to advertisers. The perlocutionary audience refers to the actual viewers and consumers of media texts, who do not necessarily coincide with the illocutionary audience. Because of the size and nature of media audiences, both kinds of audience are almost impossible to 'know' empirically – who they are, how many of them, what demographics they belong to – despite the existence of such measuring tools as television 'ratings', market research questionnaires and focus groups.

closure The point in a narrative at which only one ending is possible. This point might come right at the end, towards the end or nearer the beginning, as in a romance text where it is obvious almost from the beginning that a particular pair of characters will end up as a couple. Not all narratives have a point of closure but may be open-ended, leaving a variety of potential resolutions for the reader or audience to consider.

cohesion This is an aspect of the 'mode' of a text (see *field, tenor, mode*); that is, how a text is organised so that its elements combine to form a coherent and complete event (or not). Different genres are distinguished by their different levels of cohesion.

context of situation This refers to the immediate context in which a text is produced and received, and which influences the ways in which the text is constructed and interpreted. Movie dialogue is unlike 'natural' conversation because of its context of situation, constructed to fit a specific scene in the film while also directed at a watching audience in a cinema. Different *registers* and *genres* define, and are defined by, different contexts of situation.

diegesis and **mimesis** (1) Two ways of presenting a narrative: 'telling' it in the narrator's own words (diegesis) or 'showing' it through the words and actions of different characters (mimesis). (2) With regard to film and television, *diegesis* refers to the filmic 'world' of the narrative, the 'reality' constructed within the film or TV program.

discourse Most generally, discourse is language in use. It is typically described in terms of the language practices of its institutional or social context: thus, 'legal discourse', 'literary discourse', 'family discourse'. Discourses are distinguished by classifications that are not absolute but are historically and socially produced. A discourse is associated with particular conventions of interpretation and production: for example, television discourse assumes a private context of reception, film discourse a public context. A discourse can have a limited or extensive context of use: the discourse of advertising is realised in many media, from billboard to radio to email spam. In traditional literary studies, the term 'genre' has been conflated with discourse, but it is helpful to use 'discourse' to refer to the conventional literary divisions: poetry, drama and prose fiction. The term 'genre' can then refer to specific text types for each discourse. (See **genre**.)

duration One of Genette's concepts, to do with the speed of a narrative. It compares how long a narrator or a film dwells on events when telling them in the narrative (that is, 'plot time' and 'screen time') with how long those events might take if actually experienced. The latter is often misleadingly called 'story time', but a story is already a mediated telling of the experience. This sleight of hand by which 'story' is equated with 'experience' contributes to the structuralist dichotomy of 'story' and 'plot'. Direct speech, quoted as it would be said, is taken as a duration of 1:1. Different media facilitate different durations. For example, prose fiction lends itself to summary (perhaps achieved by a voice-over in a film) whereas film and television can elongate the narrative with a 'slow motion' sequence of shots or with the 'real time' of dialogue.

field, tenor, mode These terms are used in systemic functional grammar, associated particularly with the linguist M. A. K. Halliday. They refer to the three aspects of the context of situation in which a message is produced or interpreted. **'Field'** refers both to the social action (for narrative, the act of telling) and to the subject matter (what is told). Field is 'realised' in choices of ideational meaning, which includes experiential meaning (for example, in language, agency or goal for a participant, or mental rather than verbal meaning for a process) and logical meaning (in language, the meanings of connectors like 'but', 'although'). **'Tenor'** refers to the social relations between people in the context of situation, and their attitude to the message – this includes the context of 'telling' (the producer of the message and its audience) and the context of 'what is told' (the diegetic characters in the narrated world). Tenor is realised in choices of interpersonal meaning, (in language, choices of mood and modality; see below). **'Mode'** refers to the medium of delivery (written, spoken, visual and their subcategories) and the organisation of the message into a more or less coherent unit in relation to its context of situation. Mode is realised in choices of textual meaning.

focalisation A category of Genette's mood: the perspective from which the narrative is told, the one who 'sees', as opposed to the one who 'tells' (the narrator). A refinement of the traditional narrative concept 'point of view'. For a helpful discussion see Rimmon-Kenan (1983, chapter 6).

genre A type or category of text, serving a particular social purpose. Texts identified as belonging to the 'same genre' typically share some structural and/or linguistic features.

Different media discourses can make use of the same genres (for example, the interview in radio and television). Particular genres might nonetheless be primarily associated with a particular *discourse*; for example, the novel is a genre of the discourse of prose fiction, the sitcom is a genre of the discourse of television.

heteroglossia   The variety of meanings that can be made by different consumers of a text, depending on their own previous experience of other texts.

ideology   *Ideology* orients interpretative habits that appear 'natural', 'common sense', not open to debate or questioning. Typically, we become aware of 'ideology' only through differences in ideology (consider the narratives purveyed by different political parties before an election). To the extent that its instantiations are universal in a particular culture, it is invisible to its practitioners. Post-structuralist critiques of institutional practices (discourses, genres, texts) usually focus on ideology.

institution   The site of power relations in a culture, with subject positions and/or roles of varying power within it, and associated social practices, verbal or non-verbal. Examples of institutions include the law, different religions, the family, sport, literature, advertising and print-culture publishing.

intertextuality   The semiotic links between texts that draw on similar linguistic and referential conventions. Each text draws on meanings that have been established in other texts and which enable audiences to recognise particular *genres* and meanings.

langue* and *parole   These French terms were used by Saussure to distinguish between a whole system, such as a language, or *langue*, and individual examples of that system put into practice – a *parole*, or a specific text or utterance. This distinction is associated with structuralist analysis, whereby a specific narrative, such as a film version of the Robin Hood legend, is analysed as a *parole* in relation to a pre-existing *langue*, in this case a perceived generic form of the Robin Hood legend. The model of *langue* and *parole* has been undermined by post-structuralist critiques which suggest that all apparent examples of *langue* are in fact themselves *paroles*. In attempting to recount the generic form of the Robin Hood legend, for example, a narrator simply constructs his or her own version of it; that is, a *parole*. See also *story* and *plot*.

metalanguage   Refers to any interpretive discourse used to explain and analyse a prior level of signification. A film, for example, can be analysed using the metalanguage of narrative criticism.

metanarrative or myth   Metanarratives, or 'myths' to use the structuralist term, are the persistent cultural stories, especially those of power relations (such as stories of gender, ethnicity and class), epistemology (ways of knowing) and ontology (ways of being), which people in that culture receive and transmit. By their habitual retelling of metanarratives in their social practices, people confirm and reconfirm the ideology of the culture. For the anthropologist Lévi-Strauss, the function of 'myth' among particular cultural groups was to reconcile contradictions between experience and belief. For Lyotard, the major metanarrative of Western culture has been that of 'science' (as he described it); that is, the elevation of the 'rational' and objective, with a repression of the subjectivity of interpretation. (Gender studies would identify the subject of that myth to be white and masculine.)

mimesis   See *diegesis*.

mise en page   Refers to what is put on the page in a printed or manuscript text, and the way the page is visually organised. Combinations of words and images, various fonts and headings and other graphological signs form a particular layout that itself generates meanings.

mise en scène   Literally the 'setting' of a narrative, but also the collocation of particular items or natural objects that conventionally signify a context. In film analysis, the term refers to the visual realisation of a setting, the composition of an image within a given shot or sequence, providing a site of signification (a place where meanings are made).

modality   Refers to the attitude of the speaker or narrative voice in relation to the truth, certainty, obligation, possibility and value of what is being narrated. A high modality, such as that found in the declarative statements of news reporting, suggests truth, certainty, factuality. Lower levels of modality, identified by the use of auxiliary verbs such as 'might' or 'could', and by modal expressions such as 'perhaps' or 'I think', suggest that the speaker or narrator is less certain of the truth of what is being claimed. Evaluative expressions, or *appraisal*, indicating positive or negative attitudes, are part of the modality of a text.

mode   The means by which a text is delivered. The basic division is between the spoken mode and the written mode. However, complex modes are associated with different genres. For a theatre drama, the mode is 'written to be performed as speech'; for a radio drama, written to be spoken as speech; for a story in a political speech, written to be spoken or performed (depending on the media) as if not-written (that is, simulating spontaneous speech); for the novel, in the twentieth century, written to be read silently; for Chaucer's narrative poetry in the fourteenth century, written to be read aloud. See also *field, tenor, mode*.

montage   A set of conventions relating to film editing; the ways in which different shots, taken at different times, are selected and spliced together to make a single narrative sequence.

myth   See *metanarrative*.

narrative/narrator   In the speech function choices of systemic functional linguistics one can give information ('tell') or give goods and services ('offer'), and one can ask for information ('question') or ask for goods and services ('command' or, more politely, 'request'). The 'mood' structures realise these different meanings: the declarative mood to tell, the interrogative mood to question, the imperative mood to request and various formulations to offer. The narrator gives information so the usual narrative mood is the declarative, making statements. The full range of mood choices appears only in the speech of characters (or usually do – so marked is the choice of the interrogative mood by a narrator that it is called a 'rhetorical question'). See also *voice*.

nominalisation   At the level of the clause within a larger piece of text, actions expressed by noun phrases instead of by verbs are said to be 'nominalised'. Thus in the clause 'Outbursts of gunfire began at daylight', the noun phrase 'outbursts of gunfire' replaces a verbal expression, such as 'Soldiers began firing at daylight'. The main effect of nominalisation, which is a defining characteristic of news reporting, is to elide agency – who is performing the action – and causality, the reasons why an action takes place. Nominalisation is therefore an effect device in the construction of an 'objective' *tenor* in news reporting.

order   One of Genette's three categories of tense: the order of events in the narrative compared to the chronological order of events.

pacing   Changes of narrative 'speed' produced by adjusting the relationship between the time occupied by particular events in a narrative and the amount of narrative space devoted to those events. See also *duration*.

point of view   See *focalisation*.

plot   See *story*.

register   A somewhat contentious term in discourse analysis, referring to the relationship between language choices and the context of situation. A text that seems believable and transparent, enabling its audience to interpret it without effort, uses a register that is entirely compatible with its context. The register of hard news reporting is characterised by formality, objectivity and an emphasis on empirical facts. The register of soap opera, on the other hand, is characterised by informal conversation and domestic references. Control of register, so that language choices are appropriate to context, is one of the ways in which genre is established.

representation   A useful term to use loosely, but it carries theoretical baggage. The prefix 're' means do again, as in 'rewind'. Thus 'represent' is re-present: the experience is already present, and in a text it can be presented again, but this time in language. But language always mediates the experience; it is more accurate to say language signifies the experience than that it represents it. A second, more subtle, problem is that if the process of 're-presenting' suggests the experience is already 'present', it effaces the *Umwelt*, the recognition that all experience is perceived, even initially, through a sign system and therefore through ideological glasses.

semiotics and semiosis   While *semiotics* is the 'science of signs', *semiosis* refers to the process of signification by which signs become meaningful. Saussure and Barthes preferred the term *semiology*, but following the usage of the American theorist Charles Peirce, *semiotics* has become standard. Structuralist semiotics studies signs and sign-systems ('being'); post-structuralist semiotics studies processes of signification, the practices of interpreting or producing meaning ('becoming'). Narrative study is a species of semiotic study; for different purposes, a structuralist or post-structuralist method of study, or both, can be found relevant.

simulacrum   For Barthes, a simulacrum was a copy that revealed the model or underlying structure of the original. Postmodernists, particularly Baudrillard, have retheorised the simulacrum as a copy that has no original, referring particularly to media and marketing texts (such as theme parks) that construct their own reality while claiming to 'reflect' reality. According to this theory, the process of simulation means that audiences increasingly experience 'reality' only through the signs and codes of commercialism and the mass media.

story and plot   These terms express a structuralist view of narrative as comprising a *langue*, or pre-existing set of events happening in chronological order (the 'story'), and a *parole*, the specific instance of this set of events (the 'plot') as organised and elaborated in one particular text. The 'story' is therefore regarded as existing before the 'plot', as if it were an unmediated account of real experience compared with the artificially produced 'plot'.

subject   (1) Grammatical subject: derived from Aristotle's logic of the proposition: the subject is that of which the proposition is asserted (the predicate). (2) Speaking subject: from Benveniste, the subject of the enunciation, the one who speaks the text. (3) Subject of speech: from Benveniste, the 'enounced' subject, the one who speaks *in* the text (the first person pronouns in the text). (4) Spoken subject: an interpretative position projected into the text that the audience is invited to occupy. In film theory, the position and angle of the camera constructs the position offered to the spoken subject. For example, an advertiser would try to project a spoken subject position thought to be attractive (by market research) to the target audience. A resistant reader might refuse to take up that position (for example, a feminist response to a traditional fairy tale in which a passive princess waits while the prince acts and acts . . .).

temporality   The way in which narrative events in a text are related to each other in terms of time. Different kinds of temporality are associated with different media genres, such as the parallel storylines of soap opera, in which simultaneous events are necessarily shown in a linear sequence.

tenor   See **field, tenor, mode**.

text   A text is a semantic unit, usually identified by its genre as a coherent known media object: a conversation, a letter, a novel, a film. The medium is sometimes explicit in its generic naming; for example, a radio play. The segmented texts of television are more problematic. One episode of a series could be described as one text, but one episode of a soap opera, with its juxtaposition of different storylines in each segment, is scarcely a text in the sense of a semantic unit, although it is a text in the sense of a finite media object.

transitivity   In narrative study, transitivity analysis is particularly relevant to understanding the power relations assumed in the text. Transitivity is the system of choices of experiential meaning in the clause (see **field, tenor, mode**) by which participants take up particular meanings in relation to the process, meanings such as who does what to whom, who has agency, who is acted upon and so on.

Umwelt   The semiotic world of the interpreter; that is, the extent of experiential reality that has meaning for an individual. *Umwelt* also includes the range of signifying practices available to an individual that enables him or her to recognise genres and interpret linguistic conventions.

vector   An actual or imaginary line, often diagonal, connecting participants (both people and objects) in an image or shot. The term is used by Kress and van Leeuwen (1996) to analyse meaning and *transitivity* in visual texts.

virtual audience   See *audience*.

voice   Generally refers to the presence of the narrator in a text, the constructed consciousness of the narrator who is telling the story as opposed to the literal author of the text. Voice can broadly be subdivided into first person (the narrative 'I' of a first-hand account, which implies a second-person 'you' who is being addressed) and third person, where the narrative voice represents participants in the text. The way in which voice is constructed in particular texts has ideological implications since the narrative voice has the power to determine how participants and actions are represented. Voice can therefore be gendered or given similar kinds of social positioning.

Bibliography

Abbott, H. Porter, *Cambridge Introduction to Narrative*, Cambridge: Cambridge University Press, 2002.

Alasuutari, Pertti (ed.), *Rethinking the Media Audience*, London: Sage Publications, 1999.

Allen, S., *News Culture*, Buckingham, UK: Open University Press, 1999.

Andrew, Dudley, 'Adaptation', in James Naremore (ed.), *Film Adaptation*, London: Athlone Press, 2000, pp. 28–37.

Bal, Mieke, 'The narrating and the focalising: A theory of agents in narrative', *Style* 17 (1983), 234–69.

— *Narratology: Introduction to the Theory of Narrative*, 2nd edn, Toronto and Buffalo: Toronto University Press, 1997 (1st edn, 1985).

Baker, R., 'Will the media be the end of us?', *Harvard International Journal of Press/Politics* 4.3 (1999), 98–105.

Barnard, S., *Studying Radio*, London and New York: Arnold, 2000.

Barthes, Roland, *Essais Critiques*, Paris: Editions du Seuil, 1964.

— *S/Z*, New York: Hill & Wang, 1974.

— *Image-Music-Text*, London: Fontana, 1977.

Baudrillard, Jean, *Simulations*, New York: Semiotext(e), 1983.

Baym, G., 'Packaging reality: Structures of form in US network news coverage of Watergate and the Clinton impeachment', *Journalism: Theory, Practice and Criticism* 5.3 (2004), 279–99.

Bell, Allan, and Peter Garrett (eds), *Approaches to Media Discourse*, Oxford: Blackwell, 1998.

Bell, P., and Theo van Leeuwen, *The Media Interview: Confession, Contest, Conversation*, Sydney: UNSW Press, 1994.

Belsey, Catherine, *Critical Practice*, London: Methuen, 1980.

Benjamin, Walter, *Illuminations*, ed. Hannah Arendt, New York: Schocken, 1969.

Bennett, T., S. Boyd-Bowman, C. Mercer and J. Woollacott (eds), *Popular Film and Television*, London: British Film Institute, 1981.

Best, Steven, and Douglas Kellner, *Postmodern Theory: Critical Interrogations*, London: Macmillan, 1991.

Bignell, Jonathan, *Media Semiotics: An Introduction*, Manchester: Manchester University Press, 1997.

Bordwell, David, and Kristin Thompson, *Film Art: An Introduction*, Reading, MA: Addison-Wesley Publishing Co., 1979.

Bordwell, David, J. Staiger and Kristin Thompson, *The Classical Hollywood Cinema: Film Style and Mode of Production to 1960*, London: Routledge, 1985.

Bourdieu, Pierre, *Distinction*, trans. Richard Nice, London and New York: Routledge & Kegan Paul, 1986 (first published 1979).

Branigan, E., *Narrative Comprehension and Film*, London: Routledge, 1992.

Briggs, S., *Those Radio Times*, London: Weidenfeld & Nicolson, 1981.

Brooks, P., *Reading for the Plot: Design and Intention in Narrative*, Cambridge MA: Harvard University Press, 1992.

Butt, David et al., *Using Functional Grammar: An Explorer's Guide*, 2nd edn, Macquarie University, Sydney: National Centre for English Language Teaching and Research, 2000.

Campbell, Joseph, *The Hero with a Thousand Faces*, New York: Pantheon, 1949.

Cartmell, Deborah, and Imelda Whelehan, *Adaptations: From Text to Screen, Screen to Text*, London and New York: Routledge, 1999.

Chandler, Daniel, *Semiotics: The Basics*, London: Routledge, 2002.

Chatman, Seymour, 'The structure of narrative transmission', in Roger Fowler (ed.), *Style and Structure in Literature*, Oxford: Blackwell, 1975, pp. 213–57.

— 'What novels can do that films can't (and vice versa)', *Critical Inquiry* 7 (1980), 121–40.

— *Story and Discourse*, Ithaca and London: Cornell University Press, 1978.

Clark, Katerina, and Michael Holquist, *Mikhail Bakhtin*, Cambridge, Mass.: Belknap Press of Harvard University Press, 1984.

Clarke, Patricia, and Dale Spender, *Life Lines, Australian Women's Letters and Diaries 1788 to 1840*, Sydney: Allen & Unwin, 1992.

Cobley, Paul, *Narrative*, London: Routledge, 2001.

Cohen, Stanley, *Folk Devils and Moral Panics: The Creation of the Mods and Rockers*, London: MacGibbon & Kee, 1972.

Cohen, Stanley, and Jock Young (eds), *The Manufacture of News: Social Problems, Deviance and Mass Media*, London: Constable, 1973.

Collins Dictionary of the English Language, Sydney: Collins, 1979.

Conley, D., *The Daily Miracle: An Introduction to Journalism*, 2nd edn, Melbourne: Oxford University Press, 2002.

Cook, David A., *A History of Narrative Film*, 3rd edn, New York and London: W. W. Norton & Co., 1996.

Cooke, L., 'The police series', in G. Creeber (ed.), *The Television Genre Book*, pp. 19–23.

Cooper, James Fenimore, *Last of the Mohicans, A Narrative of 1757*, rev. edn, Paris: Baudry's European Library, 1835.

— *The Pioneers* (first published 1822), New York: Airmont, 1964.

Cortazzi, Martin, *Narrative Analysis*, London: Falmer, 1993.

Cottle, Simon, 'Analysing visuals: Still and moving images' in Anders Hansen et al., *Mass Communication Research Methods*, pp. 189–224.

Cranny-Francis, Anne, and Patricia Palmer Gillard, 'Soap opera as gender training: Teenage girls and TV', in Terry Threadgold and Anne Cranny-Francis (eds), *Feminine, Masculine and Representation*, Sydney: Allen & Unwin, 1990, pp. 171–89.

Creeber, G. (ed.), *The Television Genre Book*, London: British Film Institute, 2001.

Crisell, Andrew, *Understanding Radio*, 2nd edn, London and New York: Routledge, 1994.

— *An Introductory History of British Broadcasting*, London and New York: Routledge, 1997.

— 'Better than Magritte: How drama on the radio became radio drama', *Journal of Radio Studies* 7.2 (2000), 464–73.

Culler, Jonathan, *Saussure*, Glasgow: Fontana, 1976.

Deely, John, *Basics of Semiotics*, Bloomington: Indiana University Press, 1990.

Dorsch, T. S., *Classical Literary Criticism, Aristotle, Horace, Longinus*, Harmondsworth: Penguin, 1965.

During, Simon (ed.), *The Cultural Studies Reader*, London: Routledge, 1993.

Dyer, R., 'Kill and kill again', in *Sight and Sound* 7.9 (1997), 14–17.

Eagleton, Terry, *The Illusions of Postmodernism*, Oxford: Blackwell, 1996.

Easthope, Antony, and Kate McGowan (eds), *A Critical and Cultural Theory Reader*, London: Allen & Unwin, 1992.

Eco, Umberto, *Semiotics and the Philosophy of Language*, London: Macmillan, 1984.

Ellis, John, *Visible Fictions: Cinema, Television, Video*, rev. edn, London and New York: Routledge, 1992.

Epstein, E. J., *Between Fact and Fiction: The Problem of Journalism*, New York: Random House, 1975.

— *News from Nowhere: Television and the News*, 2nd edn, New York: Random House, 2000.

Ericson, R., P. Baranek and J. Chan, *Visualizing Deviance: A Study of News Organization*, Milton Keynes: Open University Press, 1987.

Fairclough, Norman, *Language and Power*, London and New York: Longman, 1989.

— *Media Discourse*, London and New York: Edward Arnold, 1995.

Fiske, John, *Television Culture*, London: Methuen, 1987.

— and Hartley, John, *Reading Television*, 2nd edn, London: Routledge, 2003.

Fowler, Roger, *Language in the News: Discourse and Ideology in the Press*, London and New York: Routledge, 1991.

— *Linguistic Criticism*, 2nd edn, Oxford: Oxford University Press, 1996.

Fraser, J. T., *Time, Conflict, and Human Values*, Urbana: Illinois University Press, 1999.

Friel, Brian, *Selected Plays*, London: Faber, 1984.

Gans, H., *Deciding What's News*, New York: Pantheon, 1979.

Garnham, Nicholas, *Capitalism and Communication*, London: Sage Publications, 1990.

Genette, Gérard, *Narrative Discourse: An Essay in Method*, trans. Jane E. Lewin, Ithaca, NY: Cornell University Press, 1980 (first published in French in 1972).

Goatly, Andrew, *Critical Reading and Writing: An Introductory Coursebook*, London and New York: Routledge, 2000.

Goffman, E., *Frame Analysis*, New York: Harper & Row, 1974.

Gordon, Lyndall, *A Private Life of Henry James*, New York and London: W. W. Norton, 1999.

Griffith, James, *Adaptations as Imitations: Films from Novels*, Newark: University of Delaware Press, 1997.

Hall, Stuart, 'The narrative construction of news', *Context: A Forum for Literary Arts and Culture* 10 (1983), online edition, www.centerforbookculture.org/context/no10/hall.html; viewed 12 October 2004.

Hall, Stuart et al., *Policing the Crisis: Mugging, the State, and Law and Order*, Basingstoke: Macmillan, 1978.

Halliday, M. A. K., *Language as Social Semiotic: The Social Interpretation of Language and Meaning*, London and New York: Edward Arnold, 1978.

— and Hasan, Ruqaiya, *Language, Context and Text: Aspects of Language in a Social-Semiotic Perspective*, Waurn Ponds, Vic.: Deakin University Press, 1985.

Hallin, D., *We Keep America on Top of the World: Television Journalism and the Public Sphere*, London and New York: Routledge, 1993.

Hansen, Anders, Simon Cottle, Ralph Negrine and Chris Newbold, *Mass Communication Research Methods*, London: Macmillan, 1998.

Hartley, John, *Understanding News*, London: Routledge, 1982.

— *Popular Reality: Journalism, Modernity, Popular Culture*, London and New York: Arnold, 1996.

Hawthorn, Jeremy (ed.), *Narrative: From Malory to Motion Pictures*, London: Edward Arnold, 1985.

Hodge, Robert, and Gunther Kress, 'Rereading as exorcism: Semiotics and the ghost of Saussure', *Southern Review* 19 (1986), 38–52.

Hurd, G., 'The television presentation of the police', in T. Bennett et al. (eds), *Popular Film and Television*.

Innis, Robert E. (ed.), *Semiotics: An Introductory Reader*, Bloomington: Indiana University Press, 1985, and as *Semiotics: An Introductory Anthology*, London: Hutchinson, 1986.

Jameson, Fredric, 'Postmodernism, or the cultural logic of late capitalism', *New Left Review* 146 (July–August 1984), 53–92.

— *Signatures of the Visible*, London: Routledge, 1992.

Kilborn, Richard, *Television Soaps*, London: Batsford, 1992.

Kress, Gunther, and Theo van Leeuwen, *Reading Images: The Grammar of Visual Design*, London and New York: Routledge, 1996.

Labov, William, *Language in the Inner City*, Philadelphia: Pennsylvania University Press, 1972.

Lacey, Nick, *Image and Representation: Key Concepts in Media Studies*, London: Macmillan, 1998.

— *Narrative and Genre: Key Concepts in Media Studies*, London: Macmillan, 2000.

Langer, John, *Tabloid Television: Popular Journalism and the 'Other News'*, London and New York: Routledge, 1998.

Lévi-Strauss, Claude, 'The structural study of myth', in *Structural Anthropology*, Harmondsworth: Penguin, 1977, pp. 206–31 (first published in French in 1958).

Lewis, P., and J. Booth, *The Invisible Medium*, Basingstoke and London: Macmillan, 1989.

Lichtenberg, Judith, 'In defence of objectivity revisited', in J. Curran and M. Gurevitch (eds), *Mass Media and Society*, 3rd edn, London: Arnold, 2000, pp. 238–54.

Livingstone, Sonia M. (1990a), *Making Sense of Television: The Psychology of Audience Interpretation*, Oxford: Pergamon, 1990.

— (1990b), 'Interpreting a television narrative: How different viewers see a story', *Journal of Communication* 40 (1990), 72–85.

— 'The rise and fall of audience research: An old story with a new ending', in Mark R. Levy and Michael Gurevitch (eds), *Defining Media Studies: Reflections on the Future of the Field*, New York: Oxford University Press, 1994, pp. 247–54.

Lowe, N. J., *The Classical Plot and the Invention of Western Narrative*, Cambridge: Cambridge University Press, 2000.

Lumby, Catharine, and J. O'Neil, 'Tabloid television', in J. Schulz (ed.), *Not Just Another Business*, Sydney: Pluto Press, 1994, pp. 149–66.

Lyotard, Jean-François, *The Postmodern Condition: A Report on Knowledge*, Manchester: Manchester University Press; Minneapolis: University of Minnesota Press, 1984.

Marris, Paul, and Sue Thornham (eds), *Media Studies, A Reader*, Edinburgh: Edinburgh University Press, 1996.

McFarlane, Brian, *Novel to Film: An Introduction to the Theory of Adaptation*, Oxford: Clarendon Press, 1996.

McGilligan, Patrick, *Alfred Hitchcock, A Life In Darkness and Light*, Chichester, UK: Wiley, 2003.

McKnight, David, 'Facts versus stories: From objective to interpretive reporting', *Media International Australia* 99 (2001), 49–58.

McLuhan, Marshall, *Understanding Media: The Extensions of Man*, New York: Routledge & Kegan Paul, 1964.

McQuail, Denis, *Media Performance: Mass Communication and the Public Interest*, London: Sage Publications, 1992.

McQuillan, Martin (ed.), *The Narrative Reader*, London and New York: Routledge, 2000.

McRobbie, Angela, *Postmodernism and Popular Culture*, London and New York: Routledge, 1985.

Mead, George Herbert, 'The nature of aesthetic experience', *International Journal of Ethics* 36 (1926), 382–93.

Metz, C., *The Imaginary Signifier: Psychoanalysis and the Cinema*, trans. Celia Britten et al., Bloomington: Indiana University Press, 1982.

Moi, Toril (ed.), *The Kristeva Reader*, New York: Columbia University Press, 1986.

Mulvey, Laura, 'Visual pleasure and narrative cinema', in Charles Harrison and Paul Wood (eds), *Art in Theory 1900–1990: An Anthology of Changing Ideas*, Oxford: Blackwell, 1992.

Neale, S.,'Studying genre' in G. Creeber (ed.), *The Television Genre Book*, pp. 1–3.

Nelmes, Jill (ed.), *An Introduction to Film Studies*, London and New York: Routledge, 1996.

O'Shaughnessy, Michael, and Jane Stadler, *Media and Society: An Introduction*, 2nd edn, Melbourne: Oxford University Press, 2002.

O'Sullivan, T., J. Hartley, D. Saunders, M. Montgomery and J. Fiske, *Key Concepts in Communication and Cultural Studies*, London: Routledge, 1994.

O'Toole, Michael, *The Language of Displayed Art*, London: Leicester University Press, 1994.

Perloff, Marjorie, *Radical Artifice: Writing Poetry in the Age of Media*, Chicago: University of Chicago Press, 1991.

Phillips, G., and M. Lindgren (eds), *The Australian Broadcast Journalism Manual*, Melbourne: Oxford University Press, 2002.

Poster, Mark, *Critical Theory and Poststructuralism: In Search of a Context*, Ithaca and London: Cornell University Press, 1989.

Postman, Neil, *Amusing Ourselves to Death*, New York: Viking, 1985.

Pöttker, H., 'News and its communicative quality: The inverted pyramid – when and why did it appear?', *Journalism Series* 4.4 (2003), 501–11.

Potts, James, *Radio in Australia*, Sydney: Allen & Unwin, 1989.

Propp, Vladimir, *Morphology of the Folktale*, 2nd edn, Austin: Texas University Press, 1968.

Putnis, P., *Displaced, Recut and Recycled: File-tape in Television News*, Centre for Journalism Research and Education, Bond University, Qld, 1994.

Pynchon, Thomas, *The Crying of Lot 49*, New York: Harper & Row, 1986.

Ray, Robert B., 'The field of "literature and film" ', in James Naremore (ed.), *Film Adaptation*, London: Athlone Press, 2000, pp. 38–53.

Reddy, Michael, 'The conduit metaphor – A case of frame conflict in our language about language', in Andrew Ortony (ed.), *Metaphor and Thought*, Cambridge: Cambridge University Press, 1979, pp. 284–324.

Ricketson, M., 'True stories: The power and the pitfalls of literary journalism', in S. Tapsall and C. Varley (eds), *Journalism Theory in Practice*, Melbourne: Oxford University Press, 2000.

Ricoeur, Paul, *Time and Narrative*, 3 vols, Chicago: University of Chicago Press, 1984–88.

Rimmon-Kenan, Shlomith, *Narrative Fiction: Contemporary Poetics*, London and New York: Methuen, 1983.

Salinger, J. D., *The Catcher in the Rye*, London: Penguin, 1994.

Saussure, Ferdinand, *Course in General Linguistics*, New York: McGraw-Hill, 1966.

Schudson, Michael, *Discovering the News: A Social History of American Newspapers*, Basic Books: New York, 1978.

Schulz, Julianne, *Reviving the Fourth Estate: Democracy, Accountability and the Media*, Cambridge: Cambridge University Press, 1998.

Selby, Keith, and Ron Cowdery, *How to Study Television*, London: Macmillan, 1995.

Shingler, M., and C. Wieringa, *On Air: Methods and Meanings of Radio*, London and New York: Arnold, 1998.

Silverman, Kaja, *The Subject of Semiotics*, New York and Oxford: Oxford University Press, 1983.

Smith, Barbara Hernstein, 'Narrative versions, narrative theories', *Critical Inquiry* 7 (1980), 209–18.

Smith, Jen, 'Tabloid television', *Polemic* 3.2 (1992), 120–3.

Sperry, Sharon, 'Television News as Narrative', in R. Adler (ed.), *Understanding Television: Essays on Television as a Social and Cultural Force*, New York: Praeger, 1981.

Spivak, Gayatri Chakravorty, 'Translator's preface', in Jacques Derrida, *Of Grammatology*, Baltimore: Johns Hopkins University Press, 1976.

Swingewood, Alan, *Cultural Theory and the Problem of Modernity*, London: Macmillan, 1998.

Tarkovsky, A., *Sculpting in Time: Reflections on the Cinema*, trans. Kitty Hunter Blair, London: Bodley Head, 1986.

Thomas, Bronwen, '"Piecing together a mirage": Adapting *The English Patient* for the screen', in Robert Giddings and Erica Sheen (eds), *The Classic Novel: From Page to Screen*, Manchester and New York: Manchester University Press, 2000, pp. 197–232.

Thompson, Geoff, *Introducing Functional Grammar*, London and New York: Edward Arnold, 1996.

Todorov, T., *The Poetics of Prose*, trans. Richard Howard, Ithaca, NY: Cornell University Press, 1977.

Toolan, Michael, *Narrative: A Critical Linguistic Introduction*, London and New York: Routledge, 1991 (first published 1988).

Truffaut, François, *Hitchcock*, rev. edn, New York: Touchstone, 1985.

Tulloch, J., *Watching Television Audiences: Cultural Theories and Methods*, London: Arnold, 2000.

Tunstall, Jeremy, *Journalists at Work*, London: Constable, 1971.

Turner, G., 'The uses and limitations of genre', 'Genre, hybridity and mutations', 'Genre, format and "live" television', in G. Creeber (ed.), *The Television Genre Book*, pp. 4–7.

Turow, Joseph, *Media Today: An Introduction to Mass Communication*, Boston and New York: Houghton Mifflin, 2003.

Uspensky, Boris, *A Poetics of Composition, The Structure of the Artistic Text and Typology of a Compositional Form*, Berkeley: University of California Press, 1973.

Vertov, D., *Kino-Eye: The Writings of Dziga Vertov*, ed. Annette Michelson, trans. Kevin O'Brien, London and Sydney: Pluto Press, 1984.

Vinaver, Eugene (ed.), *Malory: Works*, 2nd edn, London: Oxford University Press, 1977.

Watson, James, *Media Communication: An Introduction to Theory and Process*, 2nd edn, Basingstoke and New York: Palgrave Macmillan, 2003.

Whitaker, Brian, *News Limited*, London: Minority Press Group, 1981.

Wilkes, G. A., *A Dictionary of Australian Colloquialisms*, Sydney: Sydney University Press, 1978.

Williams, Kevin, *Understanding Media Theory*, London: Arnold, 2003.

Williams, Raymond, *Problems in Materialism and Culture: Selected Essays*, London: Verso, 1980.

— *Television: Technology and Cultural Form*, 2nd edn, London: Routledge, 1990.

Ytreberg, Espen, 'Moving out of the inverted pyramid: Narratives and descriptions in television news', *Journalism Studies* 2.3 (2001), 357–71.

Žižek, Slavoj, 'The obscene object of postmodernity', in Elizabeth Wright and Edmond Wright (eds), *The Žižek Reader*, Oxford: Blackwell, 1999, pp. 37–52.

⌨ Websites

Archival Moving Image Materials of the United States Library of Congress: www.itsmarc.com/crs/arch0391.htm; viewed 6 November 2004.

Australian Broadcasting Corporation, Radio National: www.abc.net.au/rn/arts/airplay/s350575.htm; viewed 9 November 2004.

British Broadcasting Corporation: www.bbc.co.uk/writersroom/writing/tvcomedy.shtml; viewed 13 October 2004.

British sit-coms: www.wordiq.com/definition/Britcom; viewed 19 October 2004.

Brown, Mary Ellen and Barwick, Linda, 'Fables and endless genealogies: Soap opera and women's culture', *Continuum: The Australian Journal of Media and Culture* 1.2 (1987), wwwmcc.murdoch.edu.au/ReadingRoom/1.2/Brown.html; viewed 19 October 2004.

Brown University media courses: www.brown.edu/Departments/MCM/courses/MC11/outline/TV_narrative_outline.htm; viewed 14 October 2004.

Chandler, Daniel: www.aber.ac.uk/media/modules/TF33120; viewed 4 September 2002.

Gough, L. (2000). *The Mermaid's Tail*: www.lucy.gough.care4free.net/TheMermaidsMonologue.htm; viewed 9 November 2004.

Grossberg, Josh: http://primetimetv.about.com; viewed 26 October 2004.

Massachusetts Institute of Technology: http://web.mit.edu/mr_mole/www/seinfeld.pdf; viewed 19 October 2004.

Playwriting: www.vcu.edu/artweb/playwriting; viewed 6 September 2002.

Sheehan, Helena: www.comms.dcu.ie/sheehanh/itvsoap.htm; viewed 2 September 2002.

Taflinger, Richard F.: www.wsu.edu:8080/~taflinge/sitcom.html; viewed 19 October 2004.

Television history: www.tvhistory.tv; viewed 12 October 2004; www.museum.tv/archives/etv/S/htmlS/soapopera/soapopera.htm; viewed 19 October 2004.

Warhol, Robyn R., 'Feminine intensities: Soap-opera viewing as a technology of gender', *Genders* 28 (1998); www.genders.org/g28/g28_intensities.html; viewed 18 October 2004.

Wikipedia: http://en.wikipedia.org/wiki/Television_series; viewed 12 October 2004; http://en.wikipedia.org/wiki/Situation_comedy; viewed 12 September 2004.

Index

Note that film and book titles starting with 'A' or 'The' are filed under their second word; i.e. *Godfather, The*